FIRE FORCE

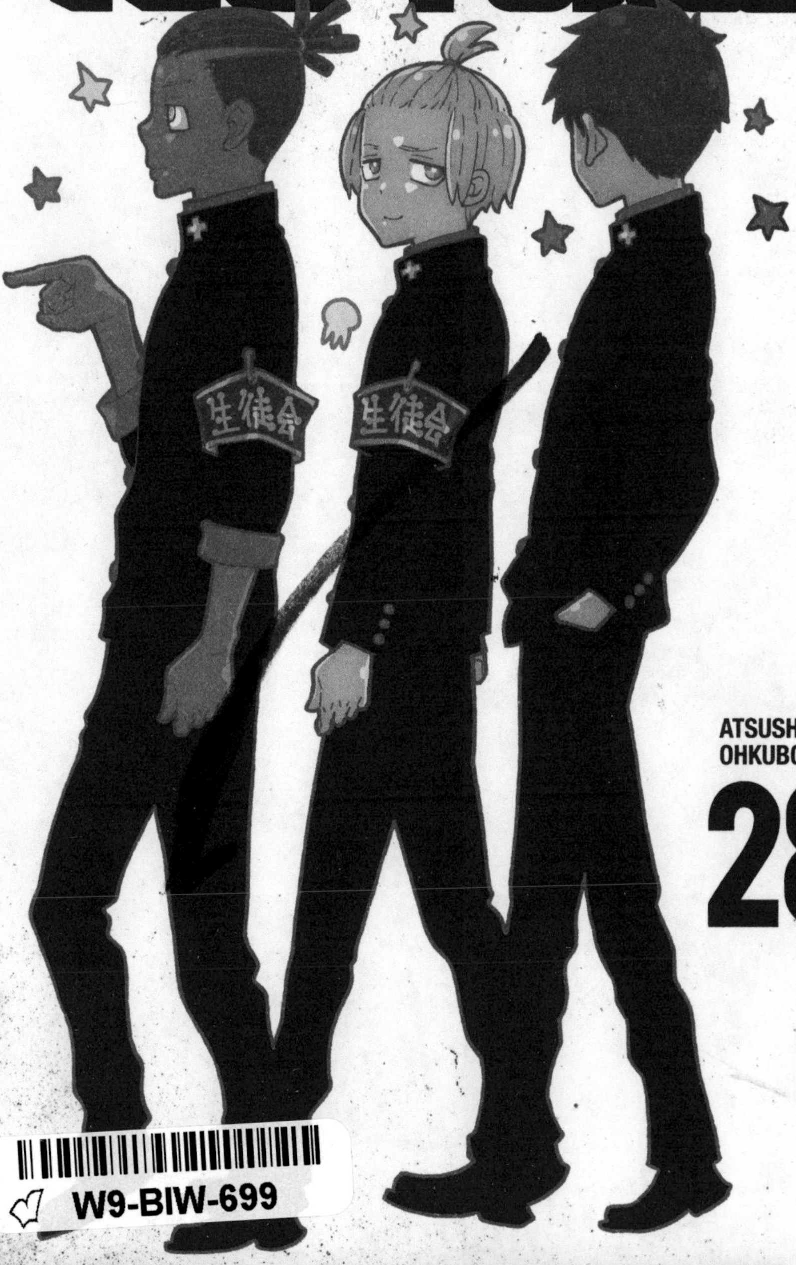

生徒会
生徒会

ATSUSHI
OHKUBO

28

down
World
ction!!

VOL.28

ATSUSHI OHKUBO

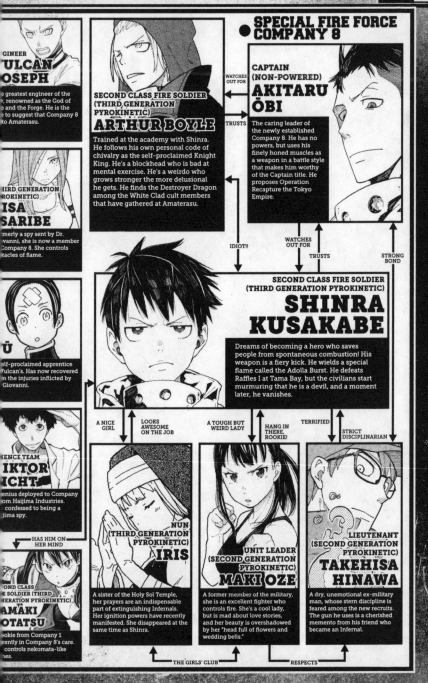

SPECIAL FIRE FORCE COMPANY 8

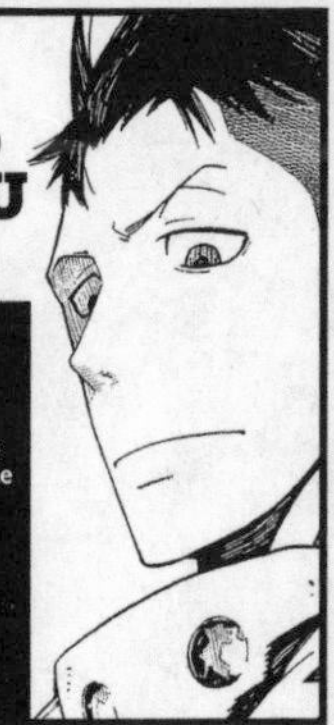

CAPTAIN
(NON-POWERED)
AKITARU ŌBI

The caring leader of the newly established Company 8. He has no powers, but uses his finely honed muscles as a weapon in a battle style that makes him worthy of the Captain title. He proposes Operation Recapture the Tokyo Empire.

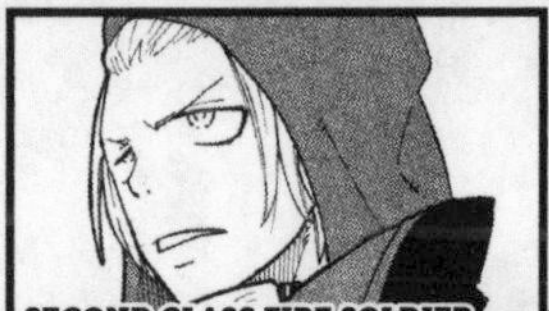

SECOND CLASS FIRE SOLDIER
(THIRD GENERATION PYROKINETIC)
ARTHUR BOYLE

Trained at the academy with Shinra. He follows his own personal code of chivalry as the self-proclaimed Knight King. He's a blockhead who is bad at mental exercise. He's a weirdo who grows stronger the more delusional he gets. He finds the Destroyer Dragon among the White Clad cult members that have gathered at Amaterasu.

WATCHES OUT FOR

TRUSTS

IDIOT!!

WATCHES OUT FOR

TRUSTS

STRONG BOND

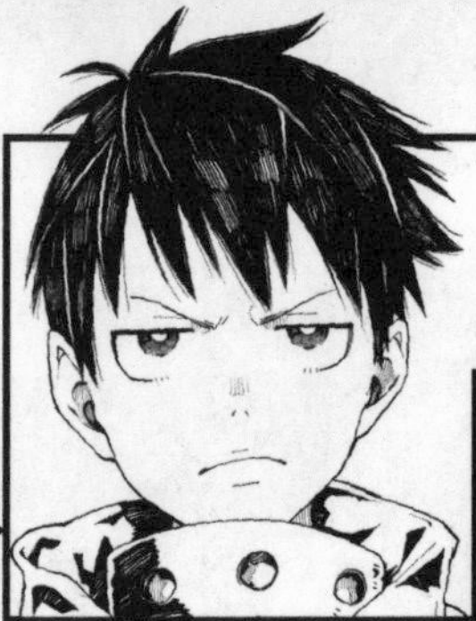

SECOND CLASS FIRE SOLDIER
(THIRD GENERATION PYROKINETIC)
SHINRA KUSAKABE

Dreams of becoming a hero who saves people from spontaneous combustion! His weapon is a fiery kick. He wields a special flame called the Adolla Burst. He defeats Raffles I at Tama Bay, but the civilians start murmuring that he is a devil, and a moment later, he vanishes.

A NICE GIRL

LOOKS AWESOME ON THE JOB

A TOUGH BUT WEIRD LADY

HANG IN THERE, ROOKIE!

TERRIFIED

STRICT DISCIPLINARIAN

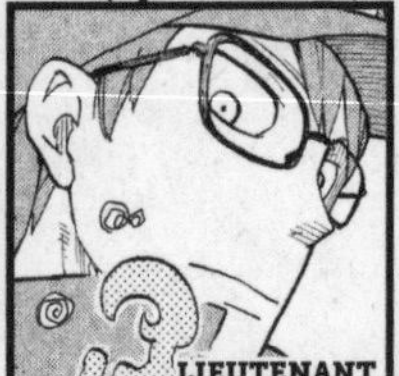

LIEUTENANT
(SECOND GENERATION PYROKINETIC)
TAKEHISA HINAWA

A dry, unemotional ex-military man, whose stern discipline is feared among the new recruits. The gun he uses is a cherished memento from his friend who became an Infernal.

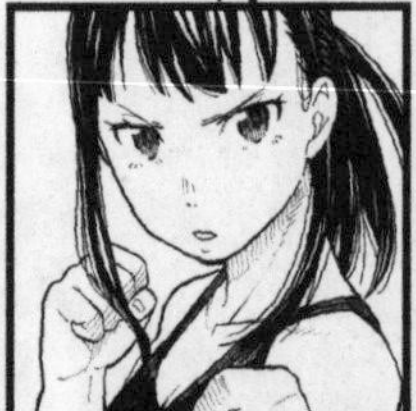

UNIT LEADER
(SECOND GENERATION PYROKINETIC)
MAKI OZE

A former member of the military, she is an excellent fighter who controls fire. She's a cool lady, but is mad about love stories, and her beauty is overshadowed by her "head full of flowers and wedding bells."

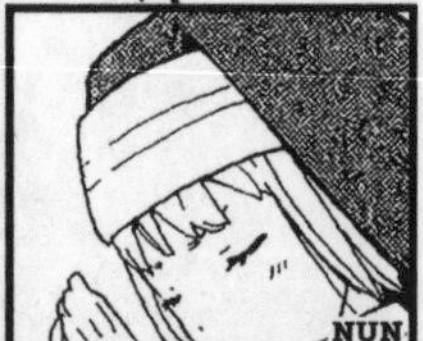

NUN
(THIRD GENERATION PYROKINETIC)
IRIS

A sister of the Holy Sol Temple, her prayers are an indispensable part of extinguishing Infernals. Her ignition powers have recently manifested. She disappeared at the same time as Shinra.

THE GIRLS' CLUB

RESPECTS

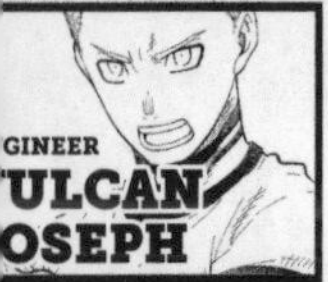

GINEER
ULCAN OSEPH

e greatest engineer of the , renowned as the God of and the Forge. He is the to suggest that Company 8 to Amaterasu.

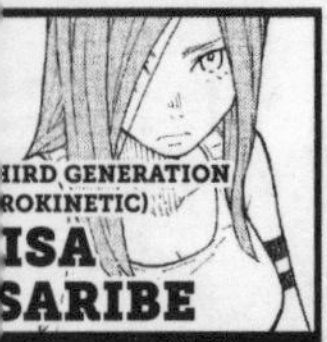

HIRD GENERATION ROKINETIC)
ISA SARIBE

merly a spy sent by Dr. vanni, she is now a member Company 8. She controls tacles of flame.

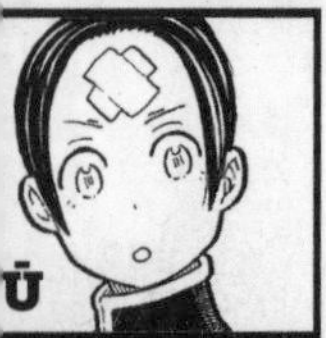

Ū

elf-proclaimed apprentice Vulcan's. Has now recovered n the injuries inflicted by Giovanni.

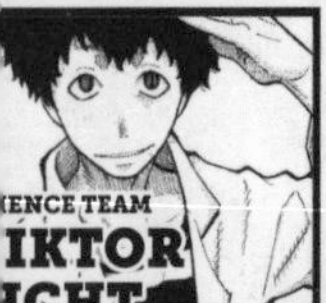

ENCE TEAM
IKTOR ICHT

enius deployed to Company om Haijima Industries. confessed to being a jima spy.

HAS HIM ON HER MIND

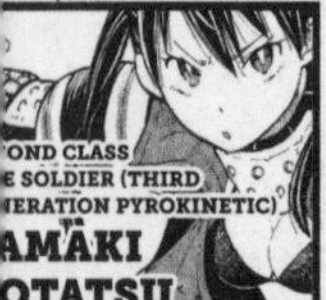

OND CLASS SOLDIER (THIRD ERATION PYROKINETIC)
AMAKI OTATSU

okie from Company 1 rently in Company 8's care. controls nekomata-like nes.

HOLY SOL TEMPLE + "EVANGELIST"

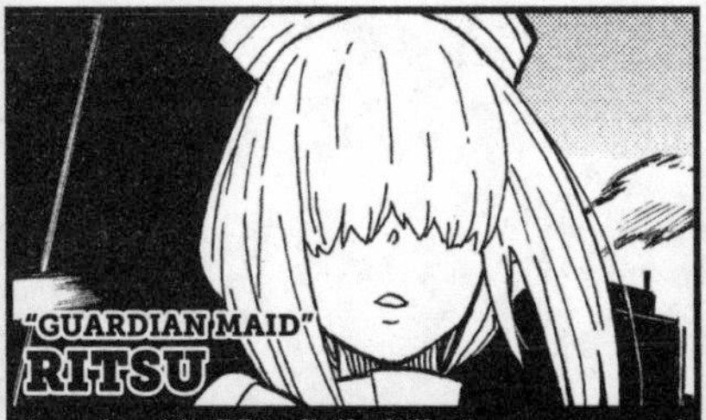

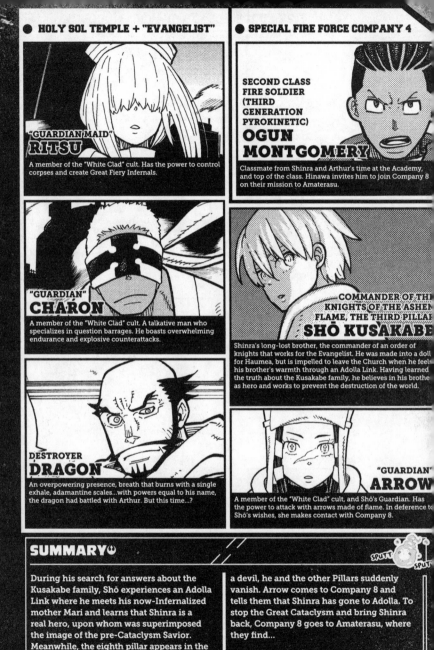

"GUARDIAN MAID"
RITSU

A member of the "White Clad" cult. Has the power to control corpses and create Great Fiery Infernals.

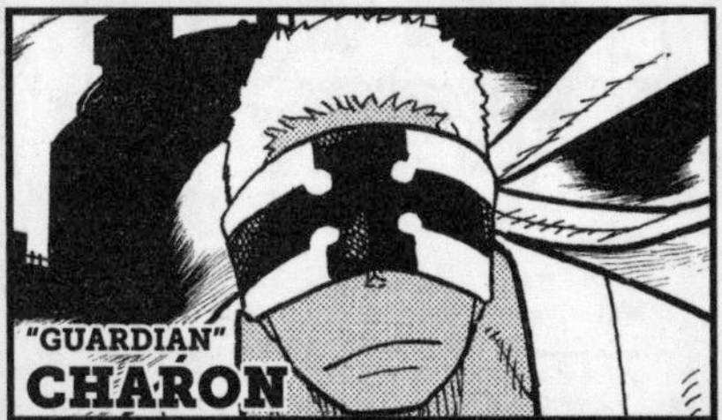

"GUARDIAN"
CHARON

A member of the "White Clad" cult. A talkative man who specializes in question barrages. He boasts overwhelming endurance and explosive counterattacks.

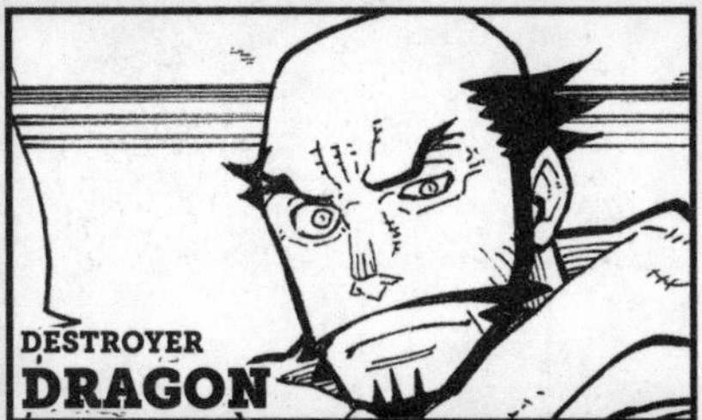

DESTROYER
DRAGON

An overpowering presence, breath that burns with a single exhale, adamantine scales...with powers equal to his name, the dragon had battled with Arthur. But this time...?

SPECIAL FIRE FORCE COMPANY 4

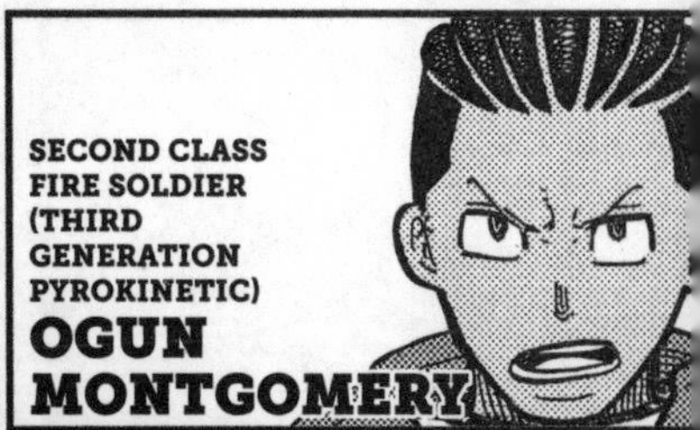

SECOND CLASS FIRE SOLDIER (THIRD GENERATION PYROKINETIC)
OGUN MONTGOMERY

Classmate from Shinra and Arthur's time at the Academy, and top of the class. Hinawa invites him to join Company 8 on their mission to Amaterasu.

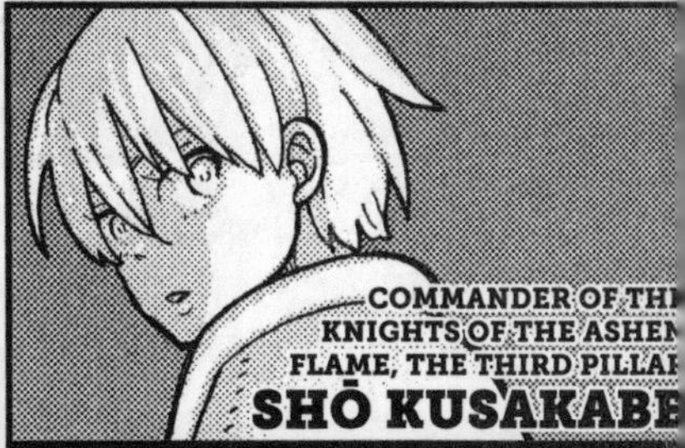

COMMANDER OF THI KNIGHTS OF THE ASHEN FLAME, THE THIRD PILLAI
SHŌ KUSAKABE

Shinra's long-lost brother, the commander of an order of knights that works for the Evangelist. He was made into a doll for Haumea, but is impelled to leave the Church when he feel his brother's warmth through an Adolla Link. Having learned the truth about the Kusakabe family, he believes in his brothe as hero and works to prevent the destruction of the world.

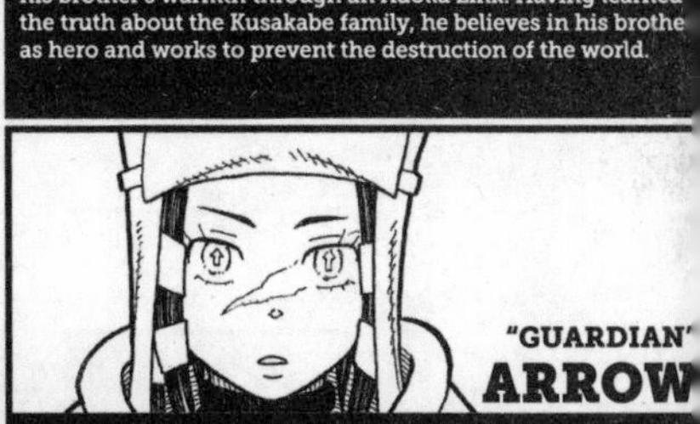

"GUARDIAN"
ARROW

A member of the "White Clad" cult, and Shō's Guardian. Has the power to attack with arrows made of flame. In deference to Shō's wishes, she makes contact with Company 8.

SUMMARY

During his search for answers about the Kusakabe family, Shō experiences an Adolla Link where he meets his now-Infernalized mother Mari and learns that Shinra is a real hero, upon whom was superimposed the image of the pre-Cataclysm Savior. Meanwhile, the eighth pillar appears in the waters of Tama Bay, and Raffles I descends upon the world. Shinra defeats Raffles I, but amid whispered accusations that he is a devil, he and the other Pillars suddenly vanish. Arrow comes to Company 8 and tells them that Shinra has gone to Adolla. To stop the Great Cataclysm and bring Shinra back, Company 8 goes to Amaterasu, where they find...

FIRE FORCE 28
CONTENTS

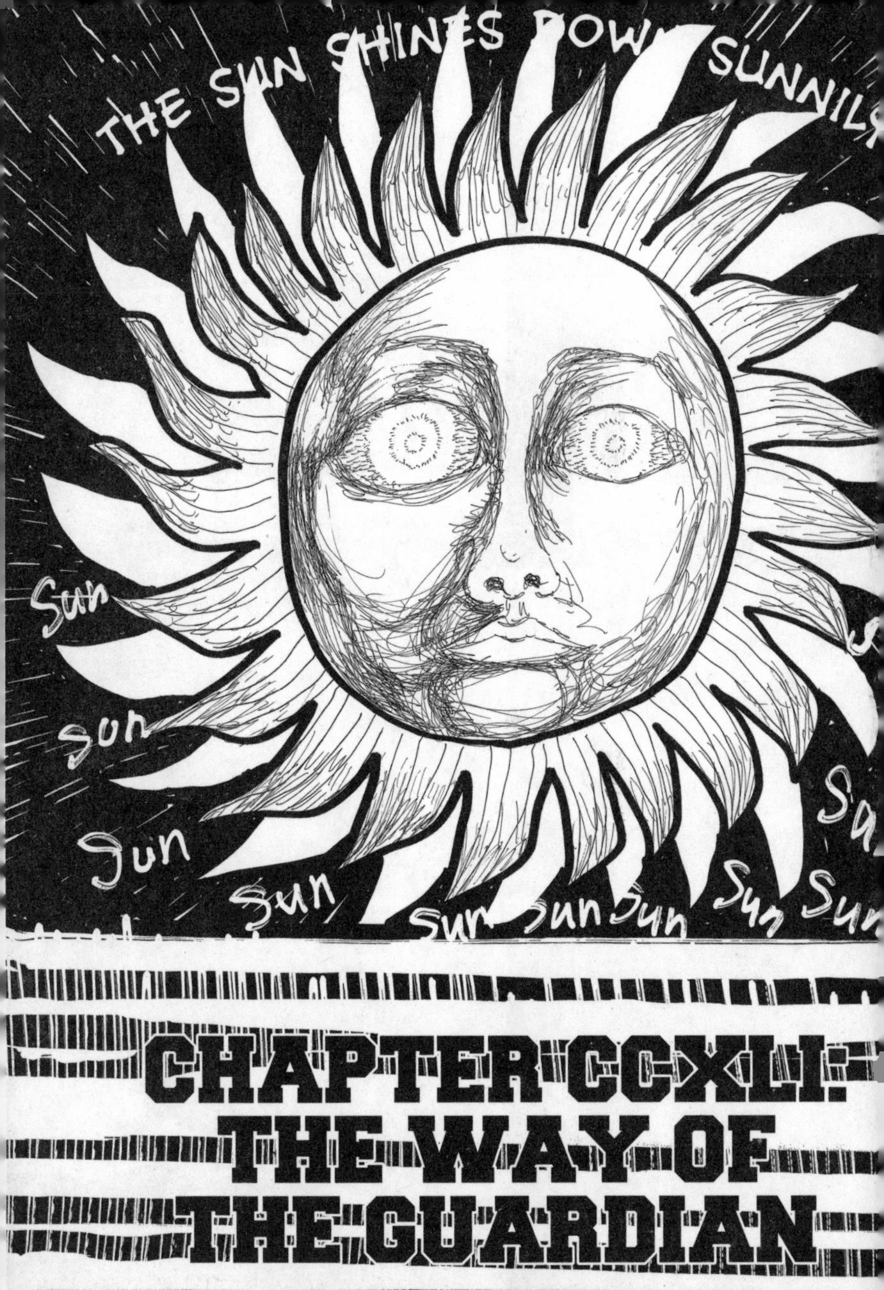
THE SUN SHINES DOW
SUNNIL
Sun
sun
Jun
Sun
Sun
Sun Jun
Sun
Sun

CHAPTER CCXLI: THE WAY OF THE GUARDIAN

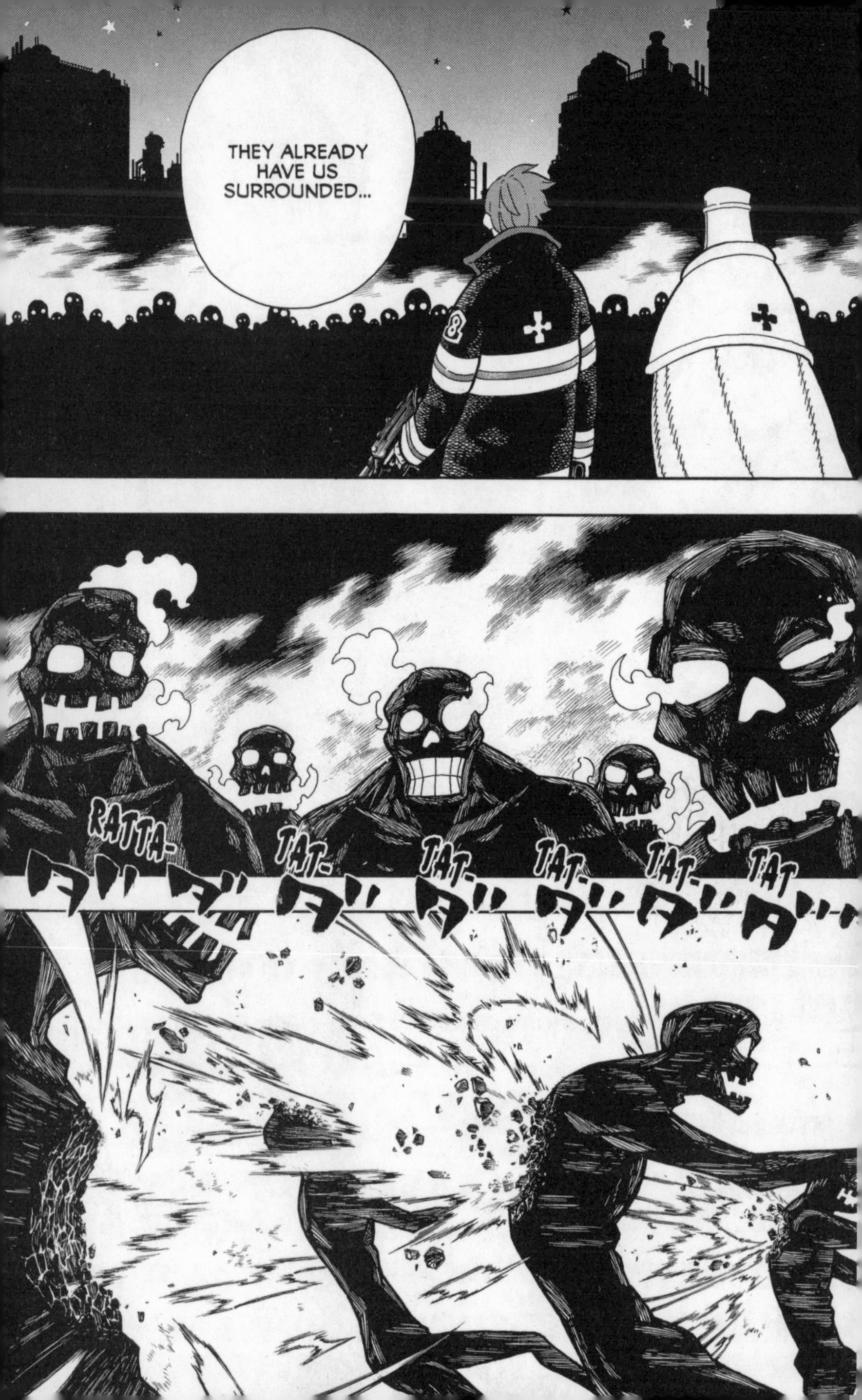
THEY ALREADY HAVE US SURROUNDED...
RATTA- TAT- TAT- TAT- TAT- TAT

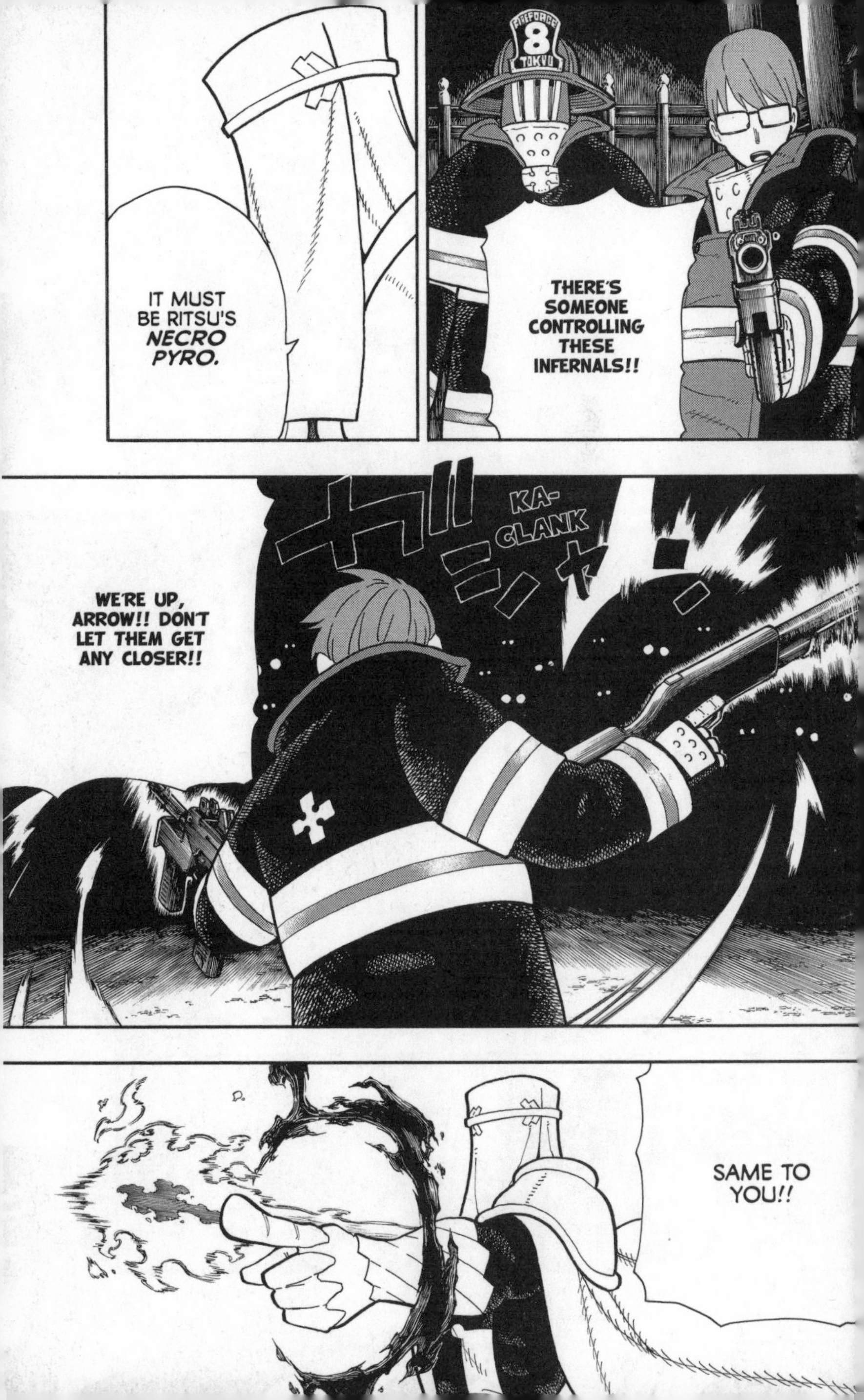
THERE'S SOMEONE CONTROLLING THESE INFERNALS!!
IT MUST BE RITSU'S *NECRO PYRO.*
KA-CLANK
WE'RE UP, ARROW!! DON'T LET THEM GET ANY CLOSER!!
SAME TO YOU!!

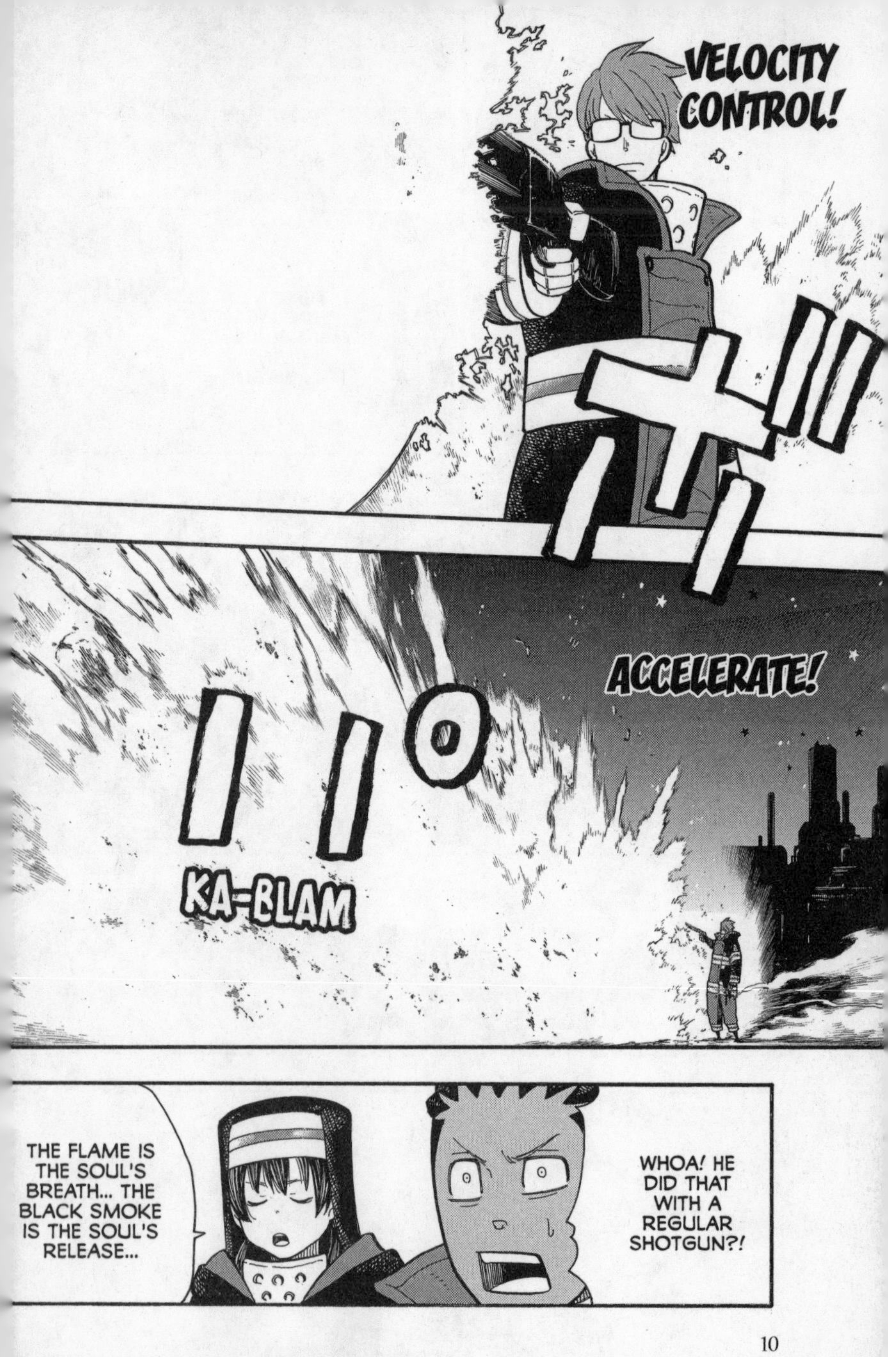
VELOCITY CONTROL!
ACCELERATE!
KA-BLAM
WHOA! HE DID THAT WITH A REGULAR SHOTGUN?!
THE FLAME IS THE SOUL'S BREATH... THE BLACK SMOKE IS THE SOUL'S RELEASE...

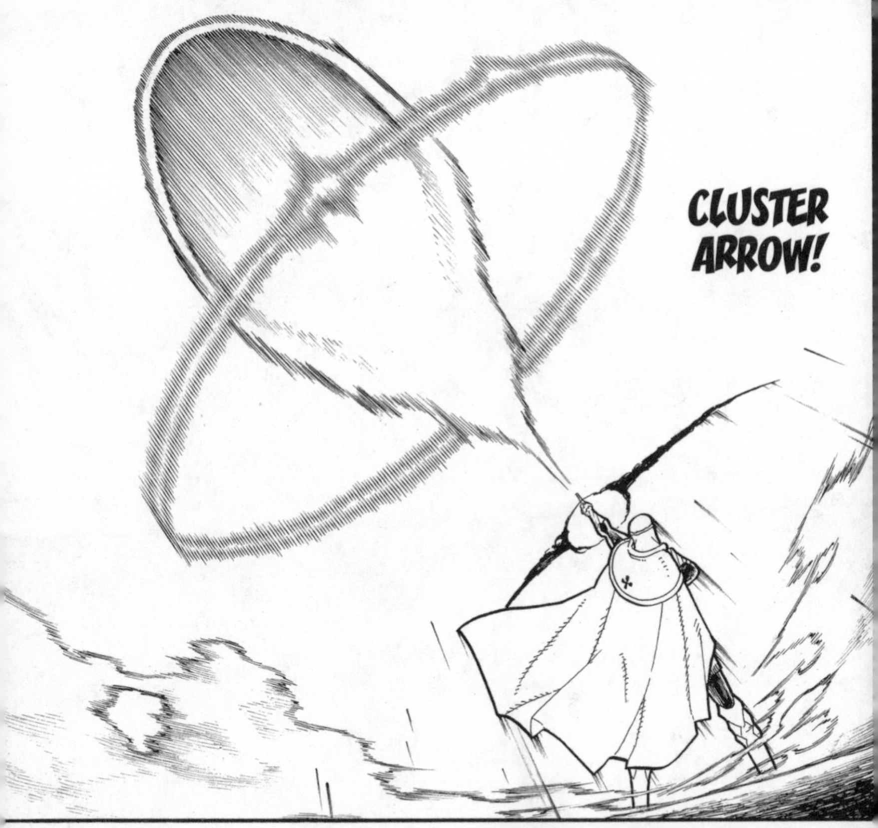
CLUSTER ARROW!

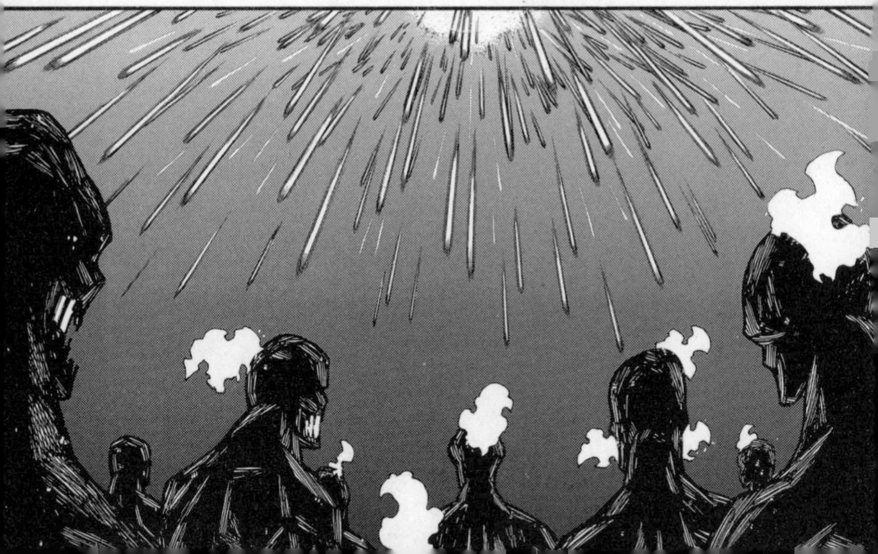

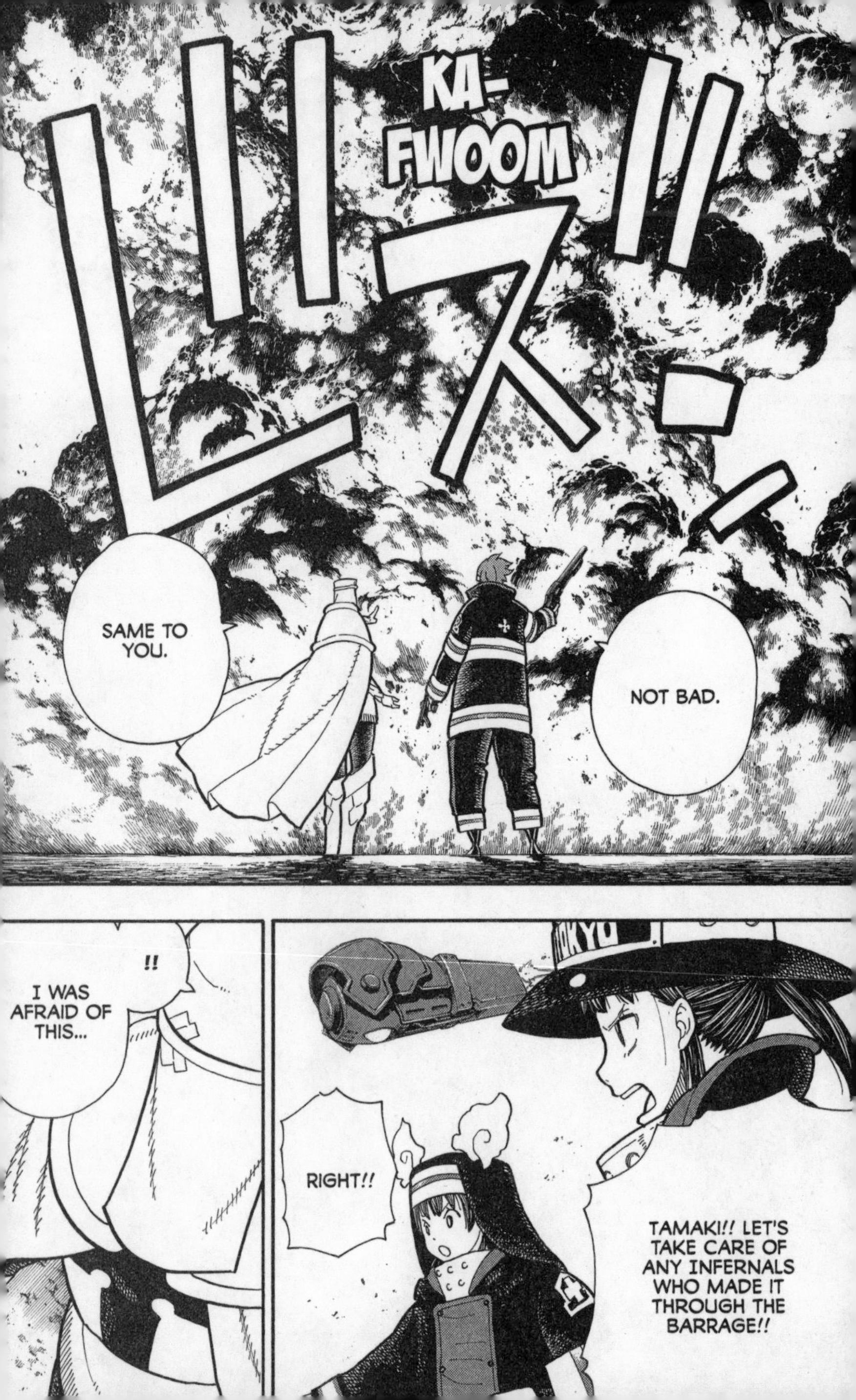
KA-FWOOM
NOT BAD.
SAME TO YOU.
TAMAKI!! LET'S TAKE CARE OF ANY INFERNALS WHO MADE IT THROUGH THE BARRAGE!!
RIGHT!!
!!
I WAS AFRAID OF THIS...

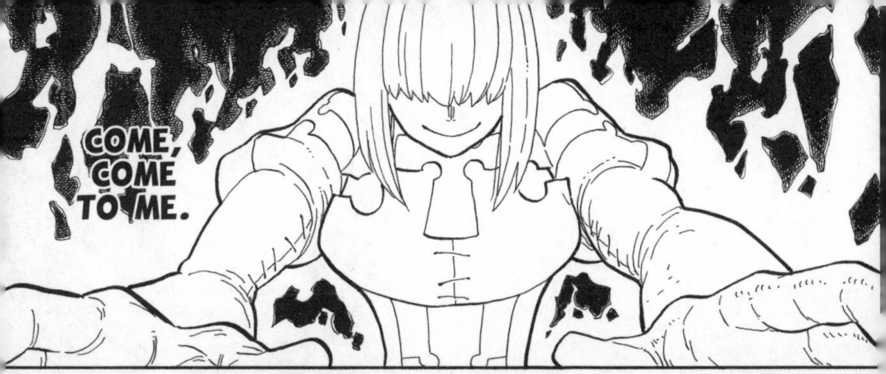
COME, COME TO ME.
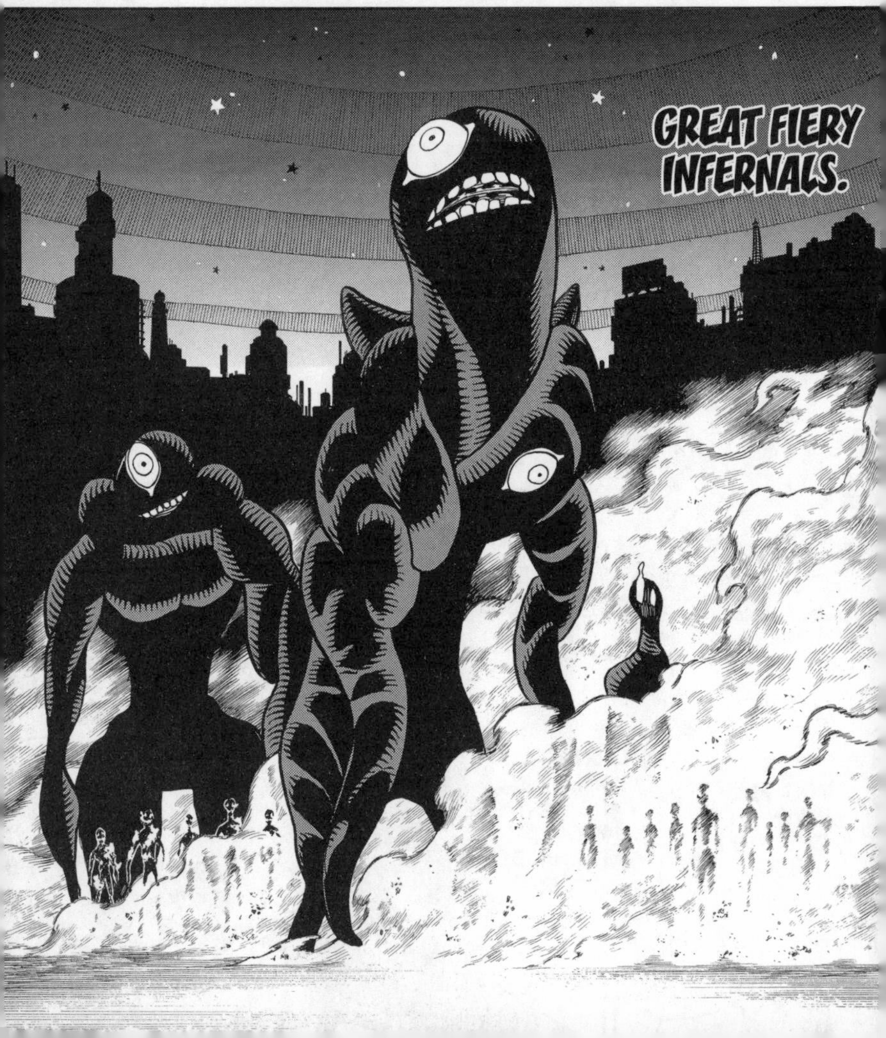
GREAT FIERY INFERNALS.

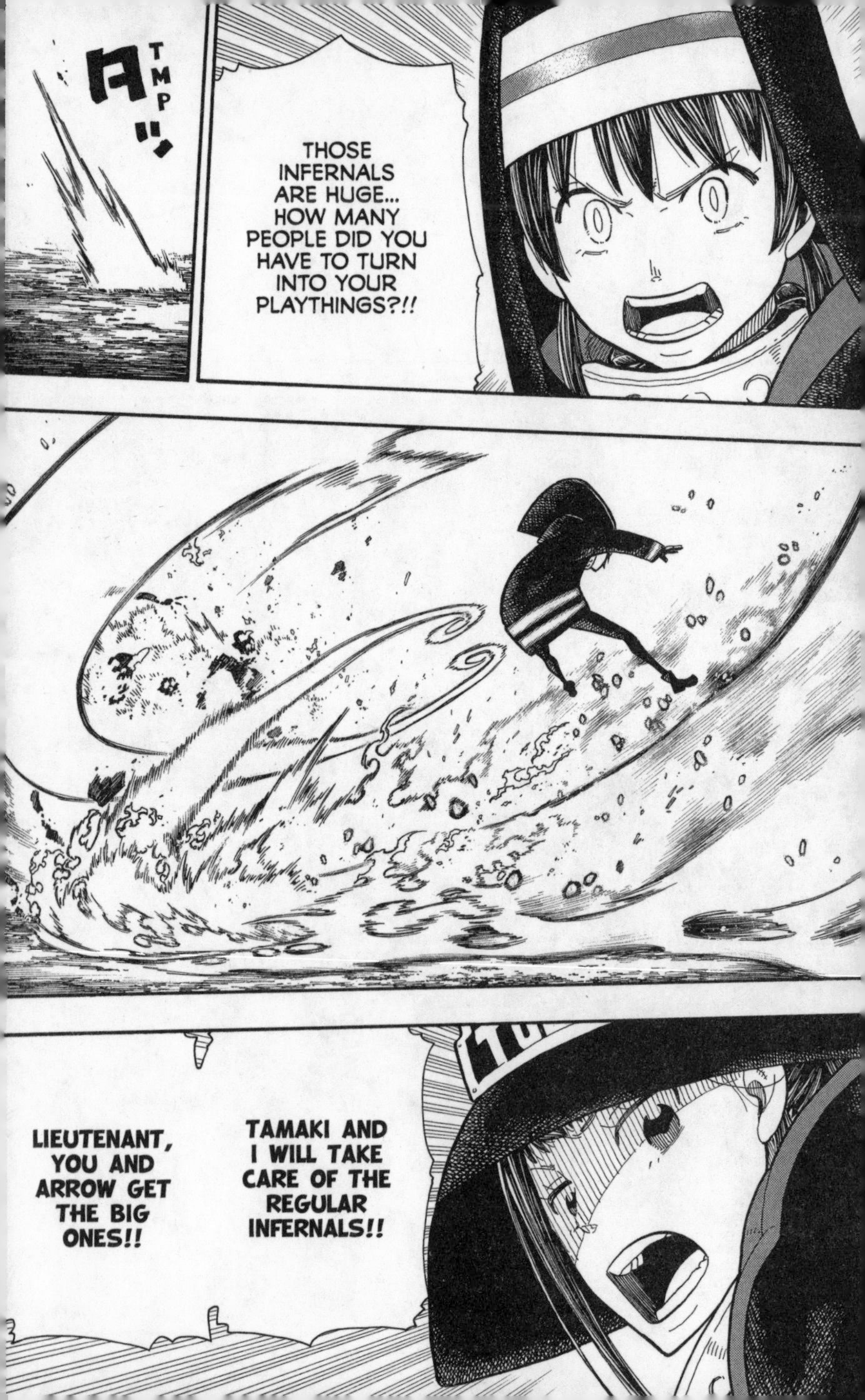
THOSE INFERNALS ARE HUGE... HOW MANY PEOPLE DID YOU HAVE TO TURN INTO YOUR PLAYTHINGS?!!
TMP
TAMAKI AND I WILL TAKE CARE OF THE REGULAR INFERNALS!!
LIEUTENANT, YOU AND ARROW GET THE BIG ONES!!

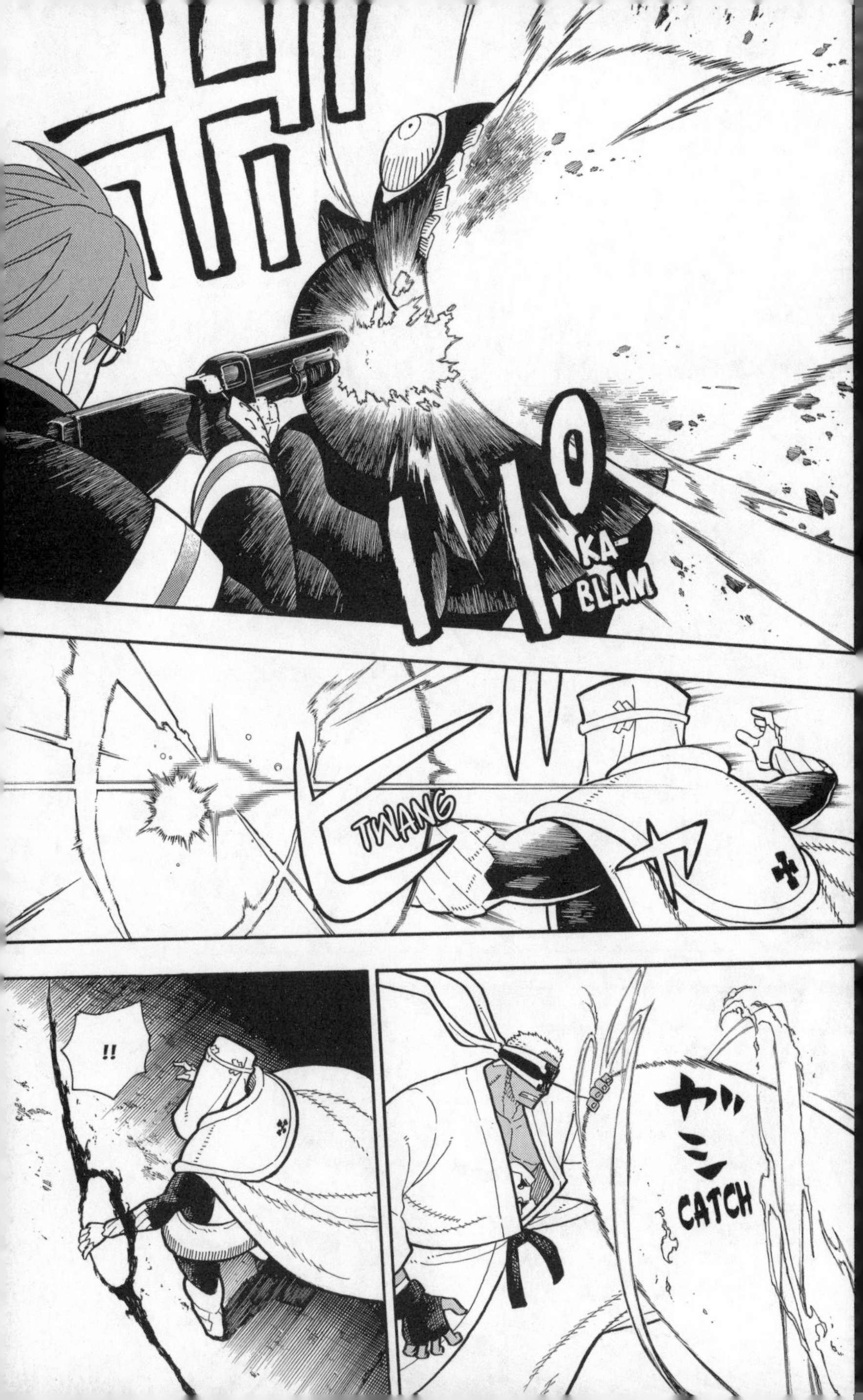
KA-
BLAM
TWANG
CATCH
!!

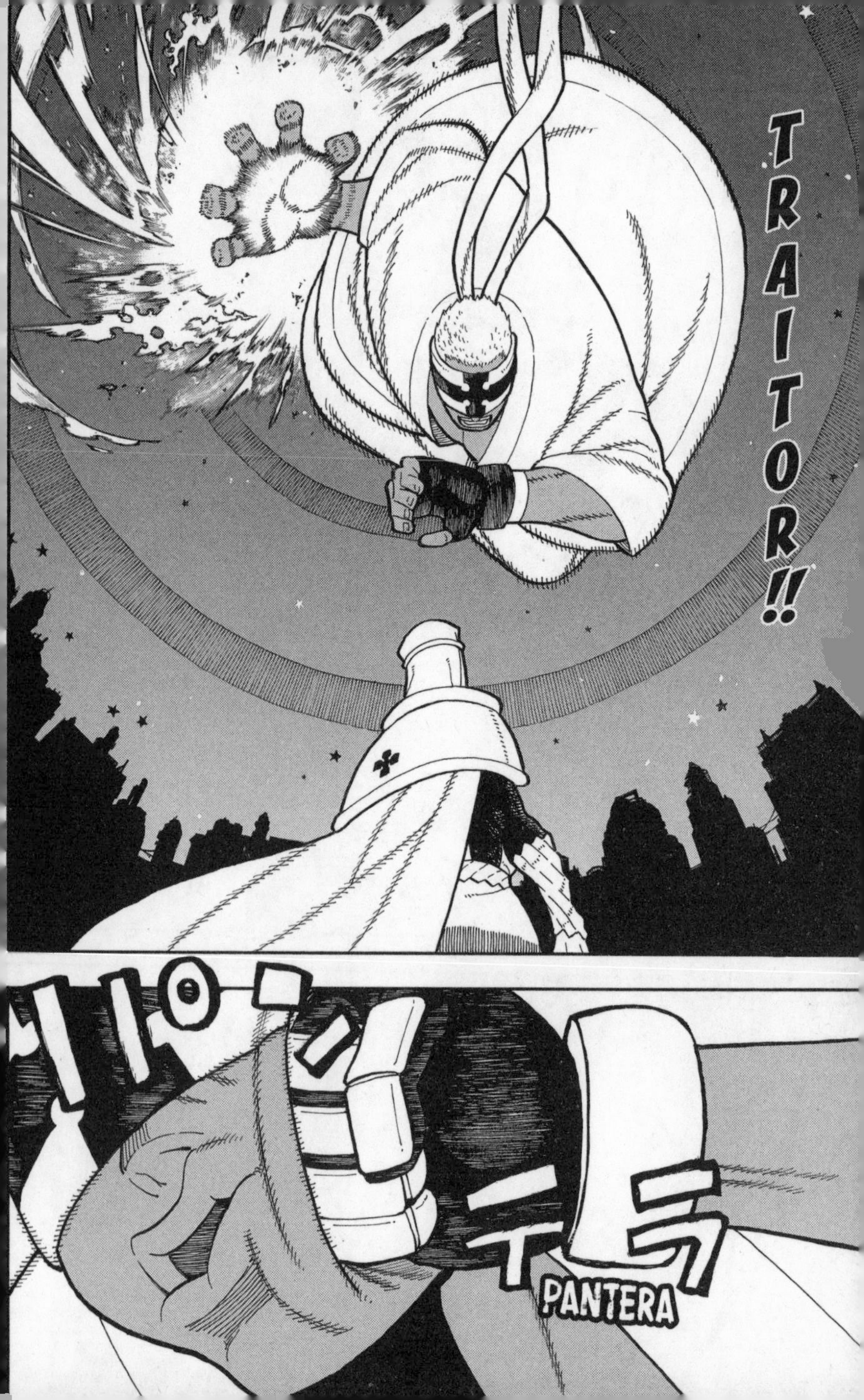
TRAITOR!!
PANTERA

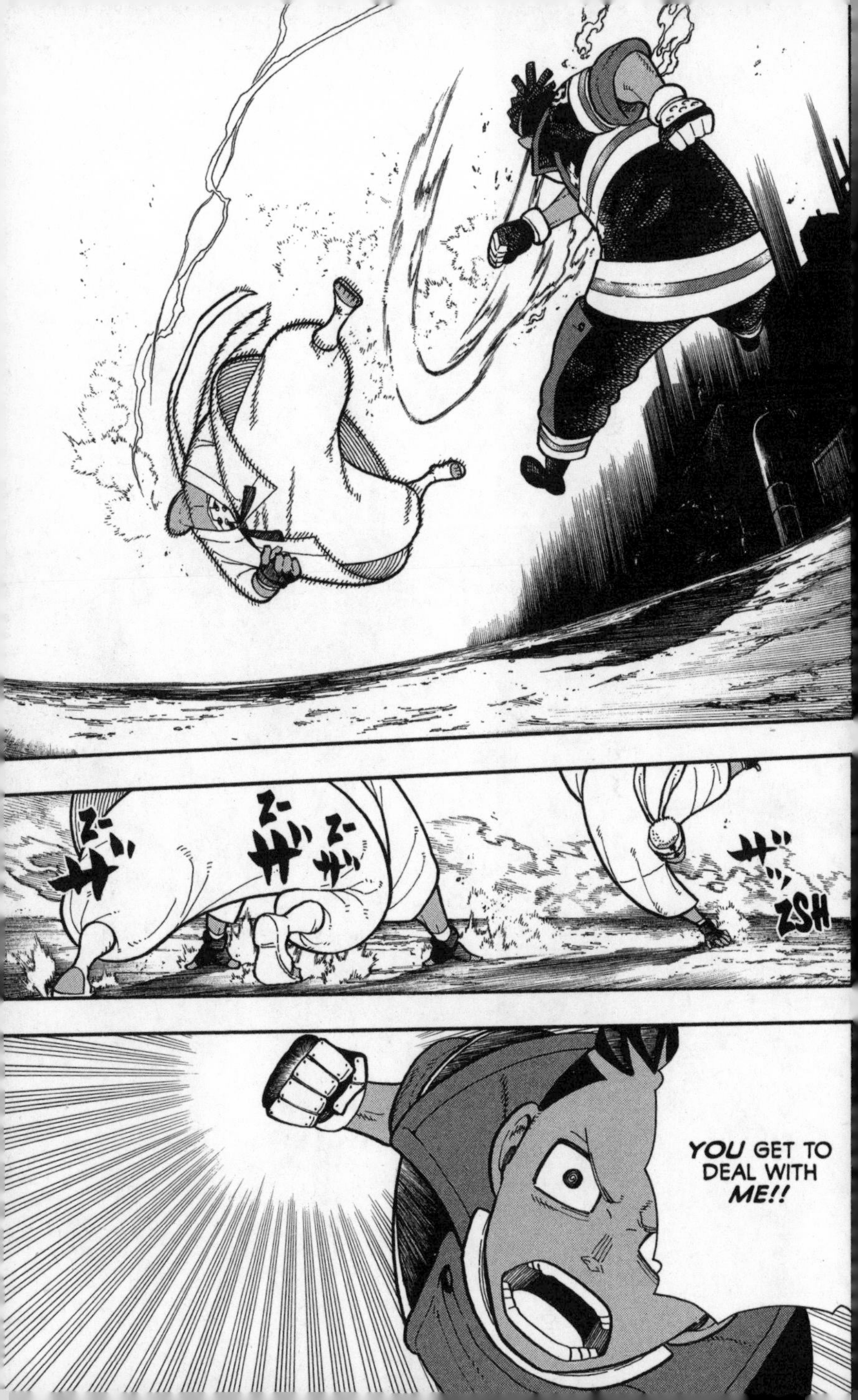
ZSH
YOU GET TO DEAL WITH ME!!

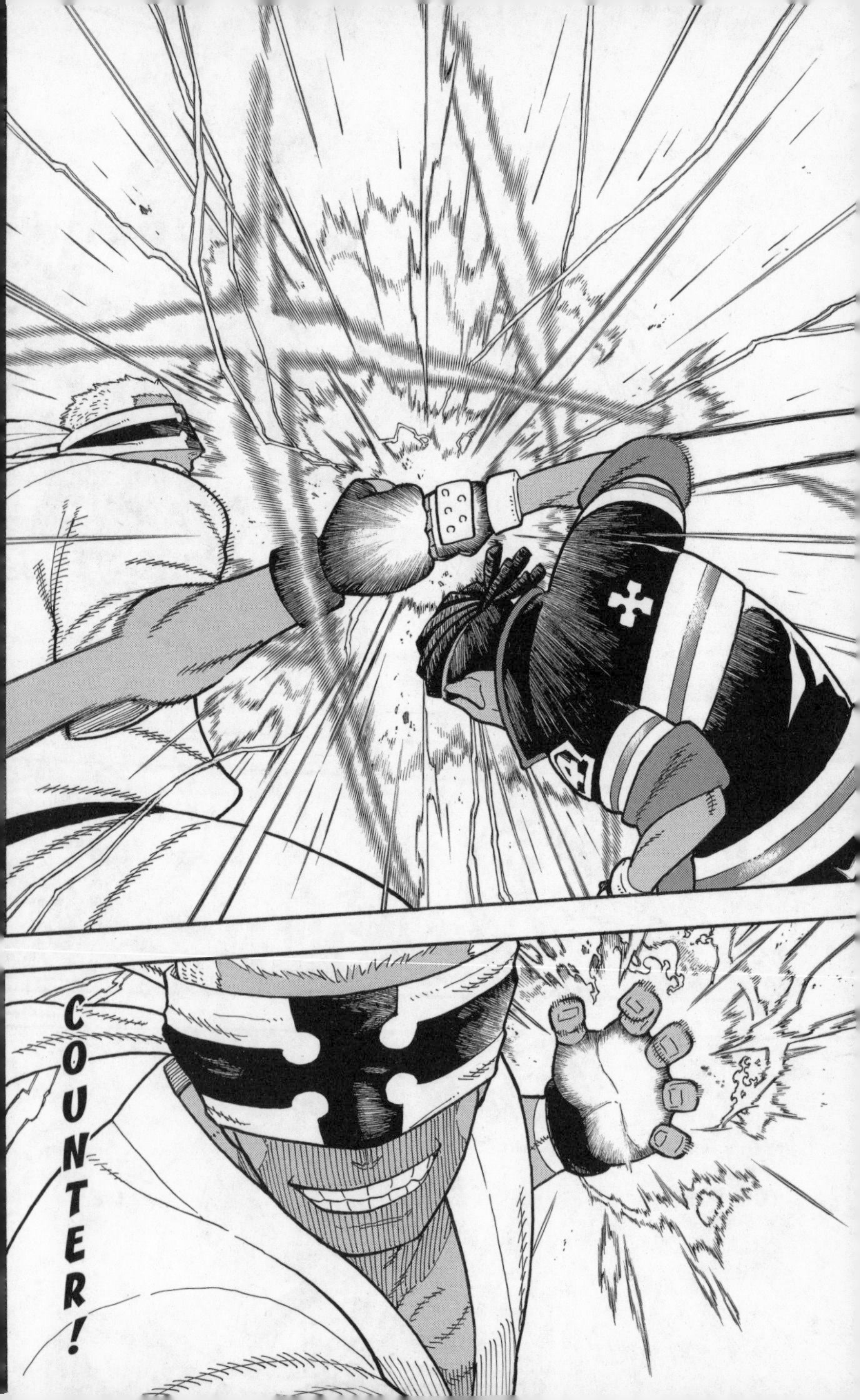
COUNTER!

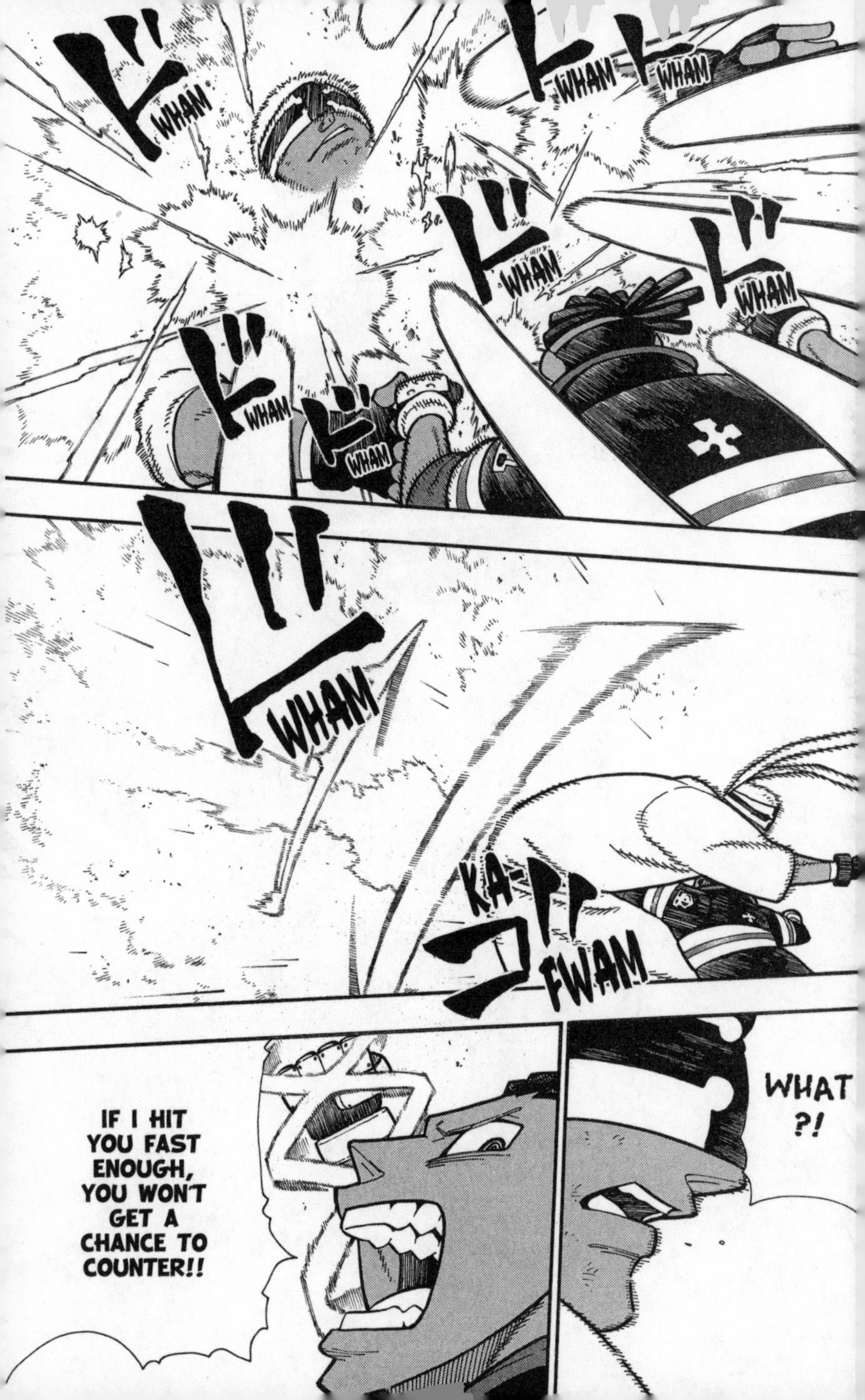

WHAM
WHAM
WHAM
WHAM
WHAM
WHAM
WHAM
WHAM
KA-
FWAM
WHAT ?!
IF I HIT YOU FAST ENOUGH, YOU WON'T GET A CHANCE TO COUNTER!!

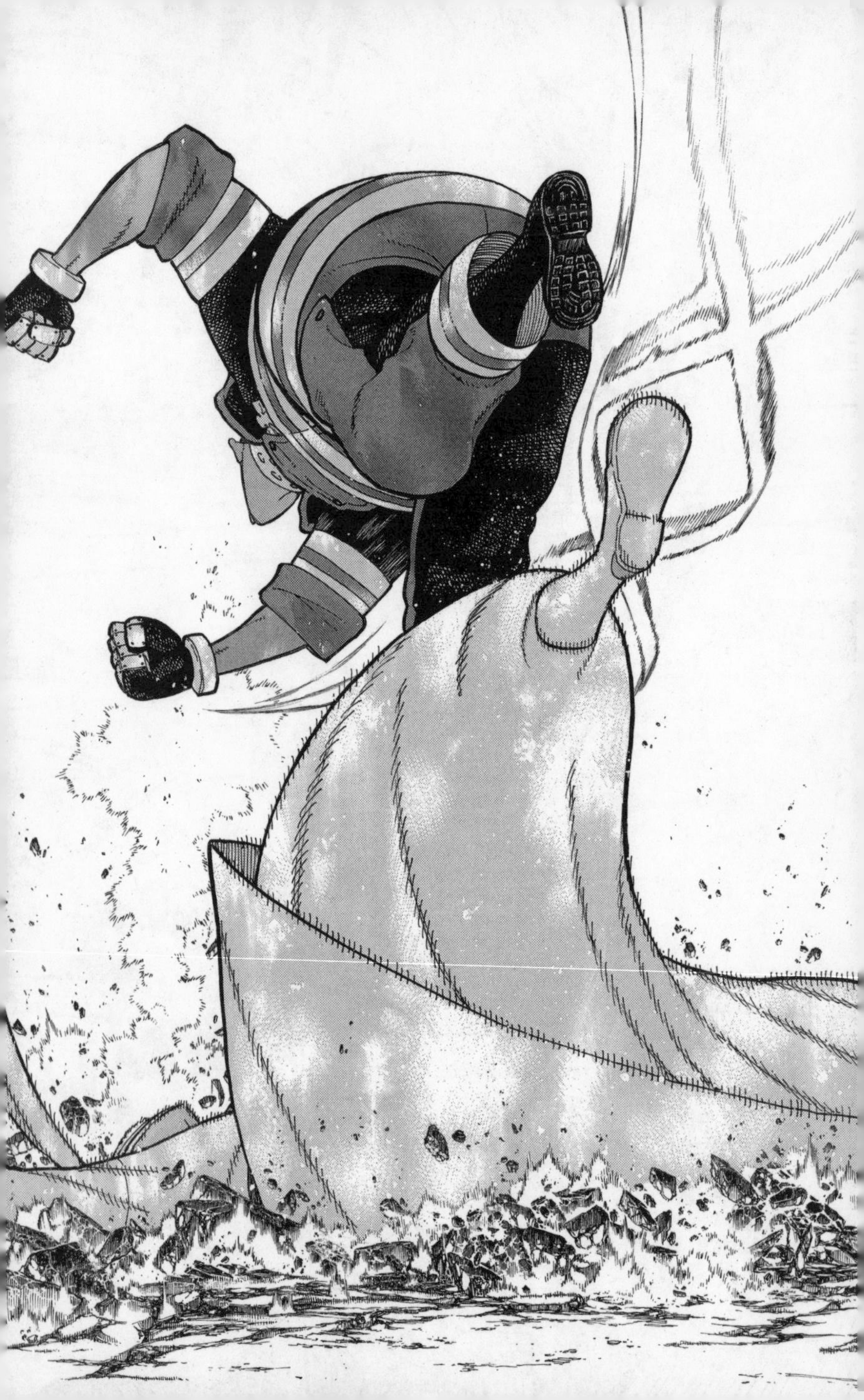

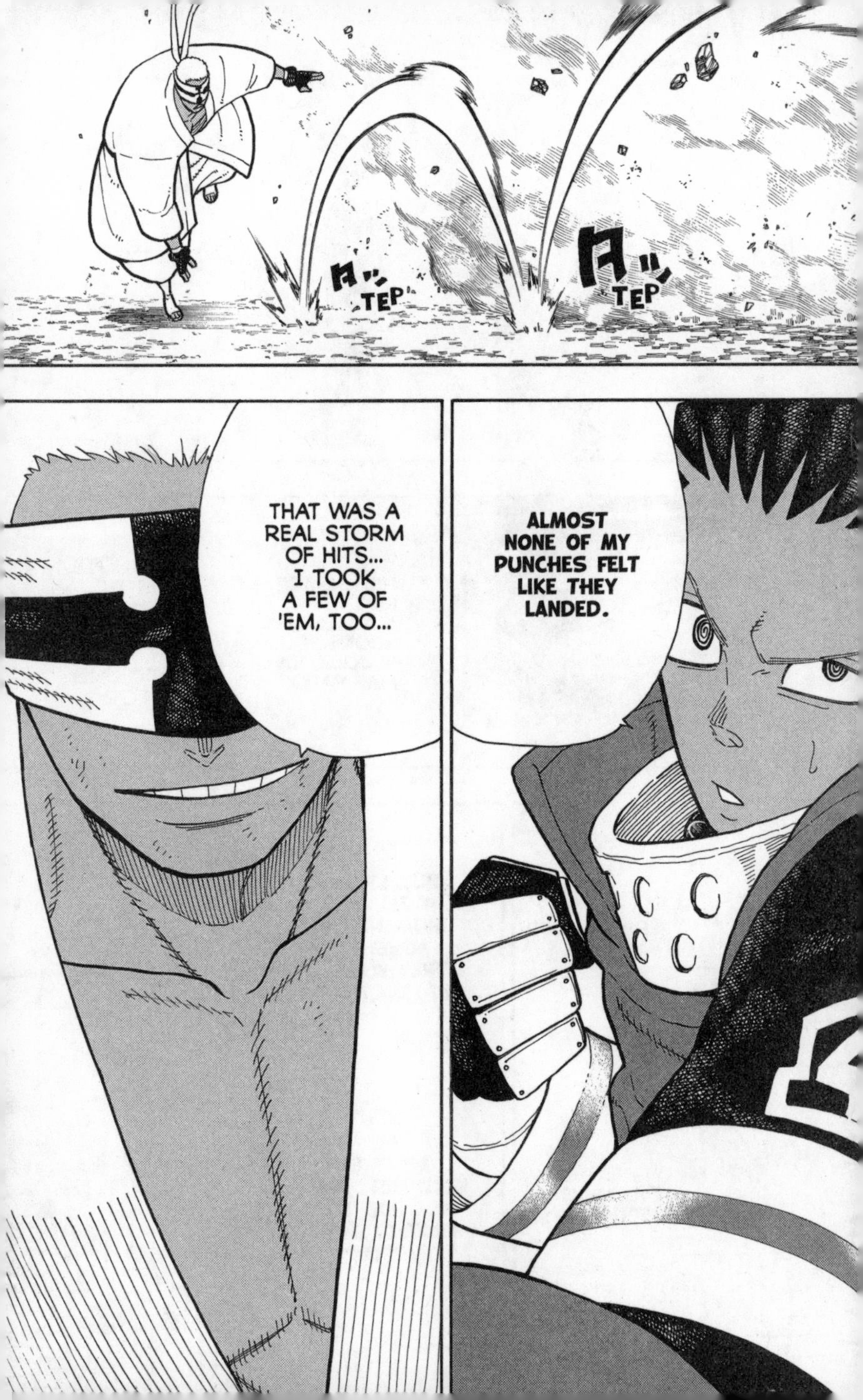
TEP
TEP
ALMOST NONE OF MY PUNCHES FELT LIKE THEY LANDED.
THAT WAS A REAL STORM OF HITS... I TOOK A FEW OF 'EM, TOO...

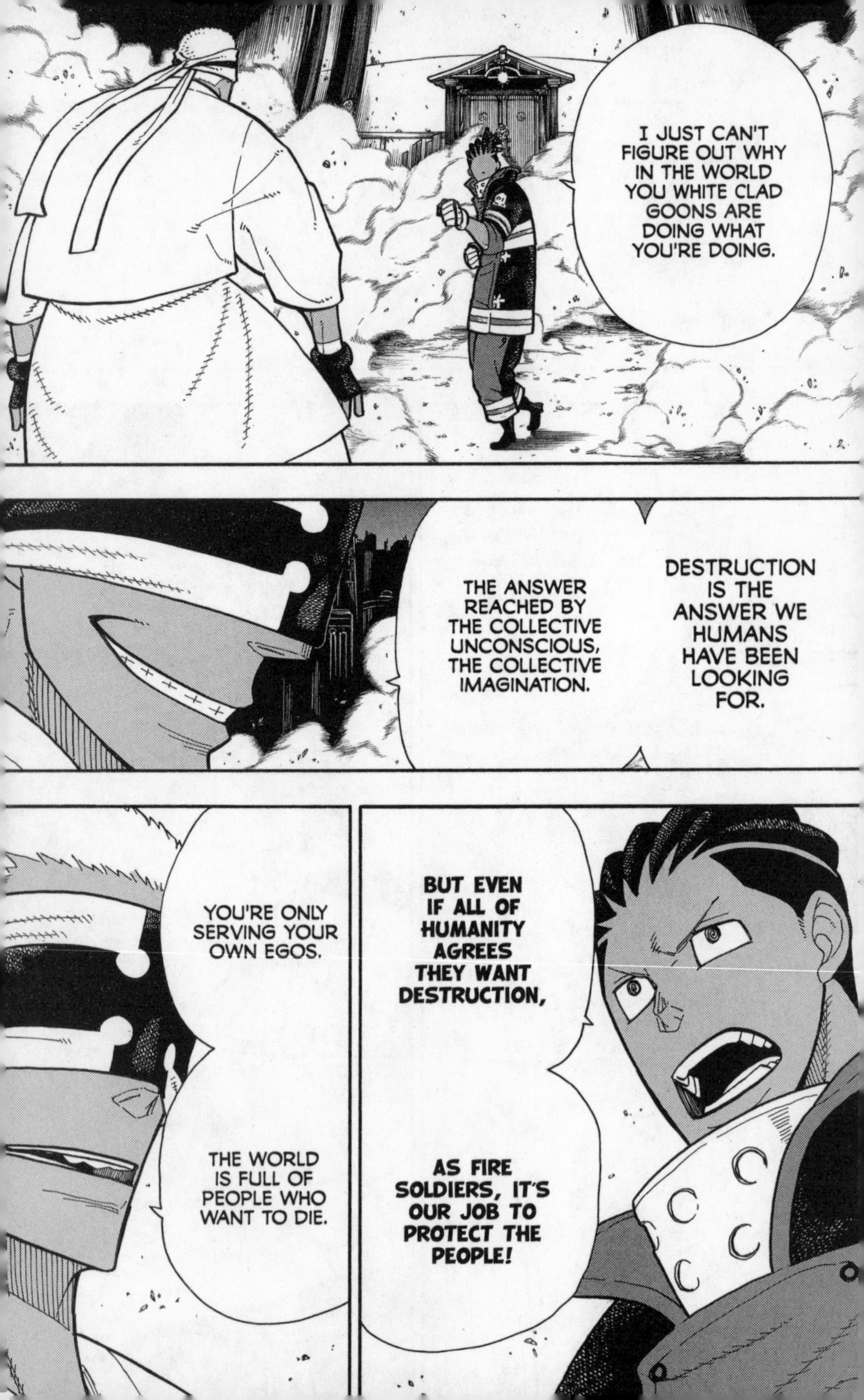
I JUST CAN'T FIGURE OUT WHY IN THE WORLD YOU WHITE CLAD GOONS ARE DOING WHAT YOU'RE DOING.
DESTRUCTION IS THE ANSWER WE HUMANS HAVE BEEN LOOKING FOR.
THE ANSWER REACHED BY THE COLLECTIVE UNCONSCIOUS, THE COLLECTIVE IMAGINATION.
BUT EVEN IF ALL OF HUMANITY AGREES THEY WANT DESTRUCTION,
AS FIRE SOLDIERS, IT'S OUR JOB TO PROTECT THE PEOPLE!
YOU'RE ONLY SERVING YOUR OWN EGOS.
THE WORLD IS FULL OF PEOPLE WHO WANT TO DIE.

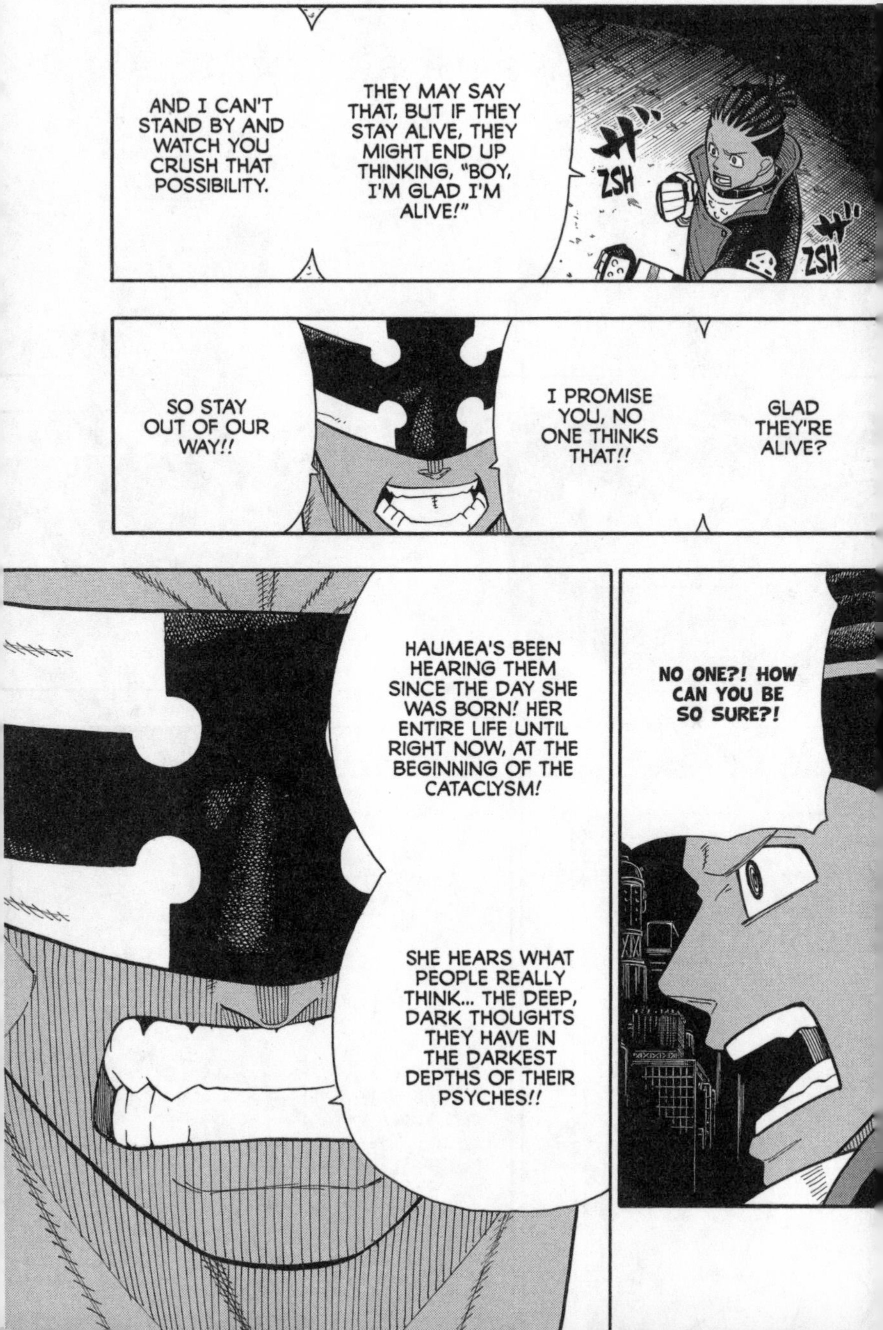
ZSH
ZSH
THEY MAY SAY THAT, BUT IF THEY STAY ALIVE, THEY MIGHT END UP THINKING, "BOY, I'M GLAD I'M ALIVE!"
AND I CAN'T STAND BY AND WATCH YOU CRUSH THAT POSSIBILITY.
GLAD THEY'RE ALIVE?
I PROMISE YOU, NO ONE THINKS THAT!!
SO STAY OUT OF OUR WAY!!
NO ONE?! HOW CAN YOU BE SO SURE?!
HAUMEA'S BEEN HEARING THEM SINCE THE DAY SHE WAS BORN! HER ENTIRE LIFE UNTIL RIGHT NOW, AT THE BEGINNING OF THE CATACLYSM!
SHE HEARS WHAT PEOPLE REALLY THINK... THE DEEP, DARK THOUGHTS THEY HAVE IN THE DARKEST DEPTHS OF THEIR PSYCHES!!

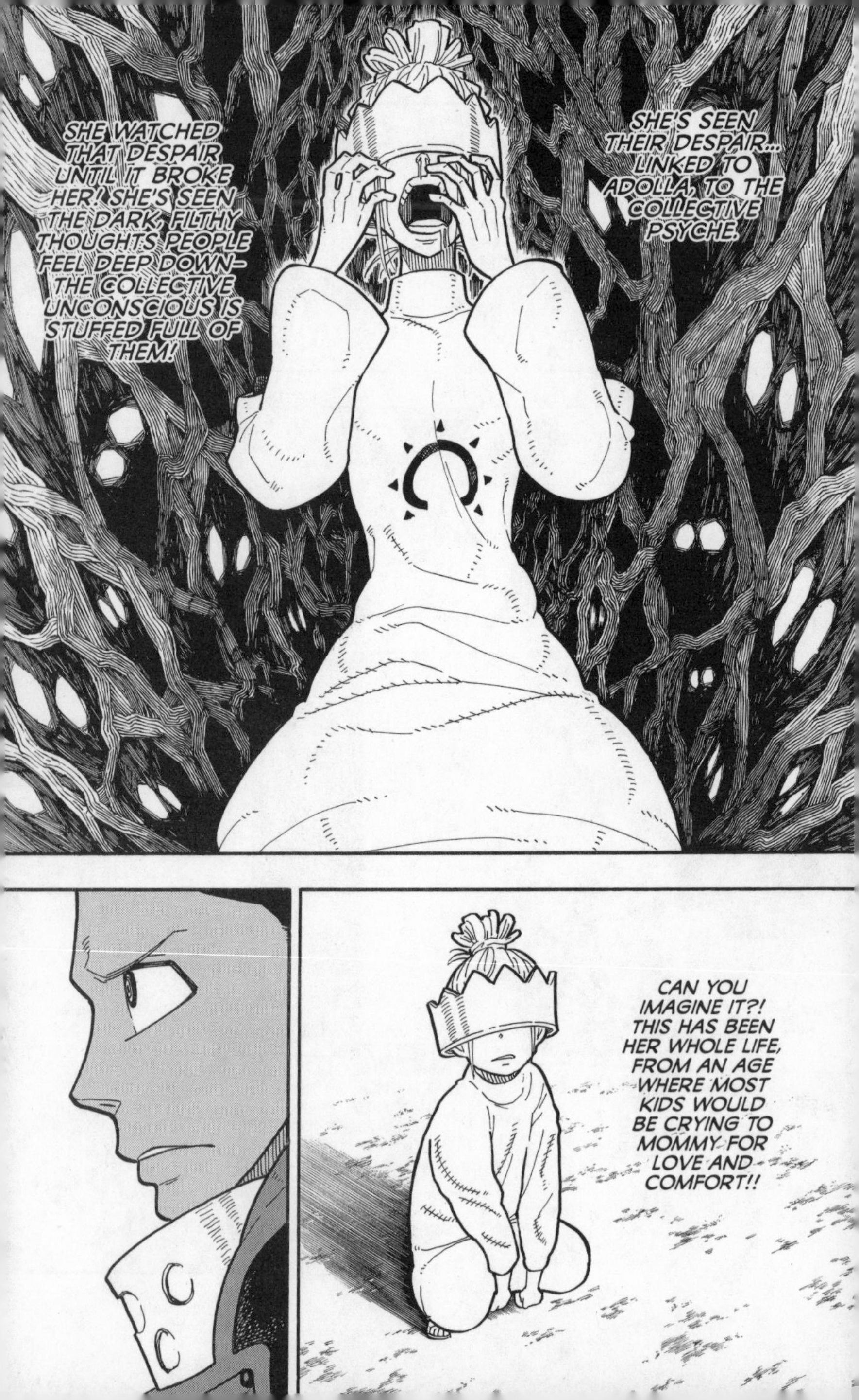
SHE'S SEEN THEIR DESPAIR... LINKED TO ADOLLA, TO THE COLLECTIVE PSYCHE.
SHE WATCHED THAT DESPAIR UNTIL IT BROKE HER! SHE'S SEEN THE DARK, FILTHY THOUGHTS PEOPLE FEEL DEEP DOWN-- THE COLLECTIVE UNCONSCIOUS IS STUFFED FULL OF THEM!
CAN YOU IMAGINE IT?! THIS HAS BEEN HER WHOLE LIFE, FROM AN AGE WHERE MOST KIDS WOULD BE CRYING TO MOMMY FOR LOVE AND COMFORT!!

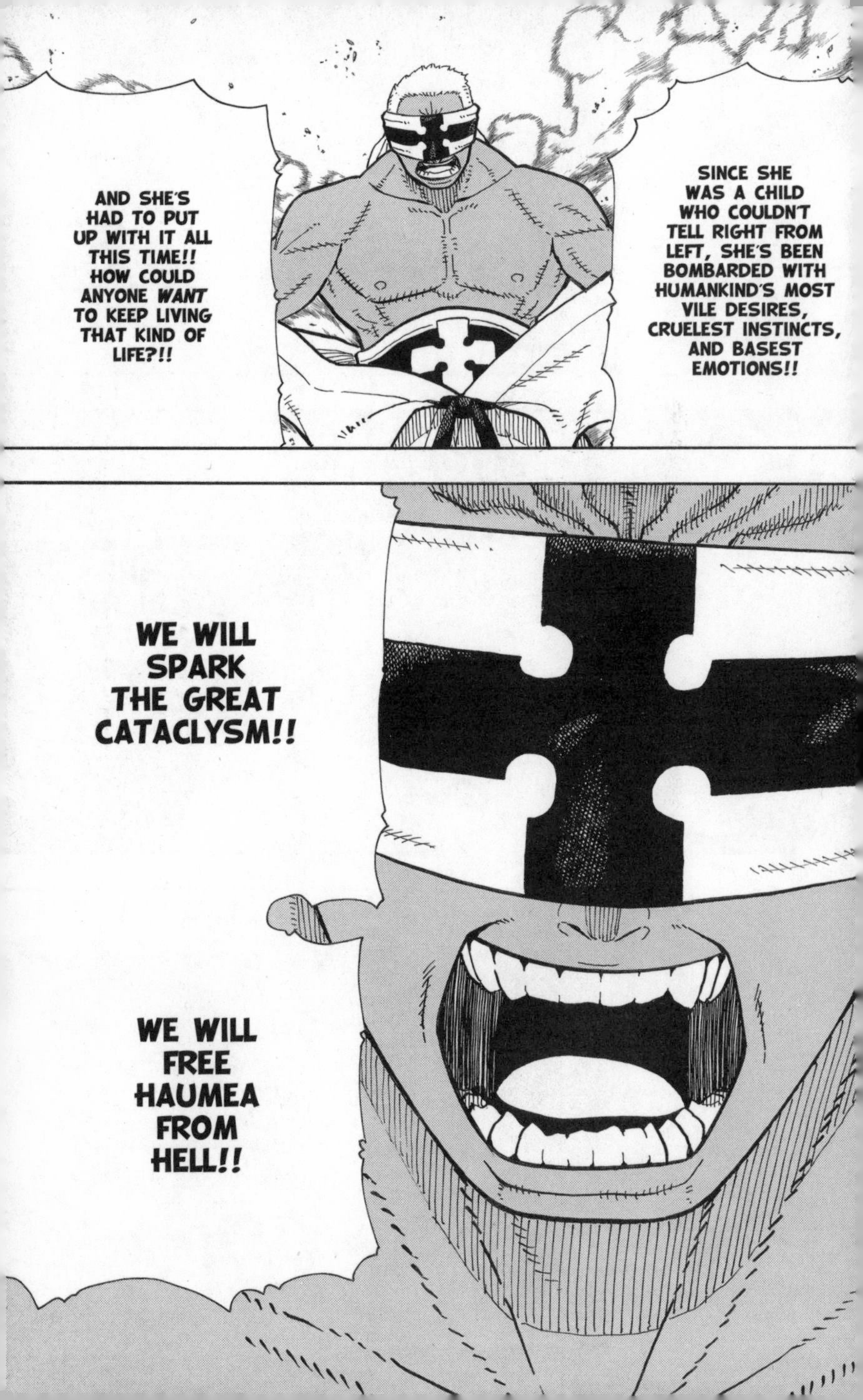
SINCE SHE WAS A CHILD WHO COULDN'T TELL RIGHT FROM LEFT, SHE'S BEEN BOMBARDED WITH HUMANKIND'S MOST VILE DESIRES, CRUELEST INSTINCTS, AND BASEST EMOTIONS!!
AND SHE'S HAD TO PUT UP WITH IT ALL THIS TIME!! HOW COULD ANYONE *WANT* TO KEEP LIVING THAT KIND OF LIFE?!!
WE WILL SPARK THE GREAT CATACLYSM!!
WE WILL FREE HAUMEA FROM HELL!!

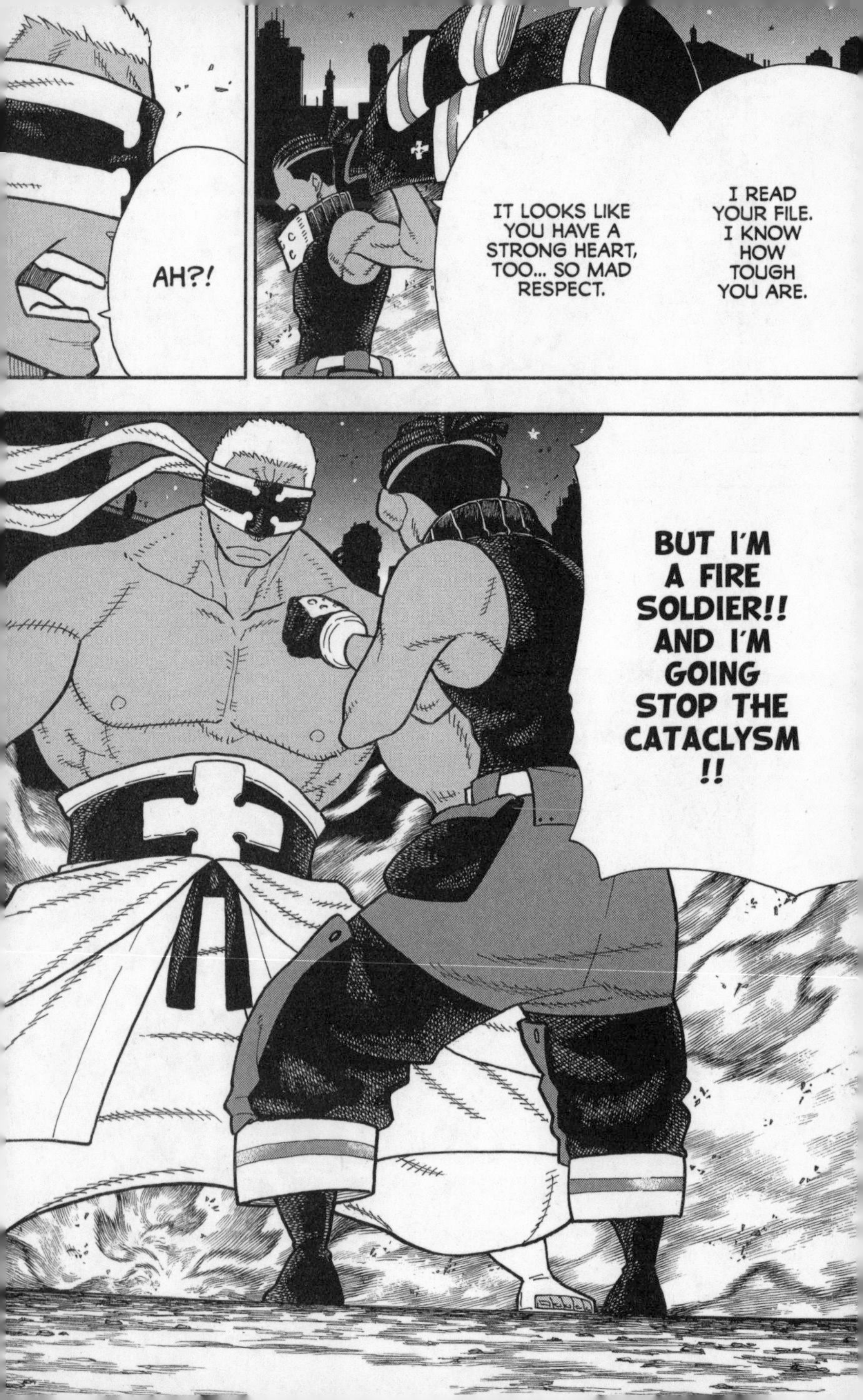
I READ YOUR FILE. I KNOW HOW TOUGH YOU ARE.
IT LOOKS LIKE YOU HAVE A STRONG HEART, TOO... SO MAD RESPECT.
AH?!
BUT I'M A FIRE SOLDIER!! AND I'M GOING STOP THE CATACLYSM!!

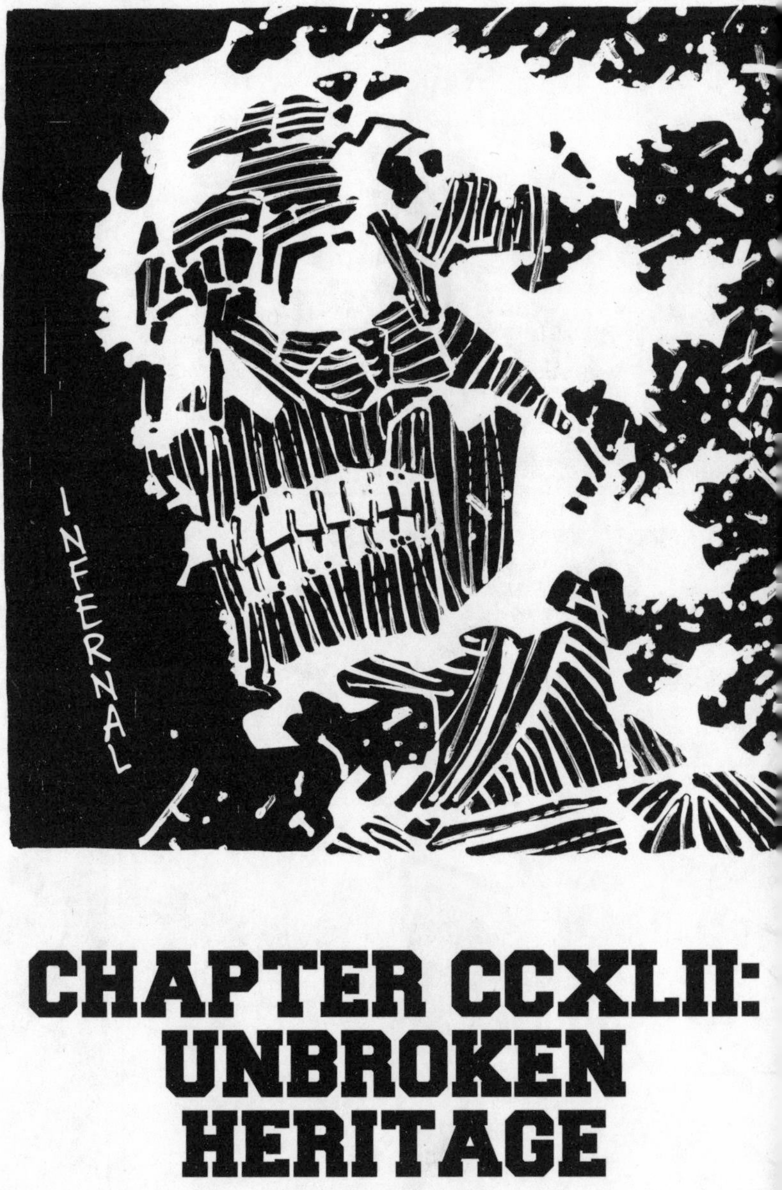
INFERNAL

CHAPTER CCXLII: UNBROKEN HERITAGE

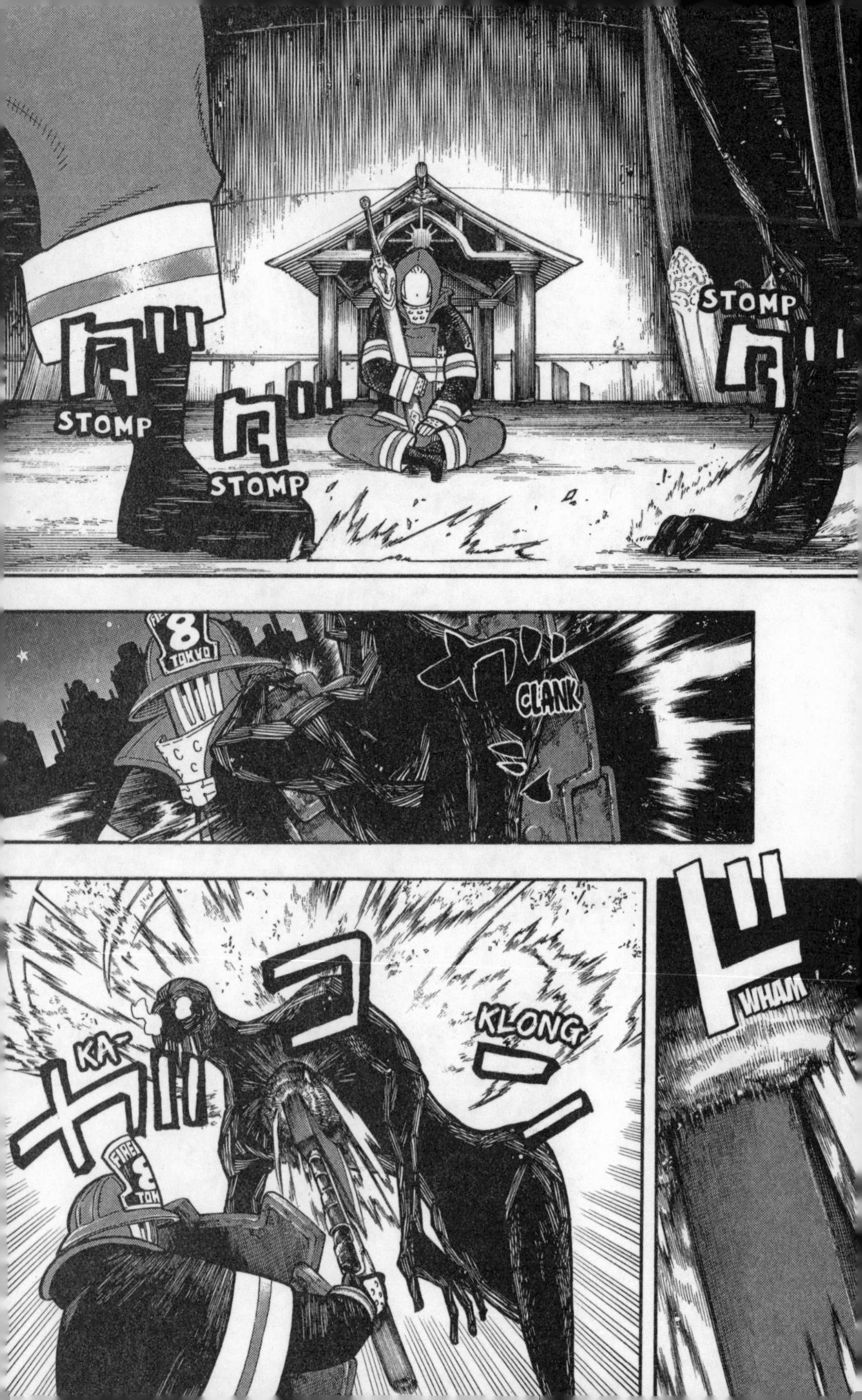
STOMP
STOMP
STOMP
CLANK
WHAM
KLONG
KA-

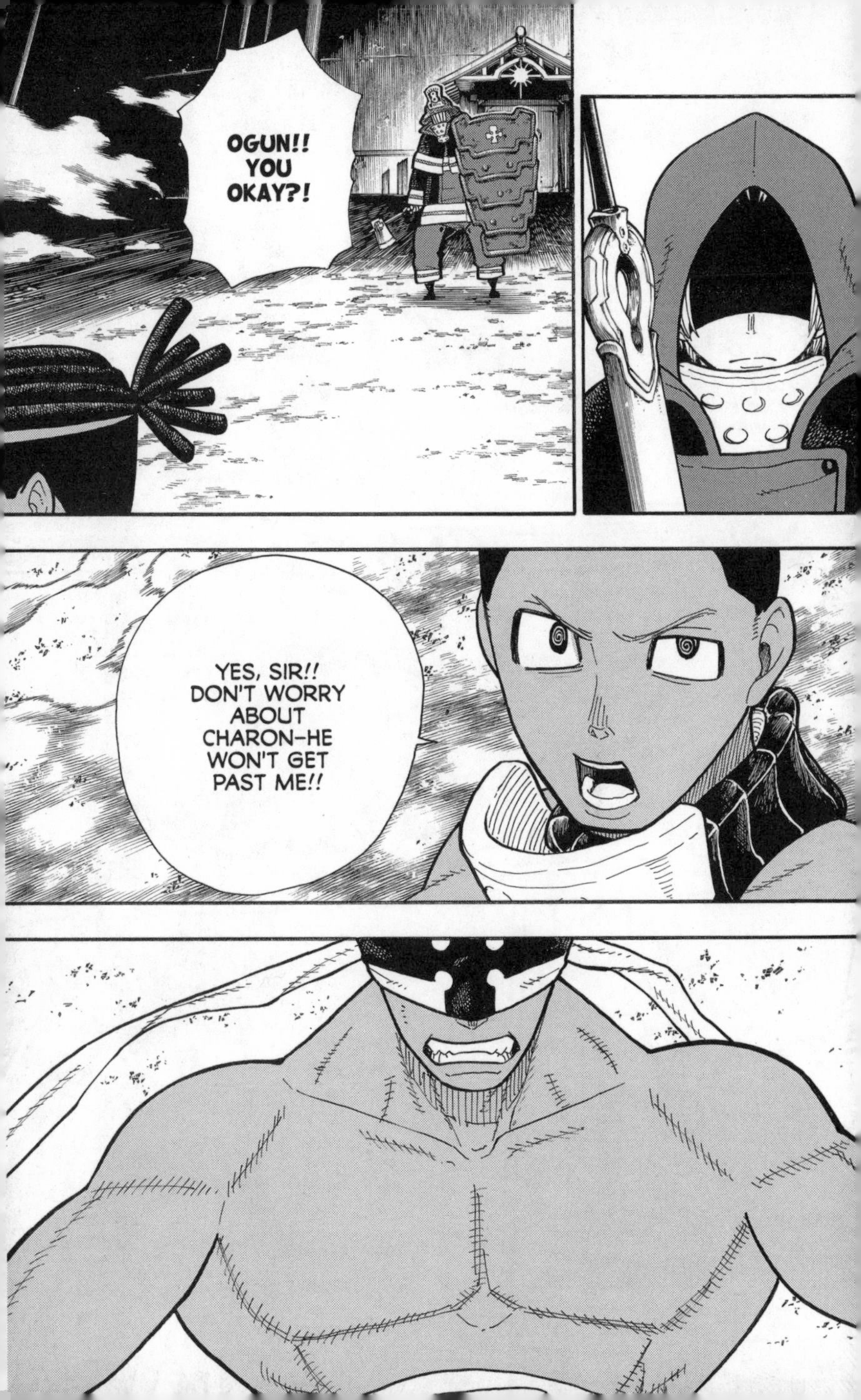
OGUN!! YOU OKAY?!
YES, SIR!! DON'T WORRY ABOUT CHARON–HE WON'T GET PAST ME!!

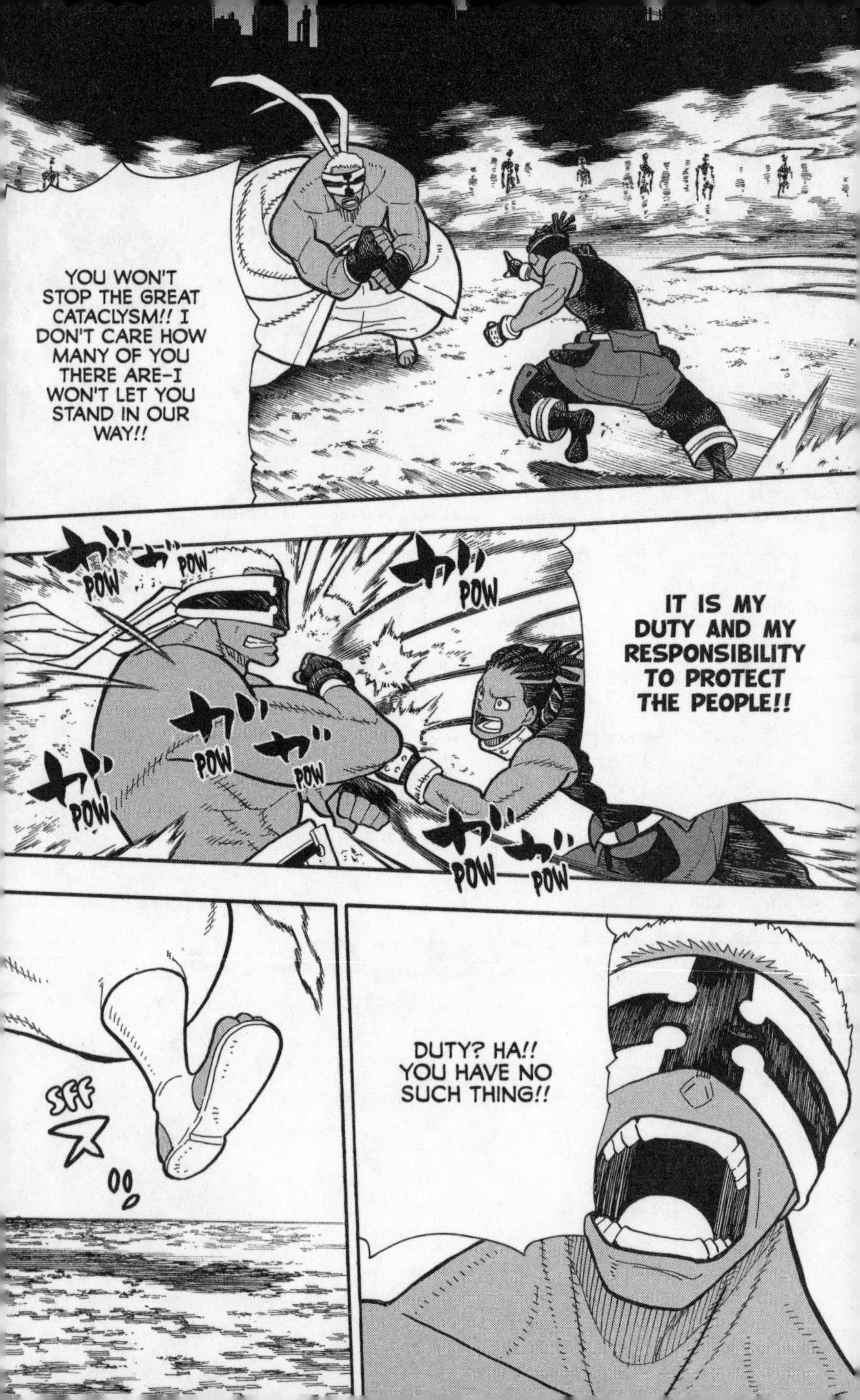
YOU WON'T STOP THE GREAT CATACLYSM!! I DON'T CARE HOW MANY OF YOU THERE ARE–I WON'T LET YOU STAND IN OUR WAY!!
POW
POW
POW
IT IS MY DUTY AND MY RESPONSIBILITY TO PROTECT THE PEOPLE!!
POW
POW
POW
POW
POW
DUTY? HA!! YOU HAVE NO SUCH THING!!
SFF

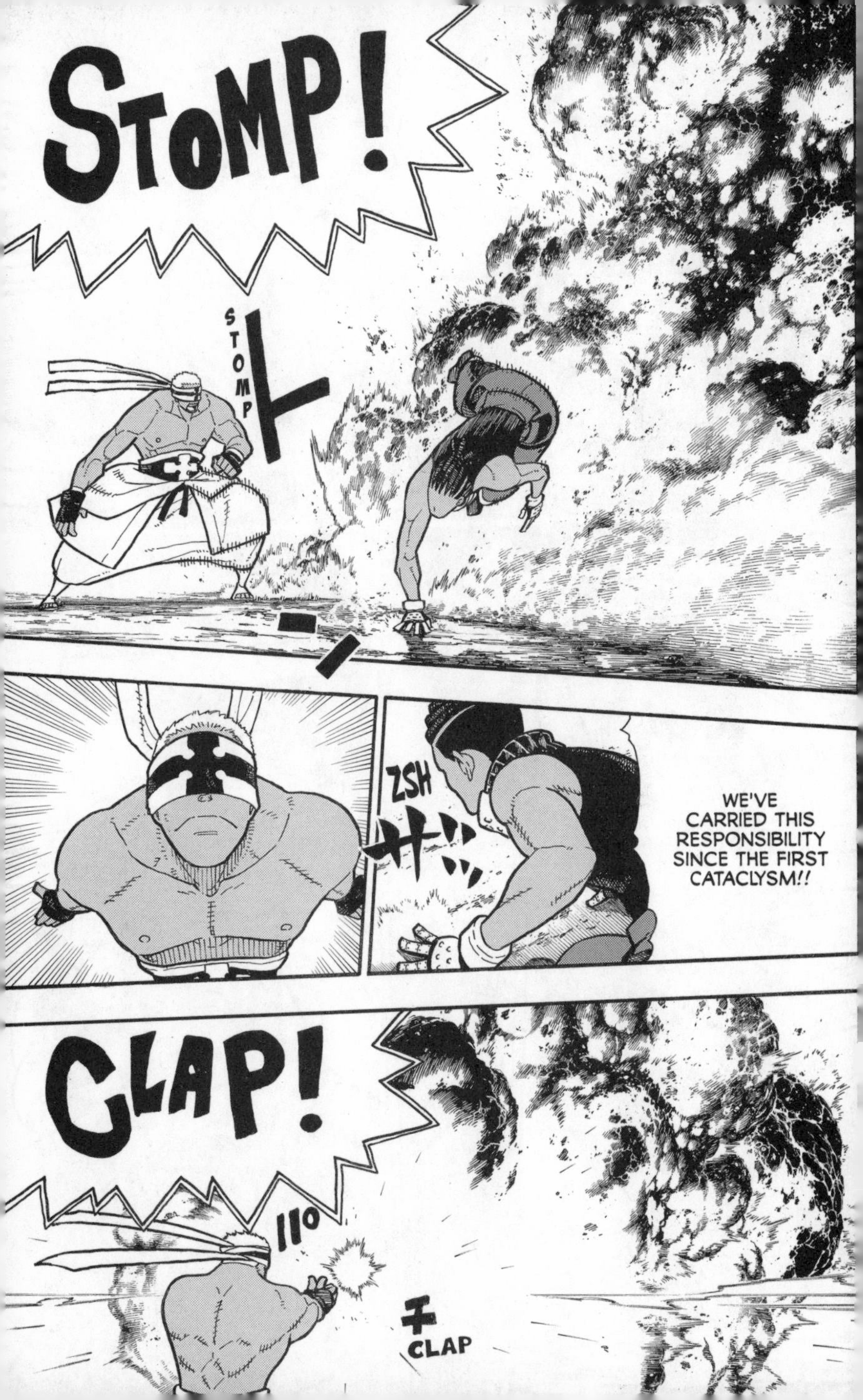
STOMP!
STOMP
WE'VE CARRIED THIS RESPONSIBILITY SINCE THE FIRST CATACLYSM!!
ZSH
CLAP!
CLAP

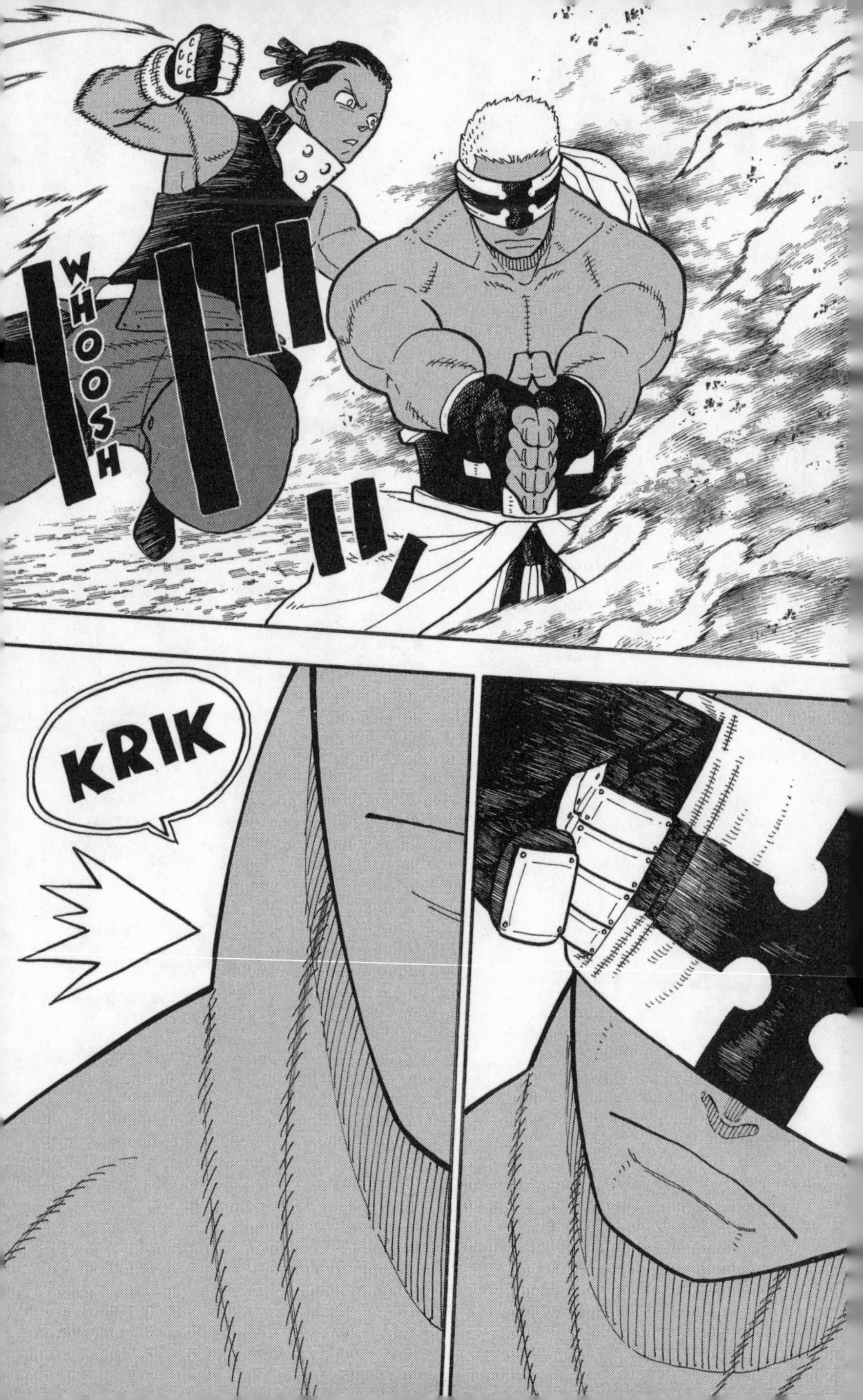
WHOOSH
KRIK

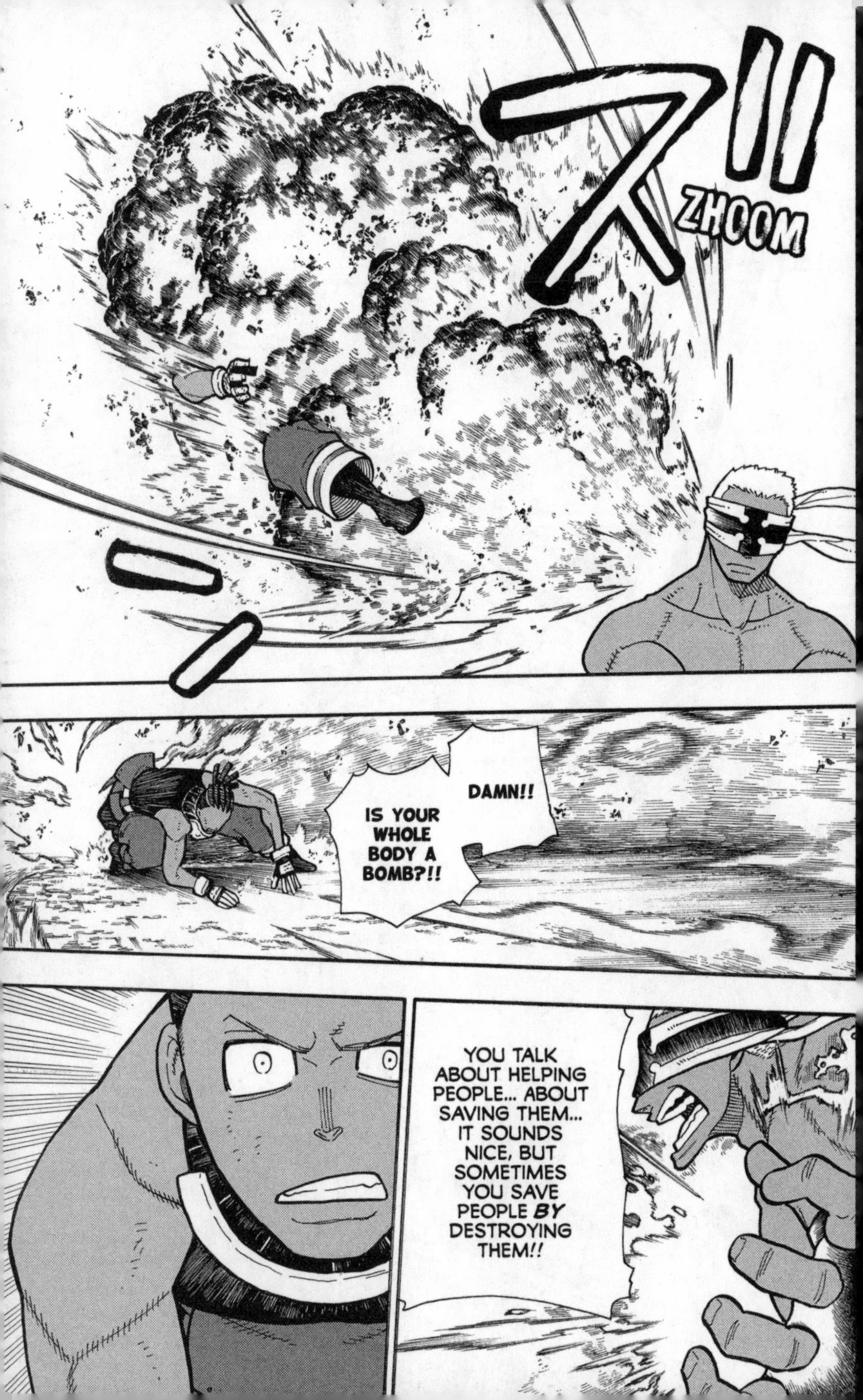
ZHOOM
DAMN!!
IS YOUR WHOLE BODY A BOMB?!!
YOU TALK ABOUT HELPING PEOPLE... ABOUT SAVING THEM... IT SOUNDS NICE, BUT SOMETIMES YOU SAVE PEOPLE *BY* DESTROYING THEM!!

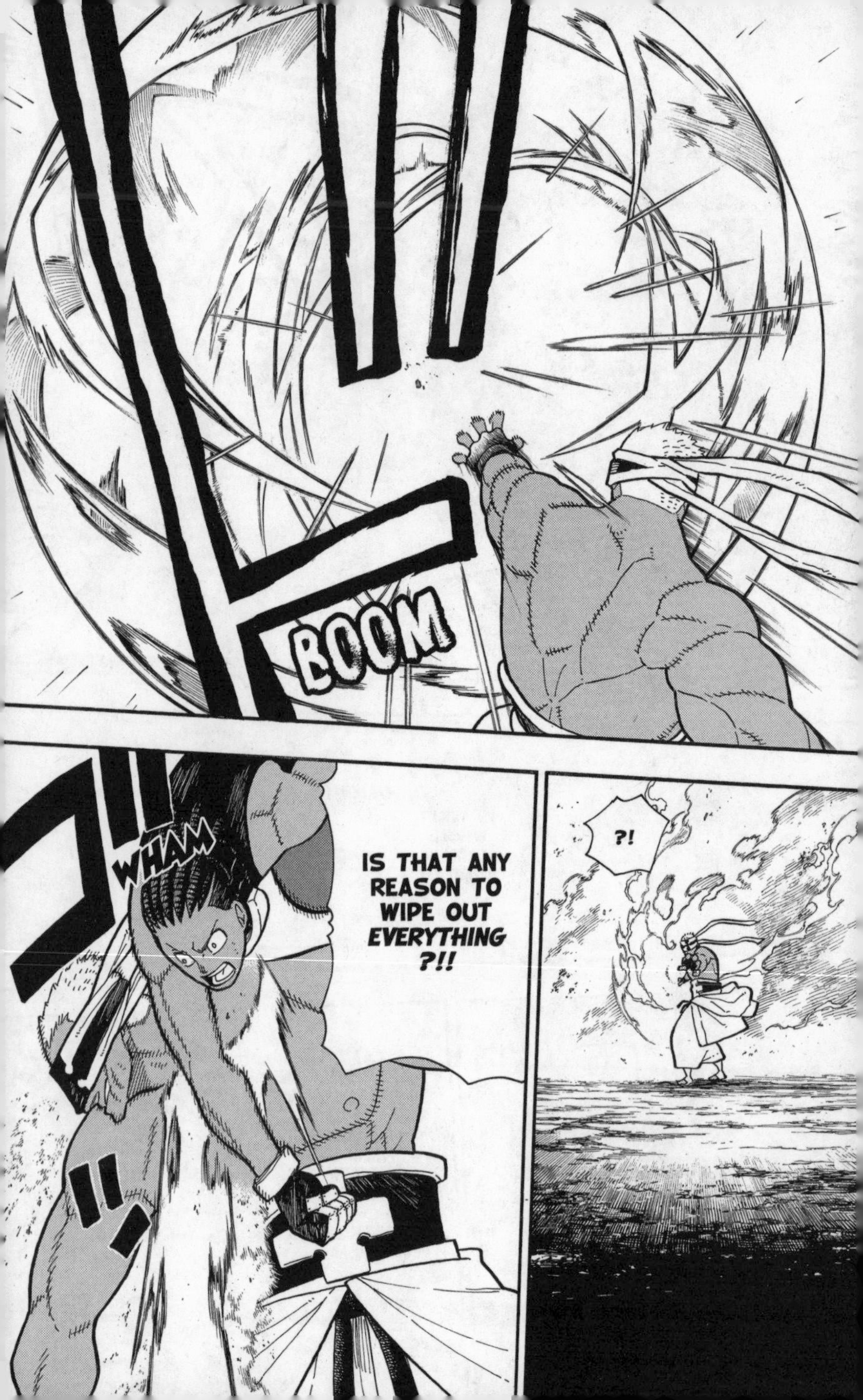
BOOM
?!
WHAM
IS THAT ANY REASON TO WIPE OUT EVERYTHING ?!!

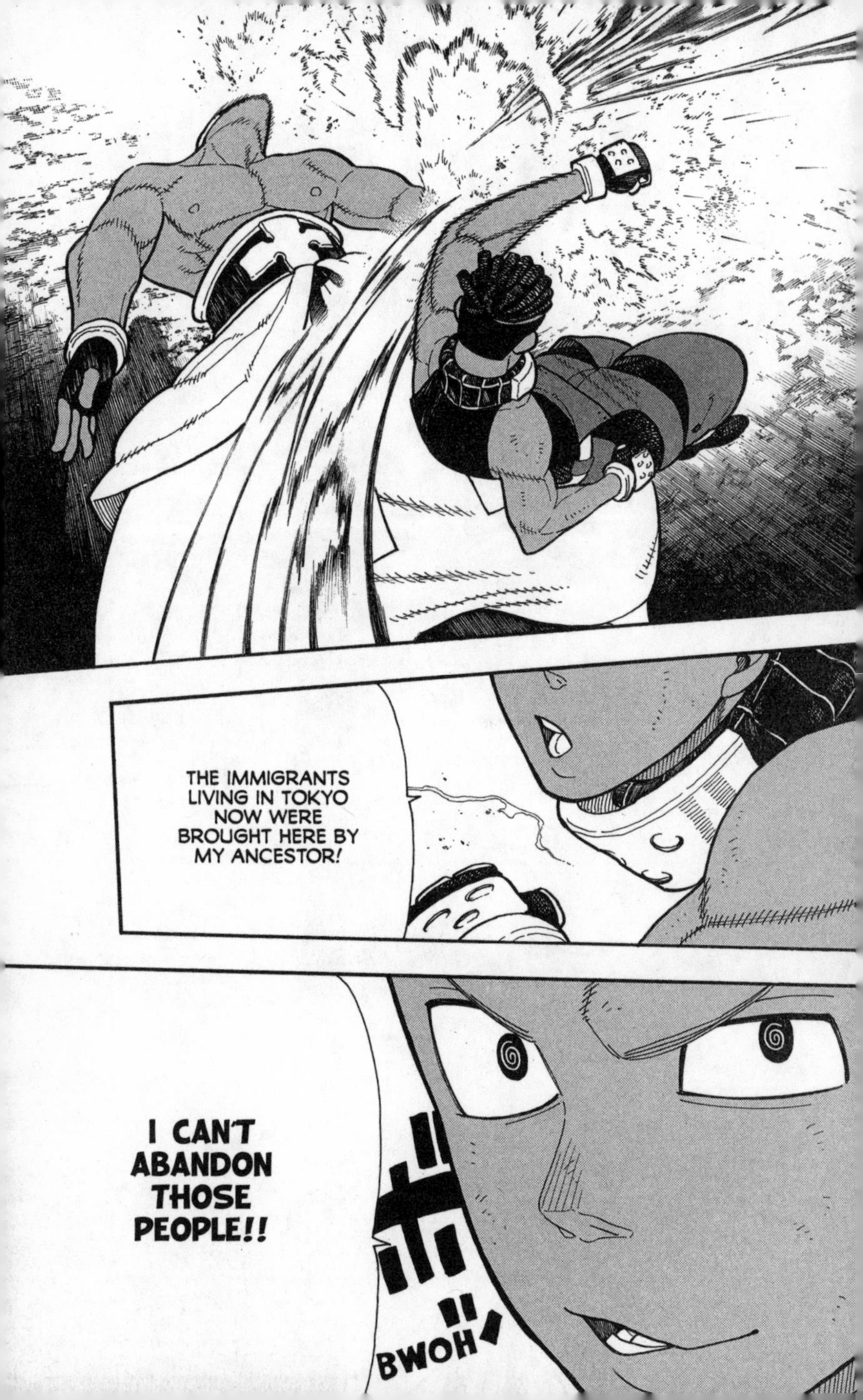
THE IMMIGRANTS LIVING IN TOKYO NOW WERE BROUGHT HERE BY MY ANCESTOR!
I CAN'T ABANDON THOSE PEOPLE!!
BWOH

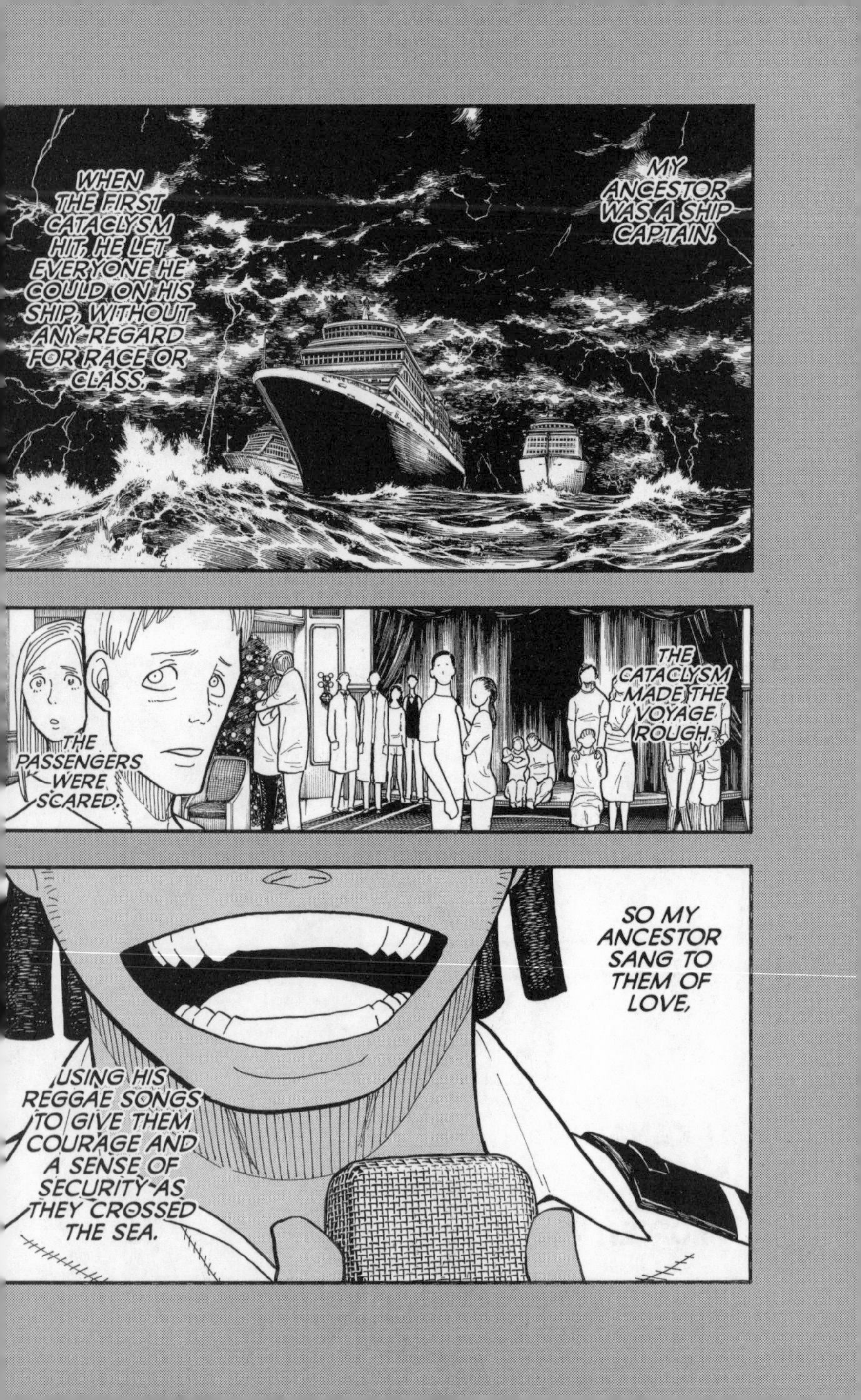
MY ANCESTOR WAS A SHIP CAPTAIN.
WHEN THE FIRST CATACLYSM HIT, HE LET EVERYONE HE COULD ON HIS SHIP, WITHOUT ANY REGARD FOR RACE OR CLASS.
THE CATACLYSM MADE THE VOYAGE ROUGH.
THE PASSENGERS WERE SCARED.
SO MY ANCESTOR SANG TO THEM OF LOVE,
USING HIS REGGAE SONGS TO GIVE THEM COURAGE AND A SENSE OF SECURITY AS THEY CROSSED THE SEA.

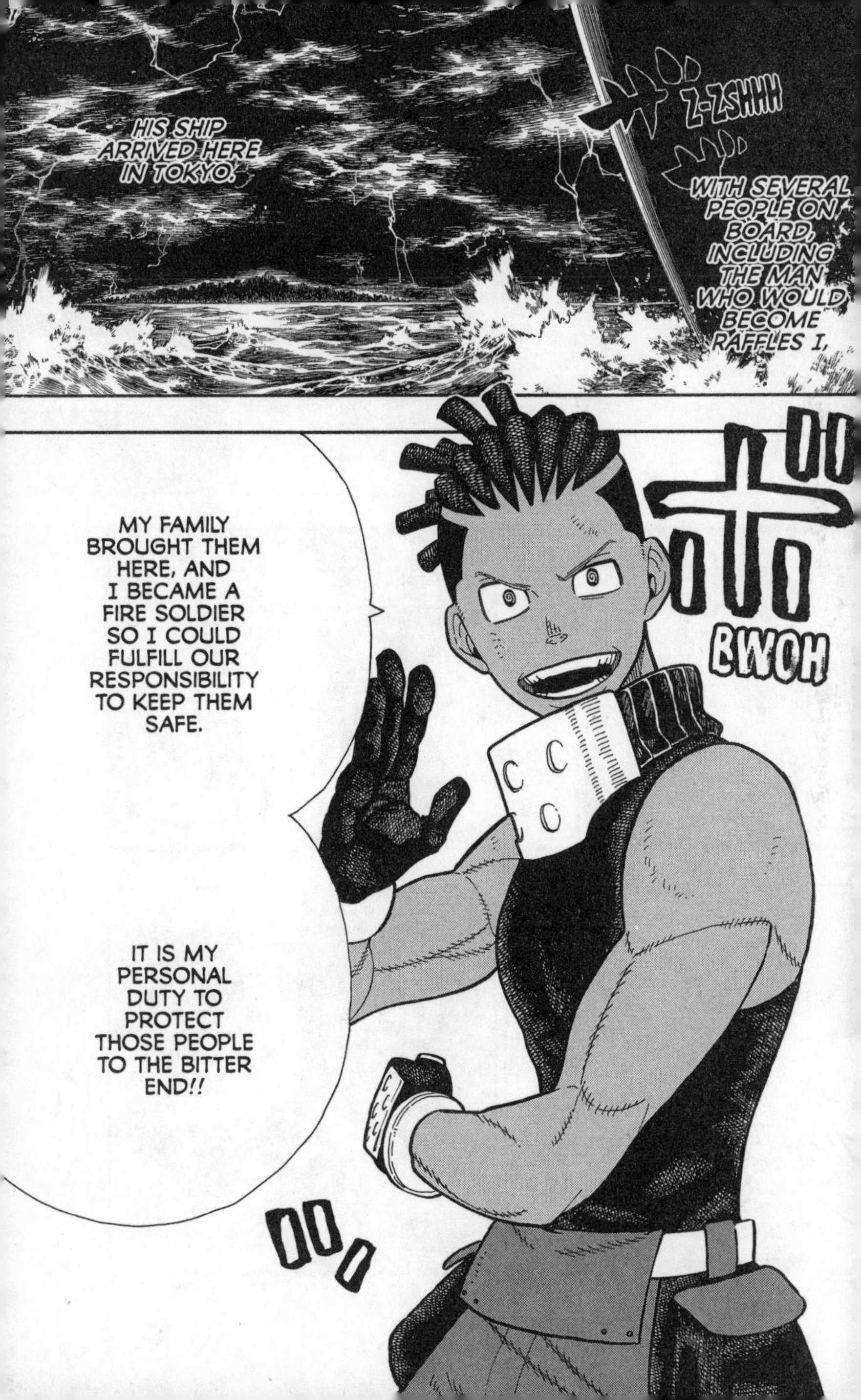
Z-ZSHHH
WITH SEVERAL PEOPLE ON BOARD, INCLUDING THE MAN WHO WOULD BECOME RAFFLES I,
HIS SHIP ARRIVED HERE IN TOKYO.
BWOH
MY FAMILY BROUGHT THEM HERE, AND I BECAME A FIRE SOLDIER SO I COULD FULFILL OUR RESPONSIBILITY TO KEEP THEM SAFE.
IT IS MY PERSONAL DUTY TO PROTECT THOSE PEOPLE TO THE BITTER END!!

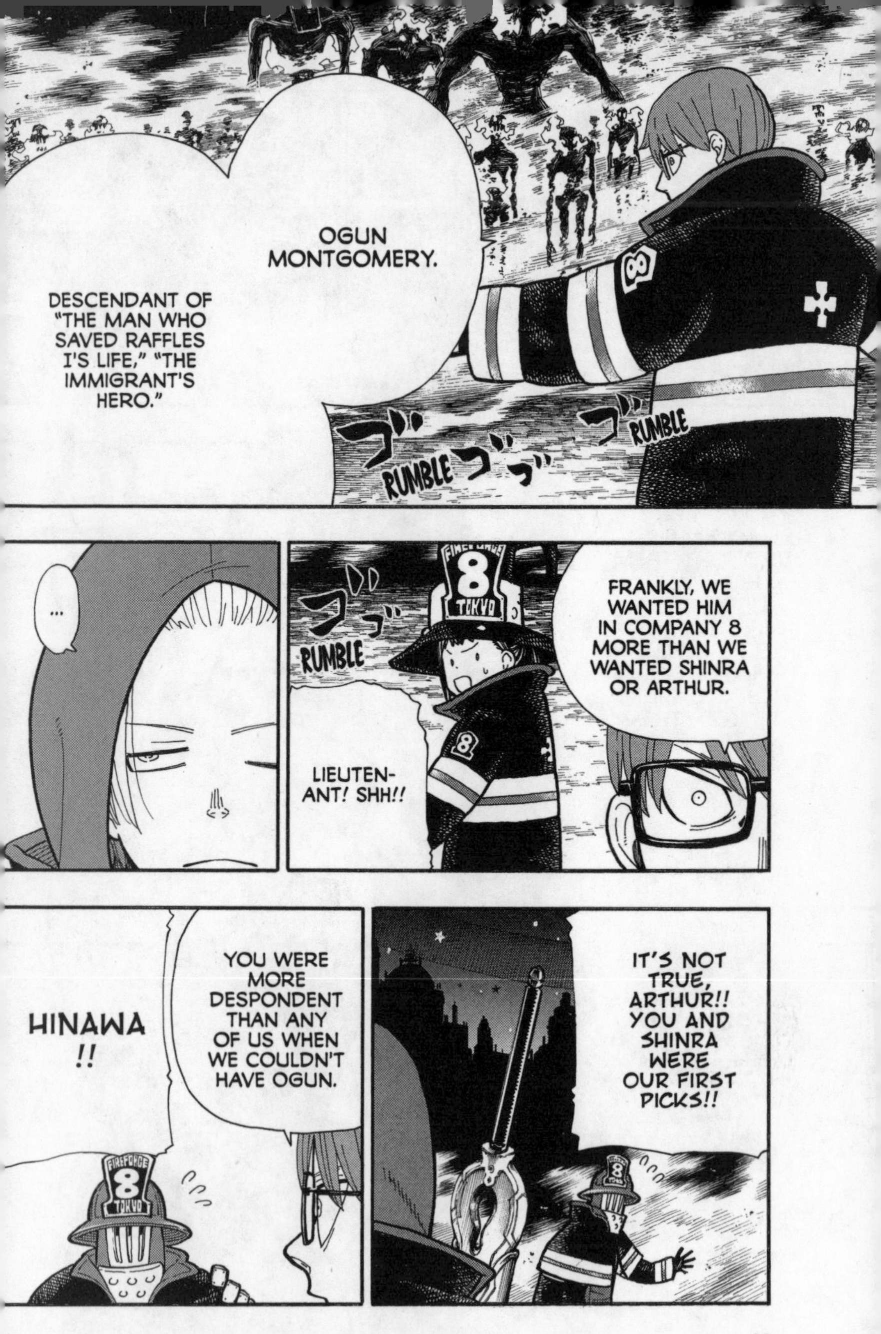
OGUN MONTGOMERY.
DESCENDANT OF "THE MAN WHO SAVED RAFFLES I'S LIFE," "THE IMMIGRANT'S HERO."
RUMBLE
RUMBLE
FRANKLY, WE WANTED HIM IN COMPANY 8 MORE THAN WE WANTED SHINRA OR ARTHUR.
RUMBLE
LIEUTEN-ANT! SHH!!
...
IT'S NOT TRUE, ARTHUR!! YOU AND SHINRA WERE OUR FIRST PICKS!!
YOU WERE MORE DESPONDENT THAN ANY OF US WHEN WE COULDN'T HAVE OGUN.
HINAWA!!

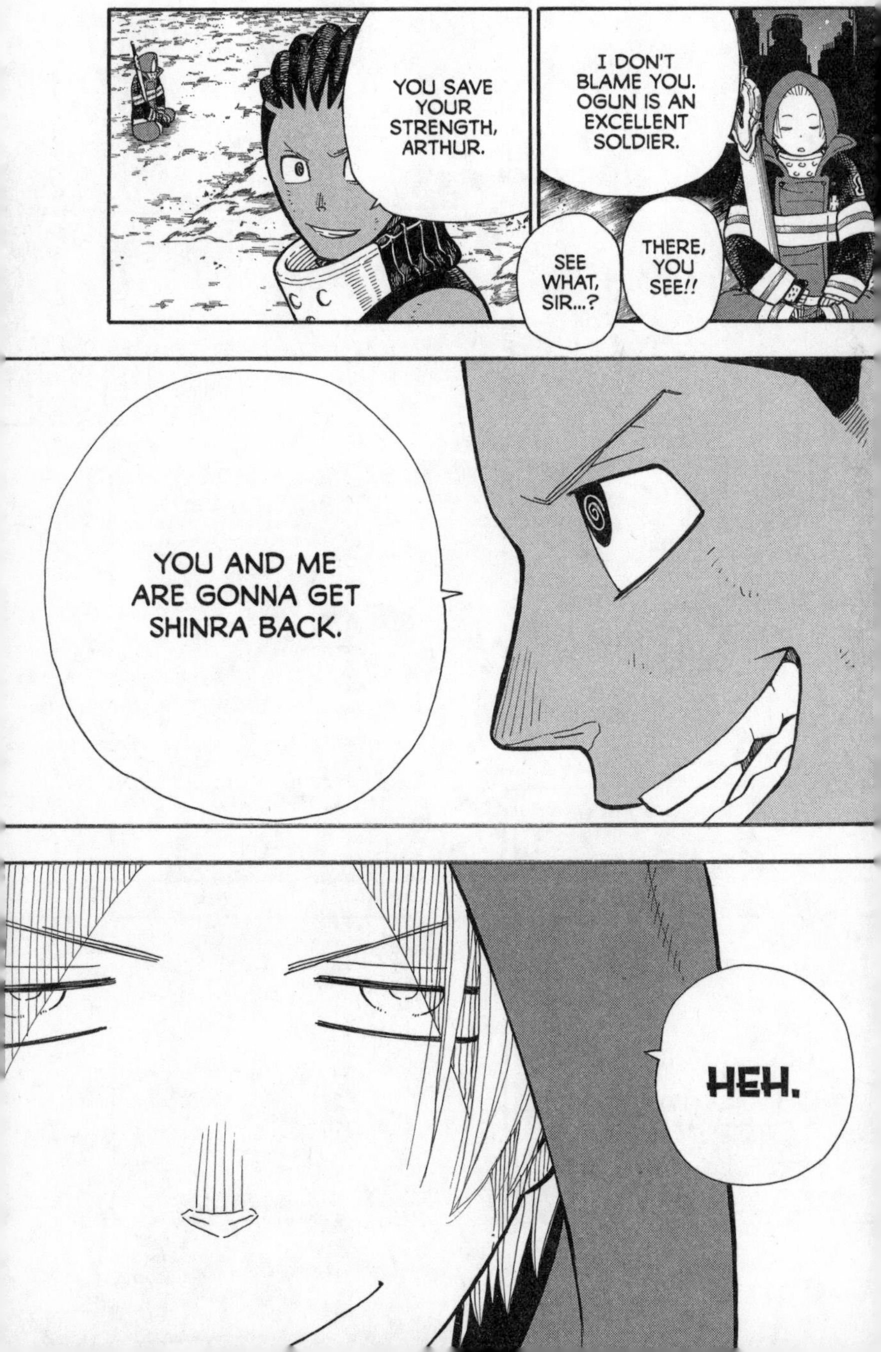
I DON'T BLAME YOU. OGUN IS AN EXCELLENT SOLDIER.
THERE, YOU SEE!!
SEE WHAT, SIR...?
YOU SAVE YOUR STRENGTH, ARTHUR.
YOU AND ME ARE GONNA GET SHINRA BACK.
HEH.

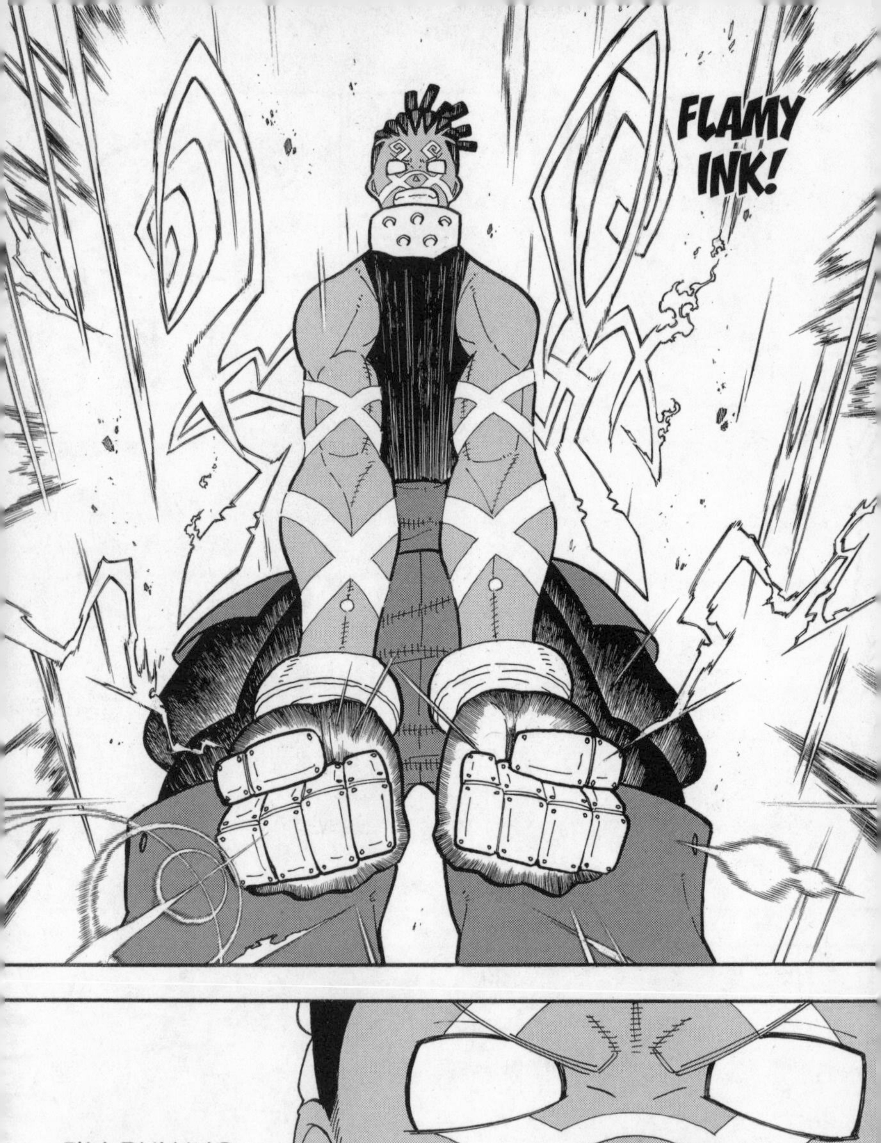
FLAMY INK!
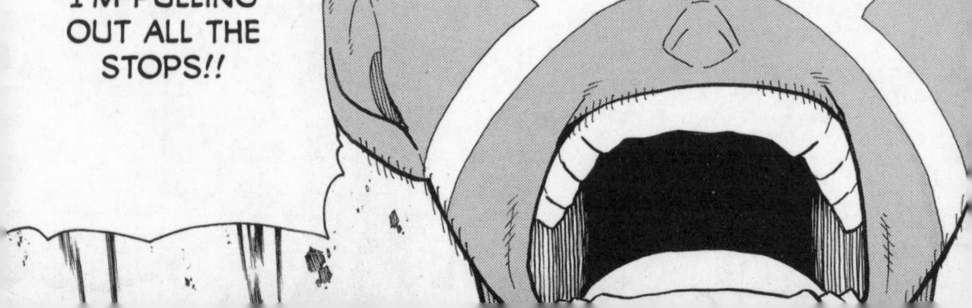
I'M PULLING OUT ALL THE STOPS!!

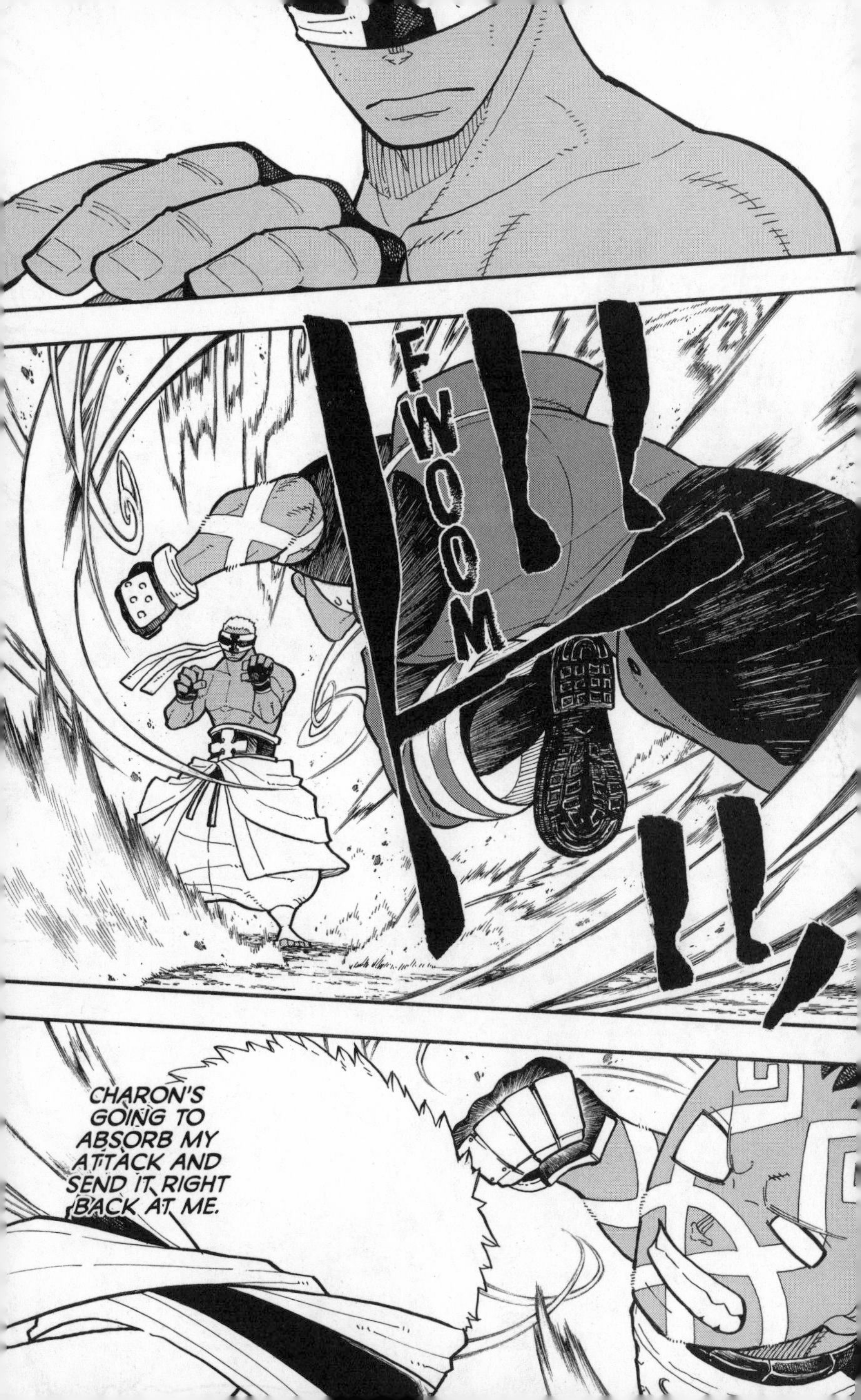
FWOOM
CHARON'S GOING TO ABSORB MY ATTACK AND SEND IT RIGHT BACK AT ME.

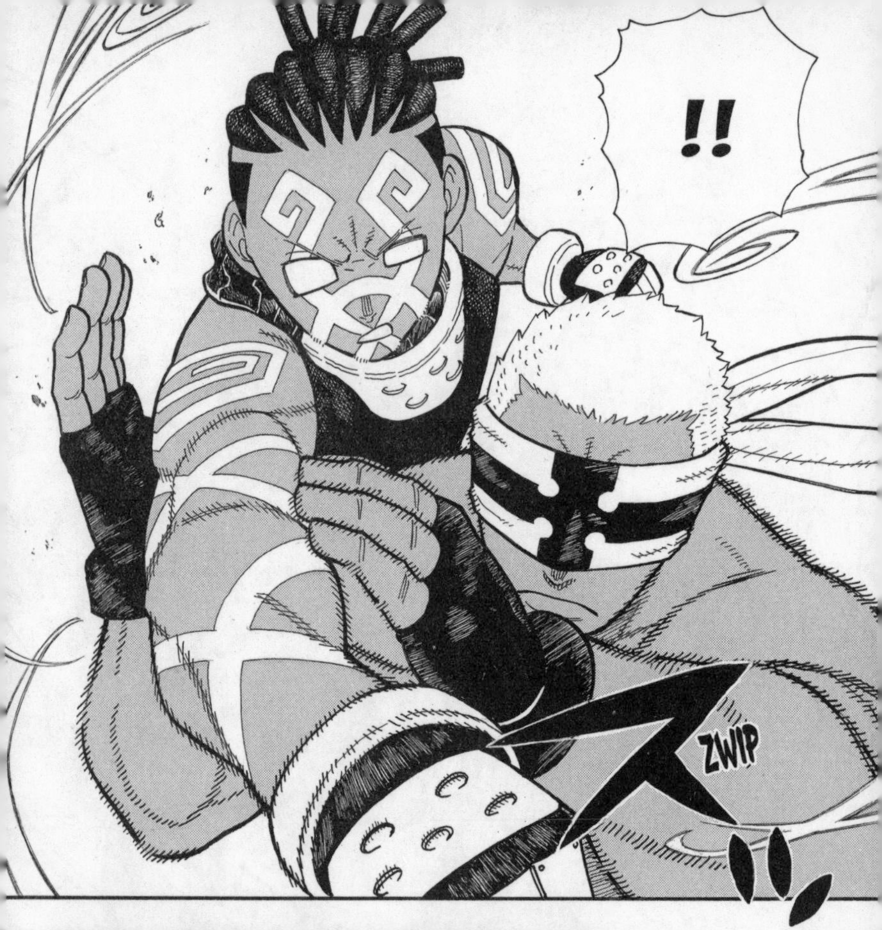
!!
ZWIP
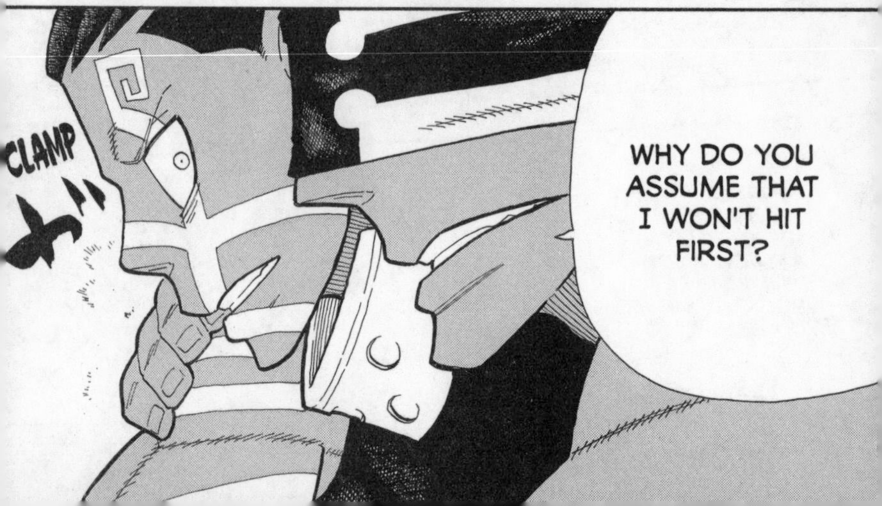
WHY DO YOU ASSUME THAT I WON'T HIT FIRST?
CLAMP

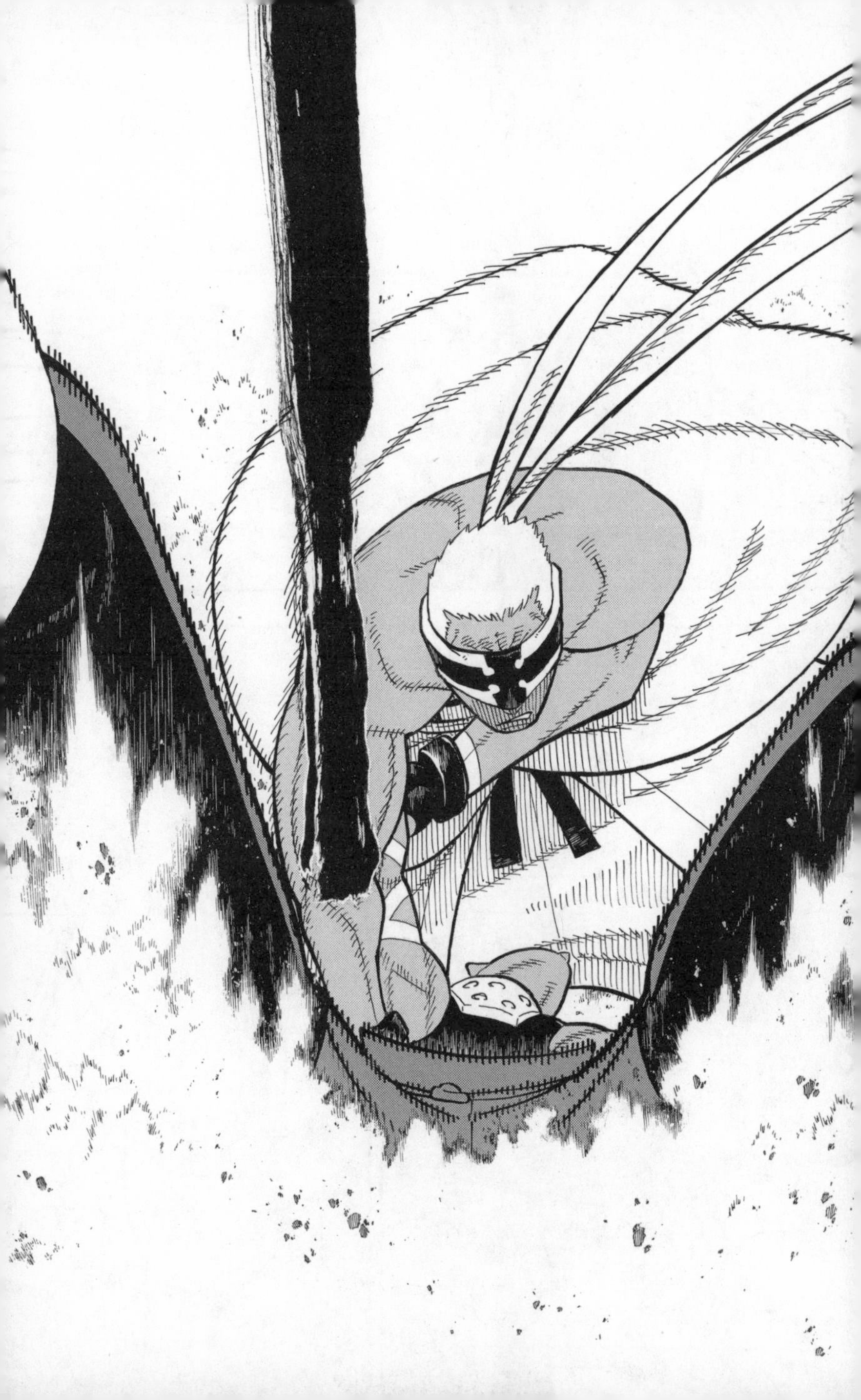

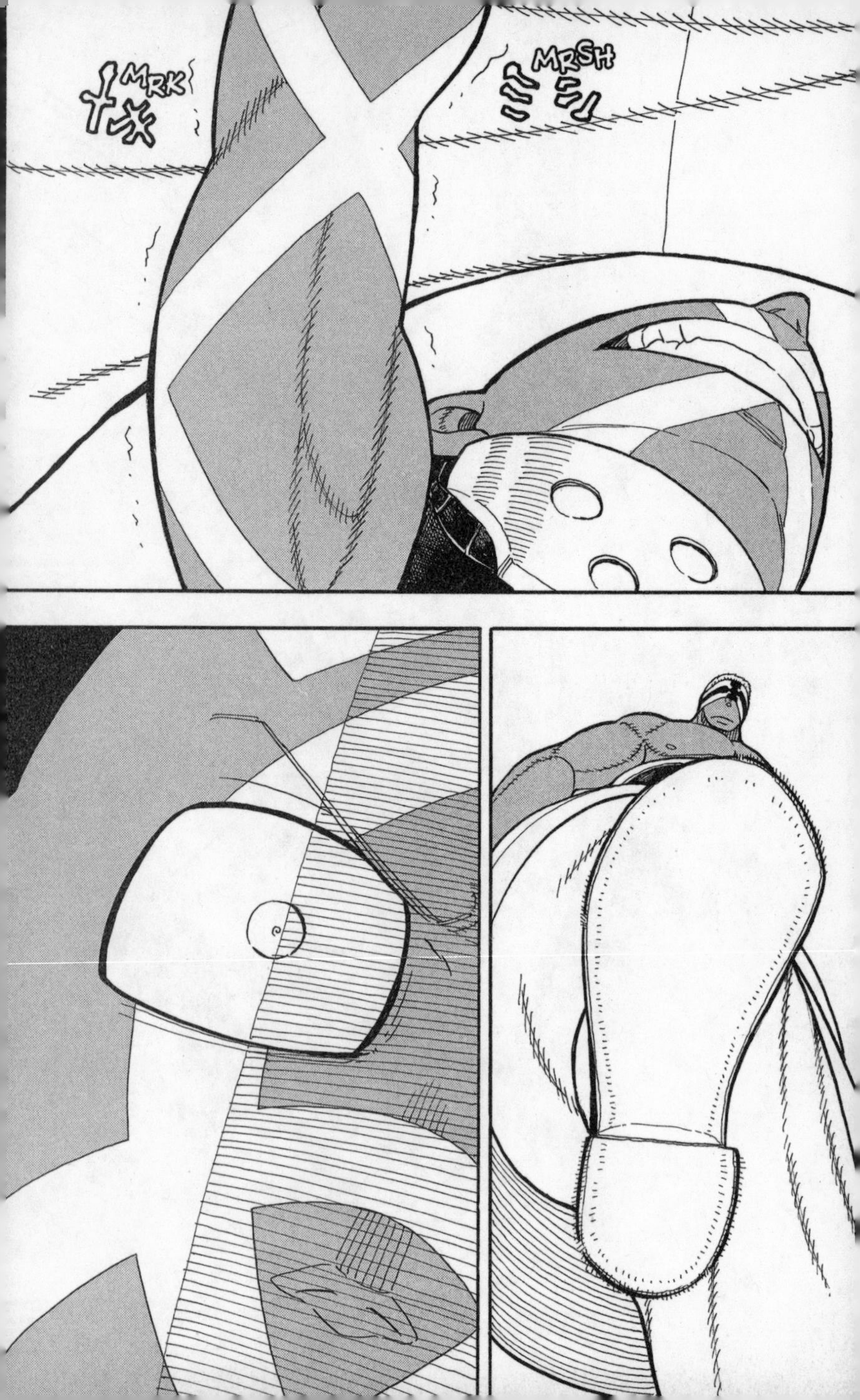
MRSH
MRK

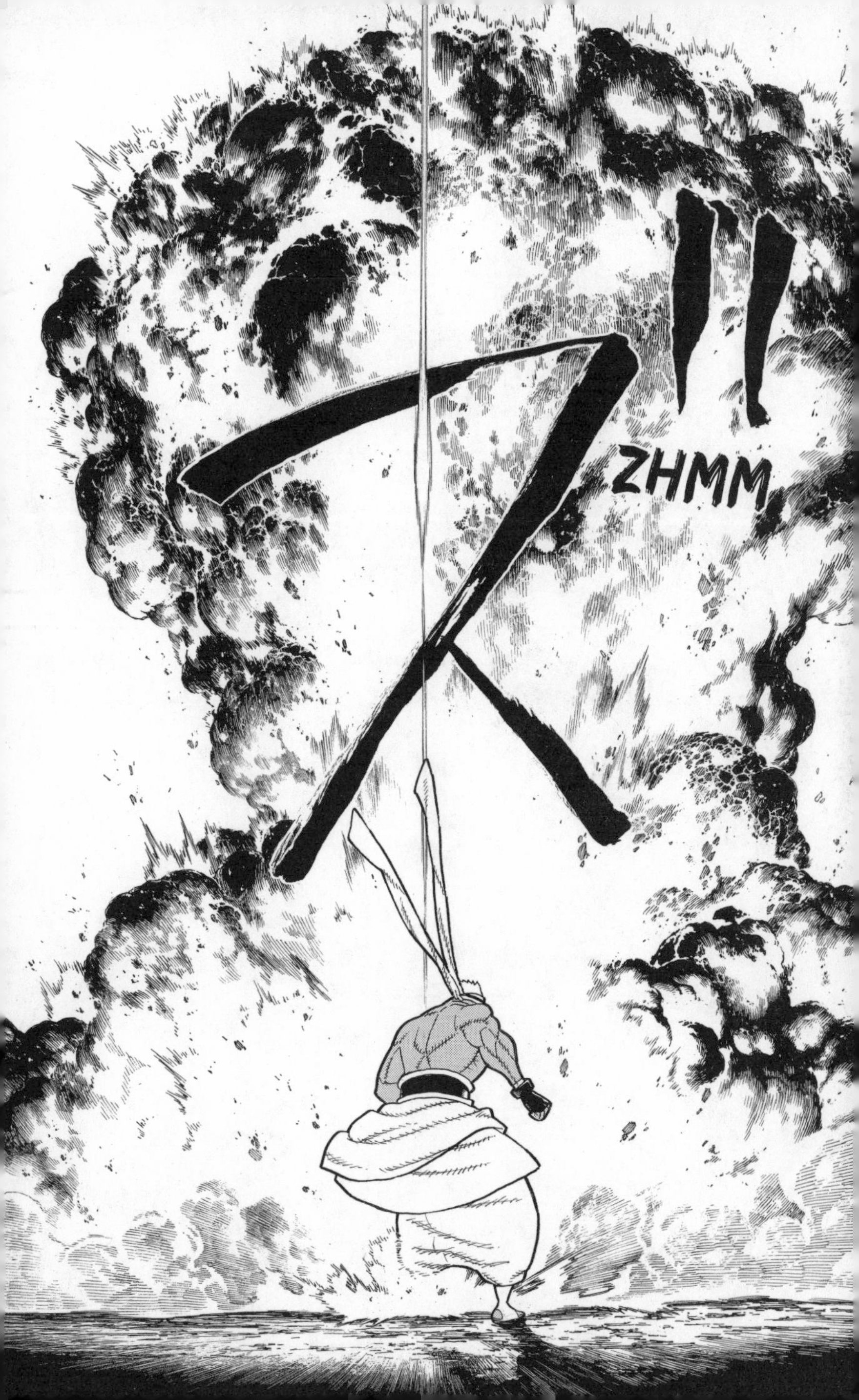
ZHMM

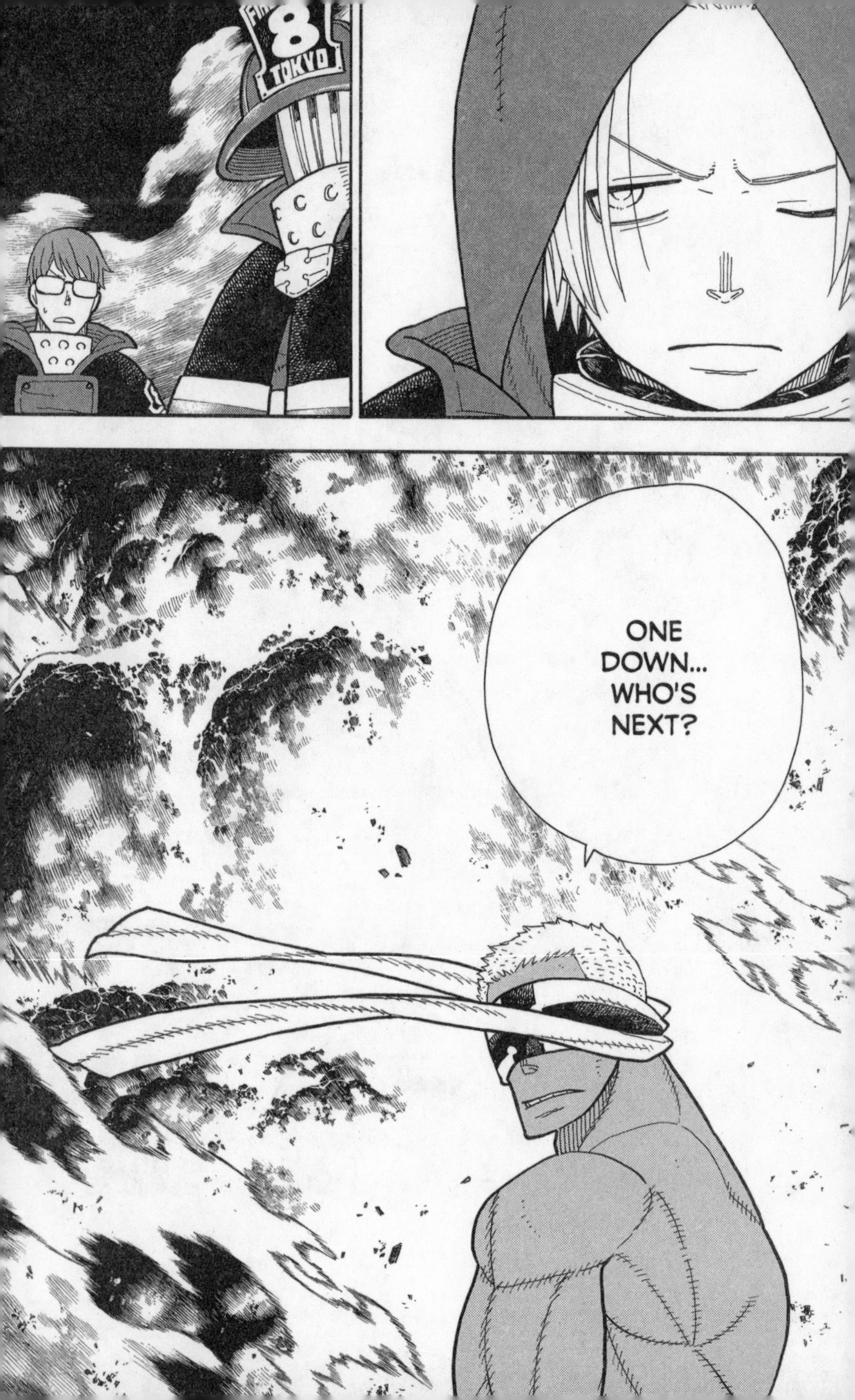
ONE DOWN... WHO'S NEXT?

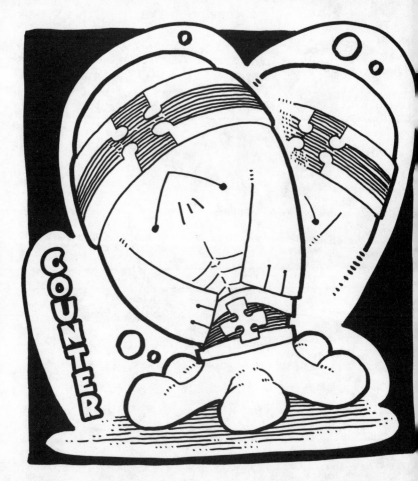

CHAPTER CCXLIII:
BACK IN THE DAY

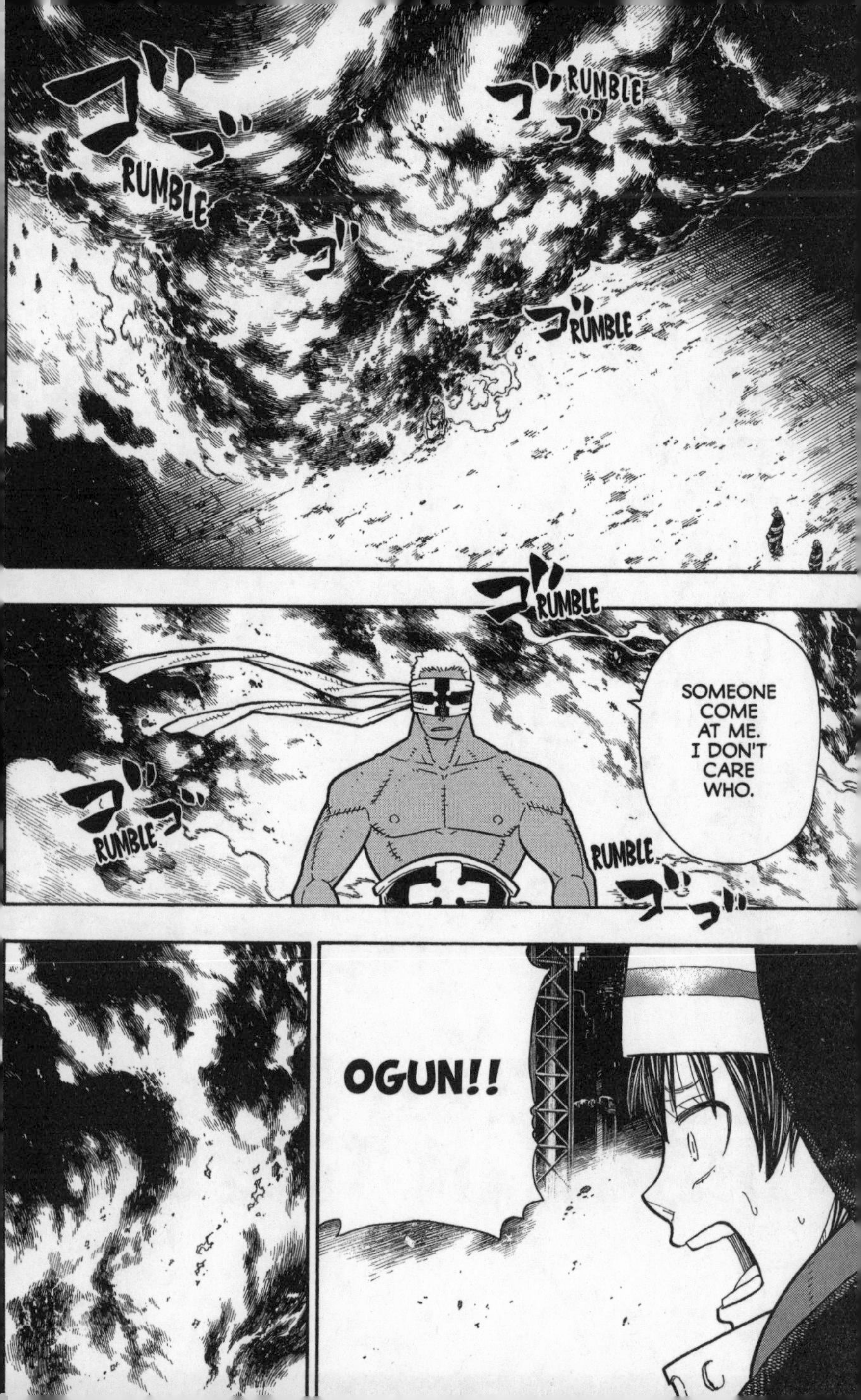

RUMBLE
RUMBLE
RUMBLE
RUMBLE
SOMEONE COME AT ME. I DON'T CARE WHO.
RUMBLE
RUMBLE
OGUN!!

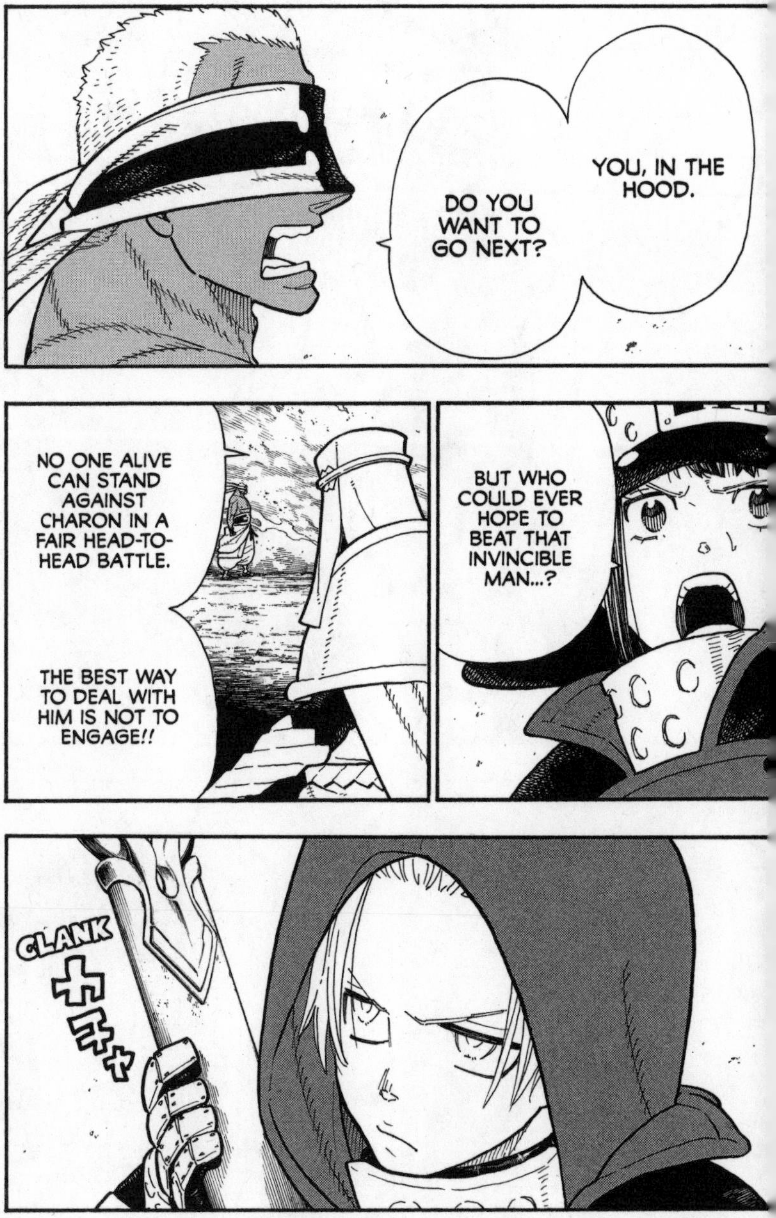
YOU, IN THE HOOD.
DO YOU WANT TO GO NEXT?
BUT WHO COULD EVER HOPE TO BEAT THAT INVINCIBLE MAN...?
NO ONE ALIVE CAN STAND AGAINST CHARON IN A FAIR HEAD-TO-HEAD BATTLE.
THE BEST WAY TO DEAL WITH HIM IS NOT TO ENGAGE!!
CLANK

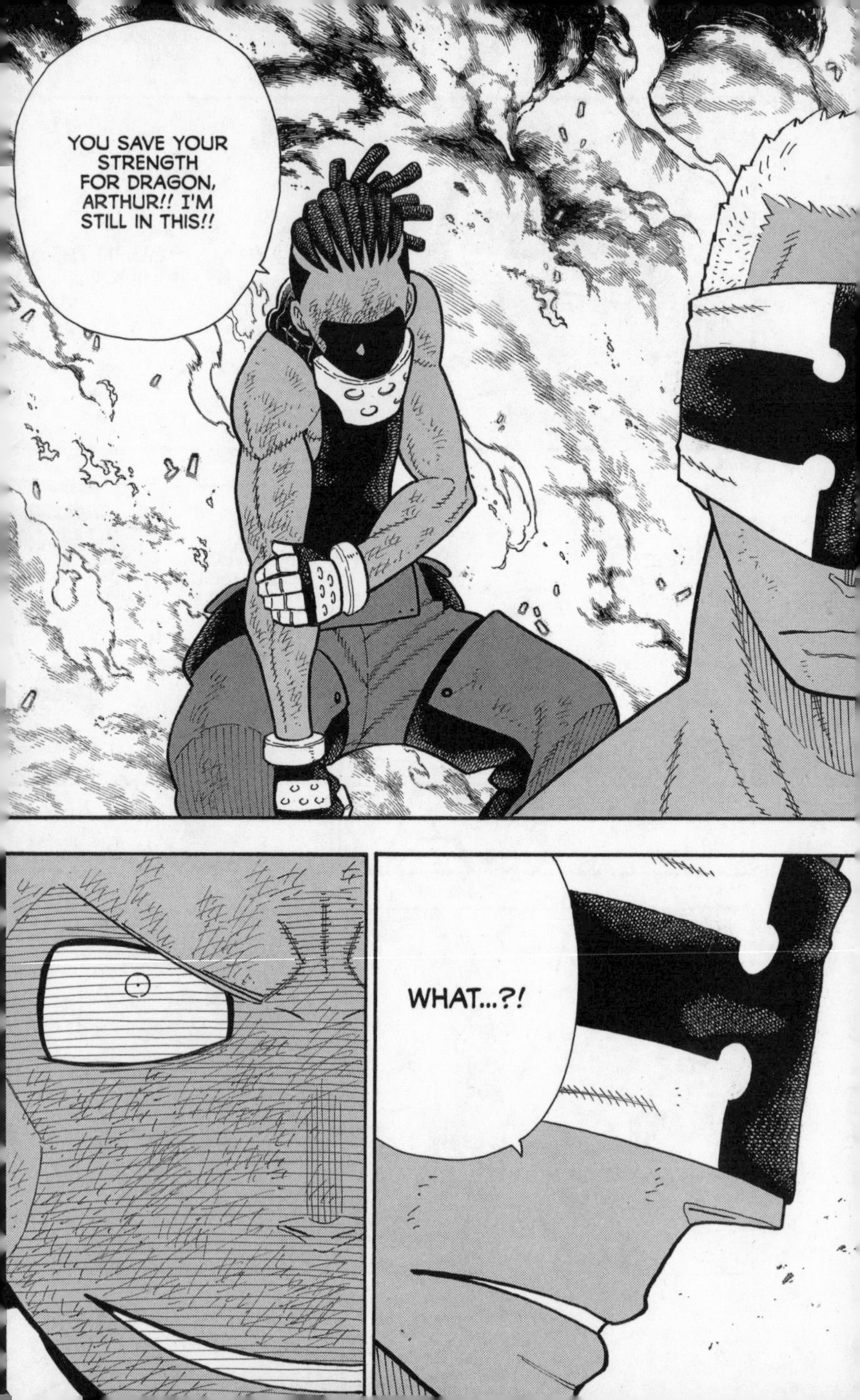
YOU SAVE YOUR STRENGTH FOR DRAGON, ARTHUR!! I'M STILL IN THIS!!
WHAT...?!

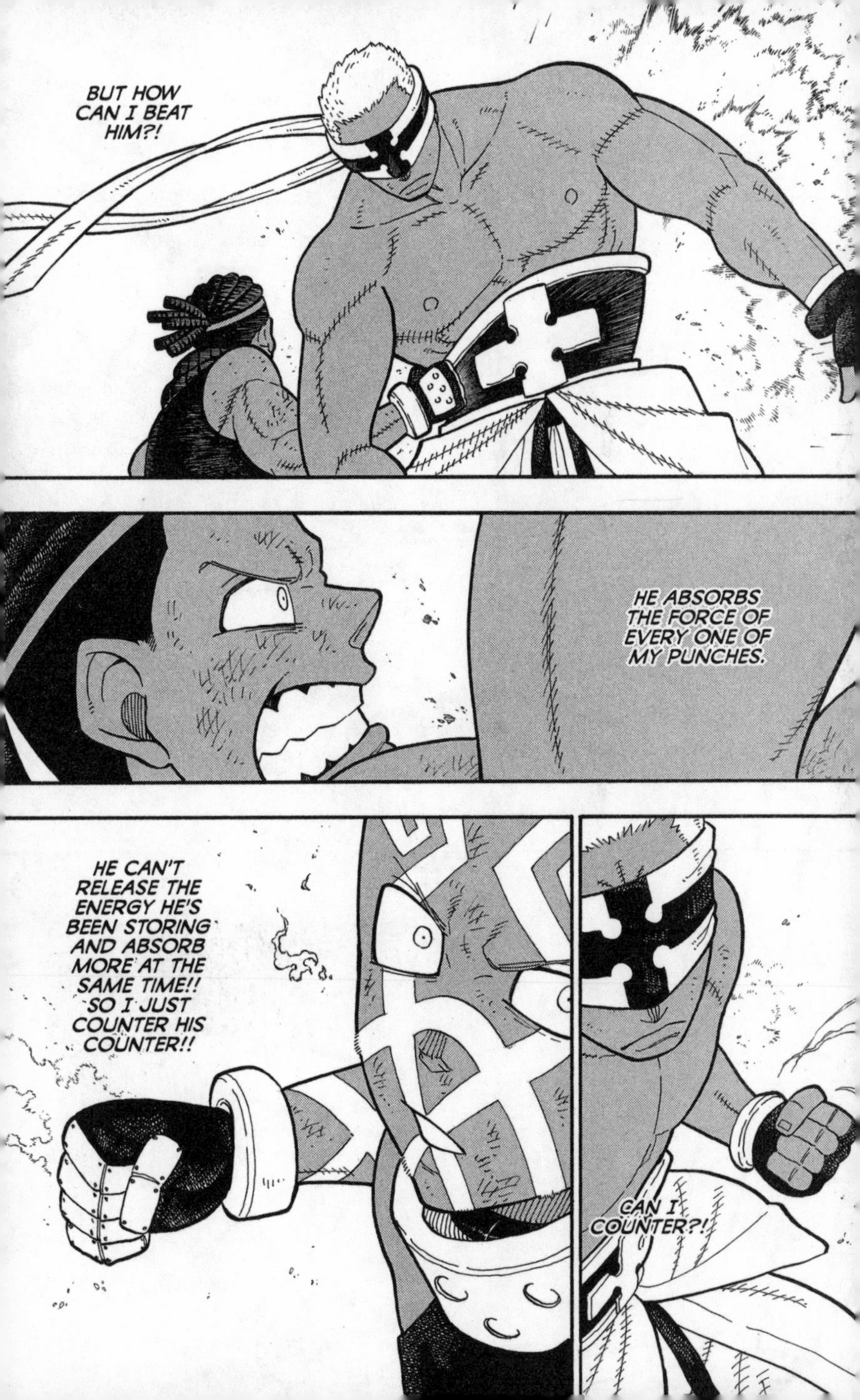
BUT HOW CAN I BEAT HIM?!
HE ABSORBS THE FORCE OF EVERY ONE OF MY PUNCHES.
CAN I COUNTER?!
HE CAN'T RELEASE THE ENERGY HE'S BEEN STORING AND ABSORB MORE AT THE SAME TIME!! SO I JUST COUNTER HIS COUNTER!!

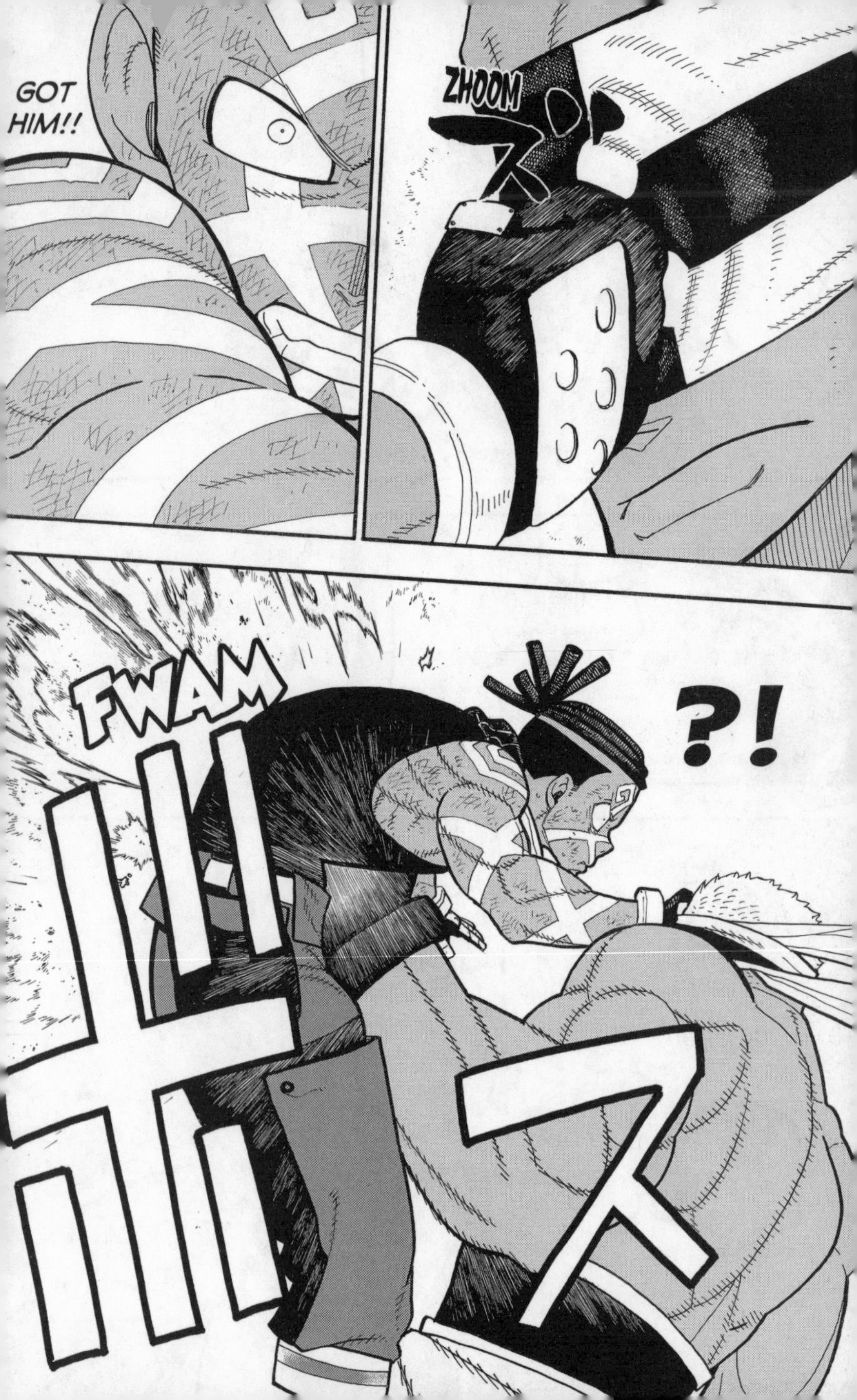
ZHOOM
GOT HIM!!
?!
FWAM

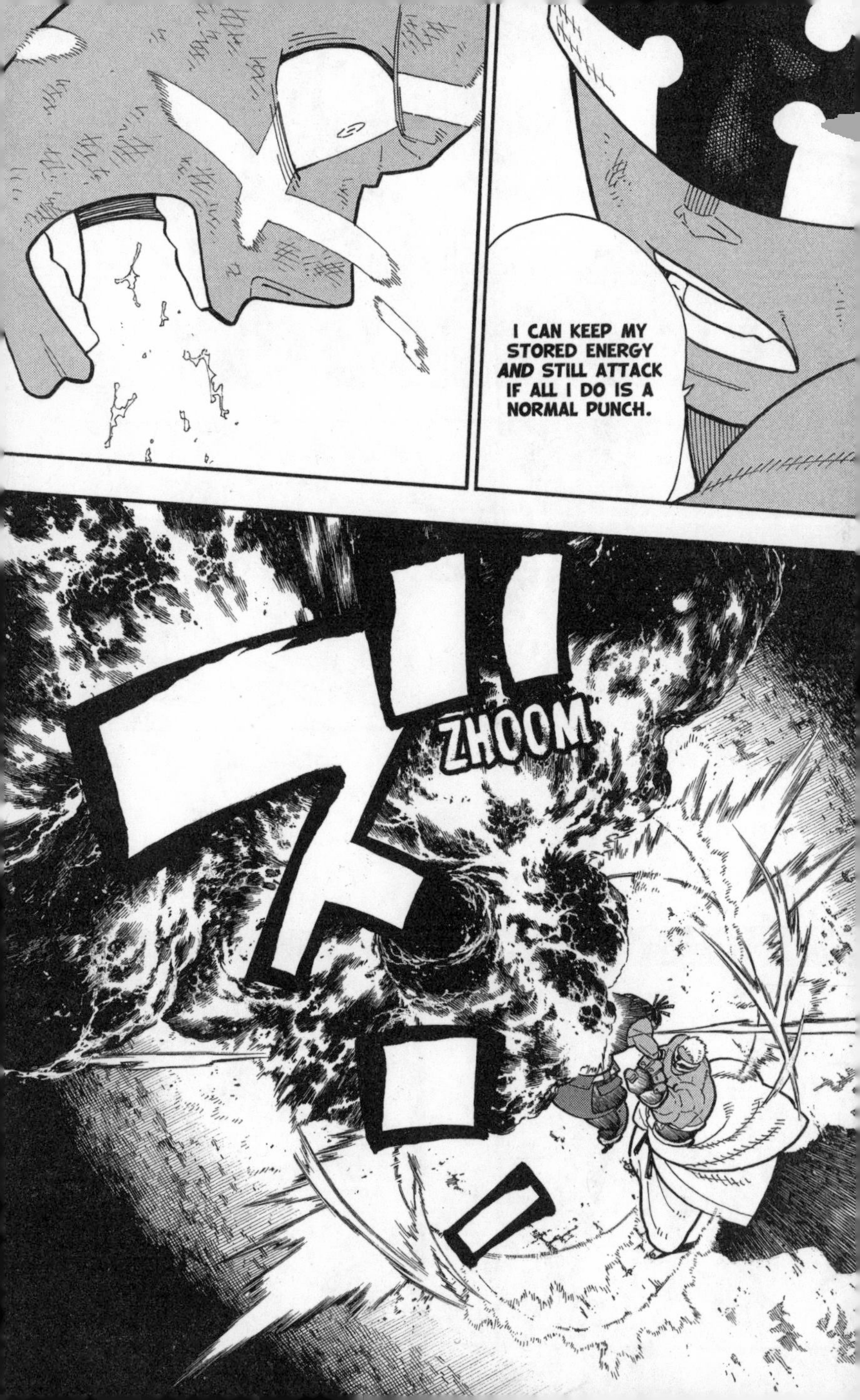
I CAN KEEP MY STORED ENERGY *AND* STILL ATTACK IF ALL I DO IS A NORMAL PUNCH.
ZHOOM

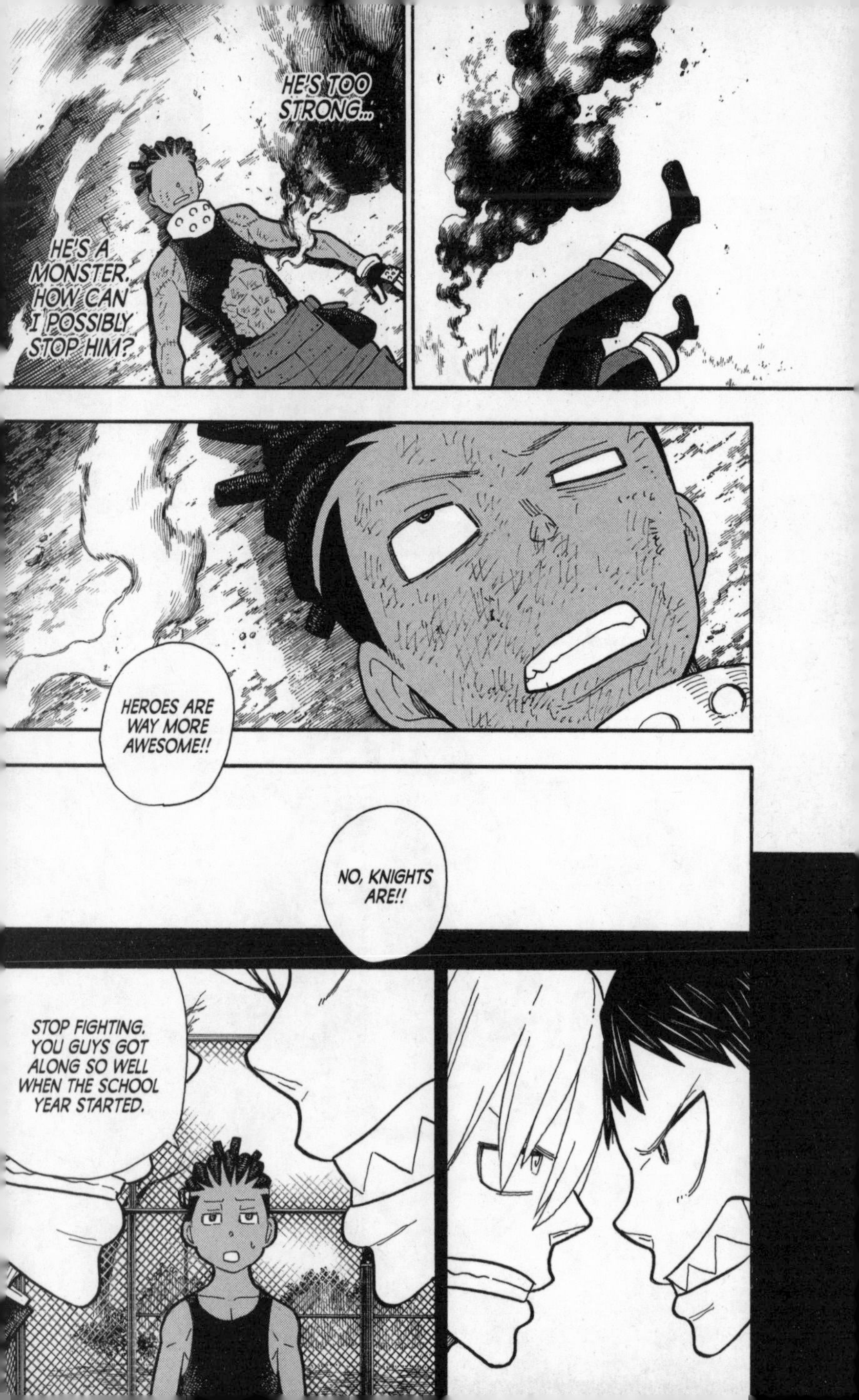
HE'S TOO STRONG...
HE'S A MONSTER. HOW CAN I POSSIBLY STOP HIM?
HEROES ARE WAY MORE AWESOME!!
NO, KNIGHTS ARE!!
STOP FIGHTING. YOU GUYS GOT ALONG SO WELL WHEN THE SCHOOL YEAR STARTED.

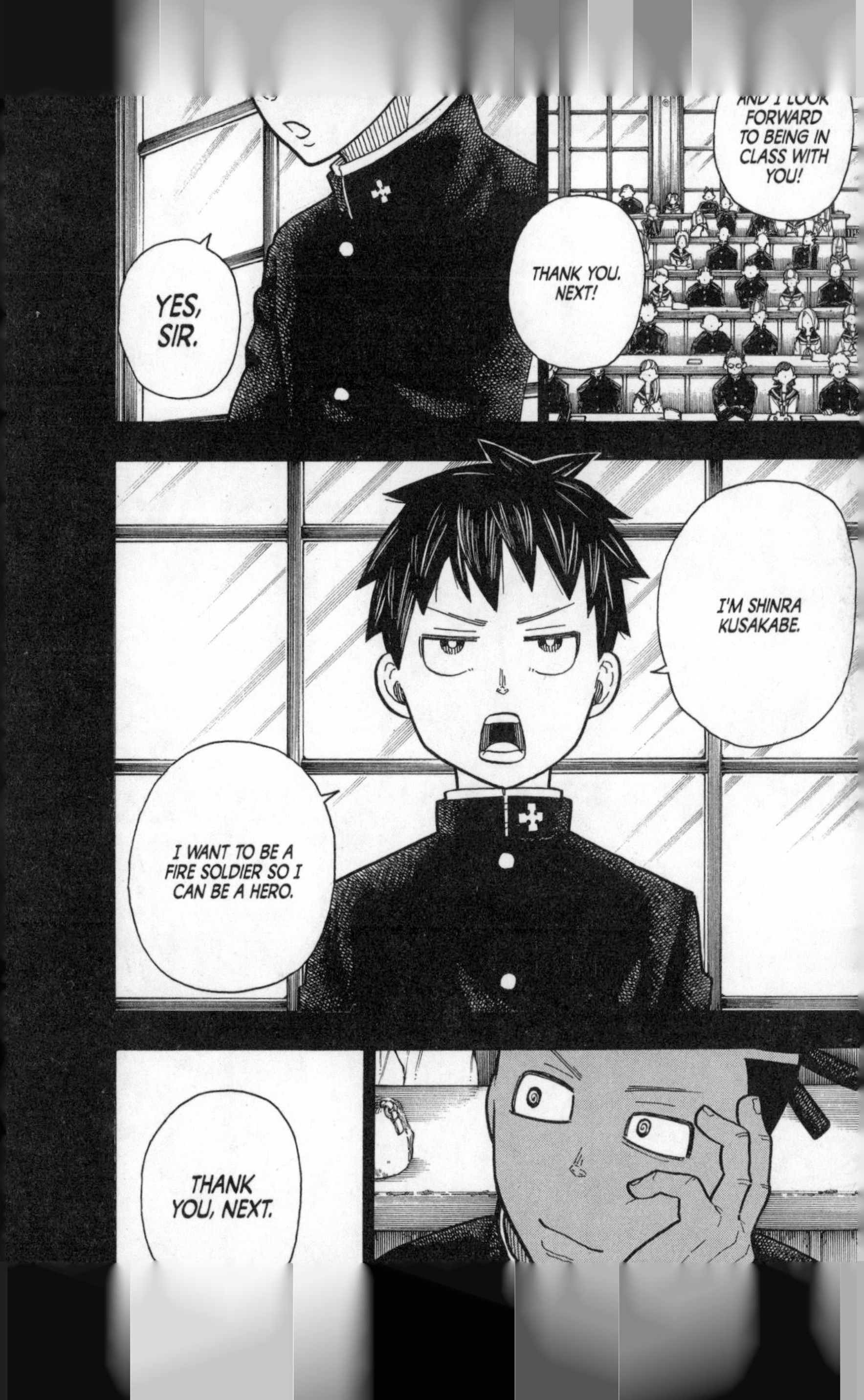
AND I LOOK FORWARD TO BEING IN CLASS WITH YOU!
THANK YOU. NEXT!
YES, SIR.
I'M SHINRA KUSAKABE.
I WANT TO BE A FIRE SOLDIER SO I CAN BE A HERO.
THANK YOU, NEXT.

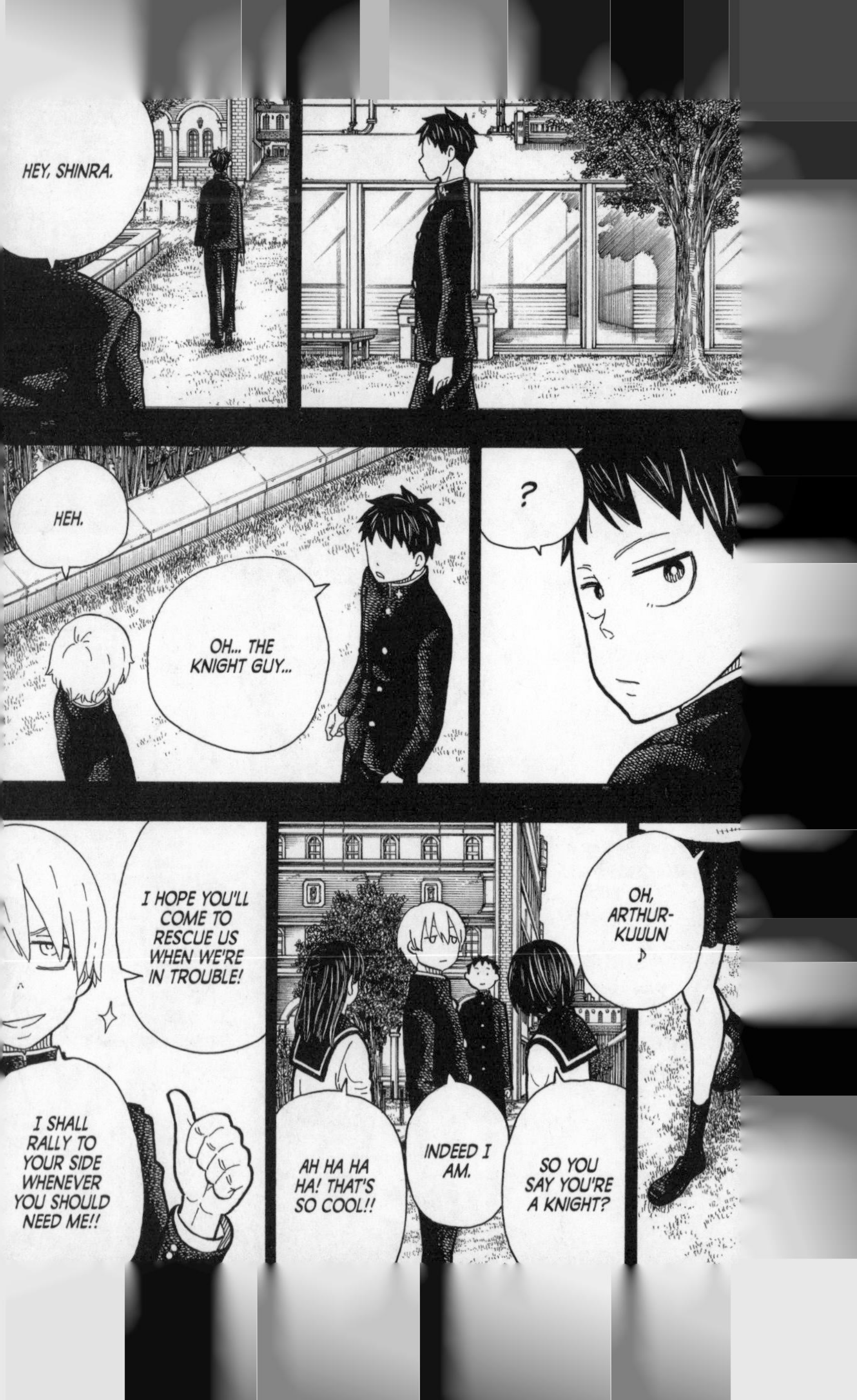
HEY, SHINRA.
?
HEH.
OH... THE KNIGHT GUY...
OH, ARTHUR-KUUUN ♪
SO YOU SAY YOU'RE A KNIGHT?
INDEED I AM.
AH HA HA HA! THAT'S SO COOL!!
I HOPE YOU'LL COME TO RESCUE US WHEN WE'RE IN TROUBLE!
I SHALL RALLY TO YOUR SIDE WHENEVER YOU SHOULD NEED ME!!

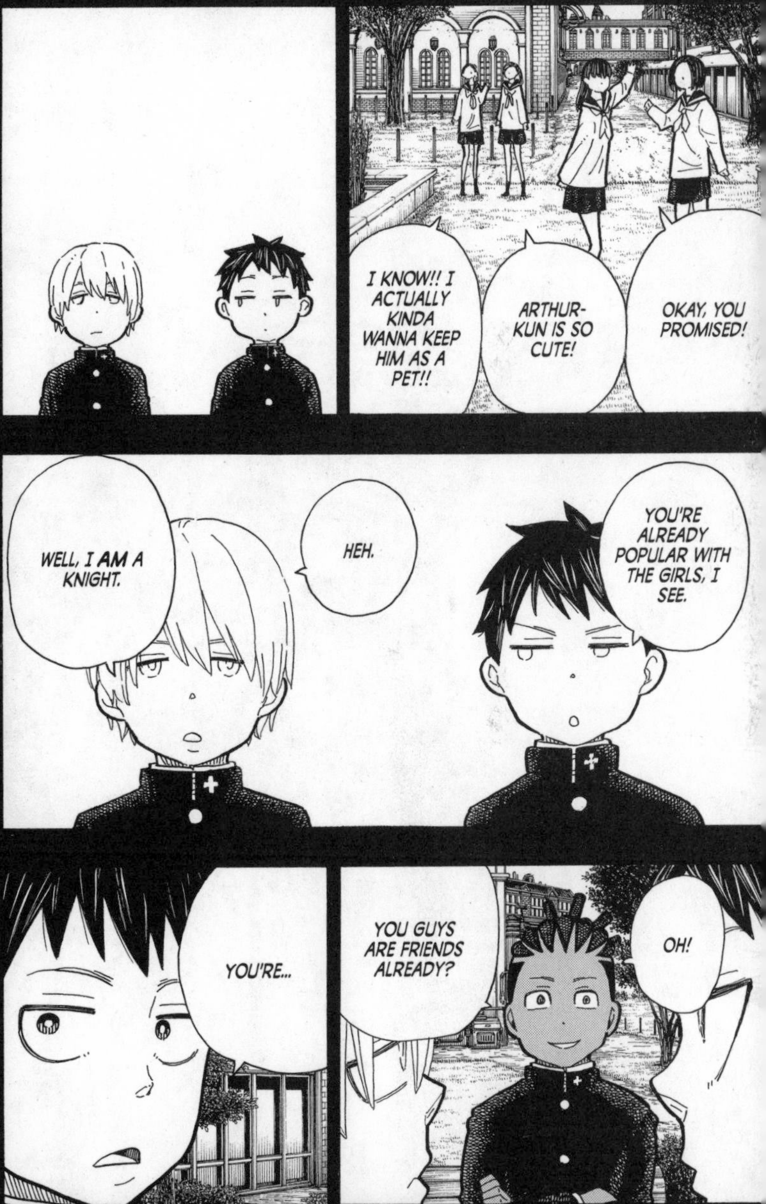
OKAY, YOU PROMISED!
ARTHUR-KUN IS SO CUTE!
I KNOW!! I ACTUALLY KINDA WANNA KEEP HIM AS A PET!!
YOU'RE ALREADY POPULAR WITH THE GIRLS, I SEE.
HEH.
WELL, I **AM** A KNIGHT.
OH!
YOU GUYS ARE FRIENDS ALREADY?
YOU'RE...

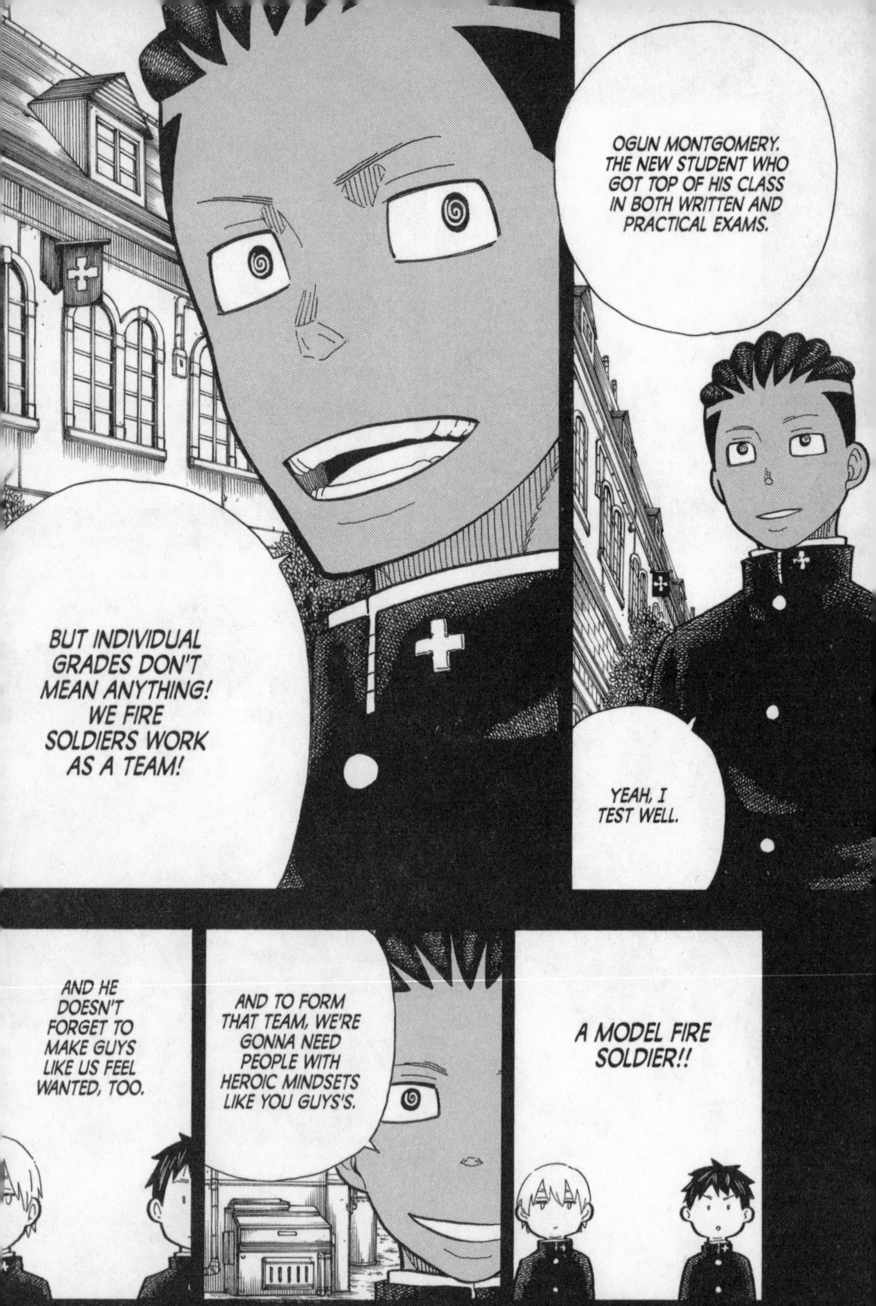
OGUN MONTGOMERY. THE NEW STUDENT WHO GOT TOP OF HIS CLASS IN BOTH WRITTEN AND PRACTICAL EXAMS.
YEAH, I TEST WELL.
BUT INDIVIDUAL GRADES DON'T MEAN ANYTHING! WE FIRE SOLDIERS WORK AS A TEAM!
A MODEL FIRE SOLDIER!!
AND TO FORM THAT TEAM, WE'RE GONNA NEED PEOPLE WITH HEROIC MINDSETS LIKE YOU GUYS'S.
AND HE DOESN'T FORGET TO MAKE GUYS LIKE US FEEL WANTED, TOO.

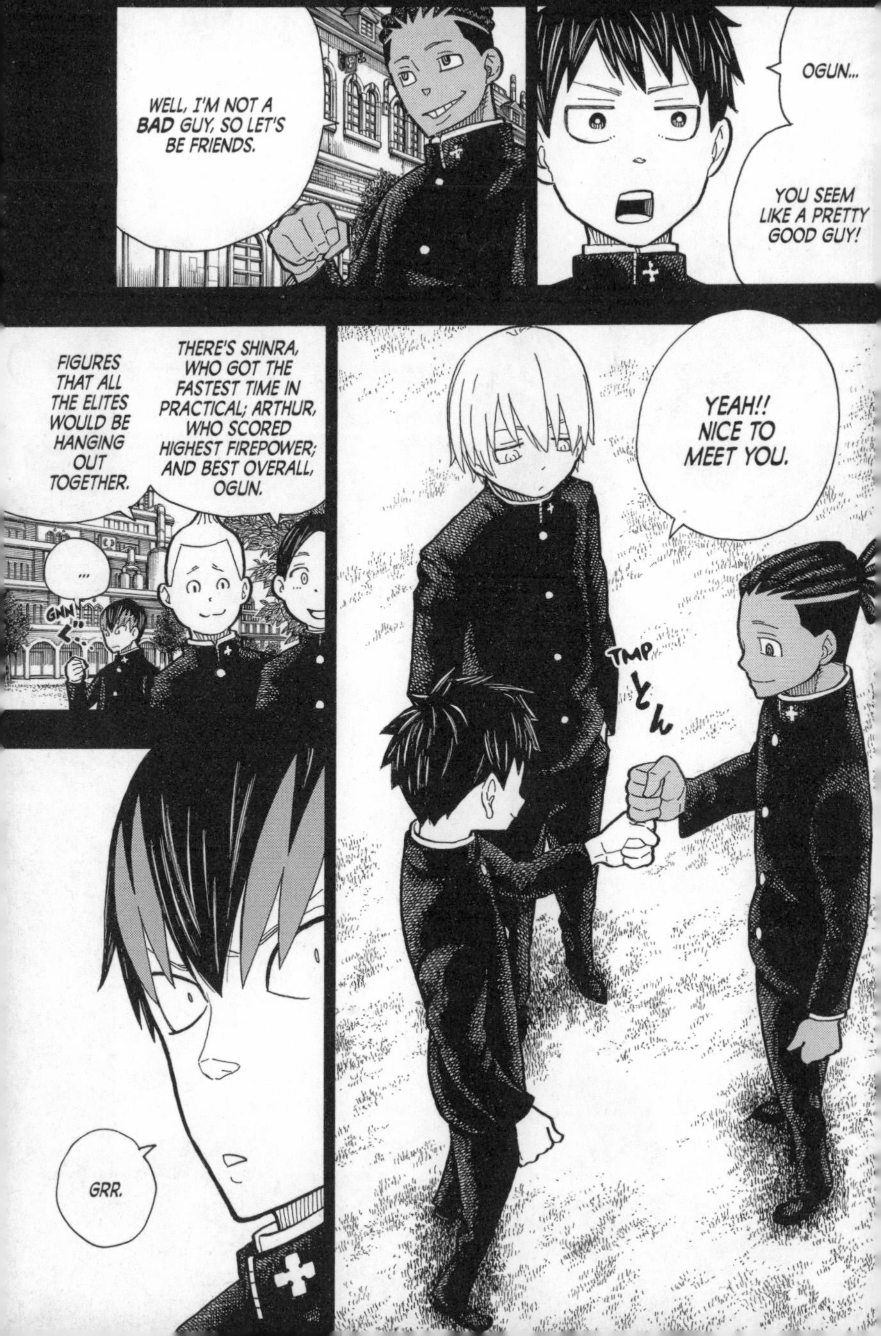
OGUN...
YOU SEEM LIKE A PRETTY GOOD GUY!
WELL, I'M NOT A BAD GUY, SO LET'S BE FRIENDS.
YEAH!! NICE TO MEET YOU.
TMP
とん
THERE'S SHINRA, WHO GOT THE FASTEST TIME IN PRACTICAL; ARTHUR, WHO SCORED HIGHEST FIREPOWER; AND BEST OVERALL, OGUN.
FIGURES THAT ALL THE ELITES WOULD BE HANGING OUT TOGETHER.
...
GNN
GRR.

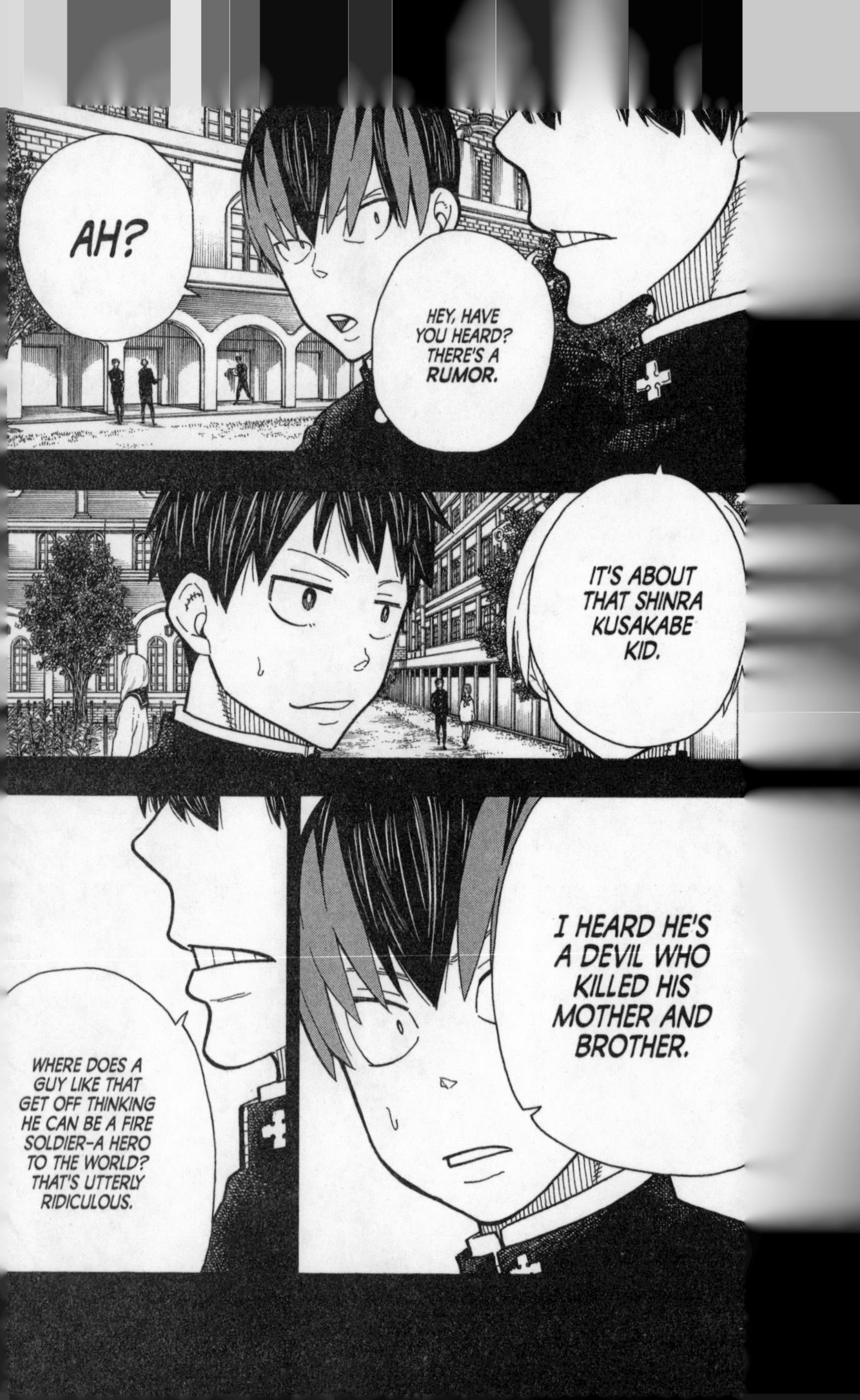
HEY, HAVE YOU HEARD? THERE'S A RUMOR.
AH?
IT'S ABOUT THAT SHINRA KUSAKABE KID.
I HEARD HE'S A DEVIL WHO KILLED HIS MOTHER AND BROTHER.
WHERE DOES A GUY LIKE THAT GET OFF THINKING HE CAN BE A FIRE SOLDIER—A HERO TO THE WORLD? THAT'S UTTERLY RIDICULOUS.

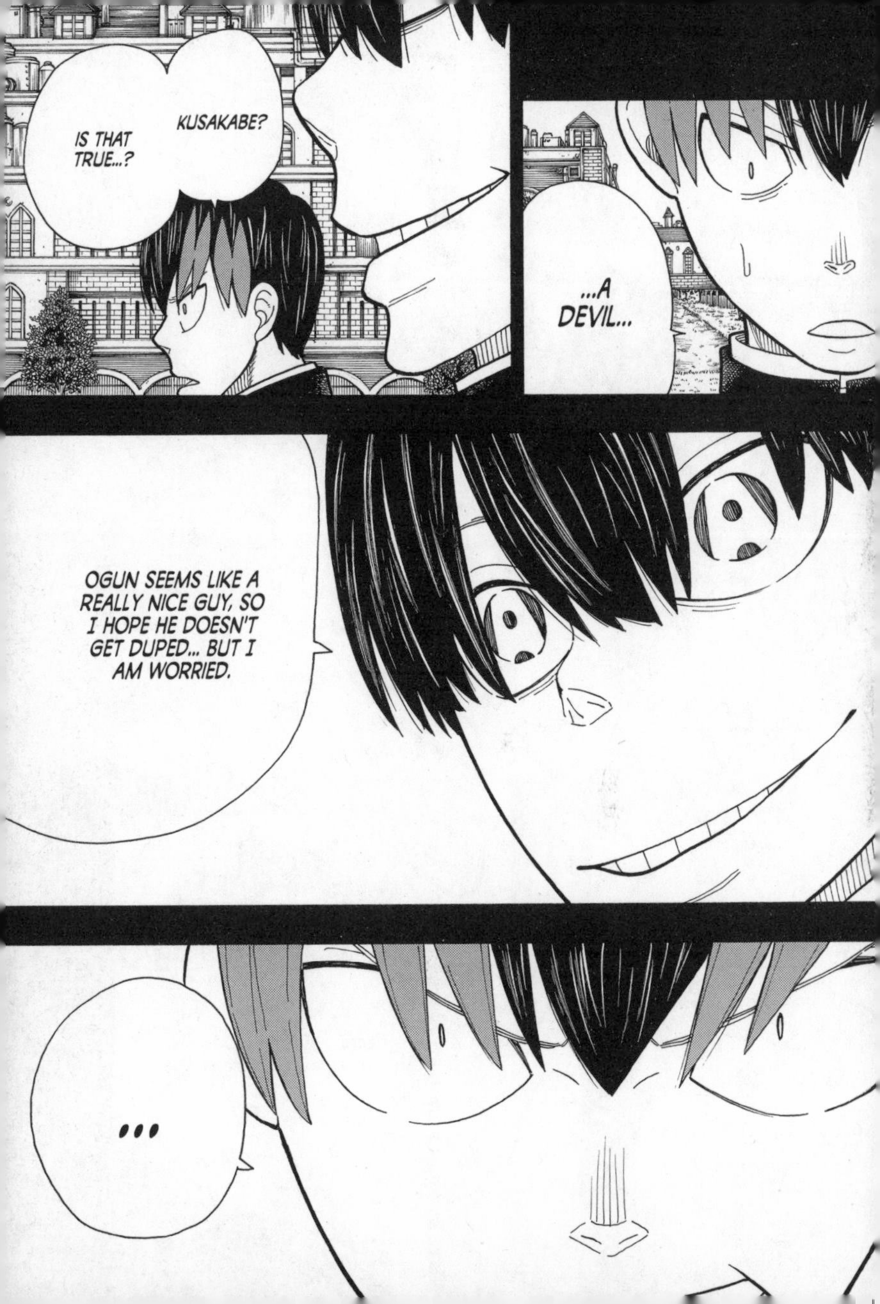
...A DEVIL...
KUSAKABE? IS THAT TRUE...?
OGUN SEEMS LIKE A REALLY NICE GUY, SO I HOPE HE DOESN'T GET DUPED... BUT I AM WORRIED.
...

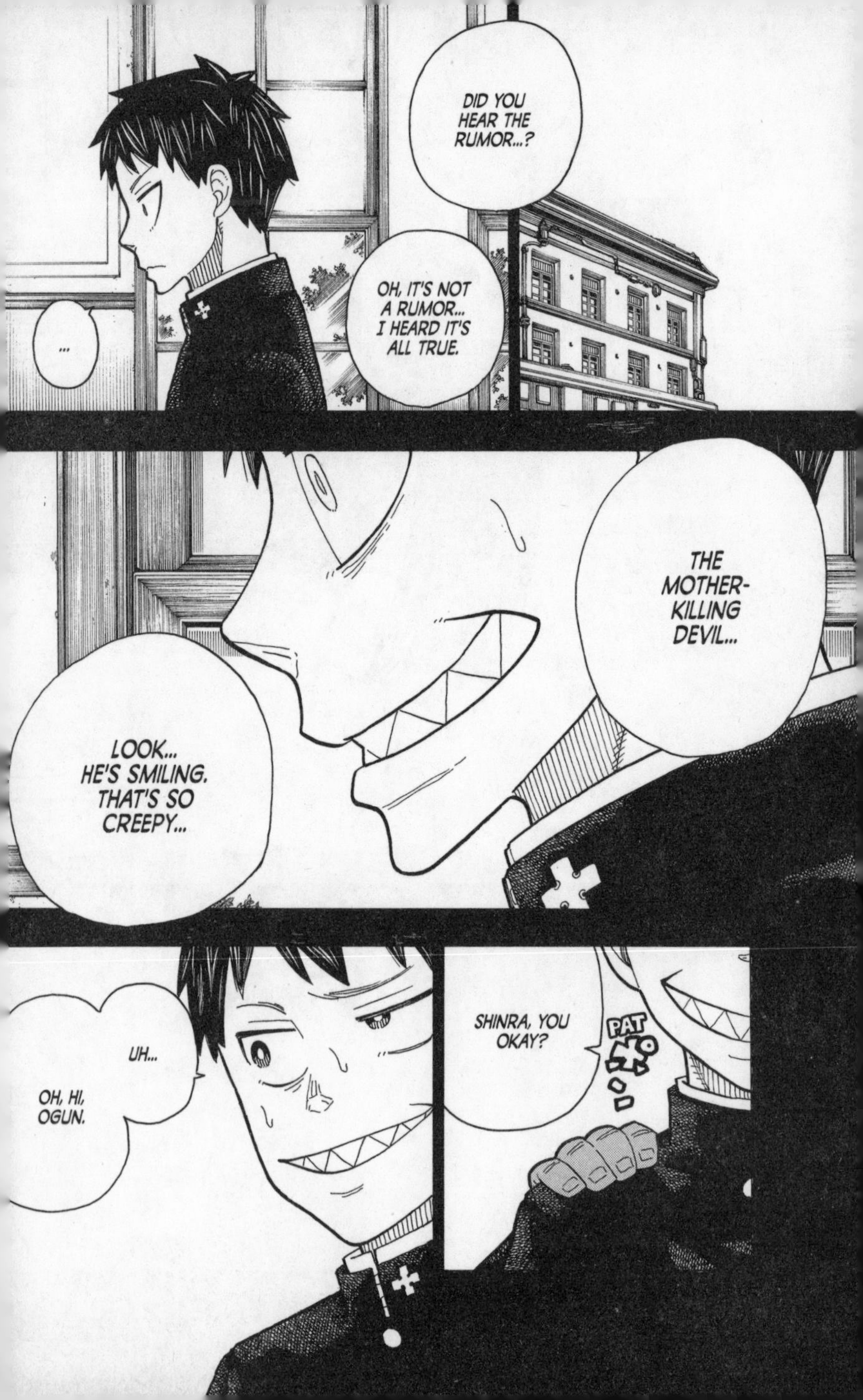
DID YOU HEAR THE RUMOR...?
OH, IT'S NOT A RUMOR... I HEARD IT'S ALL TRUE.
...
THE MOTHER-KILLING DEVIL...
LOOK... HE'S SMILING. THAT'S SO CREEPY...
SHINRA, YOU OKAY?
PAT
UH...
OH, HI, OGUN.

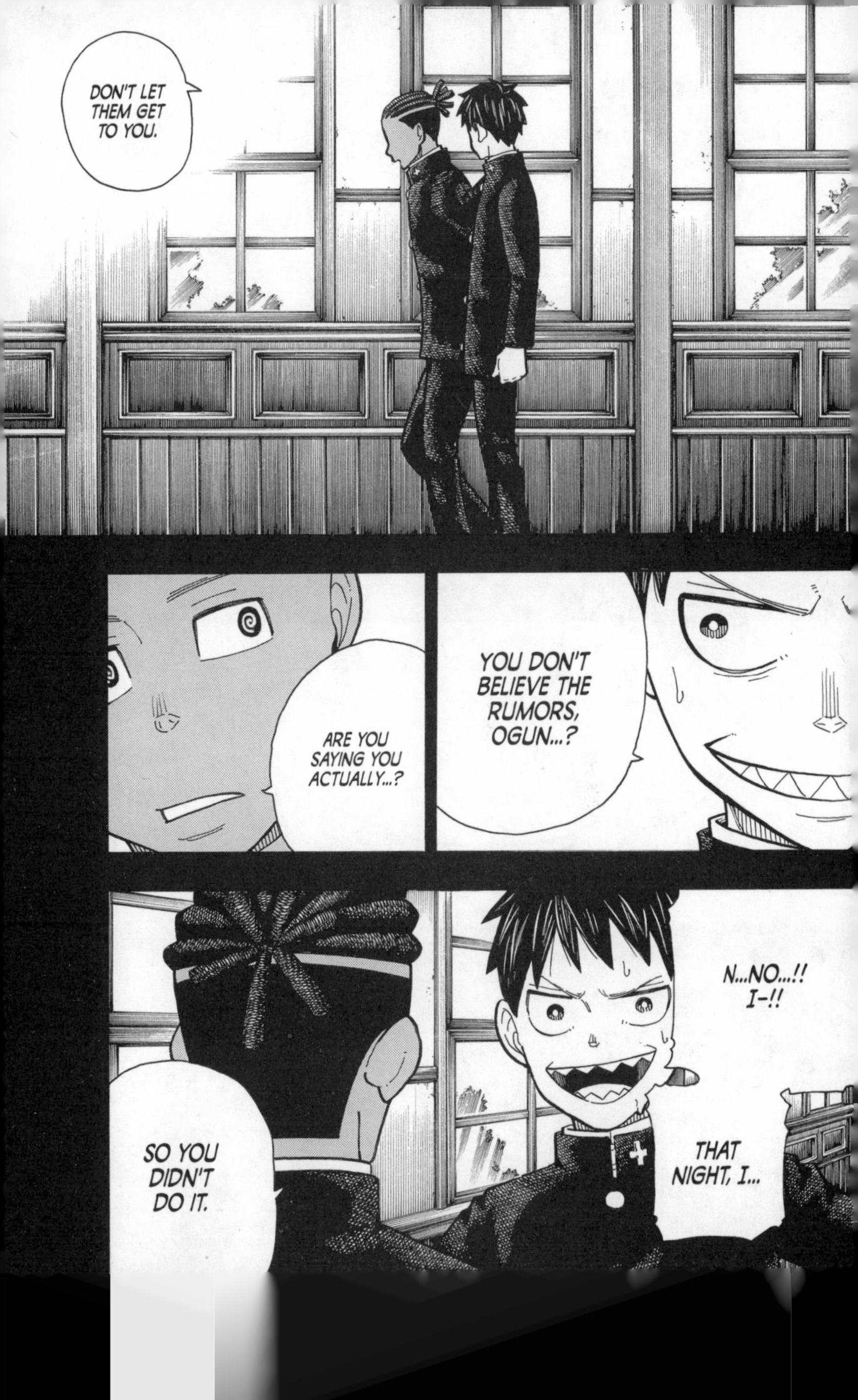
DON'T LET THEM GET TO YOU.
YOU DON'T BELIEVE THE RUMORS, OGUN...?
ARE YOU SAYING YOU ACTUALLY...?
N...NO...!! I-!!
THAT NIGHT, I...
SO YOU DIDN'T DO IT.

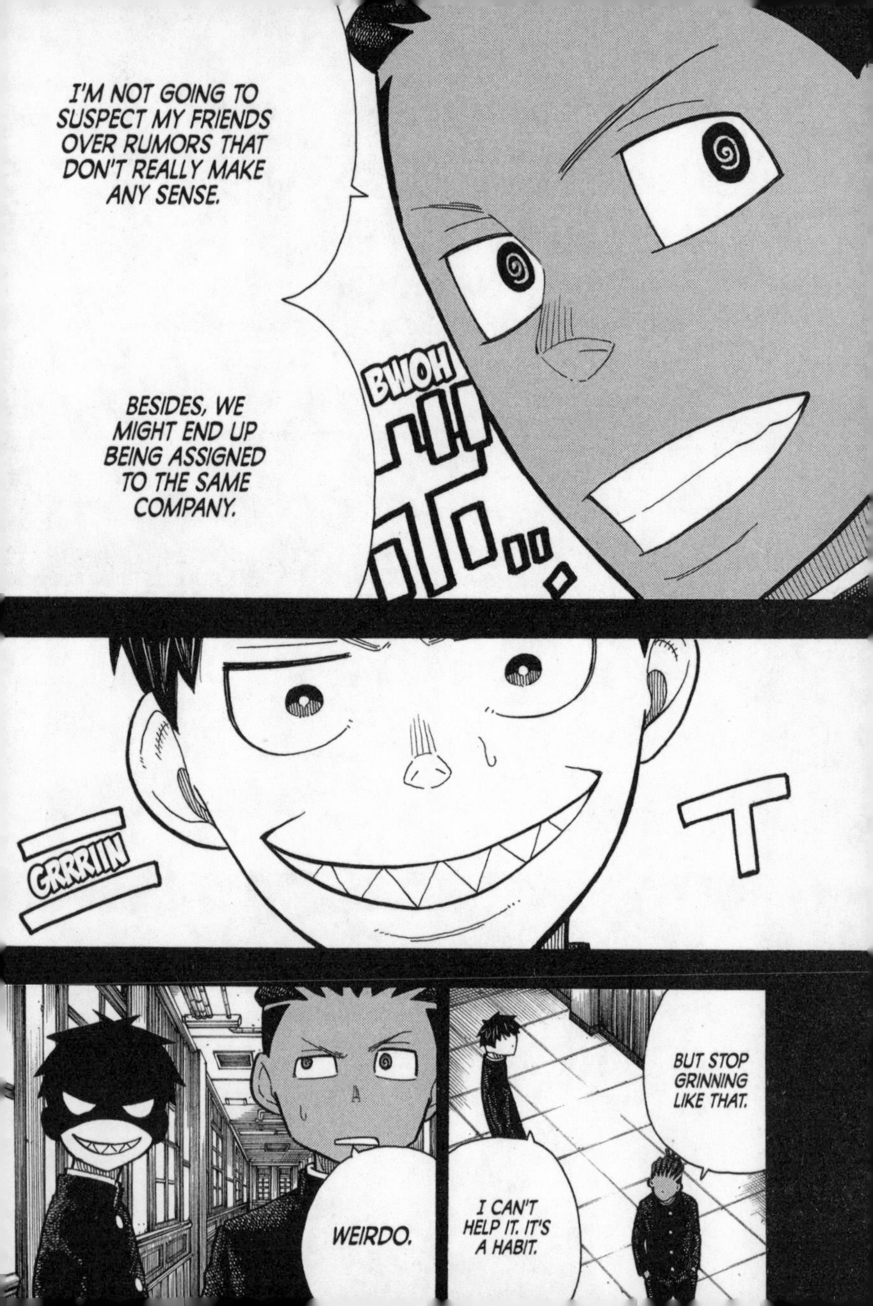
I'M NOT GOING TO SUSPECT MY FRIENDS OVER RUMORS THAT DON'T REALLY MAKE ANY SENSE.
BWOH
BESIDES, WE MIGHT END UP BEING ASSIGNED TO THE SAME COMPANY.
GRRRIIN
BUT STOP GRINNING LIKE THAT.
I CAN'T HELP IT. IT'S A HABIT.
WEIRDO.

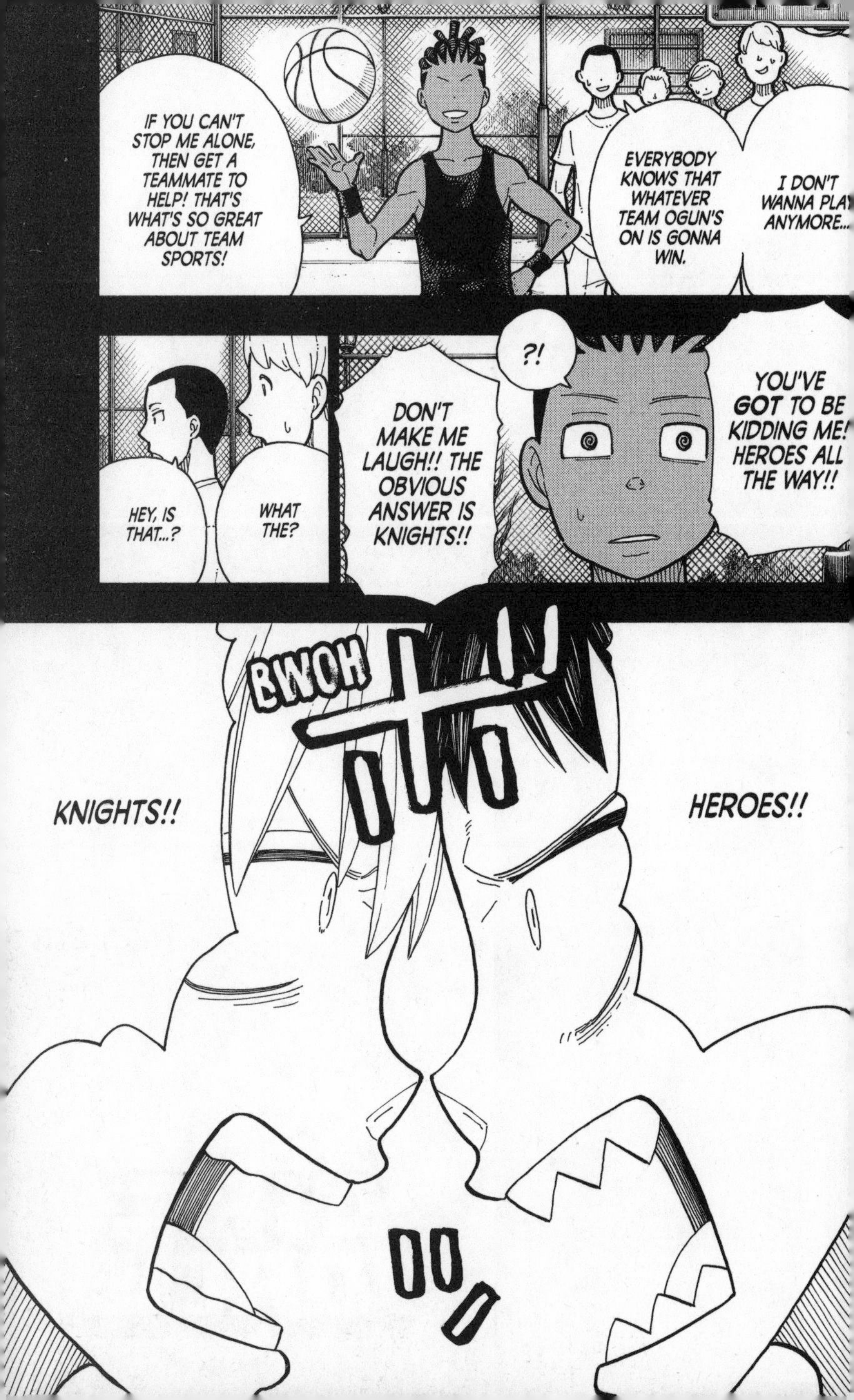
I DON'T WANNA PLAY ANYMORE...
EVERYBODY KNOWS THAT WHATEVER TEAM OGUN'S ON IS GONNA WIN.
IF YOU CAN'T STOP ME ALONE, THEN GET A TEAMMATE TO HELP! THAT'S WHAT'S SO GREAT ABOUT TEAM SPORTS!
YOU'VE GOT TO BE KIDDING ME! HEROES ALL THE WAY!!
?!
DON'T MAKE ME LAUGH!! THE OBVIOUS ANSWER IS KNIGHTS!!
WHAT THE?
HEY, IS THAT...?
HEROES!!
BWOH
KNIGHTS!!

FIRE FORCE

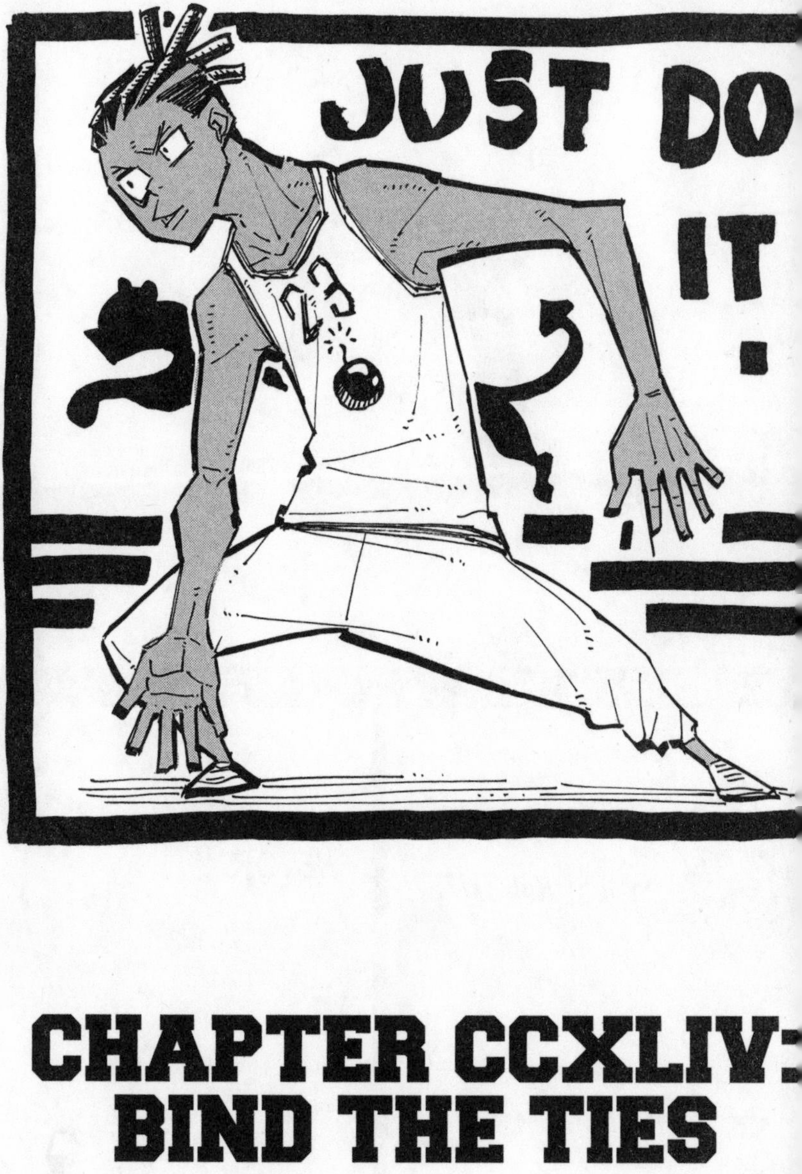
JUST DO IT!

CHAPTER CCXLIV: BIND THE TIES

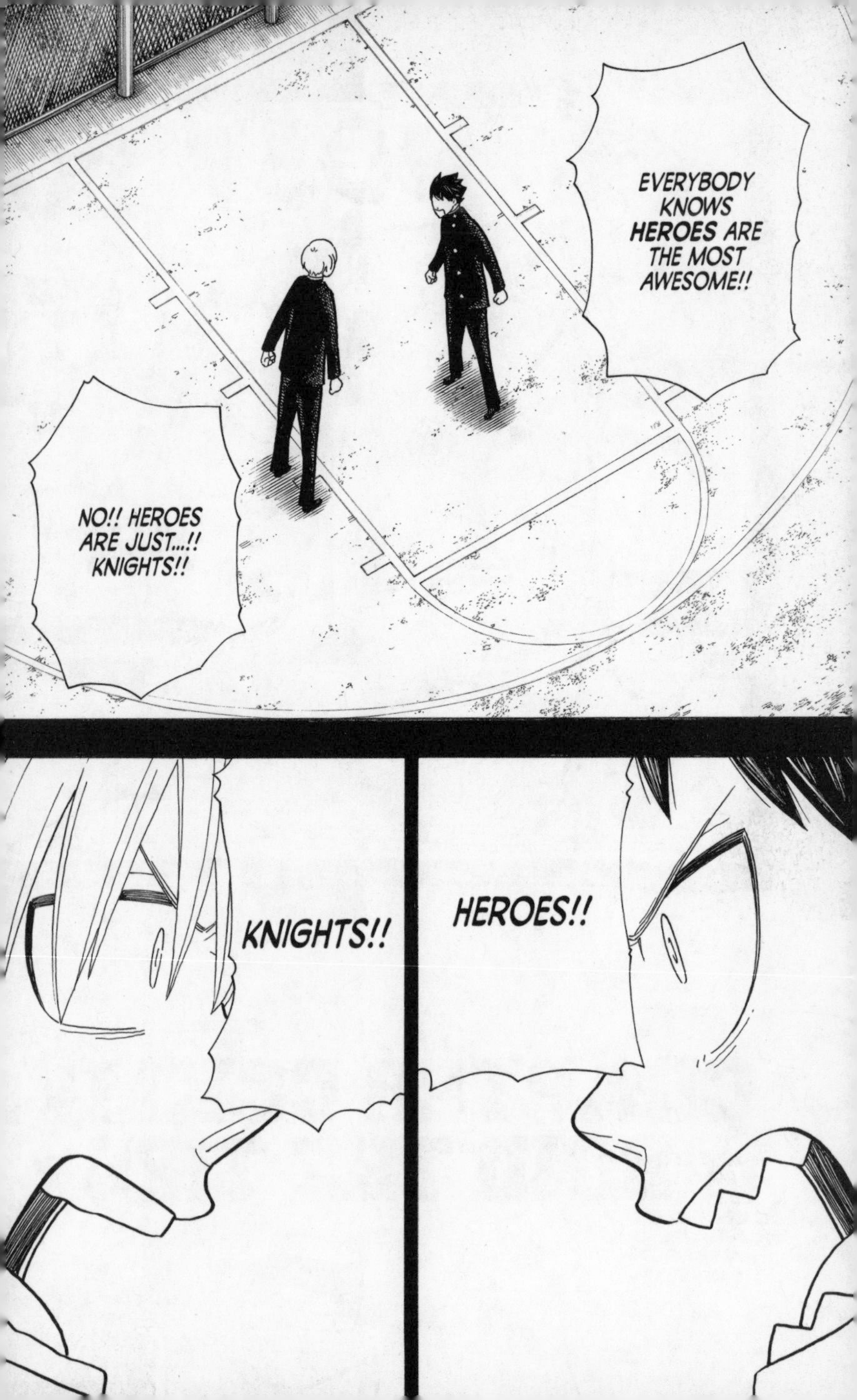
EVERYBODY KNOWS HEROES ARE THE MOST AWESOME!!
NO!! HEROES ARE JUST...!! KNIGHTS!!
HEROES!!
KNIGHTS!!

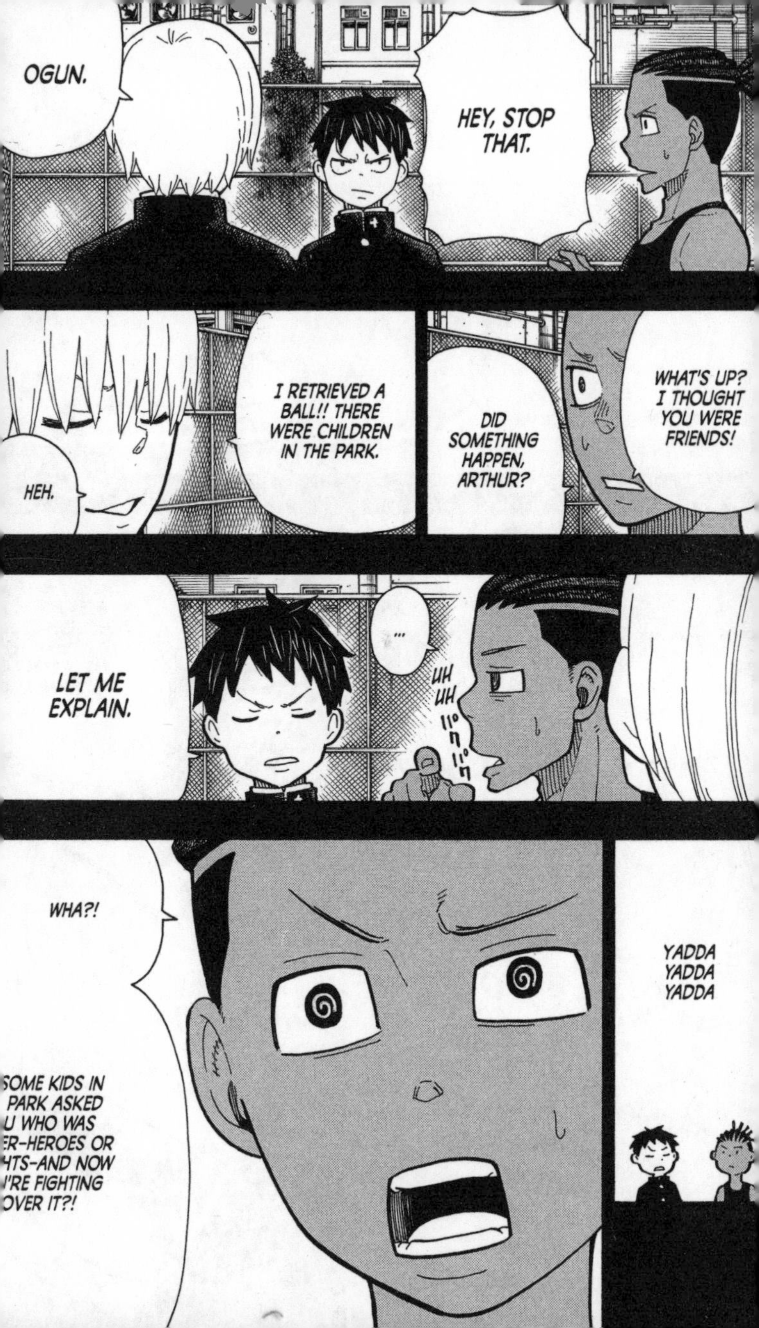
HEY, STOP THAT.
OGUN.
WHAT'S UP? I THOUGHT YOU WERE FRIENDS!
DID SOMETHING HAPPEN, ARTHUR?
I RETRIEVED A BALL!! THERE WERE CHILDREN IN THE PARK.
HEH.
...
UH UH
パクパク
LET ME EXPLAIN.
YADDA YADDA YADDA
WHA?!
SOME KIDS IN PARK ASKED U WHO WAS ER-HEROES OR HTS-AND NOW 'RE FIGHTING OVER IT?!

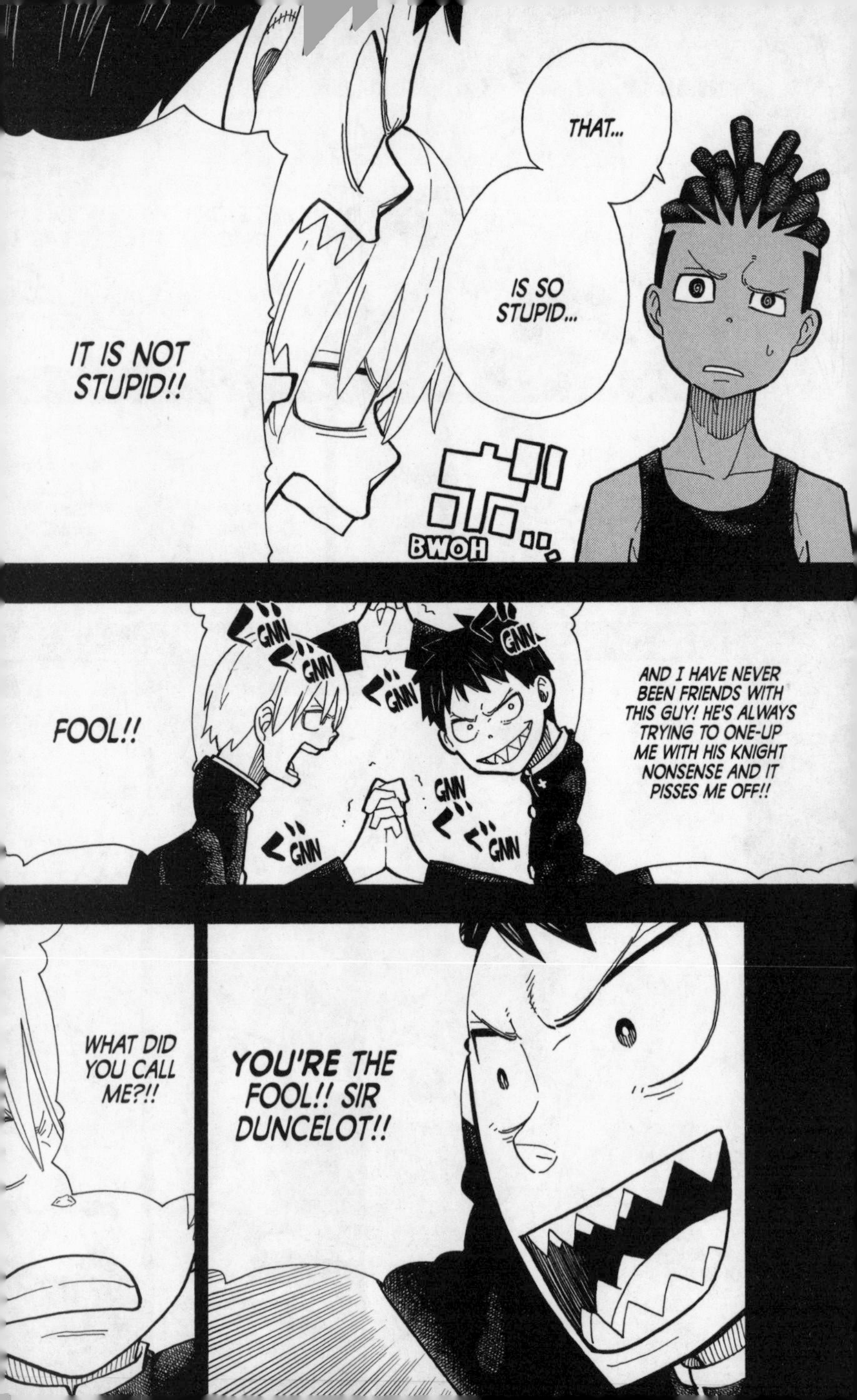
THAT...
IS SO STUPID...
BWOH
IT IS NOT STUPID!!
AND I HAVE NEVER BEEN FRIENDS WITH THIS GUY! HE'S ALWAYS TRYING TO ONE-UP ME WITH HIS KNIGHT NONSENSE AND IT PISSES ME OFF!!
GNN
GNN
GNN
GNN
GNN
GNN
GNN
FOOL!!
YOU'RE THE FOOL!! SIR DUNCELOT!!
WHAT DID YOU CALL ME?!!

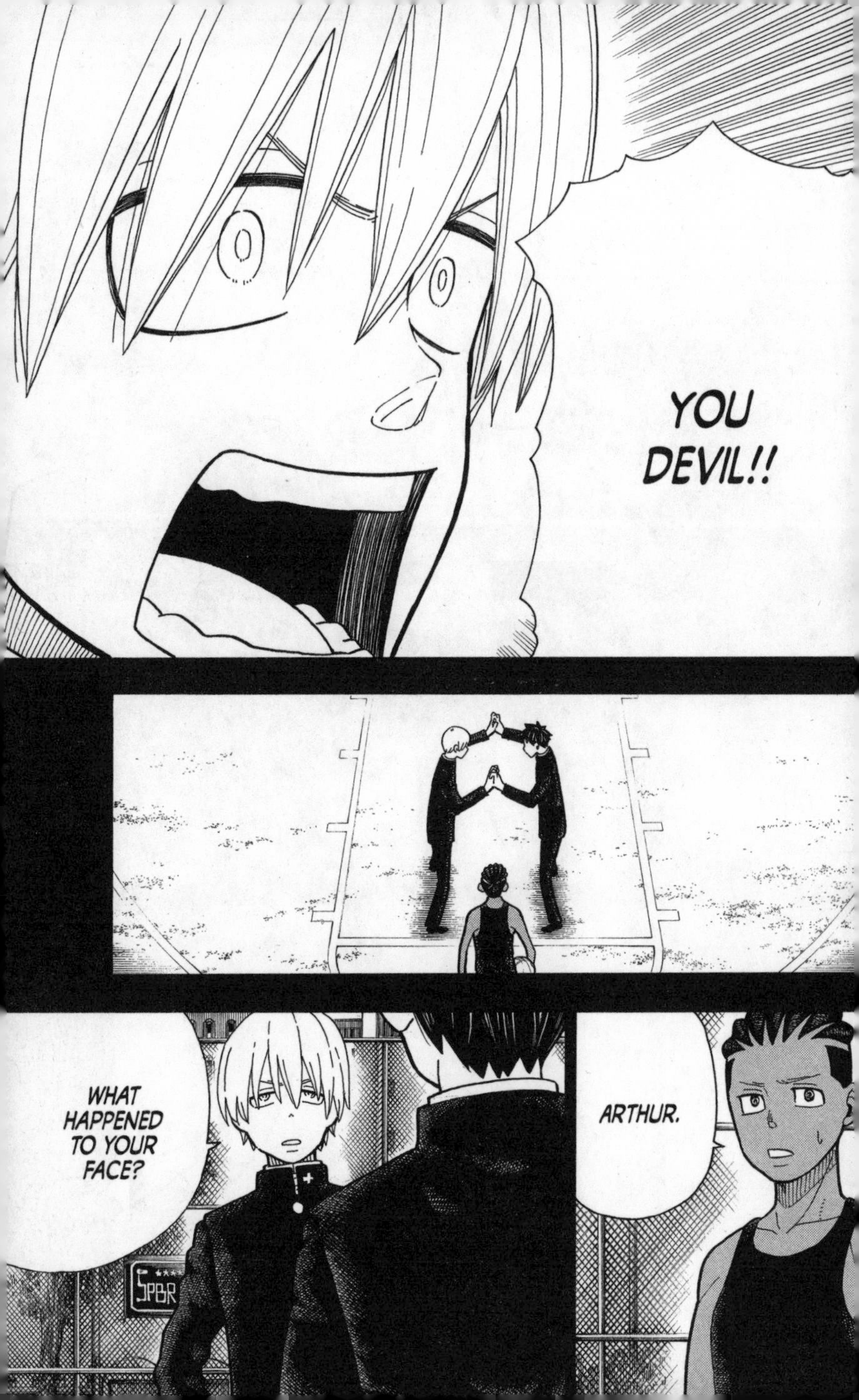
YOU DEVIL!!
ARTHUR.
WHAT HAPPENED TO YOUR FACE?
SPBR

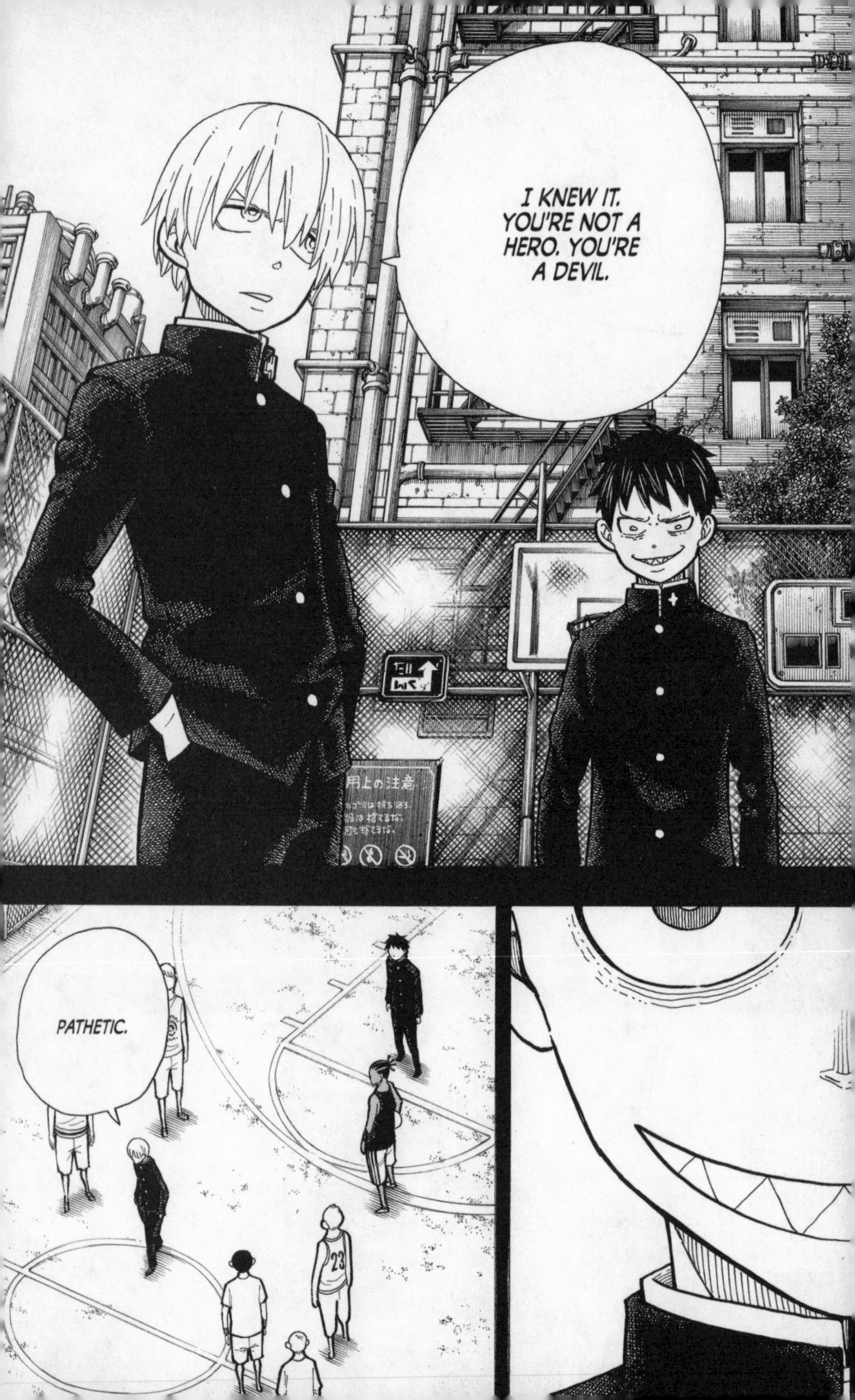
I KNEW IT. YOU'RE NOT A HERO. YOU'RE A DEVIL.
PATHETIC.

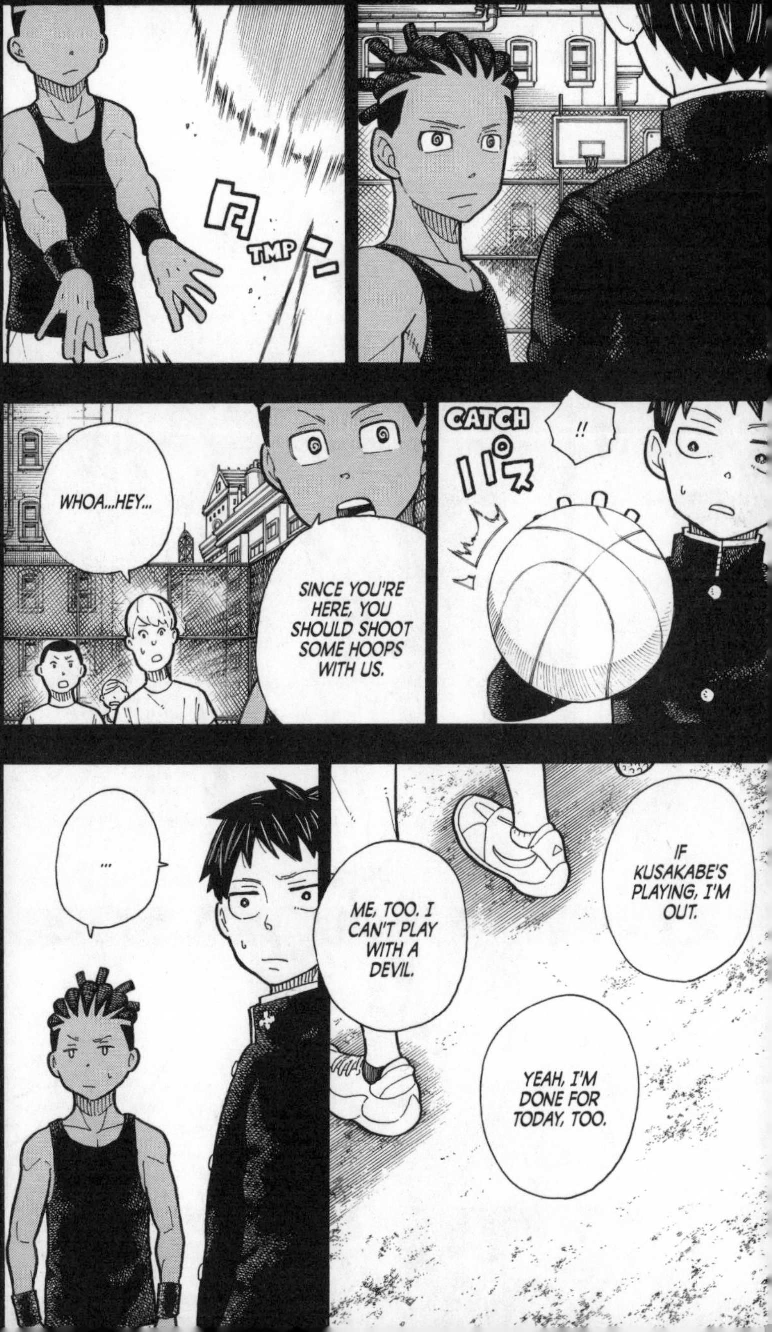
TMP
CATCH
!!
WHOA...HEY...
SINCE YOU'RE HERE, YOU SHOULD SHOOT SOME HOOPS WITH US.
IF KUSAKABE'S PLAYING, I'M OUT.
ME, TOO. I CAN'T PLAY WITH A DEVIL.
YEAH, I'M DONE FOR TODAY, TOO.
...

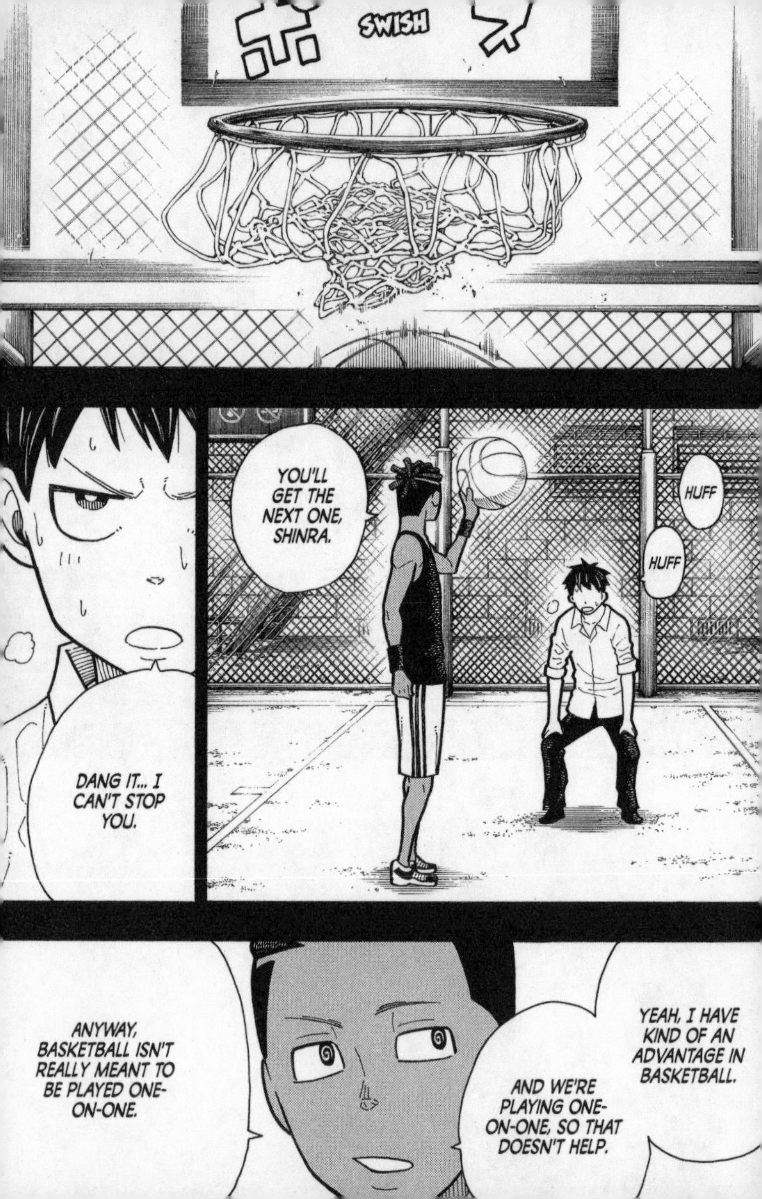
SWISH
HUFF
HUFF
YOU'LL GET THE NEXT ONE, SHINRA.
DANG IT... I CAN'T STOP YOU.
YEAH, I HAVE KIND OF AN ADVANTAGE IN BASKETBALL.
AND WE'RE PLAYING ONE-ON-ONE, SO THAT DOESN'T HELP.
ANYWAY, BASKETBALL ISN'T REALLY MEANT TO BE PLAYED ONE-ON-ONE.

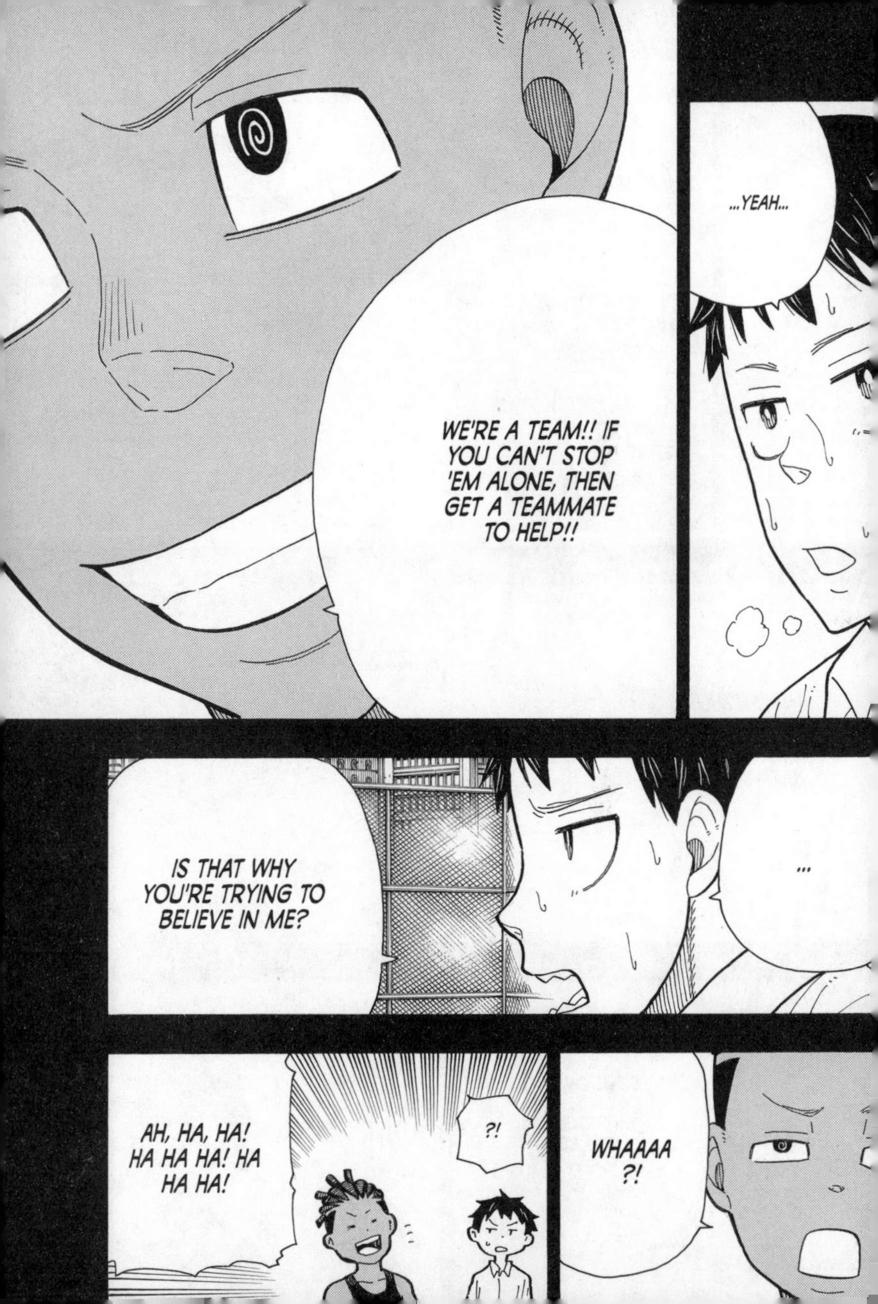
...YEAH...
WE'RE A TEAM!! IF YOU CAN'T STOP 'EM ALONE, THEN GET A TEAMMATE TO HELP!!
...
IS THAT WHY YOU'RE TRYING TO BELIEVE IN ME?
WHAAAA ?!
?!
AH, HA, HA! HA HA HA! HA HA HA!

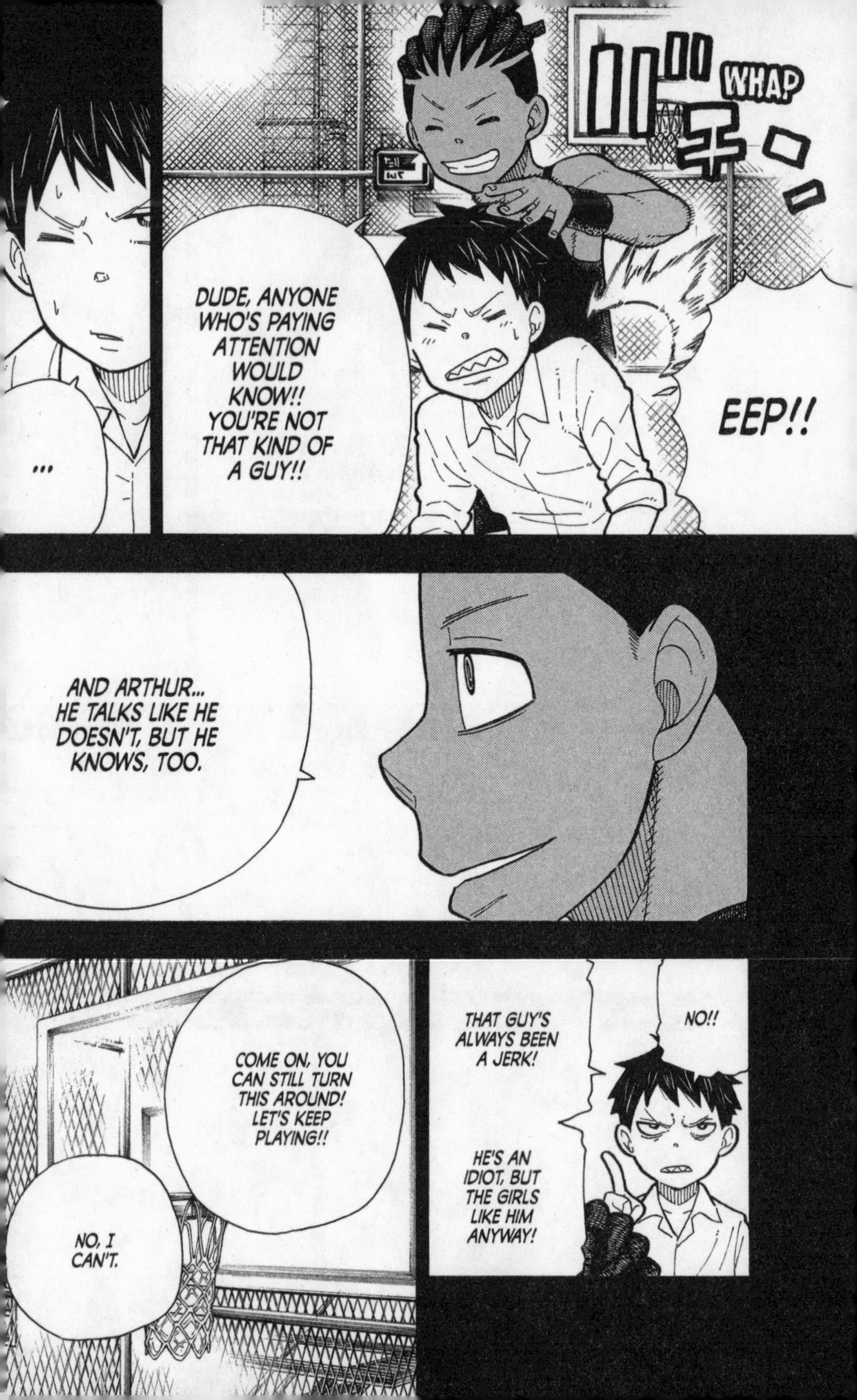
WHAP
EEP!!
DUDE, ANYONE WHO'S PAYING ATTENTION WOULD KNOW!! YOU'RE NOT THAT KIND OF A GUY!!
...
AND ARTHUR... HE TALKS LIKE HE DOESN'T, BUT HE KNOWS, TOO.
NO!!
THAT GUY'S ALWAYS BEEN A JERK!
HE'S AN IDIOT, BUT THE GIRLS LIKE HIM ANYWAY!
COME ON, YOU CAN STILL TURN THIS AROUND! LET'S KEEP PLAYING!!
NO, I CAN'T.

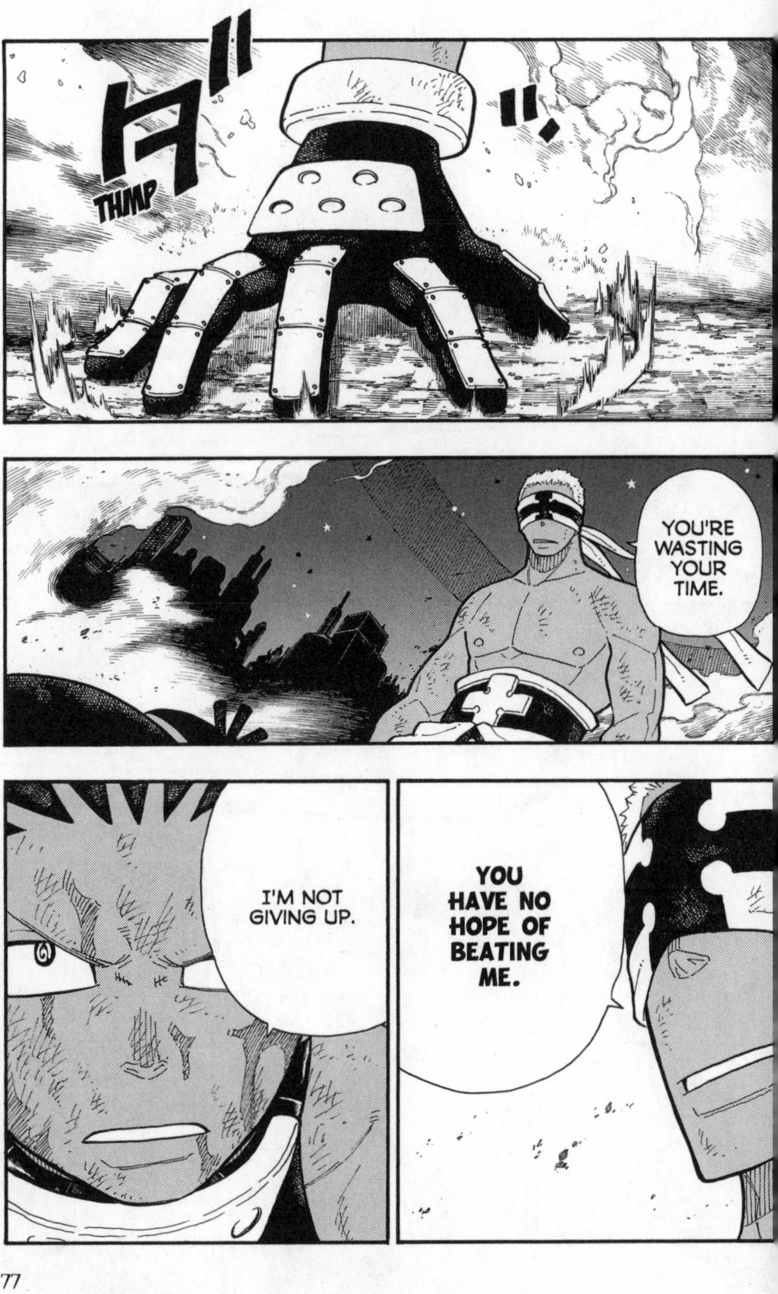
THMP
YOU'RE WASTING YOUR TIME.
YOU HAVE NO HOPE OF BEATING ME.
I'M NOT GIVING UP.

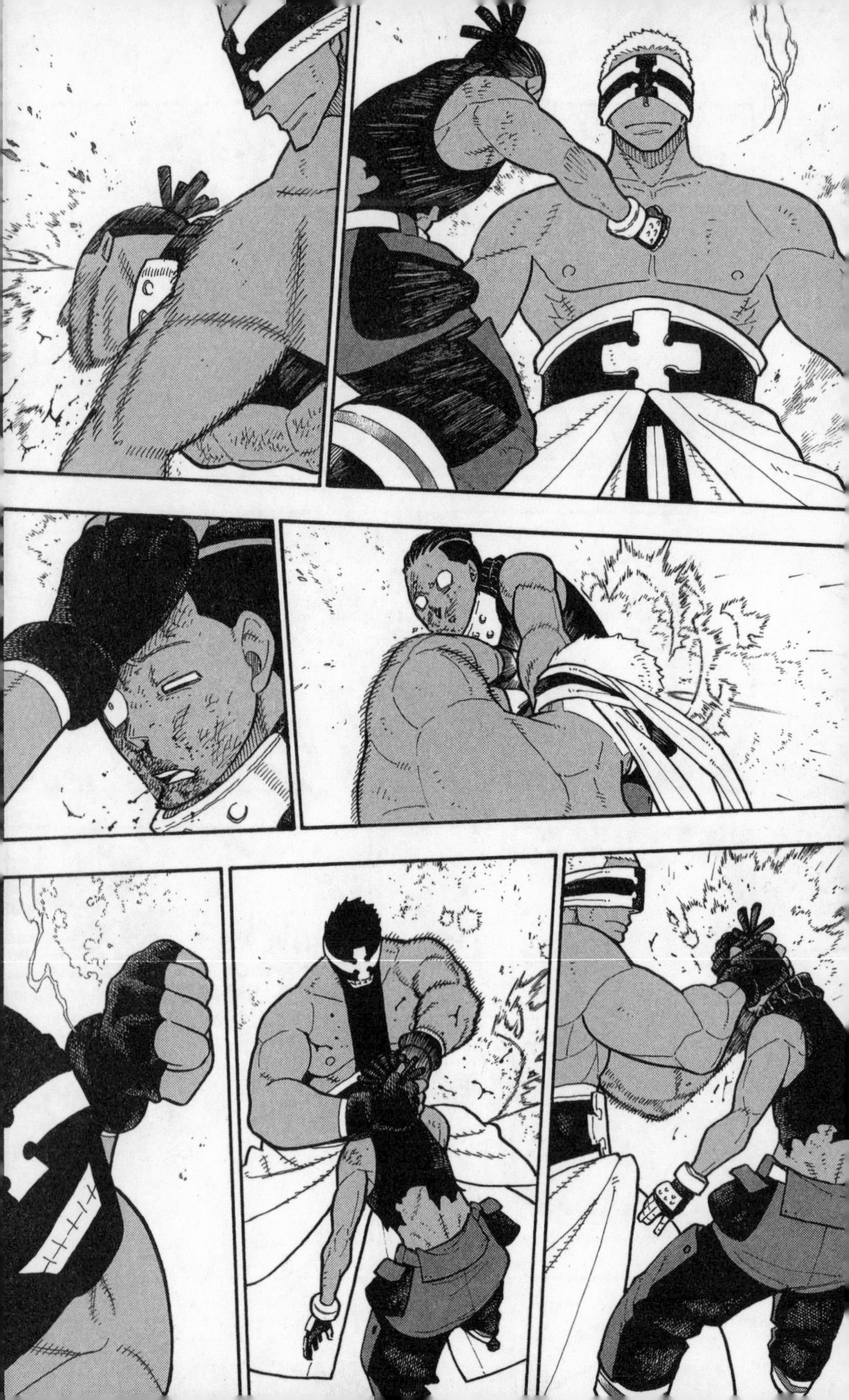

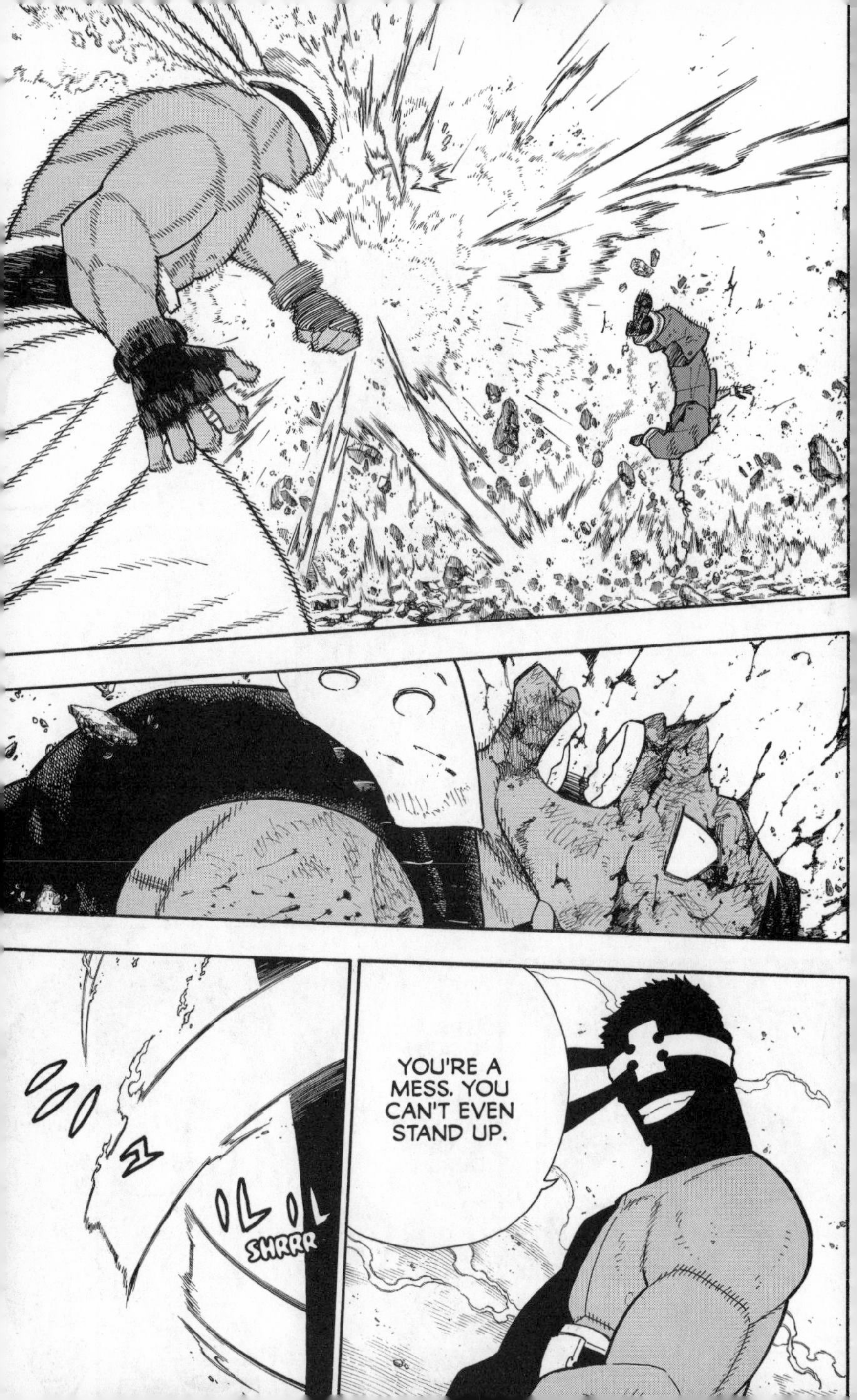
YOU'RE A MESS. YOU CAN'T EVEN STAND UP.
SHRRR

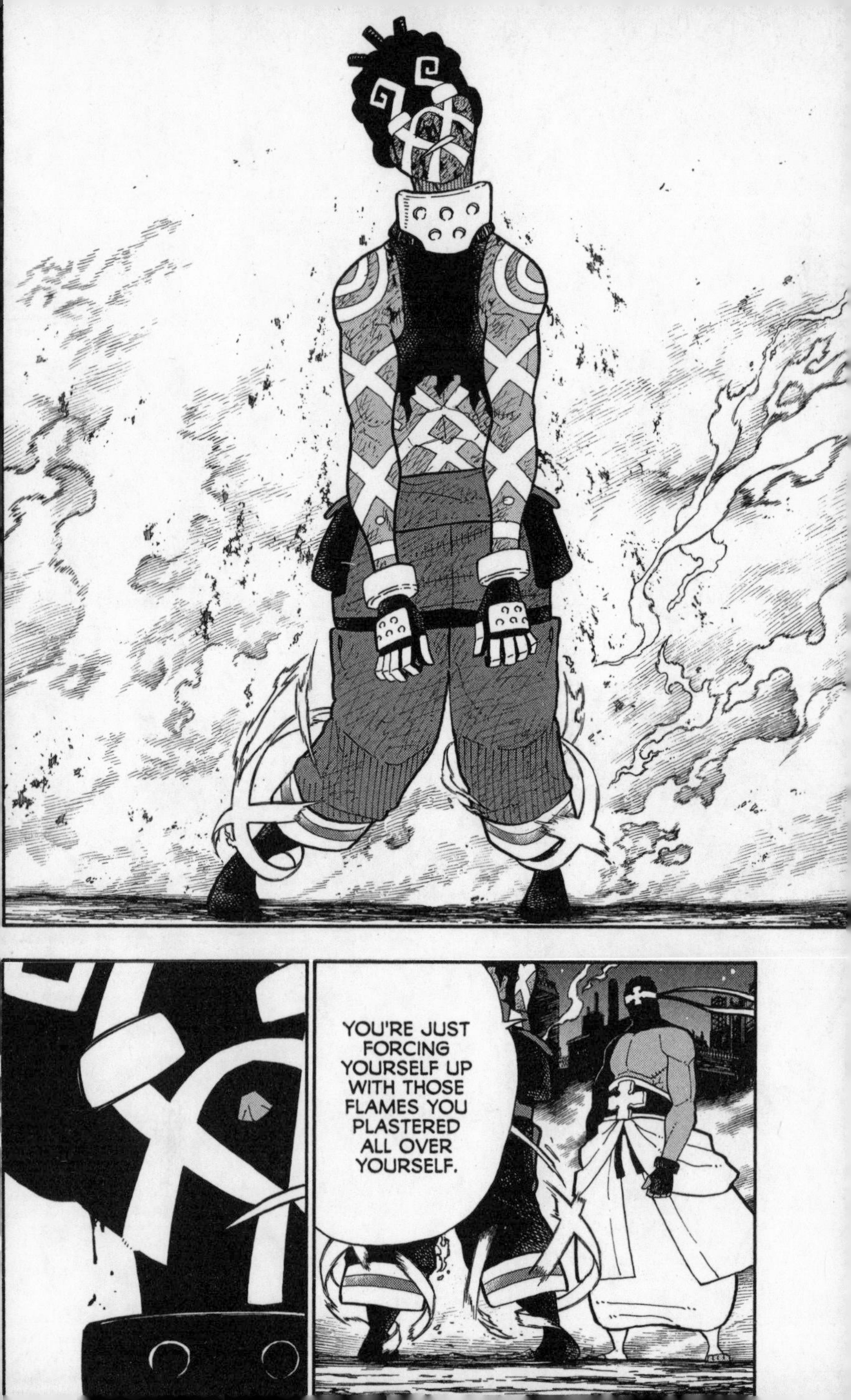
YOU'RE JUST FORCING YOURSELF UP WITH THOSE FLAMES YOU PLASTERED ALL OVER YOURSELF.

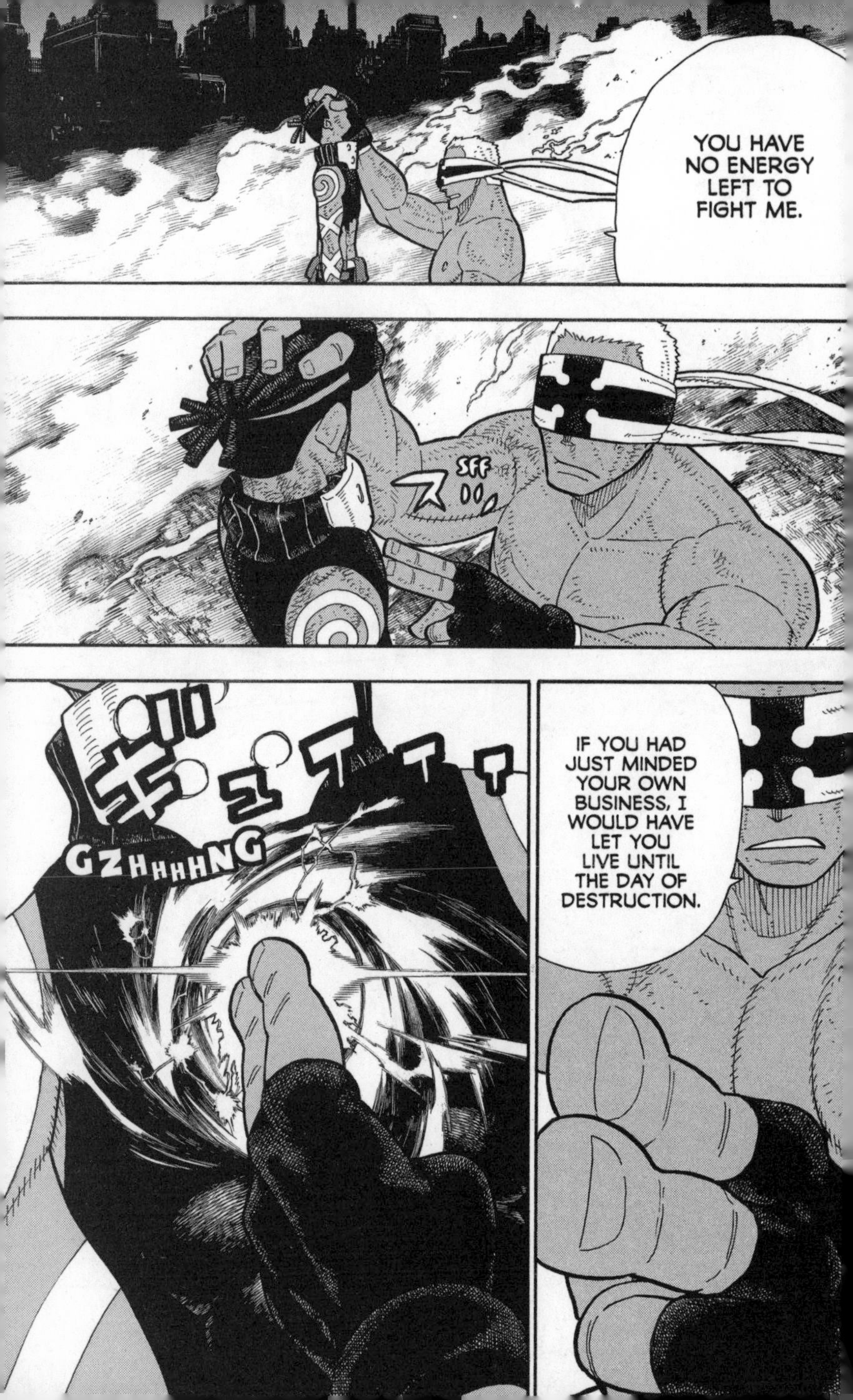
YOU HAVE NO ENERGY LEFT TO FIGHT ME.
SFF
IF YOU HAD JUST MINDED YOUR OWN BUSINESS, I WOULD HAVE LET YOU LIVE UNTIL THE DAY OF DESTRUCTION.
GZHHHHNG

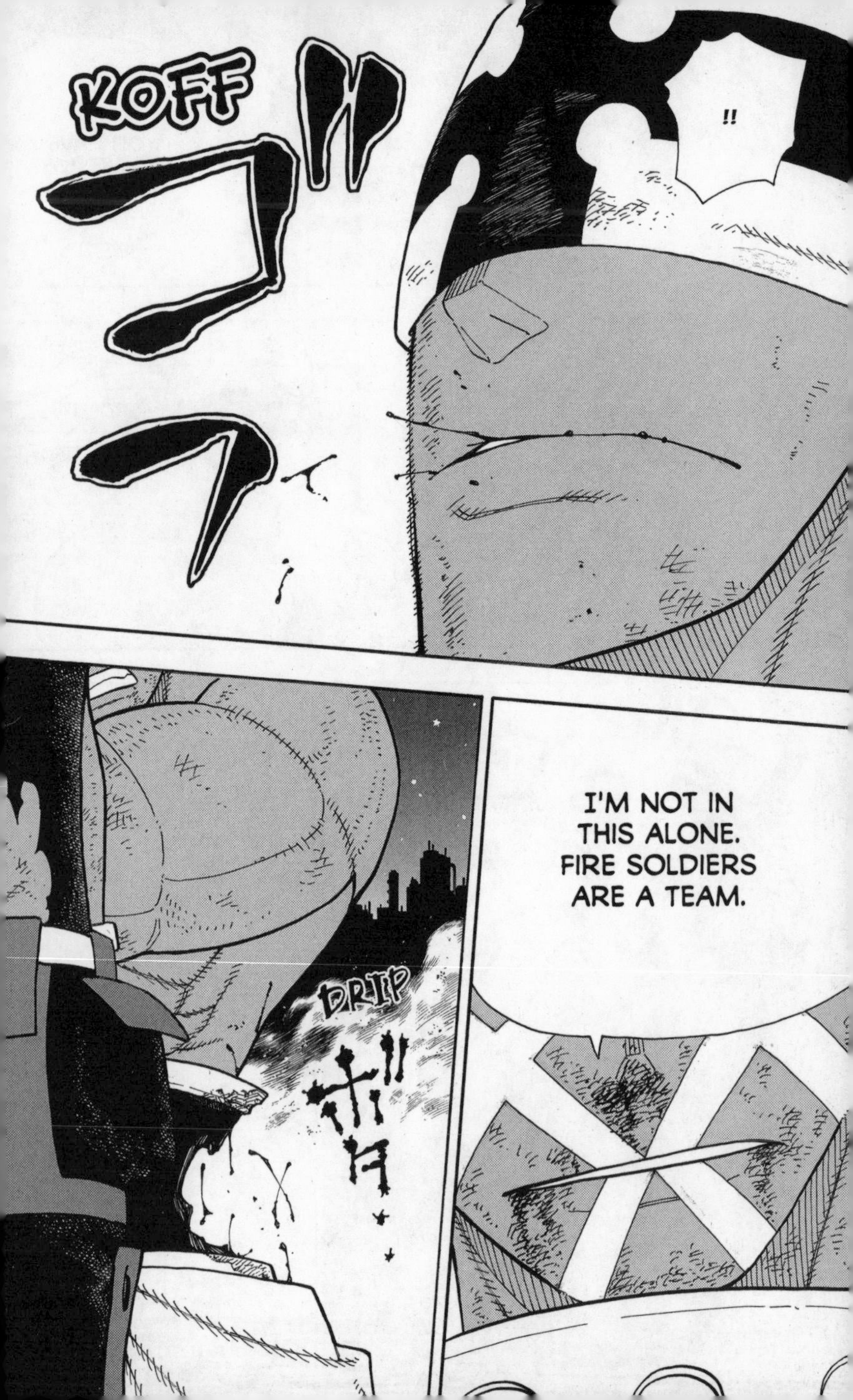
!!
KOFF
I'M NOT IN THIS ALONE. FIRE SOLDIERS ARE A TEAM.
DRIP

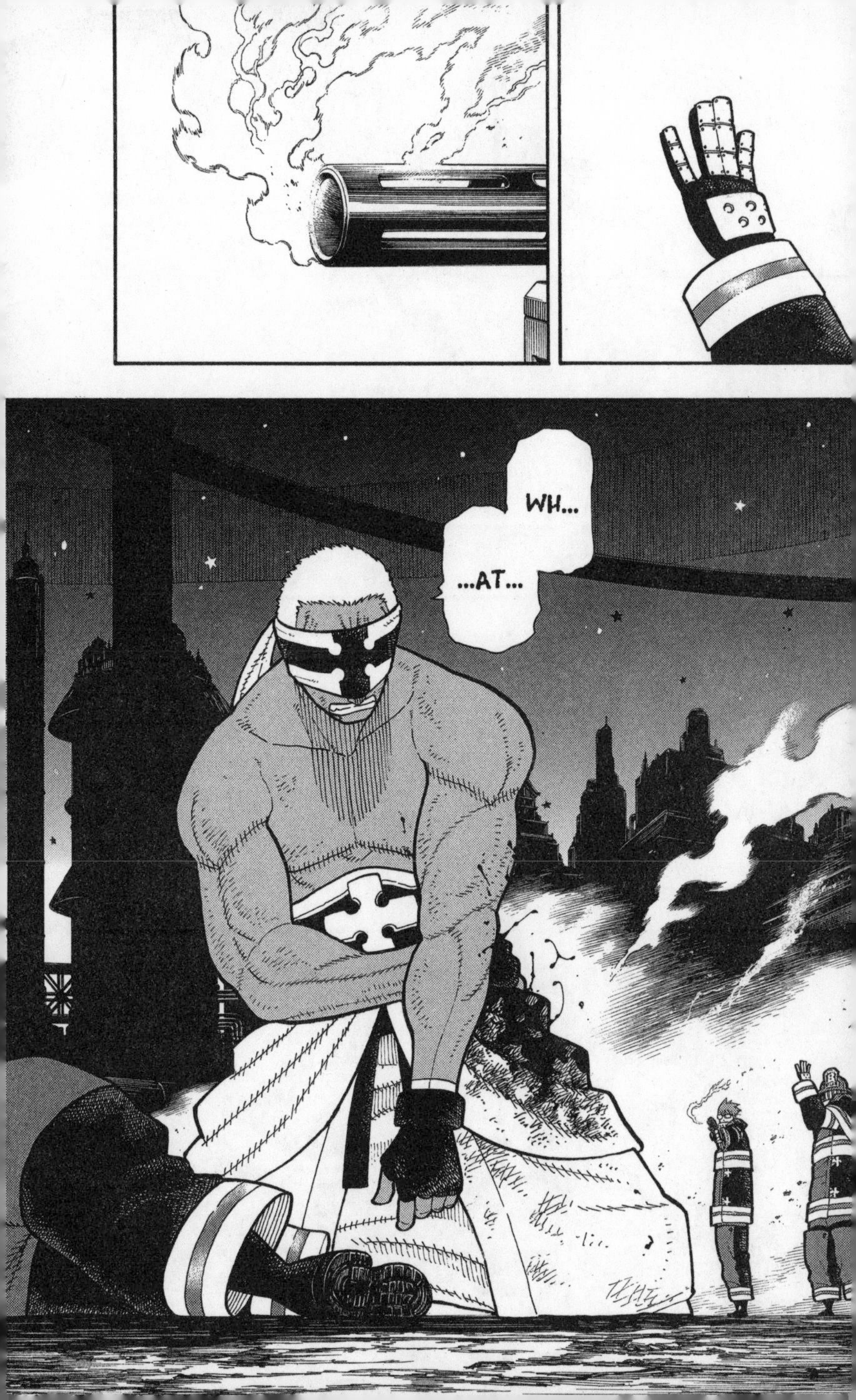
WH...
...AT...

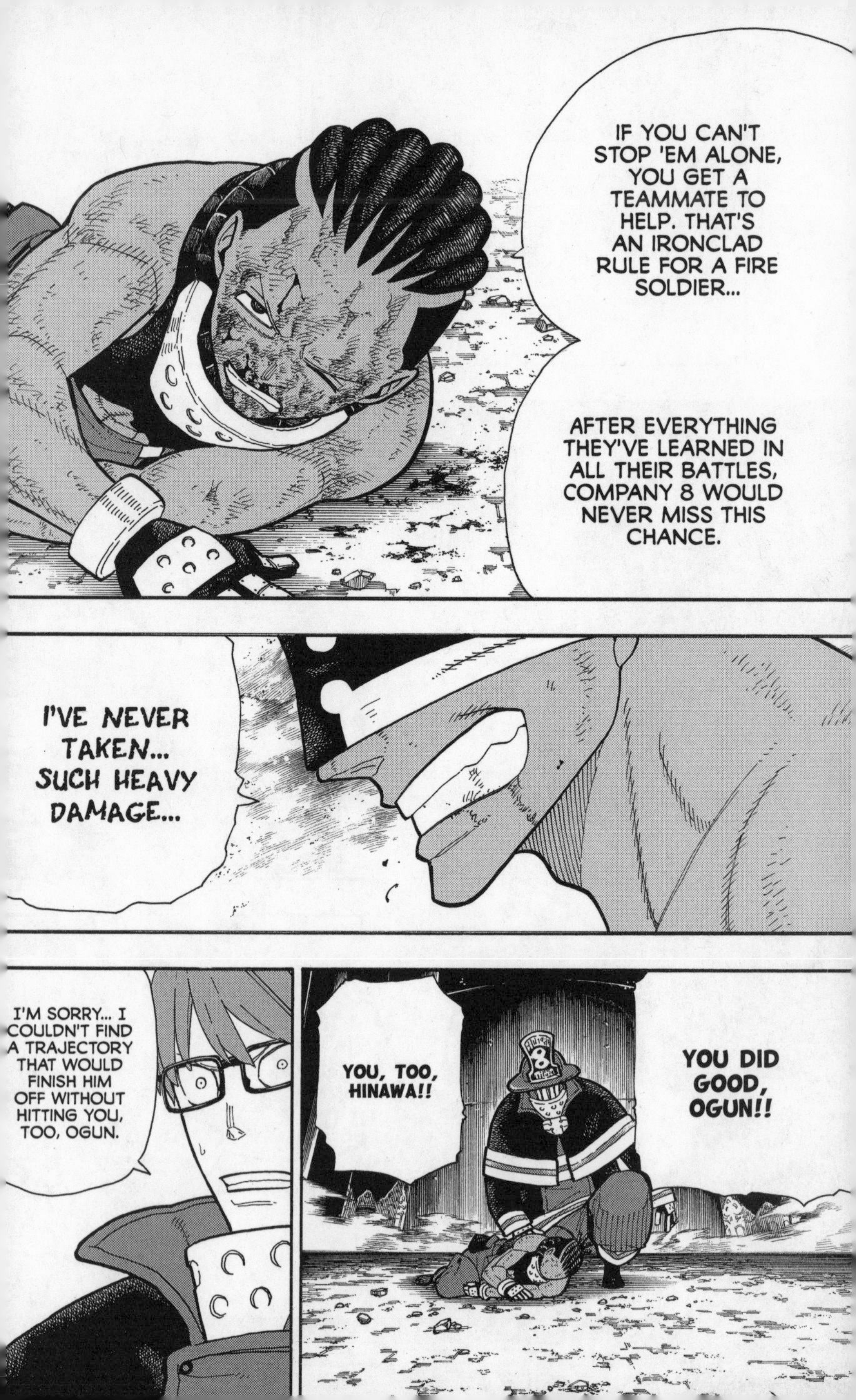
IF YOU CAN'T STOP 'EM ALONE, YOU GET A TEAMMATE TO HELP. THAT'S AN IRONCLAD RULE FOR A FIRE SOLDIER...
AFTER EVERYTHING THEY'VE LEARNED IN ALL THEIR BATTLES, COMPANY 8 WOULD NEVER MISS THIS CHANCE.
I'VE NEVER TAKEN... SUCH HEAVY DAMAGE...
YOU DID GOOD, OGUN!!
YOU, TOO, HINAWA!!
I'M SORRY... I COULDN'T FIND A TRAJECTORY THAT WOULD FINISH HIM OFF WITHOUT HITTING YOU, TOO, OGUN.

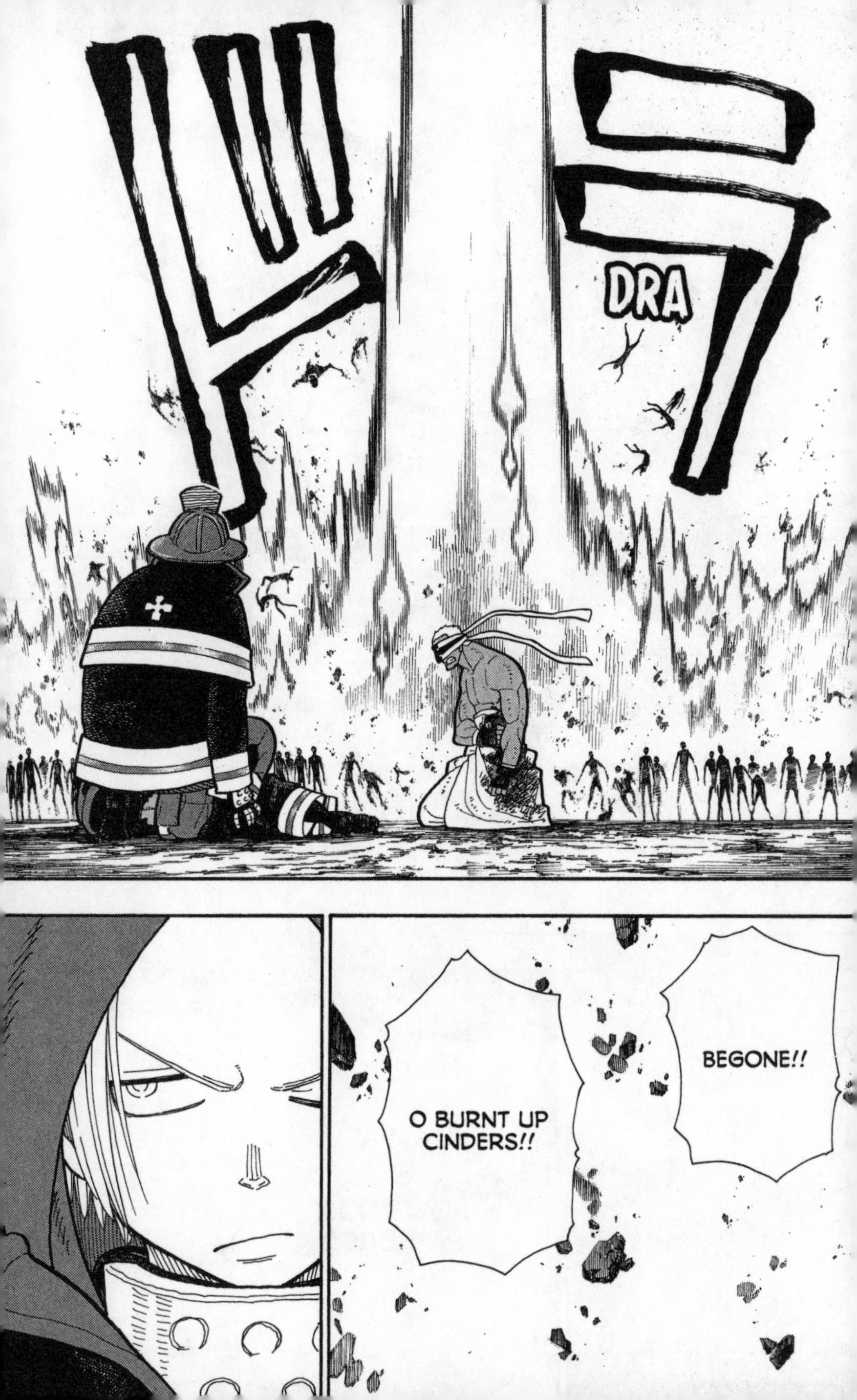
ドラ
DRA
BEGONE!!
O BURNT UP CINDERS!!

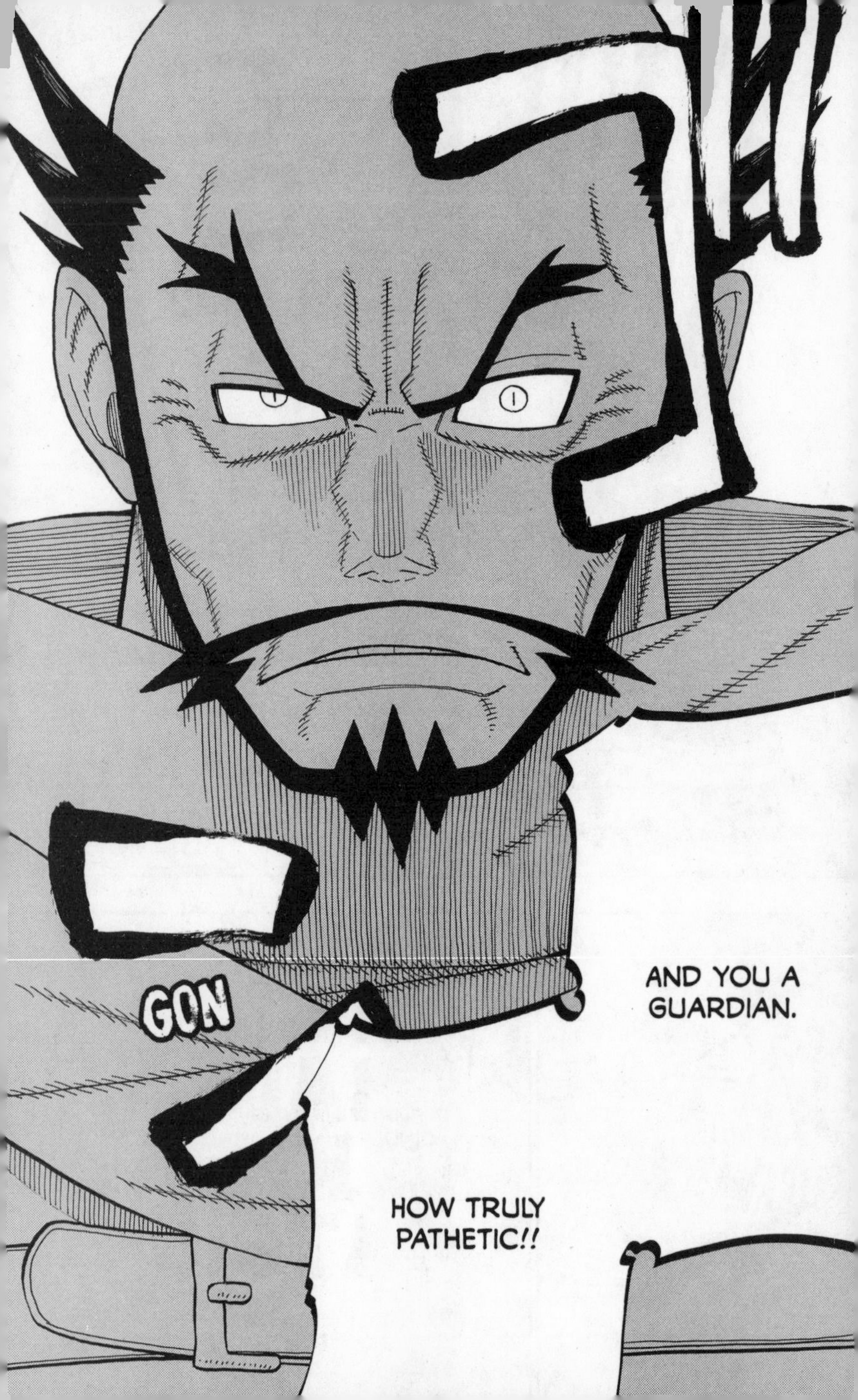
GON
AND YOU A GUARDIAN.
HOW TRULY PATHETIC!!

YOUR FRIEND MARU-KUN! NOW AVAILABLE IN KNIGHT FORM!!
I WANT ONE!!
SHA-KING

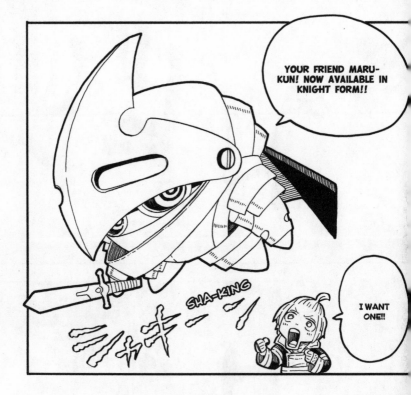

CHAPTER CCXLV: THE DRAGON AND THE KNIGHT: REMATCH

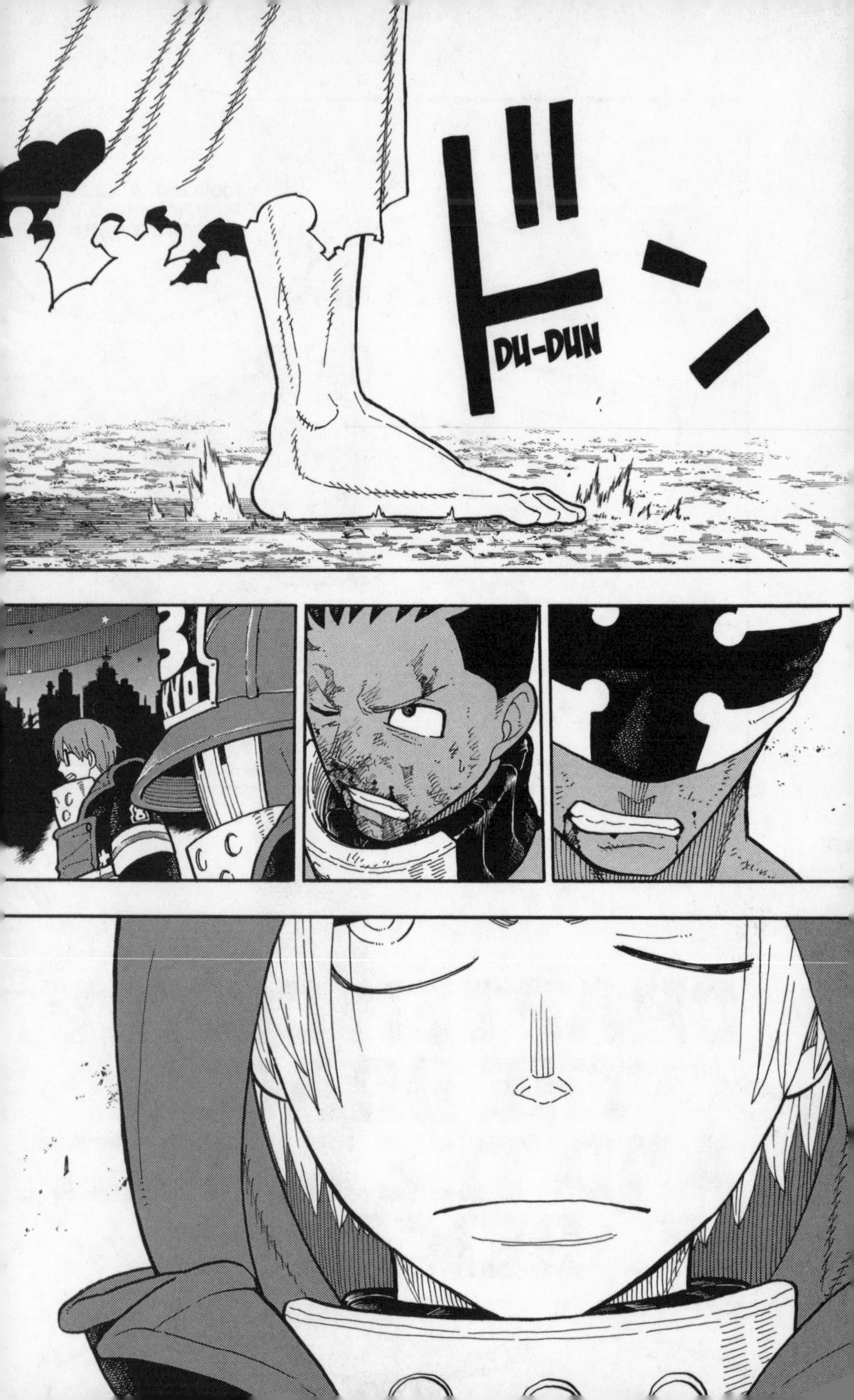
DU-DUN

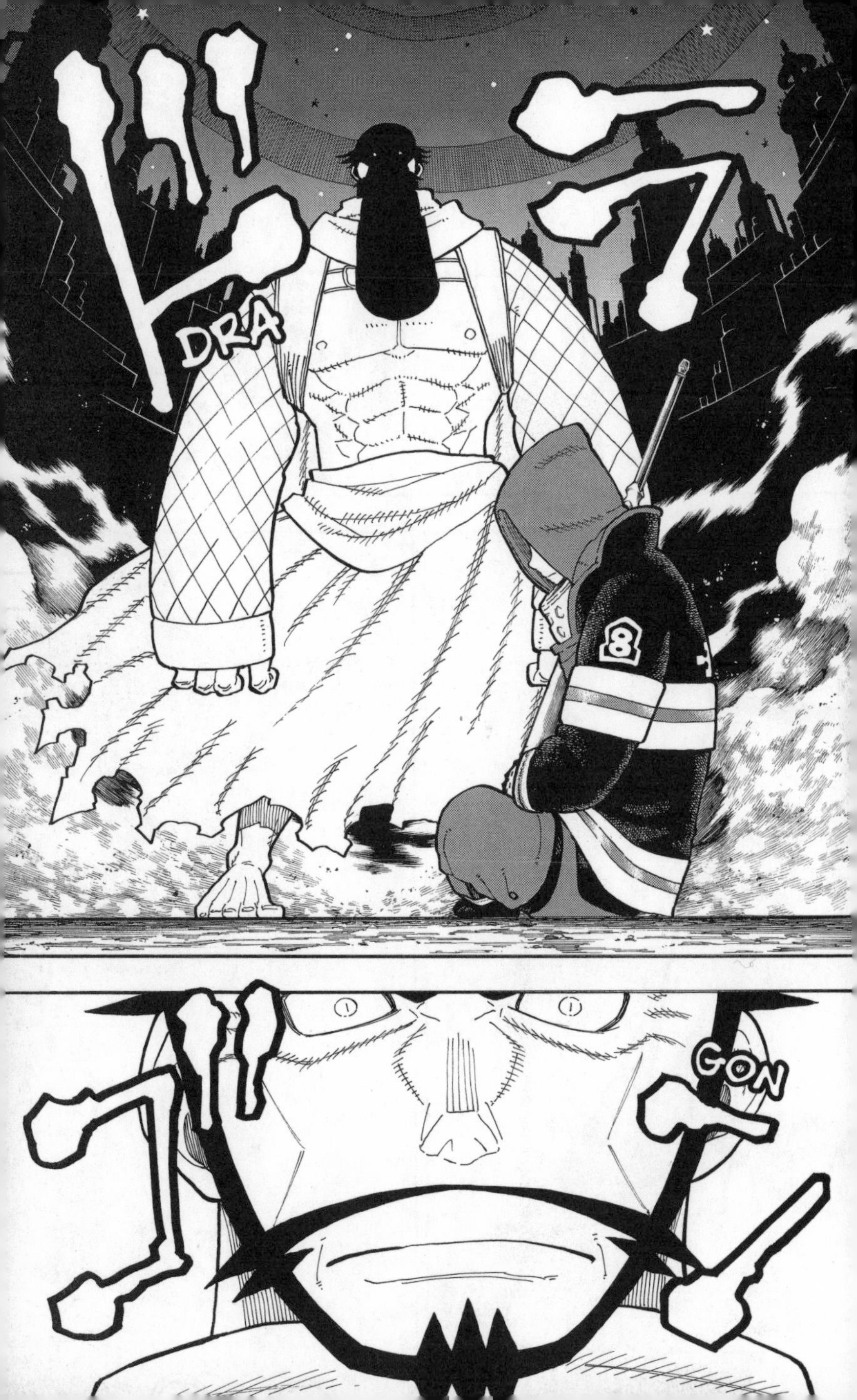
DRA
GON

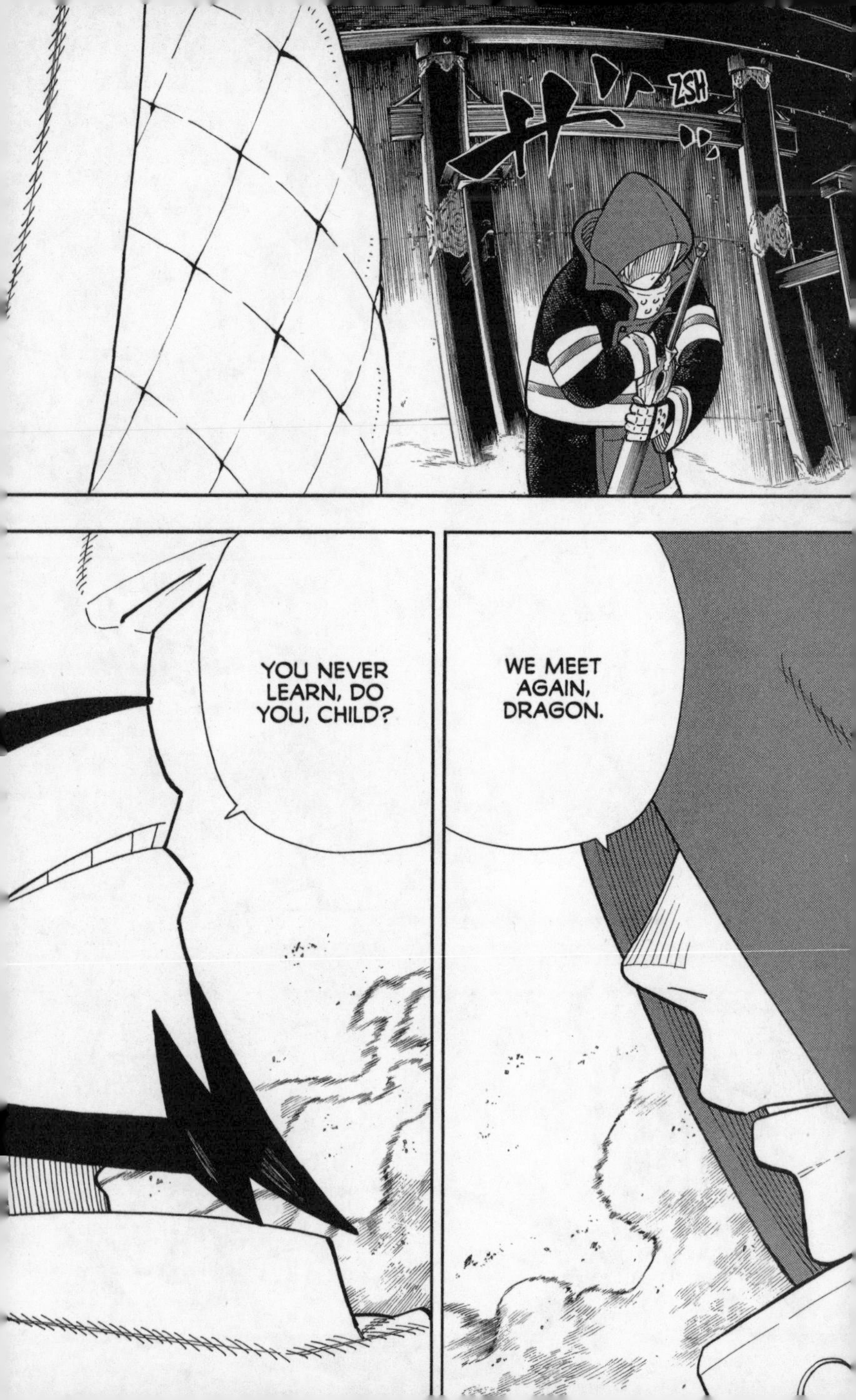
ZSH
WE MEET AGAIN, DRAGON.
YOU NEVER LEARN, DO YOU, CHILD?

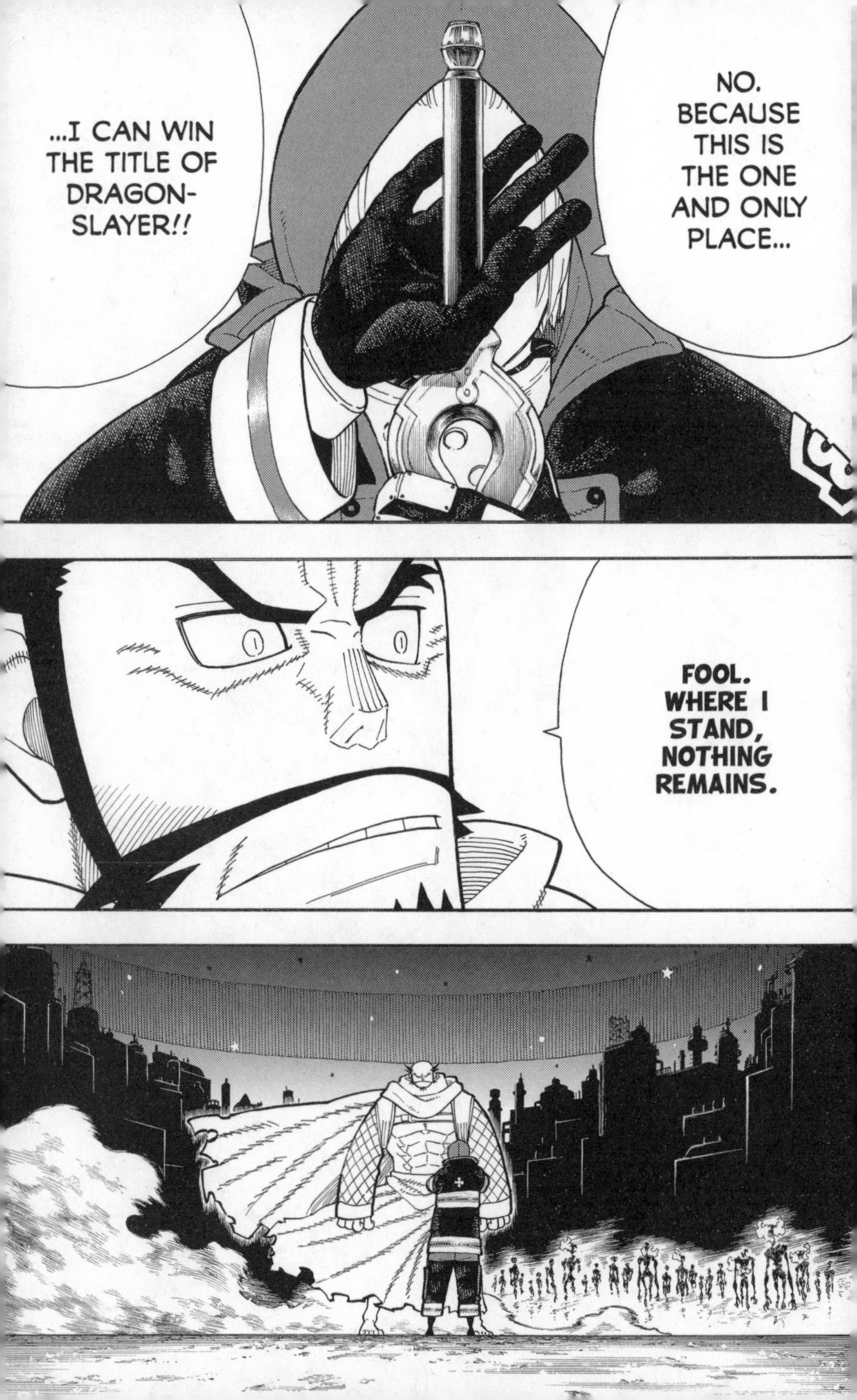
NO. BECAUSE THIS IS THE ONE AND ONLY PLACE...
...I CAN WIN THE TITLE OF DRAGON-SLAYER!!
FOOL. WHERE I STAND, NOTHING REMAINS.

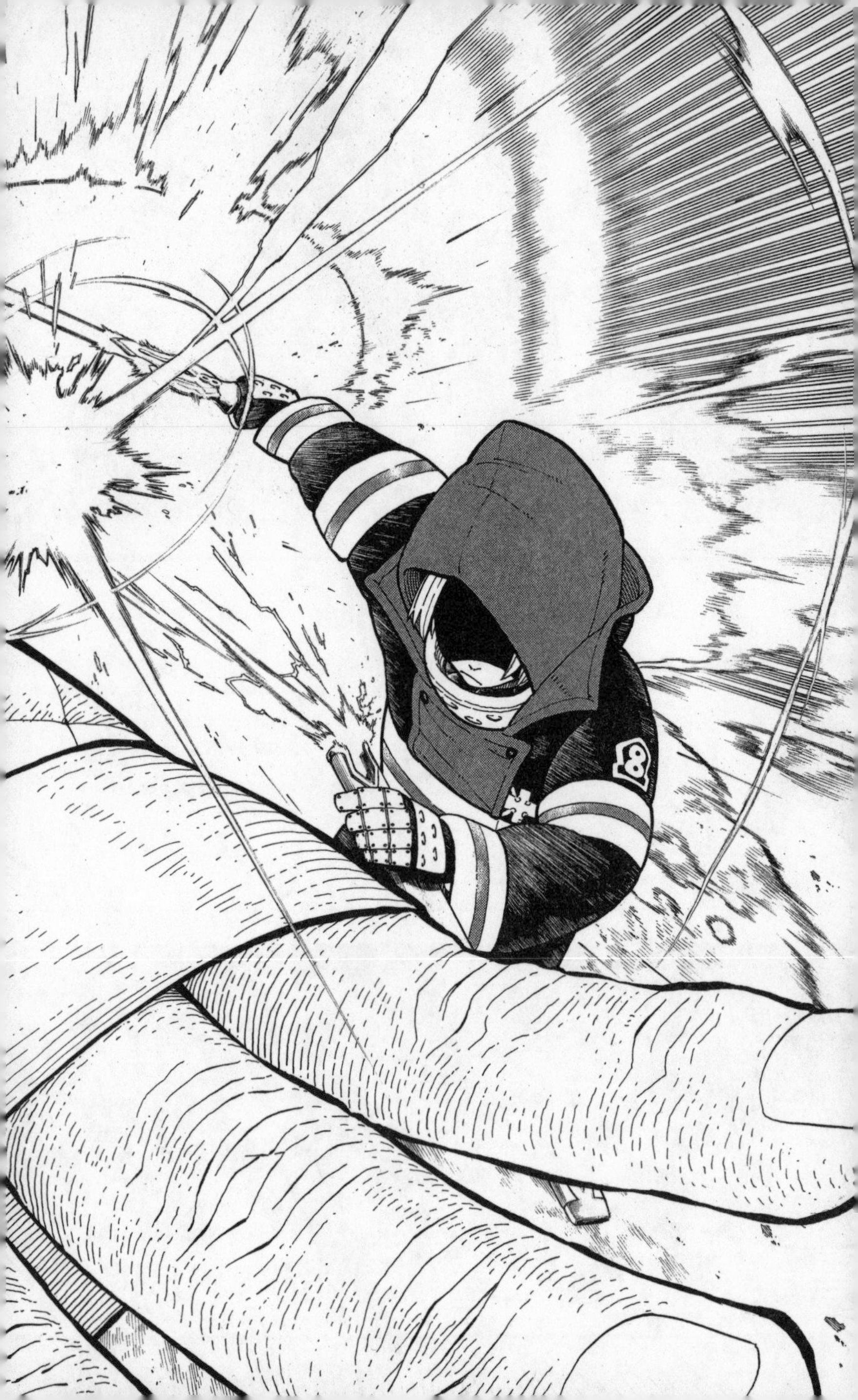

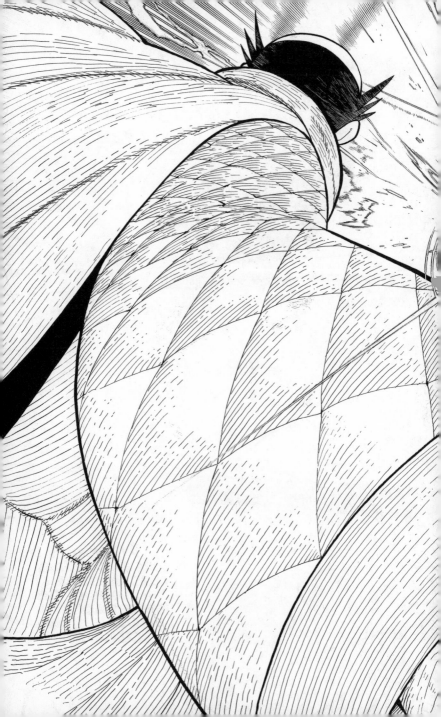

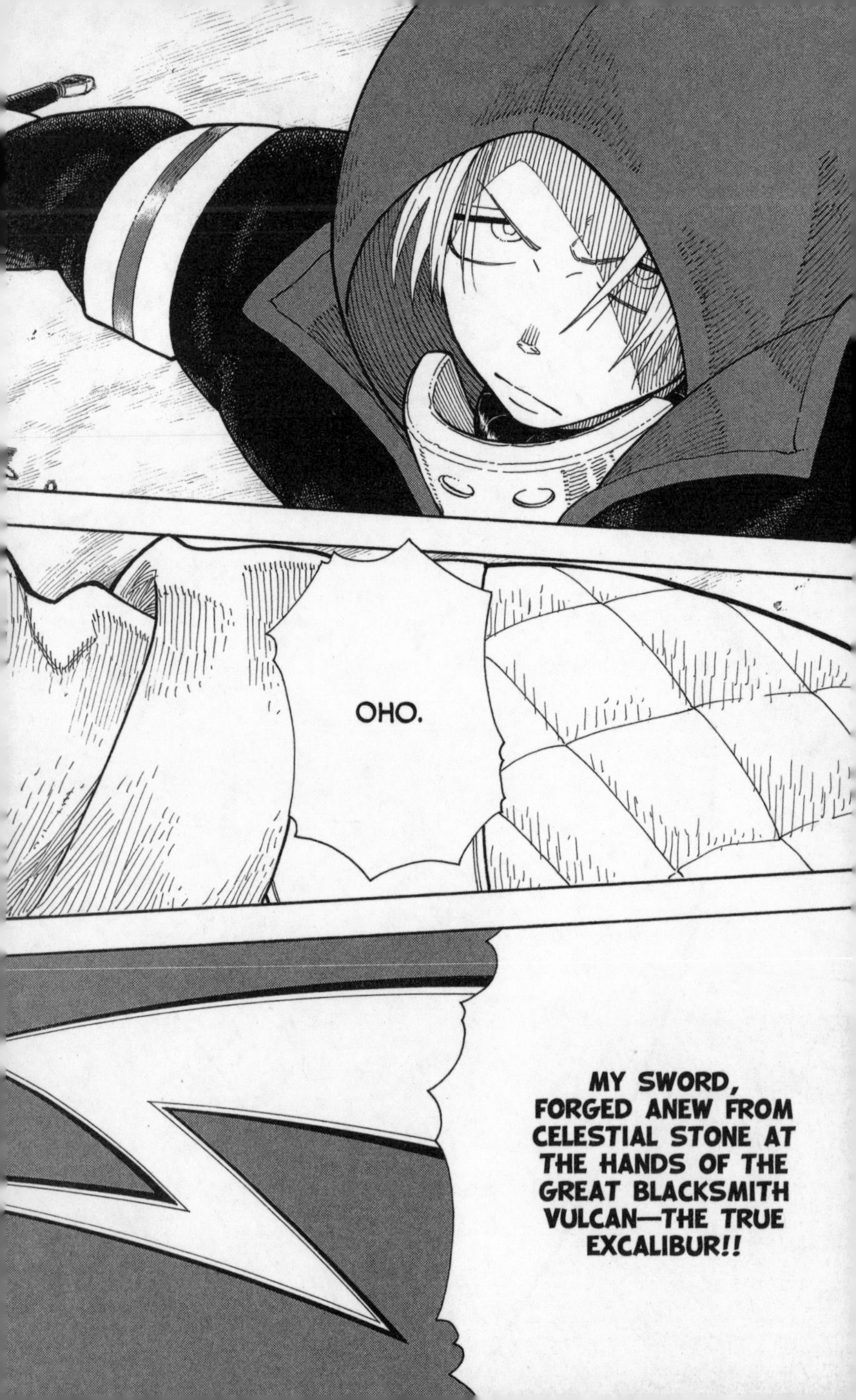
OHO.
MY SWORD, FORGED ANEW FROM CELESTIAL STONE AT THE HANDS OF THE GREAT BLACKSMITH VULCAN—THE TRUE EXCALIBUR!!

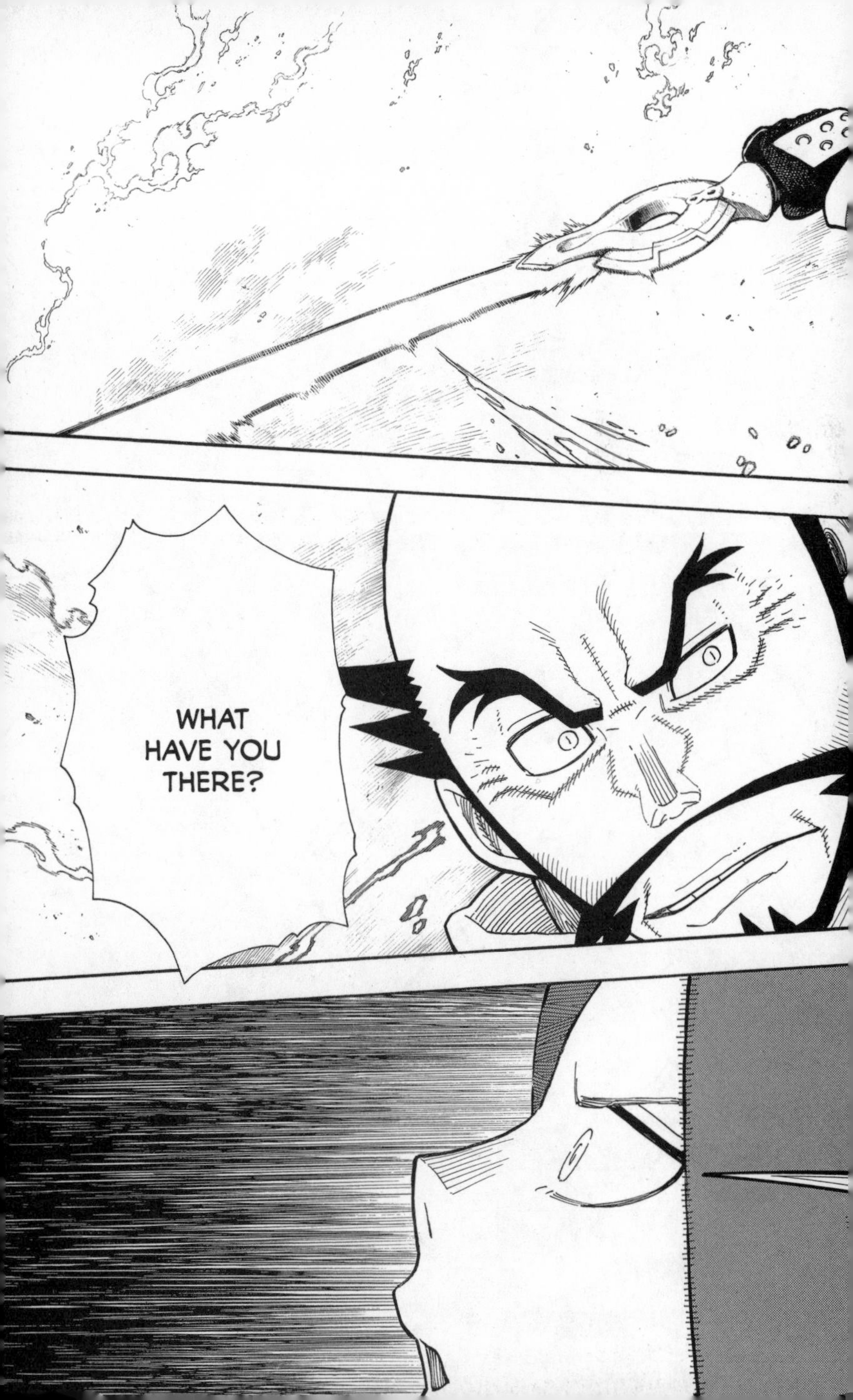
WHAT HAVE YOU THERE?

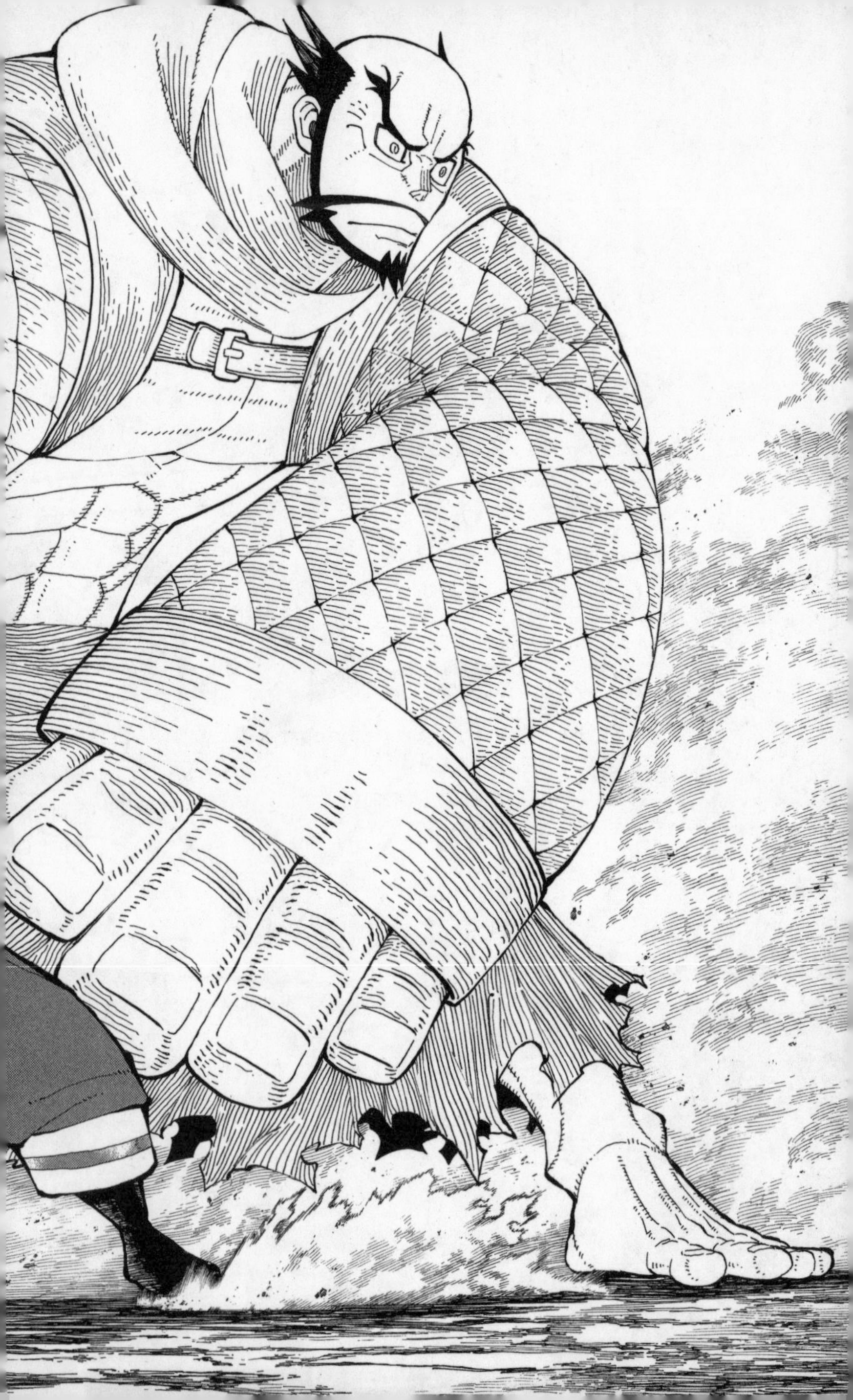

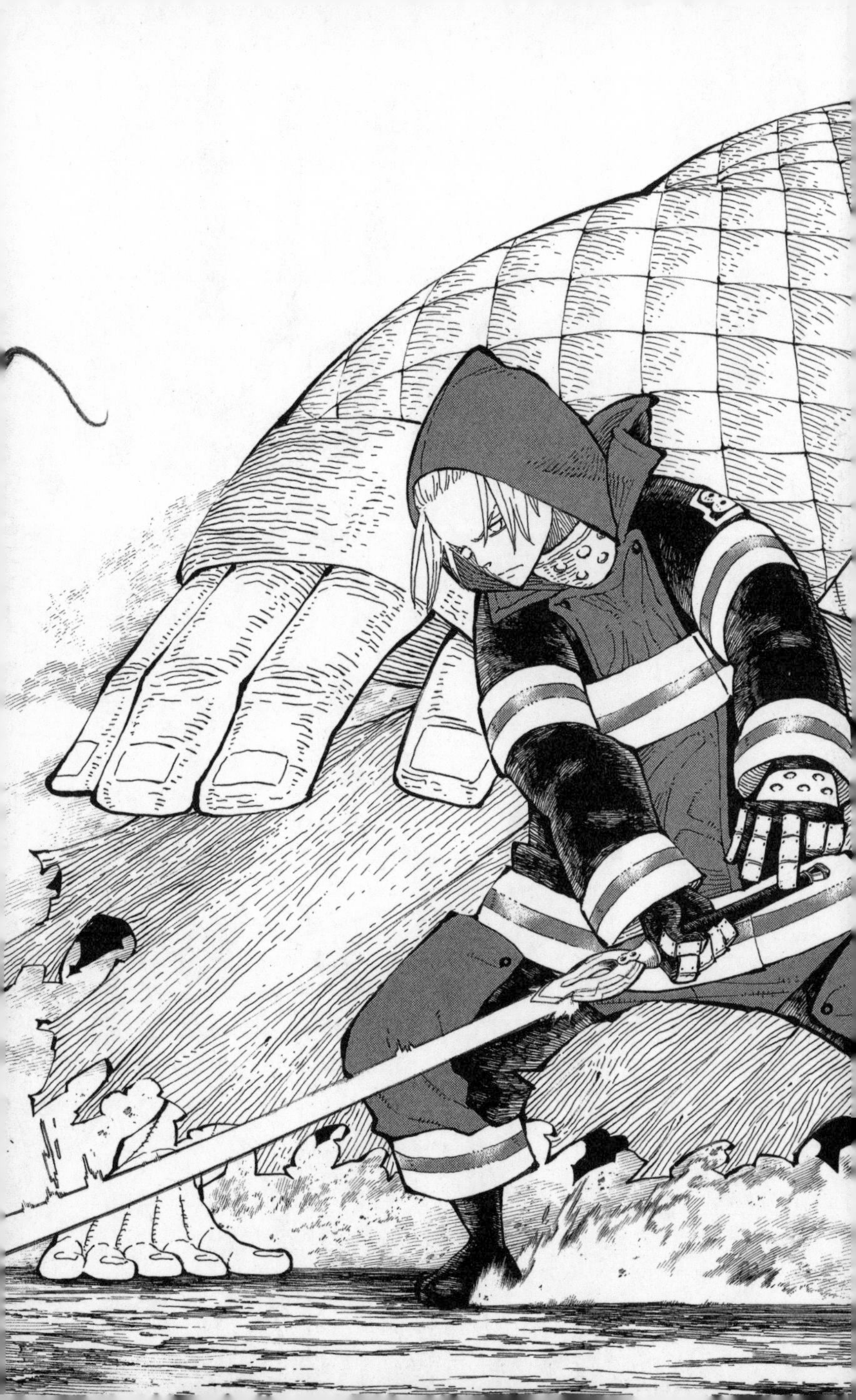

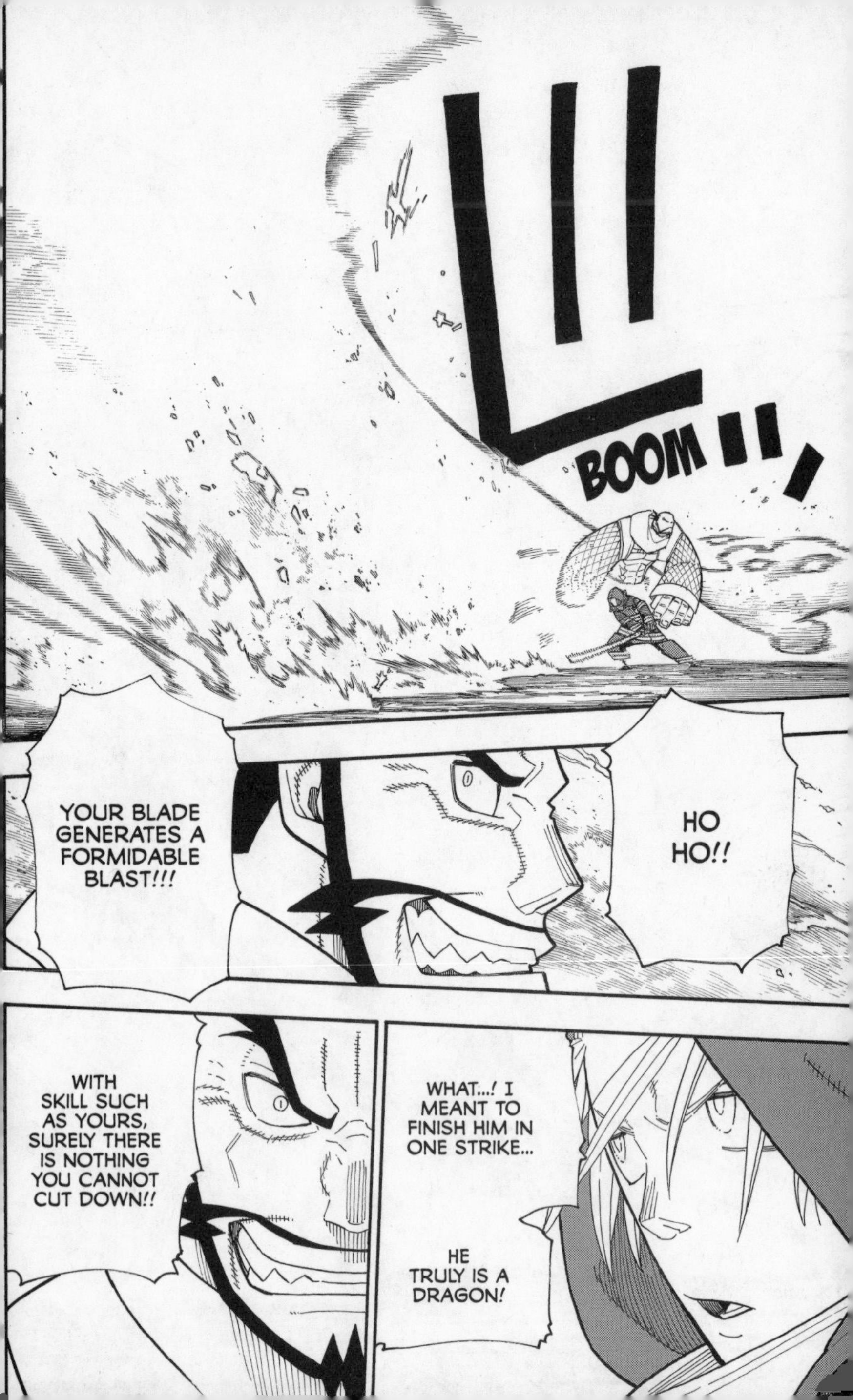
BOOM!!
HO HO!!
YOUR BLADE GENERATES A FORMIDABLE BLAST!!!
WHAT...! I MEANT TO FINISH HIM IN ONE STRIKE...
HE TRULY IS A DRAGON!
WITH SKILL SUCH AS YOURS, SURELY THERE IS NOTHING YOU CANNOT CUT DOWN!!

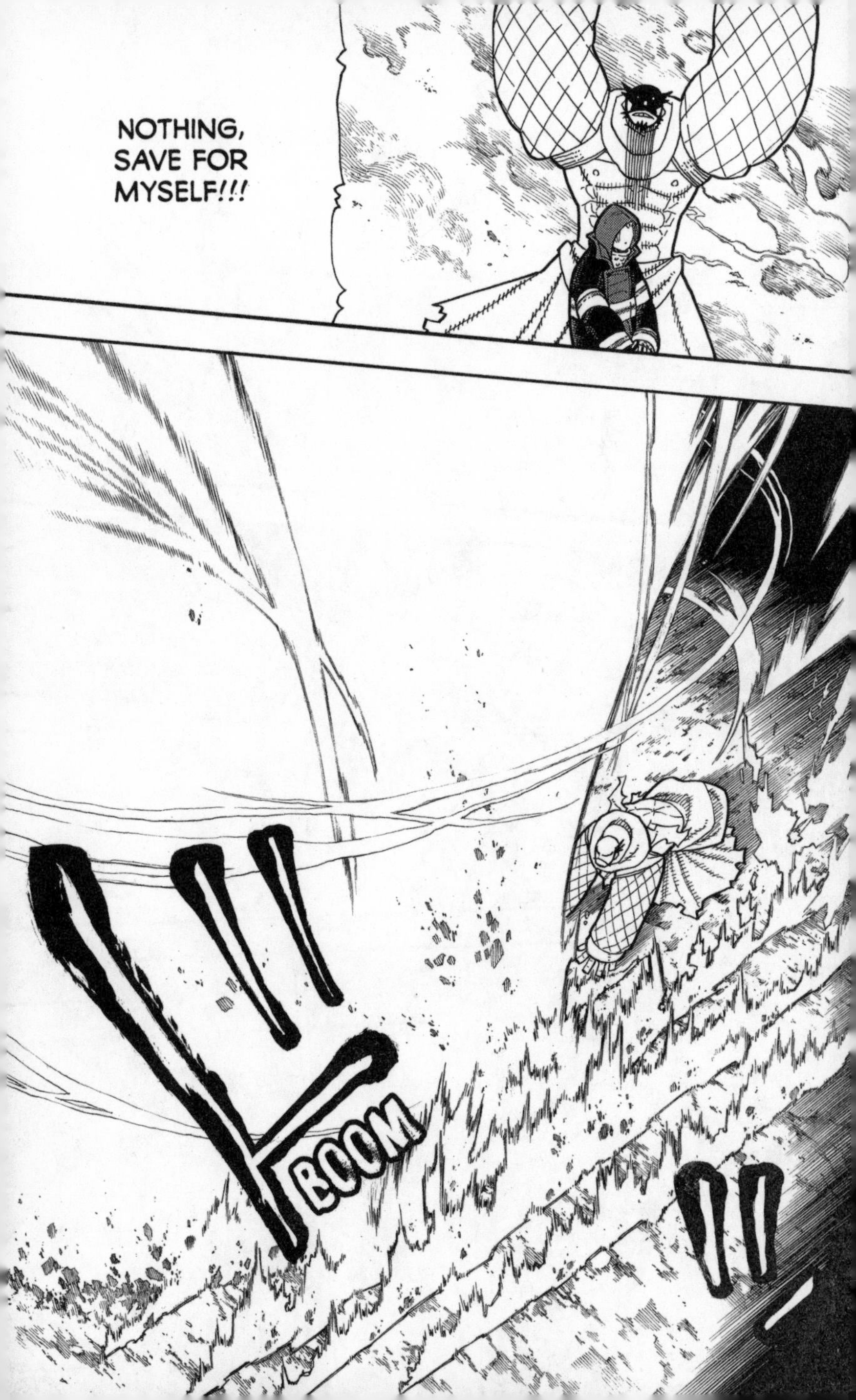
NOTHING, SAVE FOR MYSELF!!!
BOOM

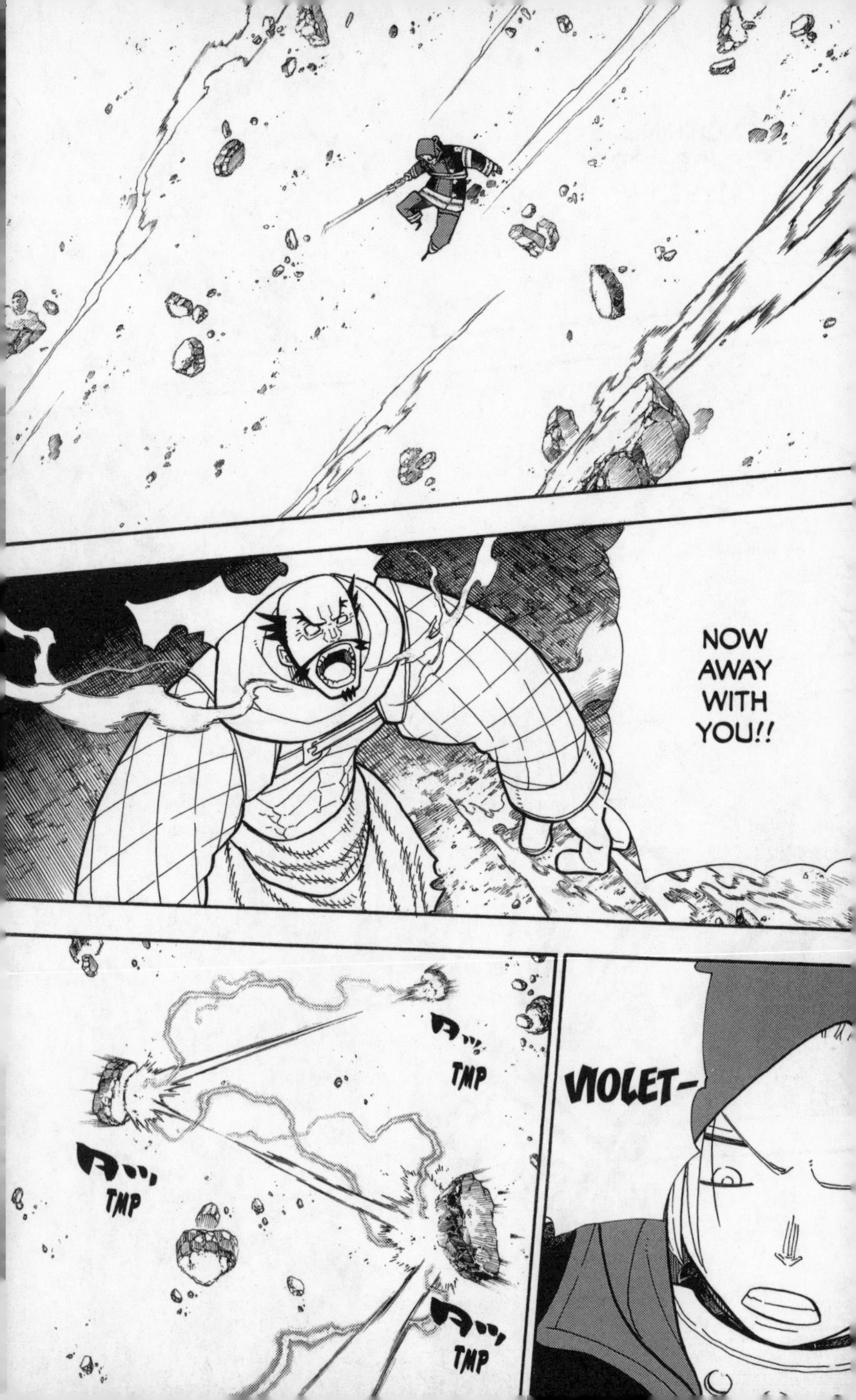
NOW AWAY WITH YOU!!
VIOLET-
TMP
TMP
TMP

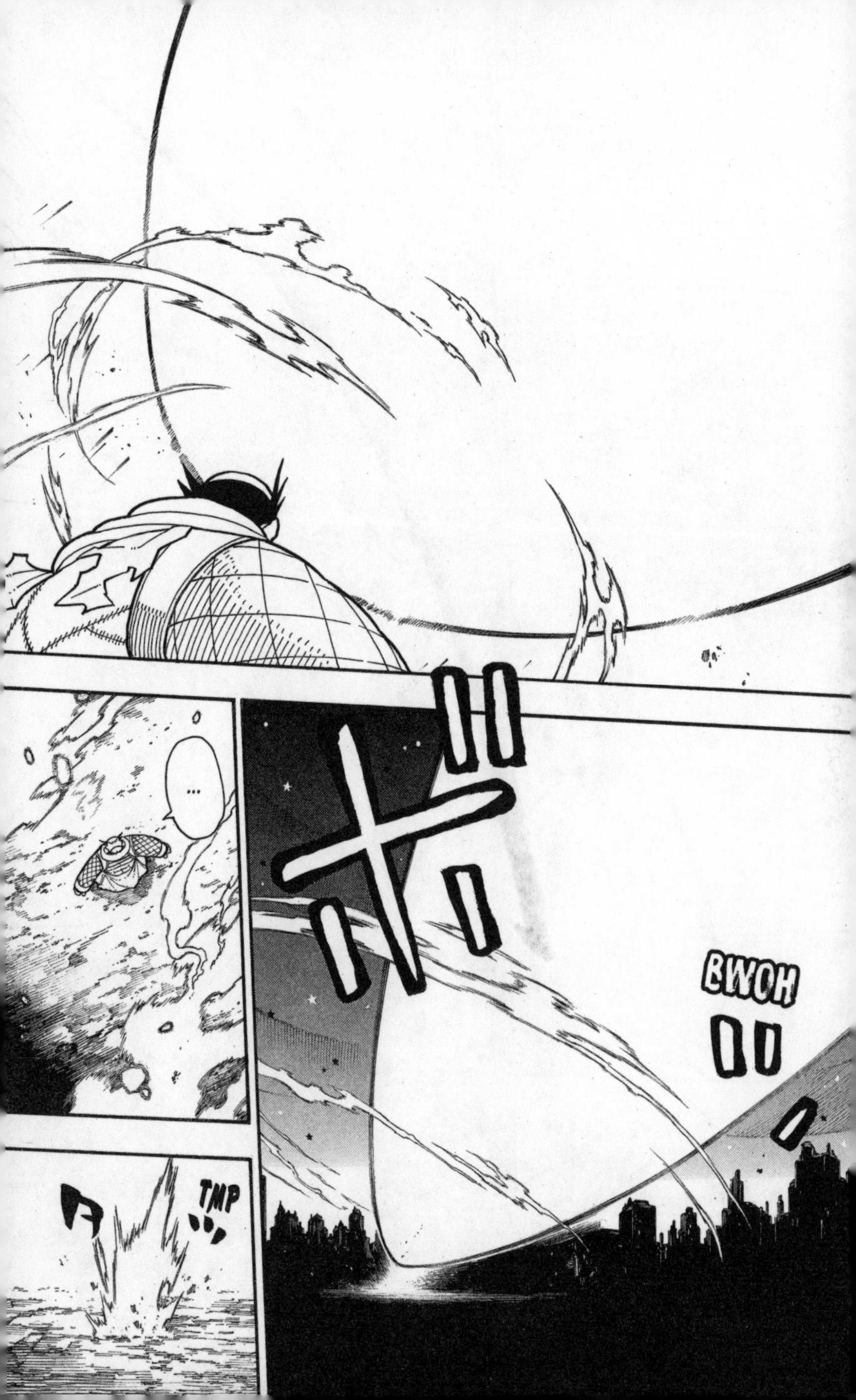
BWOH
...
TMP

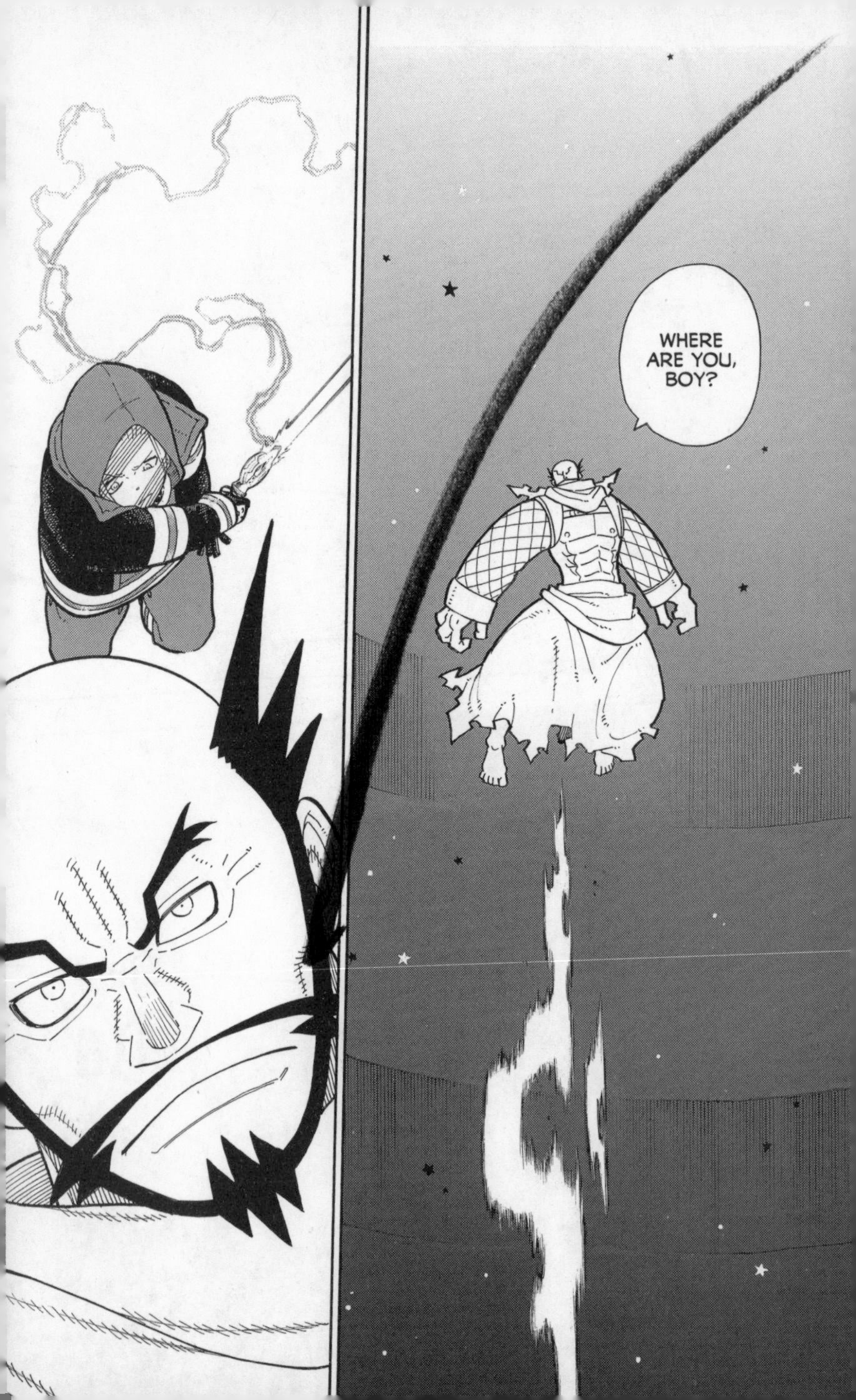
WHERE ARE YOU, BOY?

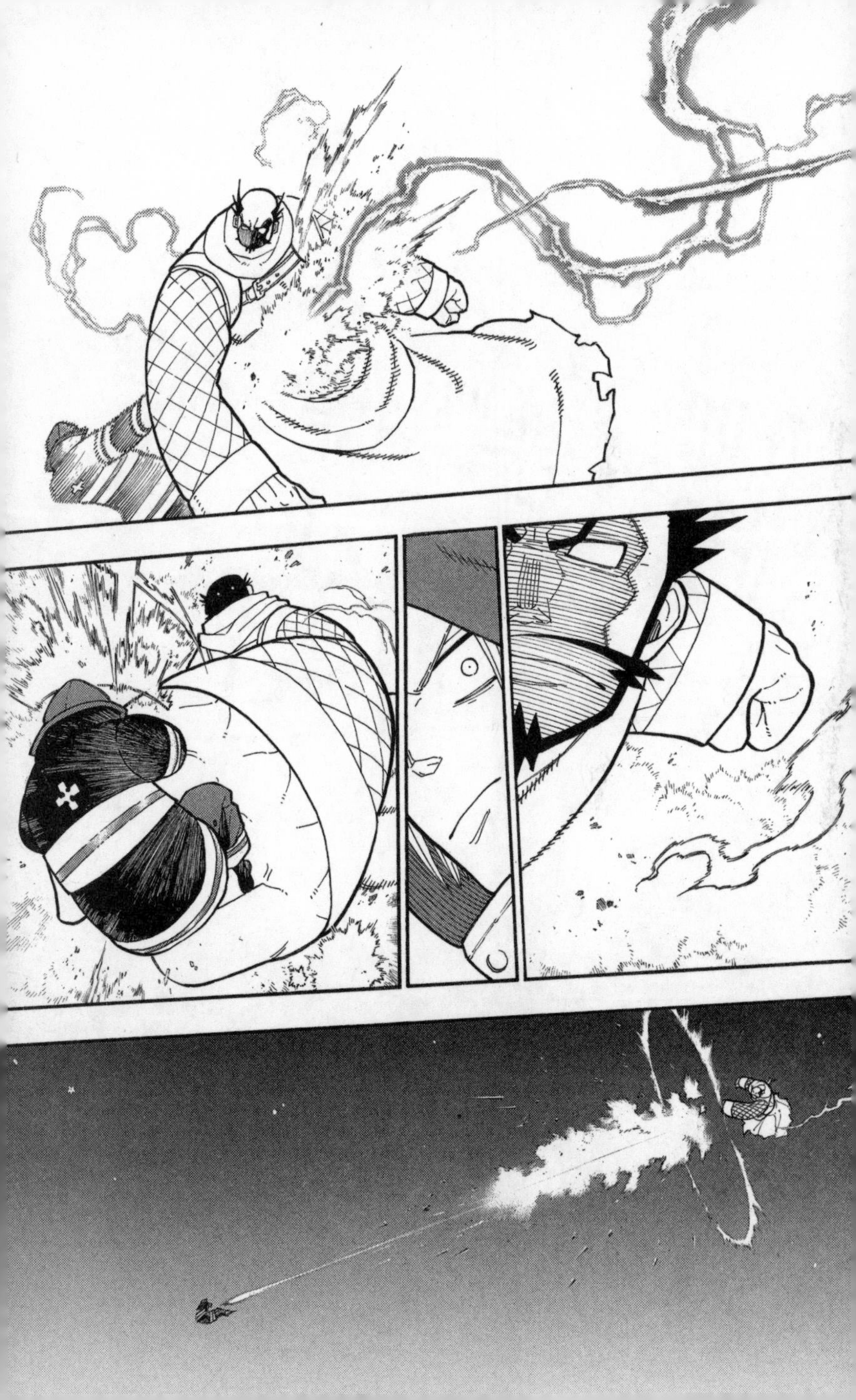

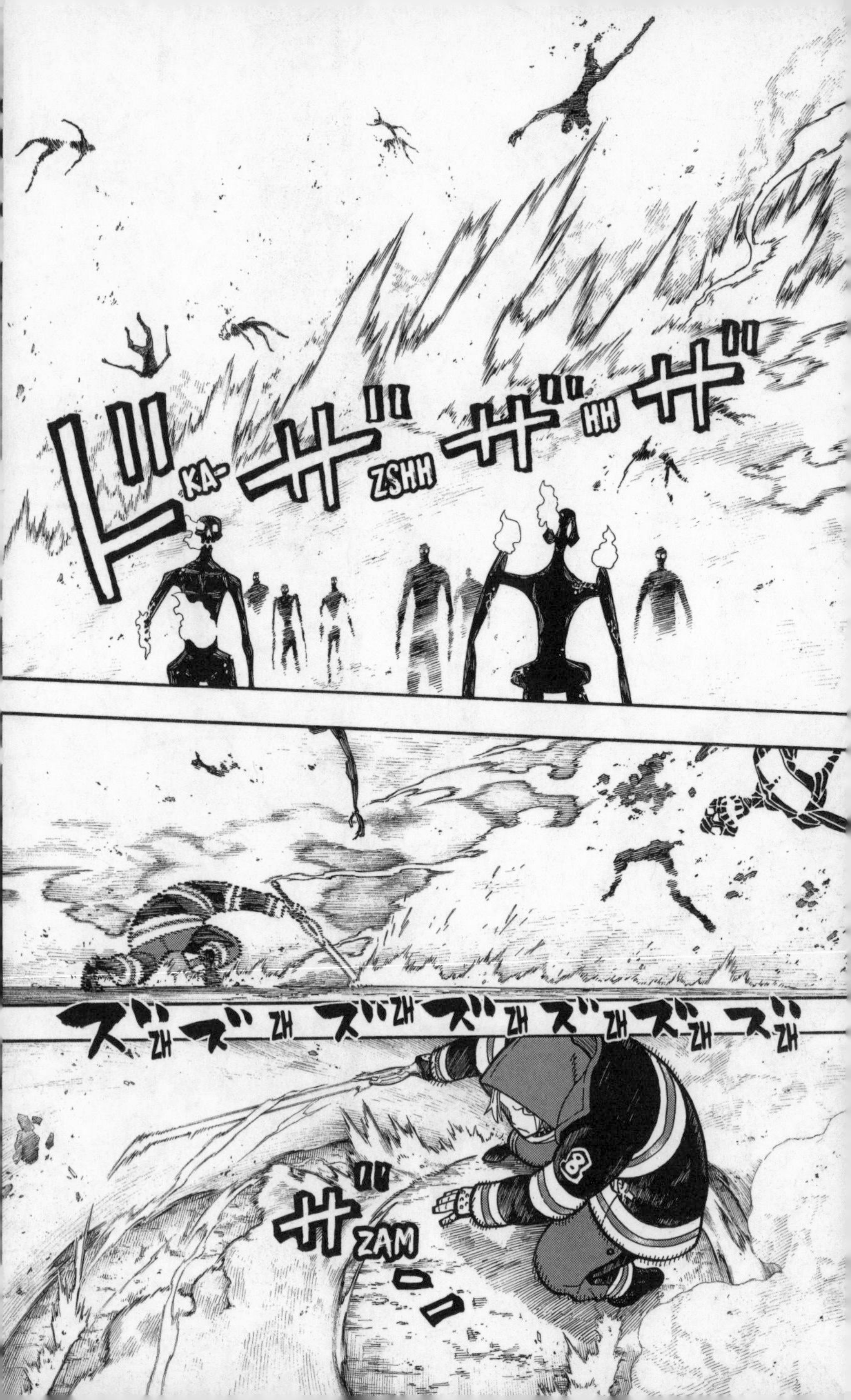
ド KA- ザ ZSHH ザ HH ザ
ズ ZH ズ ZH ズ ZH ズ ZH ズ ZH ズ ZH ズ ZH
ザ ZAM

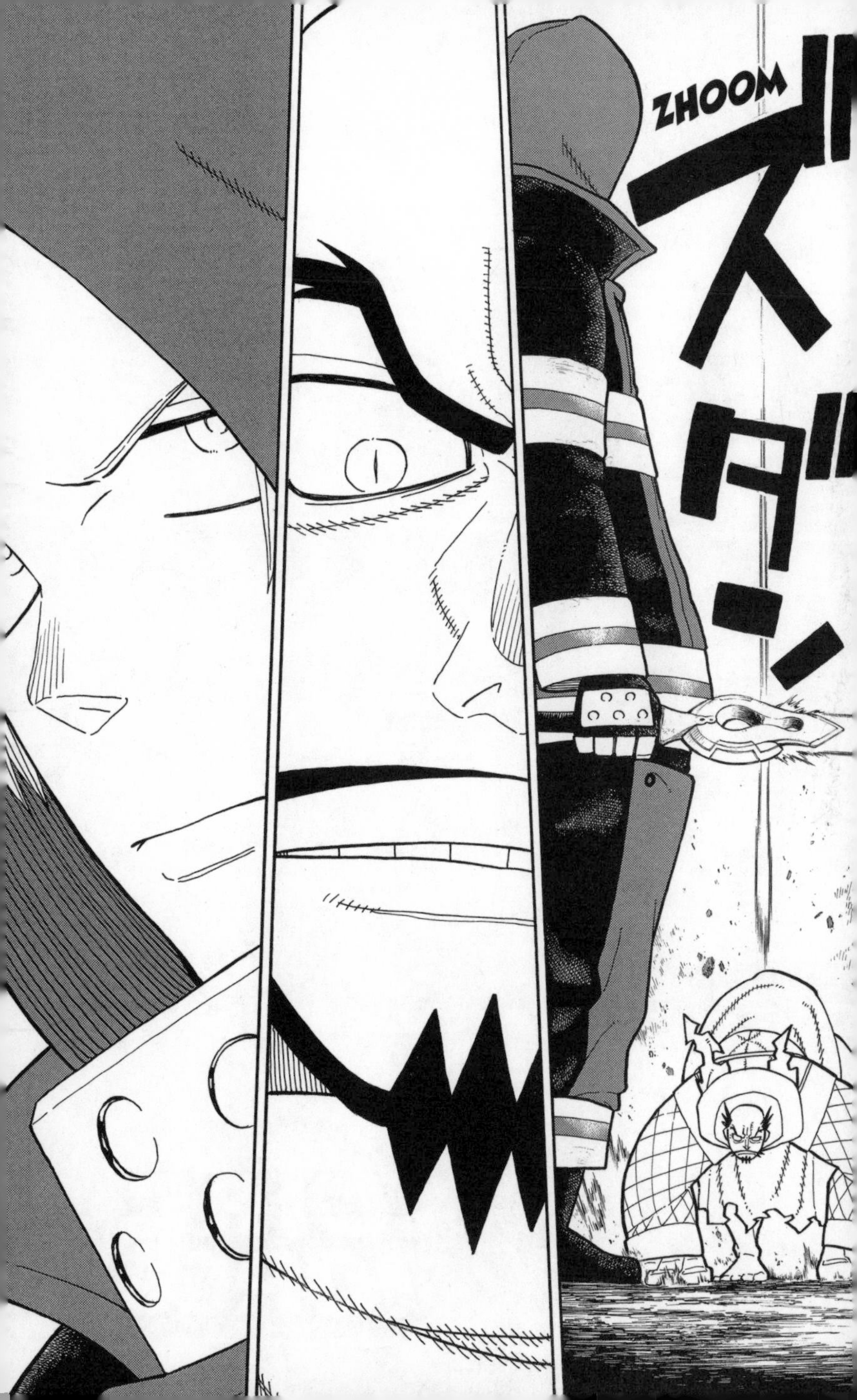
ZHOOM
ズダーン

FIRE FORCE

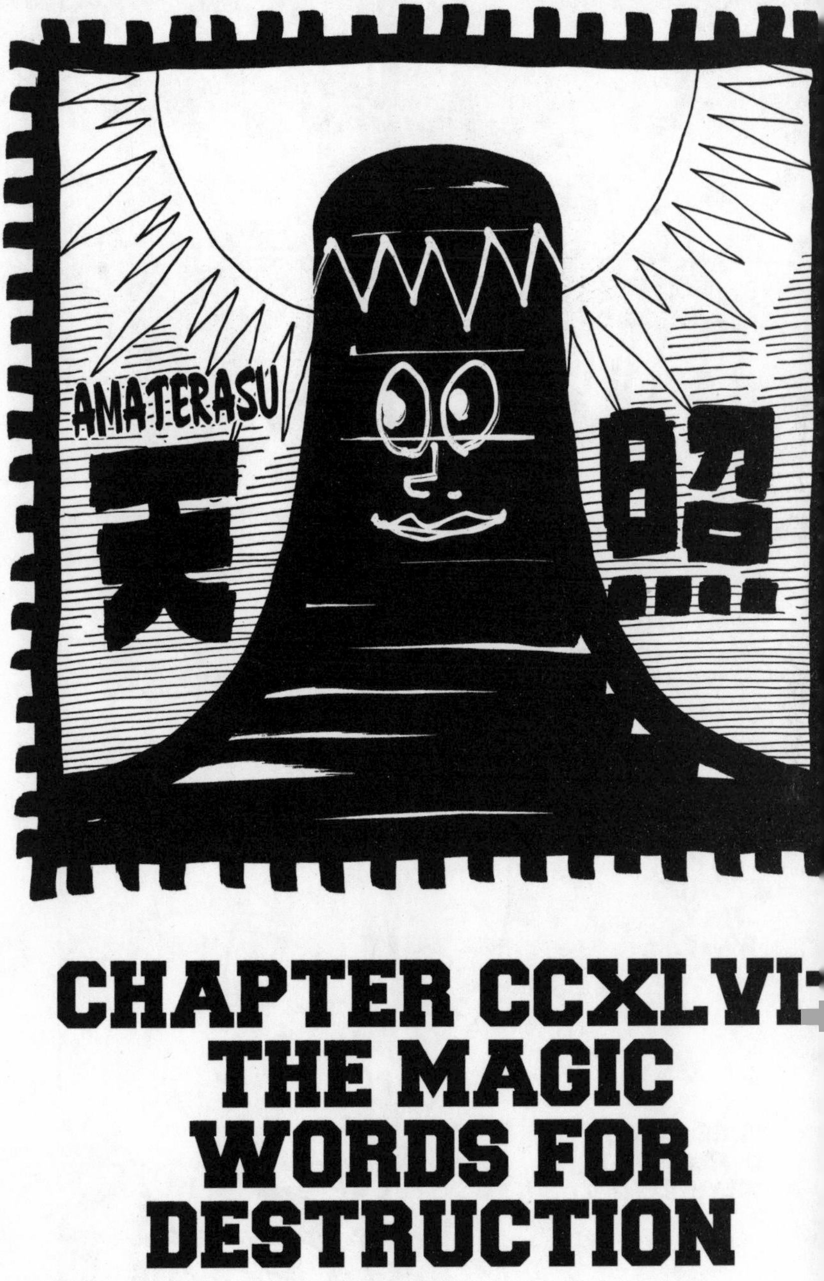
AMATERASU
天
照...

CHAPTER CCXLVI: THE MAGIC WORDS FOR DESTRUCTION

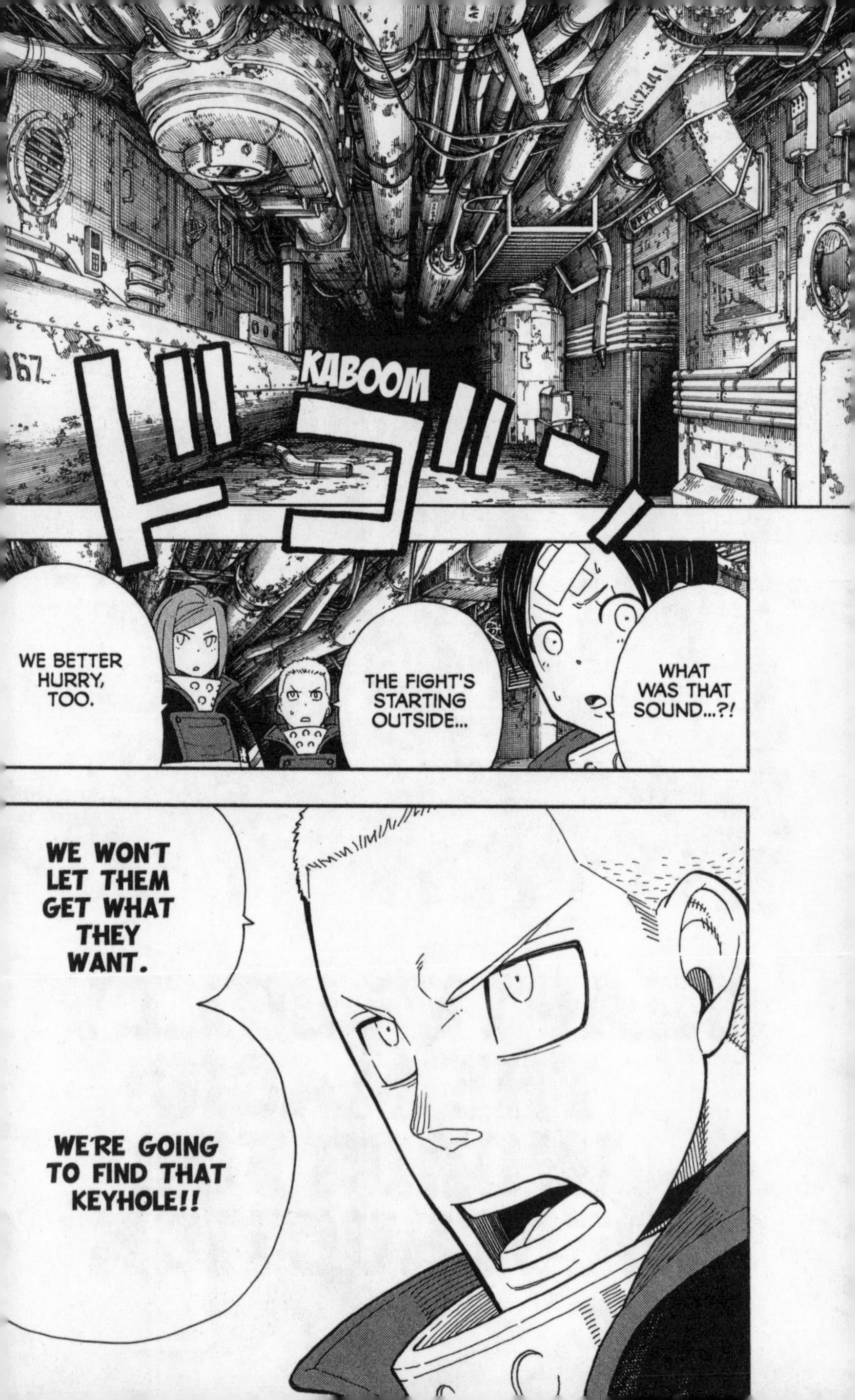
KABOOM
WHAT WAS THAT SOUND...?!
THE FIGHT'S STARTING OUTSIDE...
WE BETTER HURRY, TOO.
WE WON'T LET THEM GET WHAT THEY WANT.
WE'RE GOING TO FIND THAT KEYHOLE!!

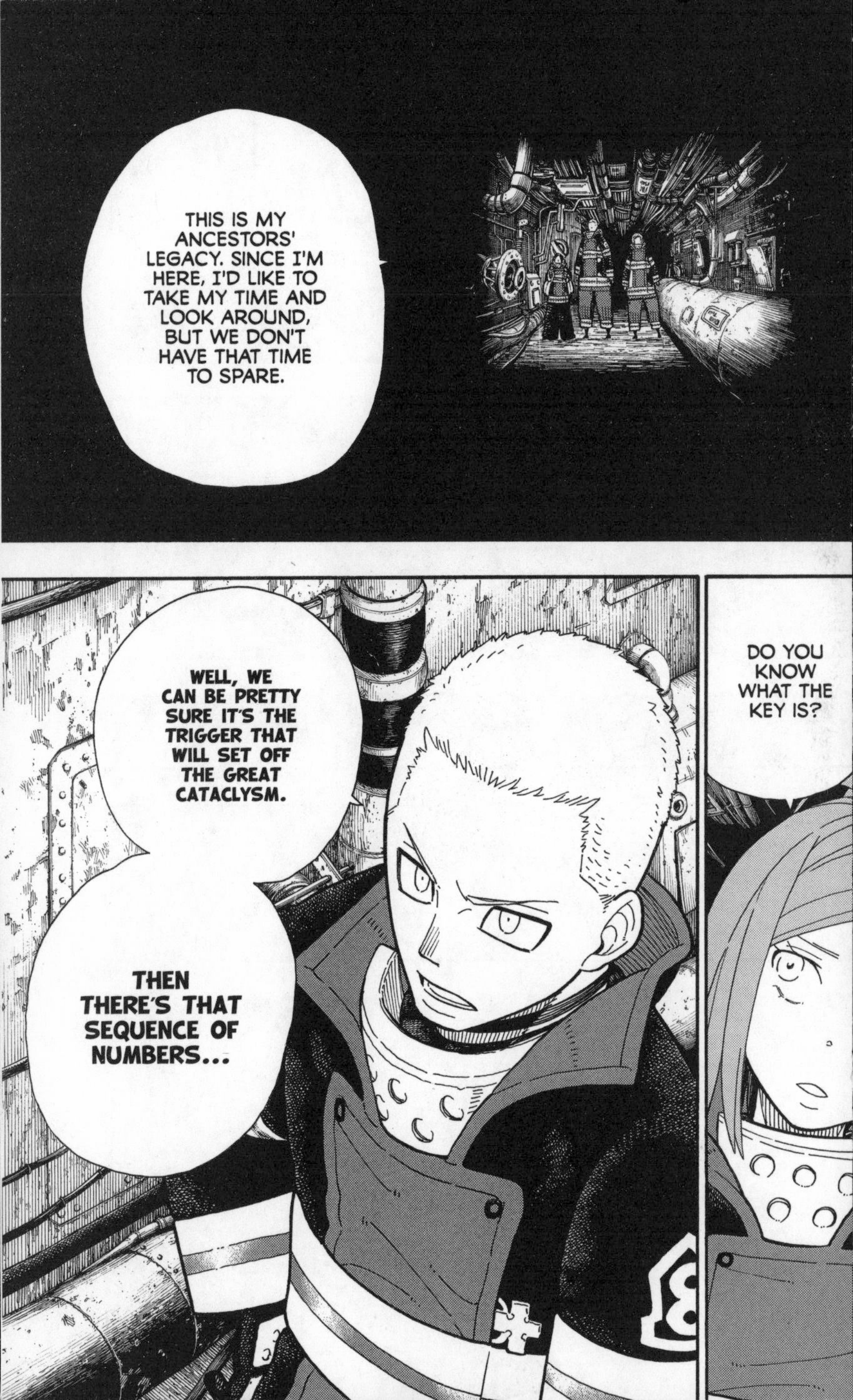
THIS IS MY ANCESTORS' LEGACY. SINCE I'M HERE, I'D LIKE TO TAKE MY TIME AND LOOK AROUND, BUT WE DON'T HAVE THAT TIME TO SPARE.
DO YOU KNOW WHAT THE KEY IS?
WELL, WE CAN BE PRETTY SURE IT'S THE TRIGGER THAT WILL SET OFF THE GREAT CATACLYSM.
THEN THERE'S THAT SEQUENCE OF NUMBERS...

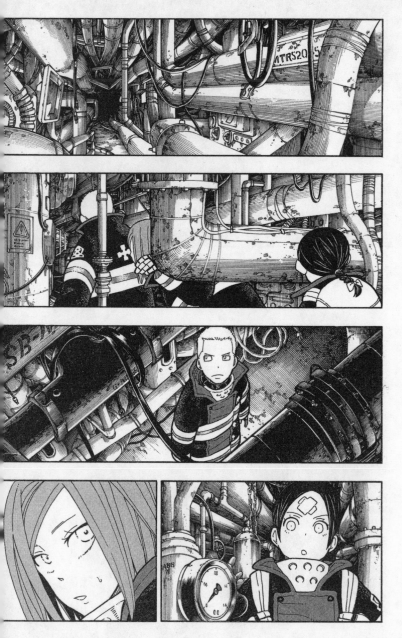

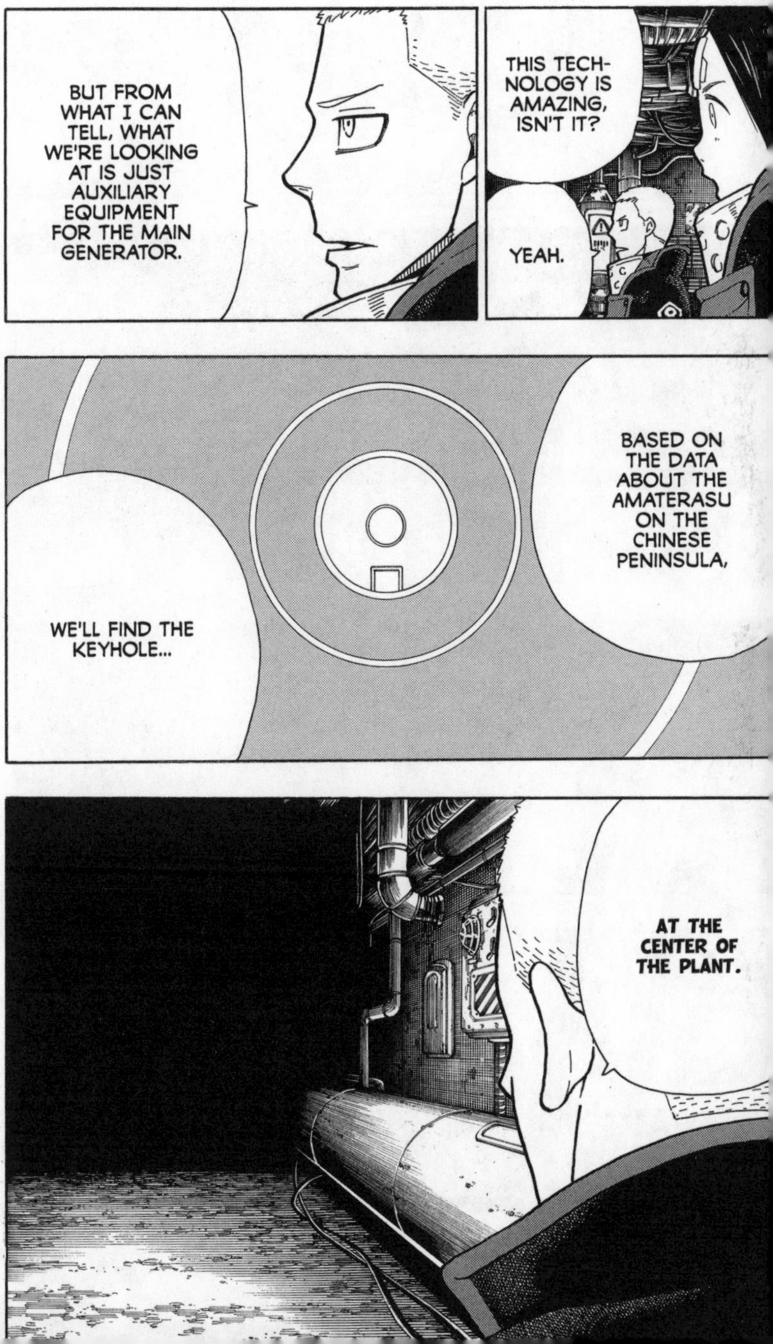
THIS TECHNOLOGY IS AMAZING, ISN'T IT?
YEAH.
BUT FROM WHAT I CAN TELL, WHAT WE'RE LOOKING AT IS JUST AUXILIARY EQUIPMENT FOR THE MAIN GENERATOR.
BASED ON THE DATA ABOUT THE AMATERASU ON THE CHINESE PENINSULA,
WE'LL FIND THE KEYHOLE...
AT THE CENTER OF THE PLANT.

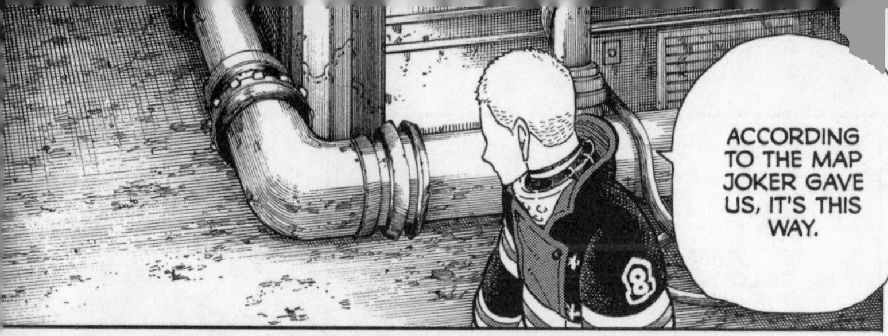
ACCORDING TO THE MAP JOKER GAVE US, IT'S THIS WAY.

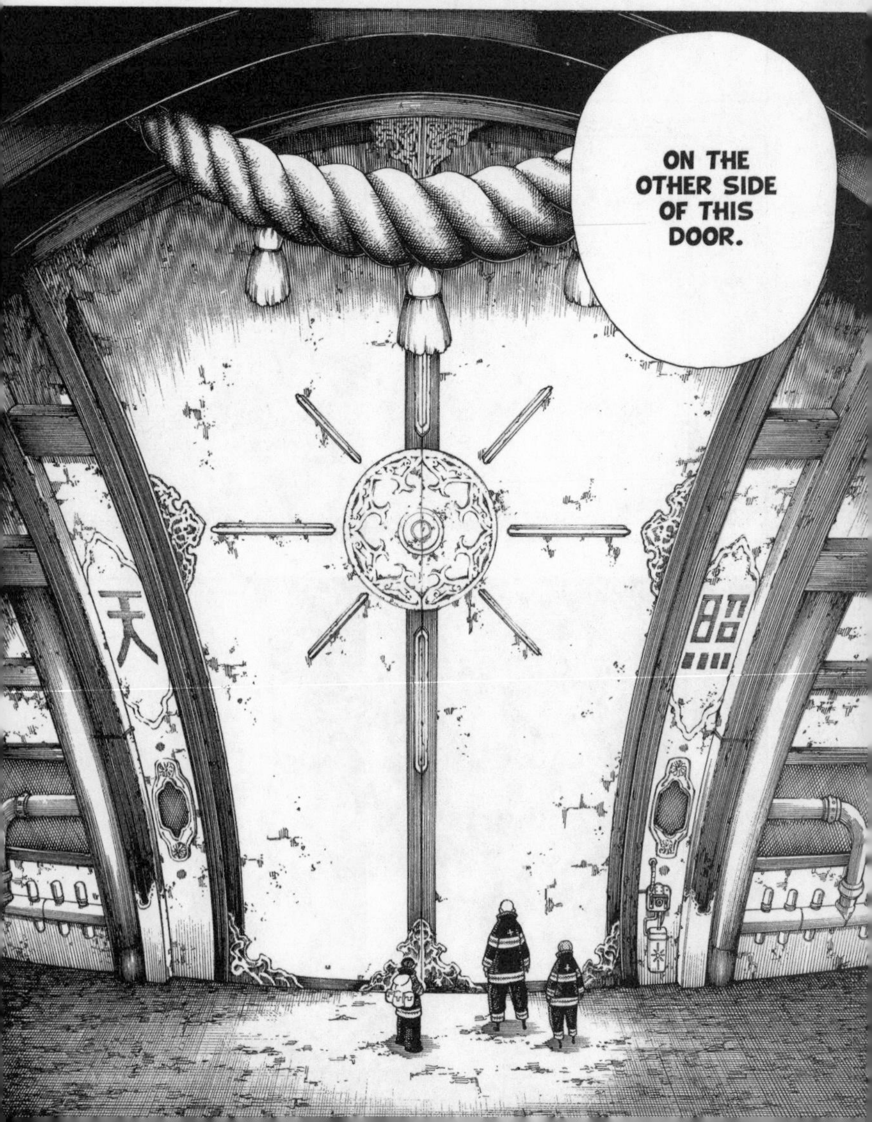
ON THE OTHER SIDE OF THIS DOOR.
天

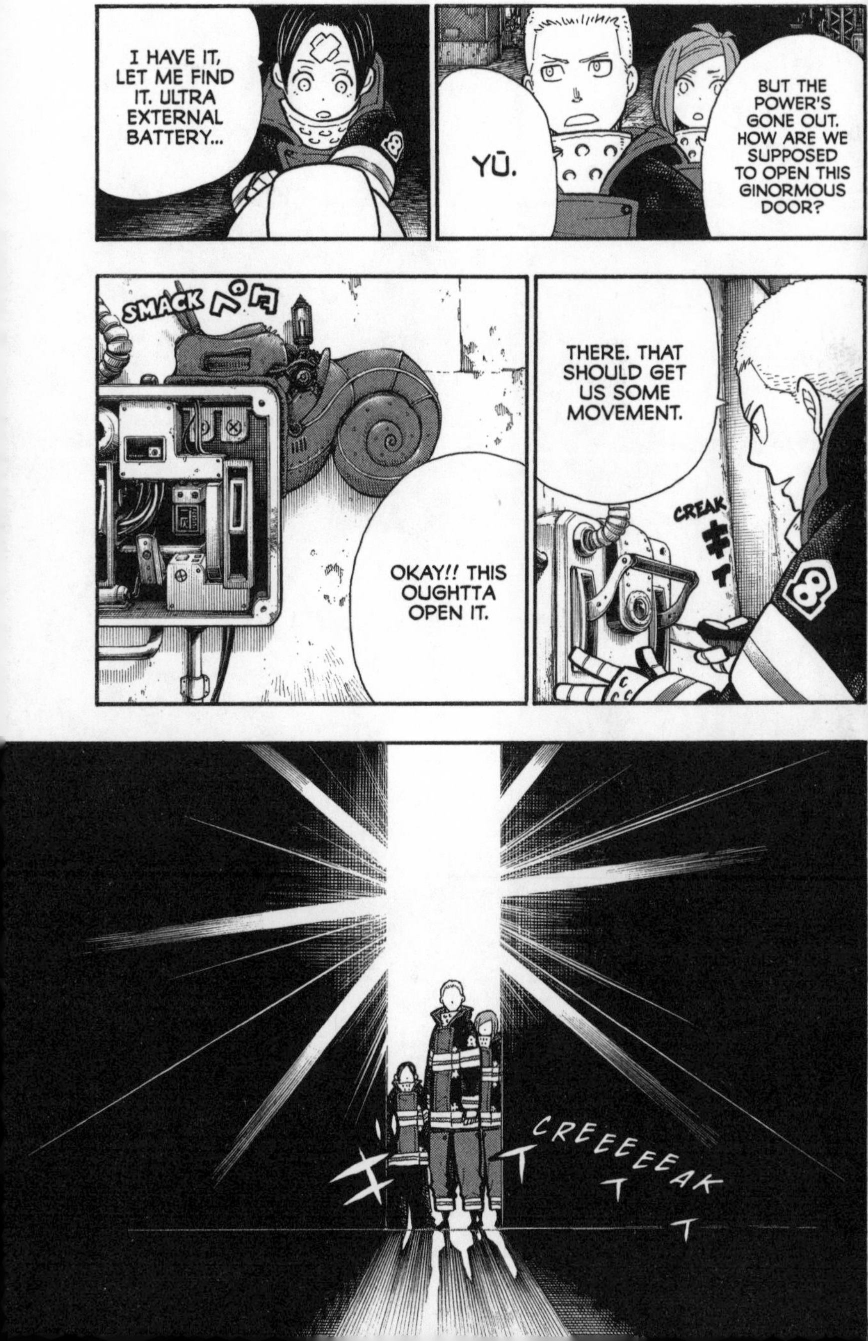
BUT THE POWER'S GONE OUT. HOW ARE WE SUPPOSED TO OPEN THIS GINORMOUS DOOR?
YŪ.
I HAVE IT, LET ME FIND IT. ULTRA EXTERNAL BATTERY...
THERE. THAT SHOULD GET US SOME MOVEMENT.
CREAK
OKAY!! THIS OUGHTTA OPEN IT.
SMACK
CREEEEEAK

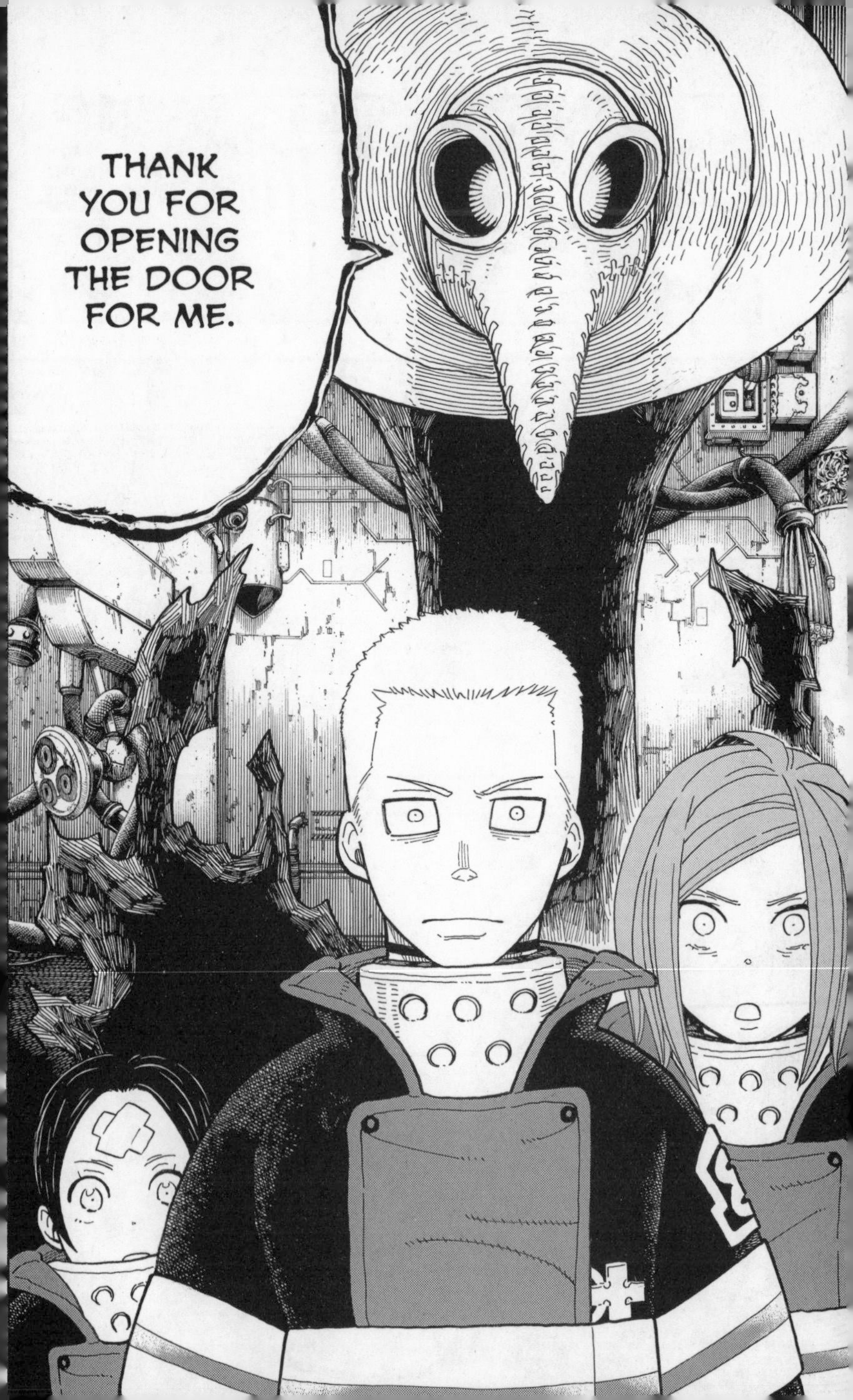
THANK YOU FOR OPENING THE DOOR FOR ME.

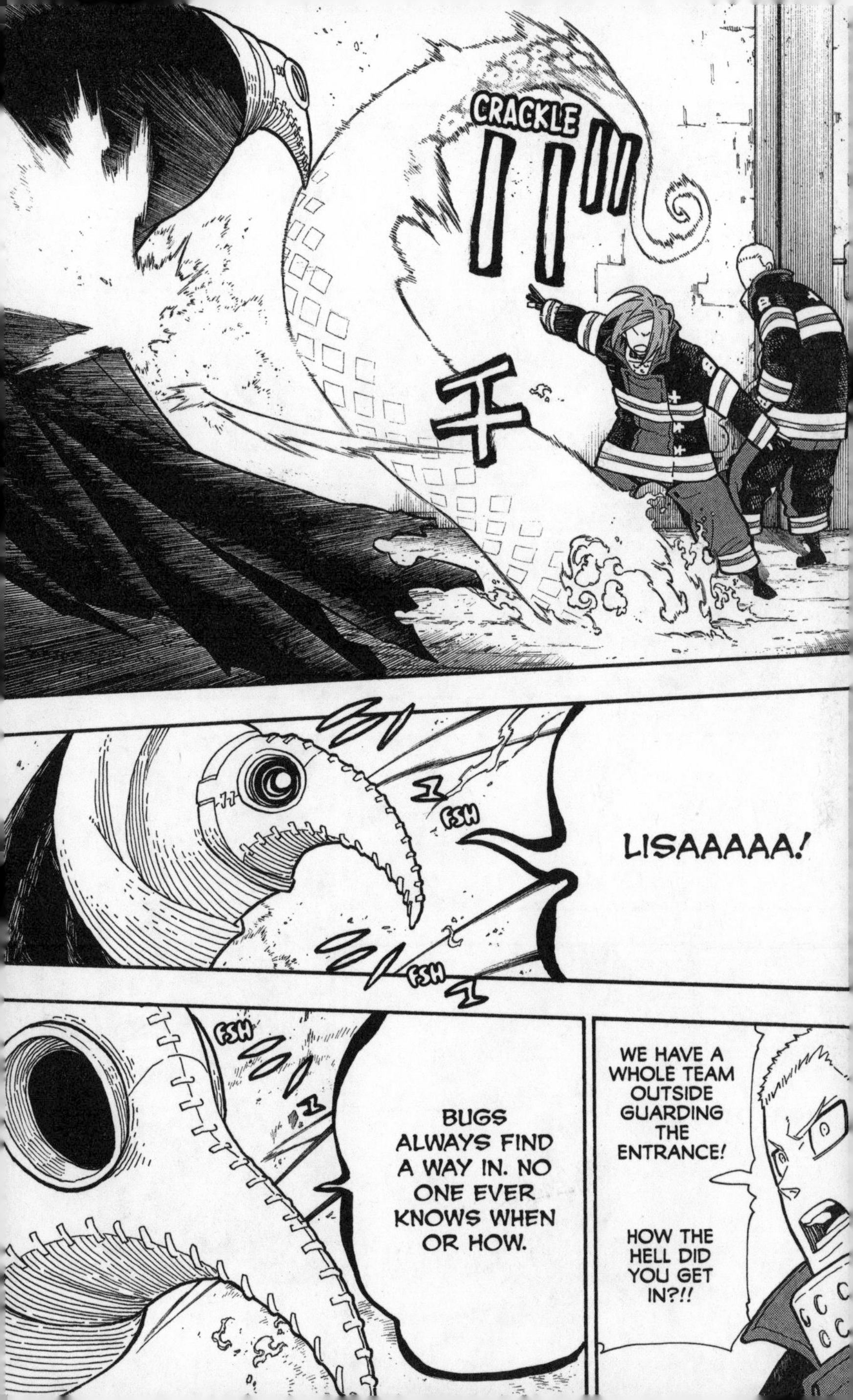
CRACKLE
LISAAAAA!
FSH
FSH
WE HAVE A WHOLE TEAM OUTSIDE GUARDING THE ENTRANCE!
HOW THE HELL DID YOU GET IN?!!
BUGS ALWAYS FIND A WAY IN. NO ONE EVER KNOWS WHEN OR HOW.
FSH

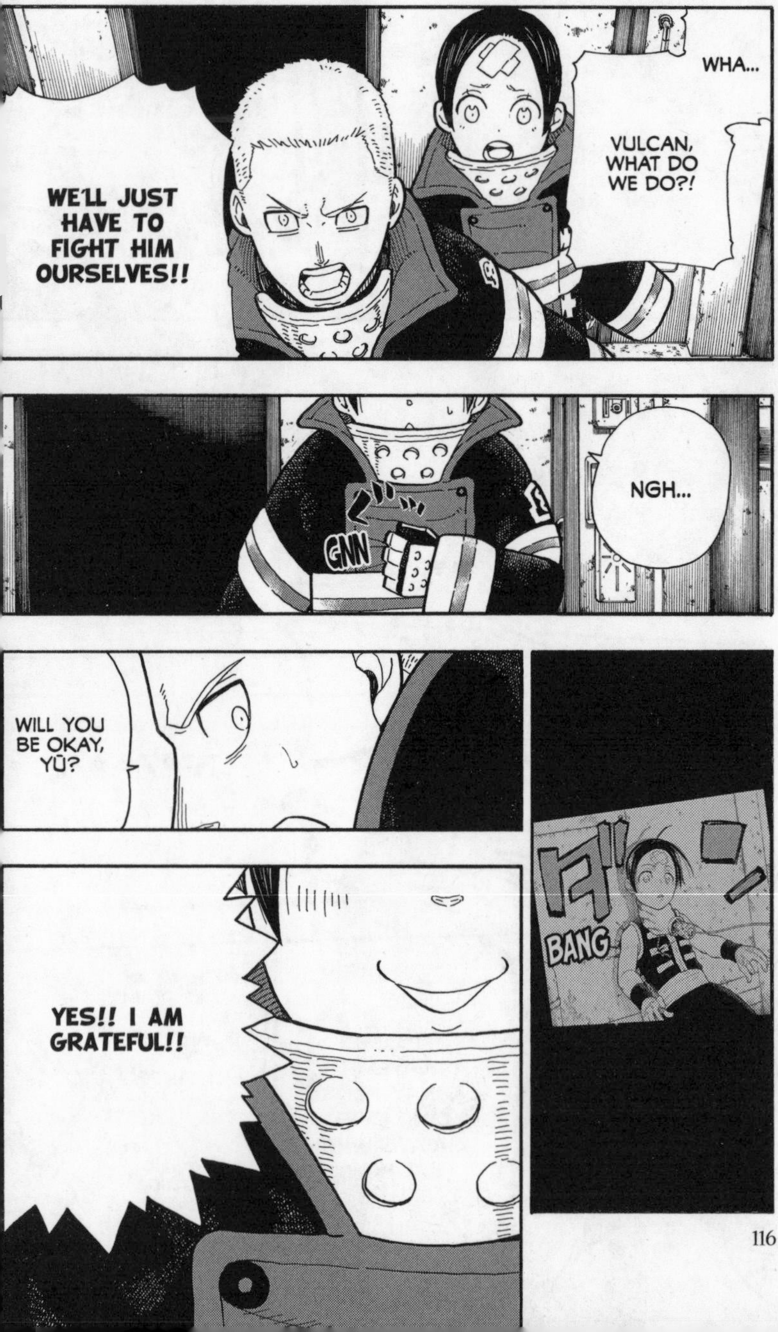
WHA...
VULCAN, WHAT DO WE DO?!
WE'LL JUST HAVE TO FIGHT HIM OURSELVES!!
NGH...
GNN
BANG
WILL YOU BE OKAY, YŪ?
YES!! I AM GRATEFUL!!

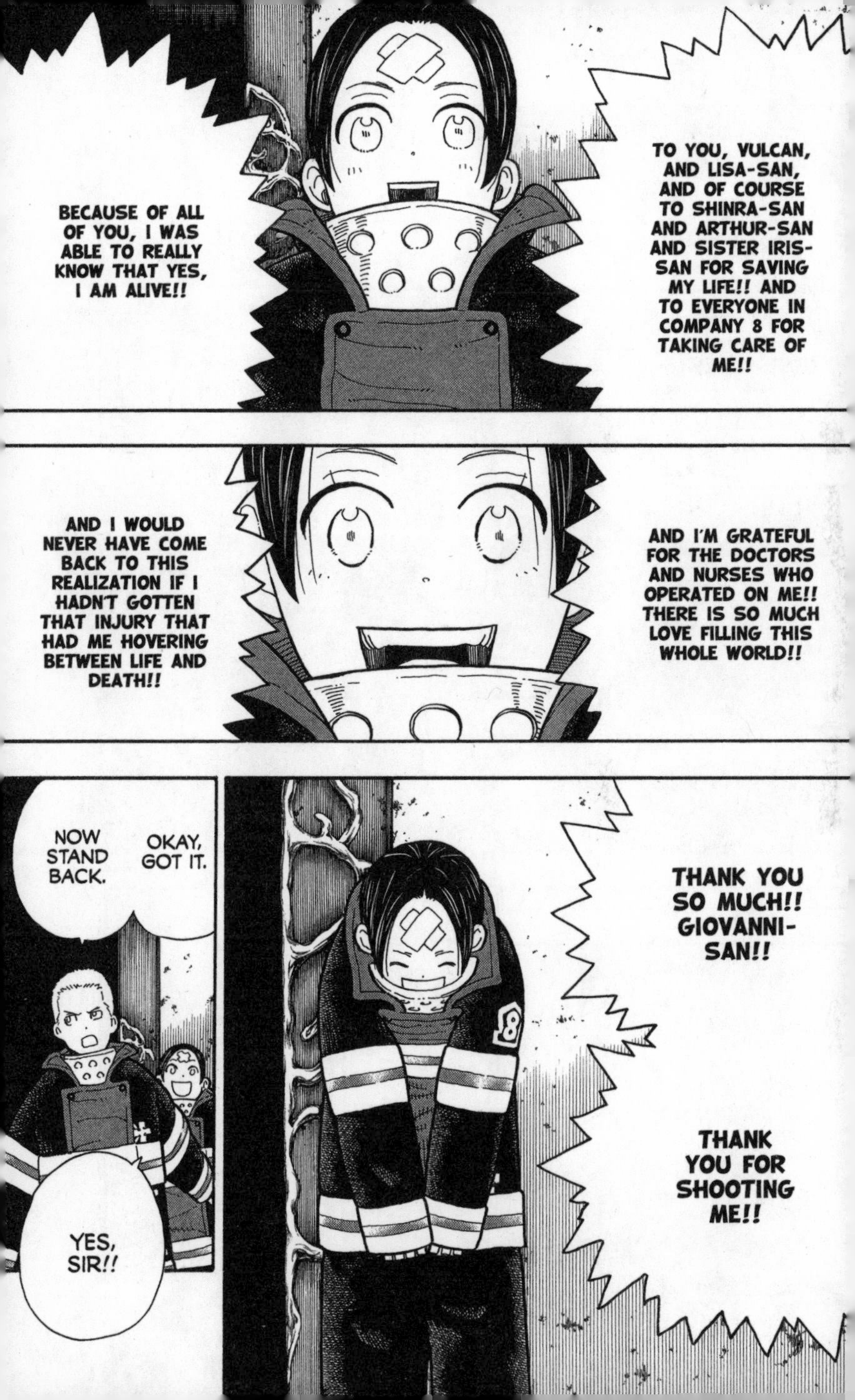
TO YOU, VULCAN, AND LISA-SAN, AND OF COURSE TO SHINRA-SAN AND ARTHUR-SAN AND SISTER IRIS-SAN FOR SAVING MY LIFE!! AND TO EVERYONE IN COMPANY 8 FOR TAKING CARE OF ME!!
BECAUSE OF ALL OF YOU, I WAS ABLE TO REALLY KNOW THAT YES, I AM ALIVE!!
AND I'M GRATEFUL FOR THE DOCTORS AND NURSES WHO OPERATED ON ME!! THERE IS SO MUCH LOVE FILLING THIS WHOLE WORLD!!
AND I WOULD NEVER HAVE COME BACK TO THIS REALIZATION IF I HADN'T GOTTEN THAT INJURY THAT HAD ME HOVERING BETWEEN LIFE AND DEATH!!
THANK YOU SO MUCH!! GIOVANNI-SAN!!
THANK YOU FOR SHOOTING ME!!
OKAY, GOT IT.
NOW STAND BACK.
YES, SIR!!

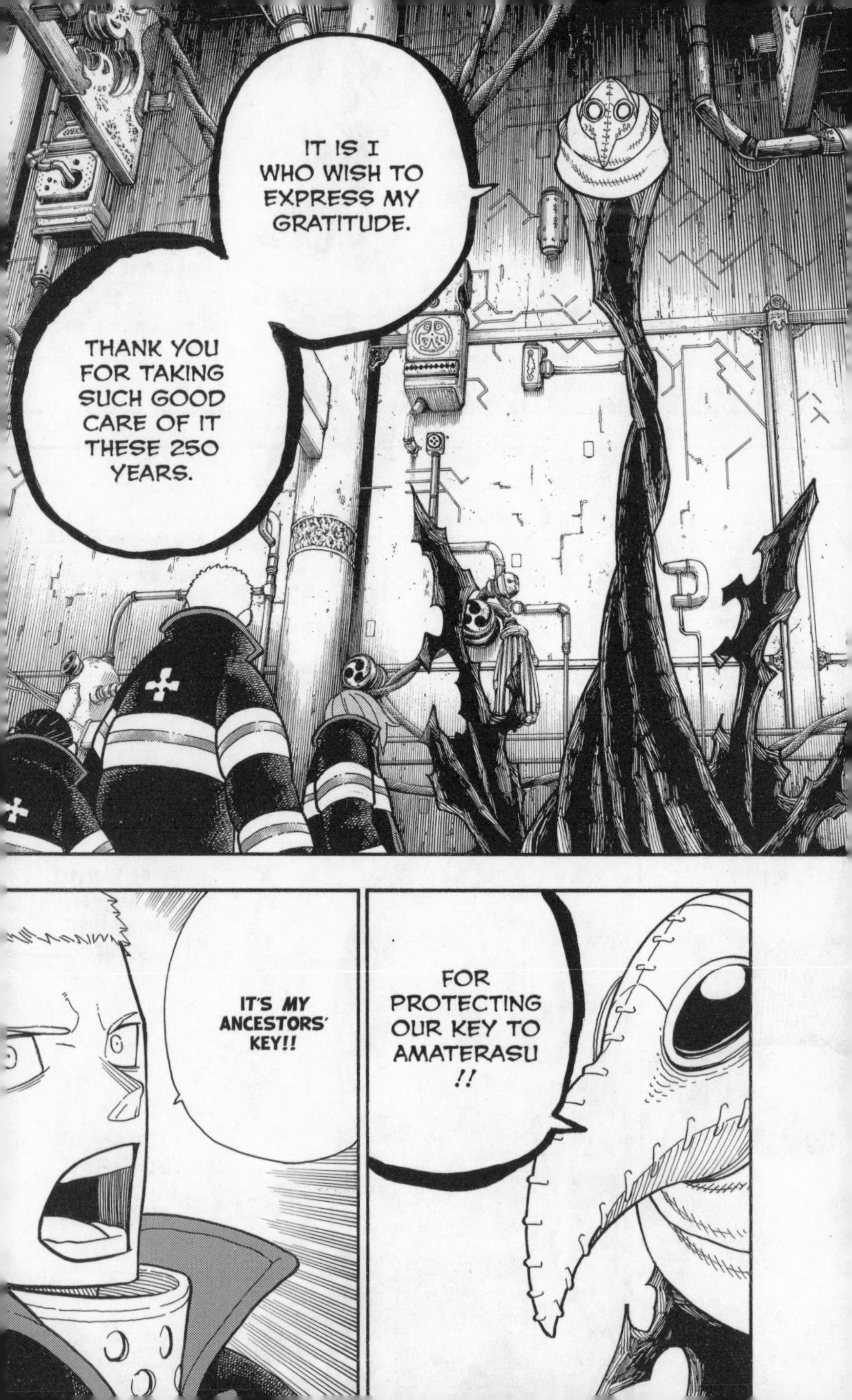
IT IS I WHO WISH TO EXPRESS MY GRATITUDE.
THANK YOU FOR TAKING SUCH GOOD CARE OF IT THESE 250 YEARS.
FOR PROTECTING OUR KEY TO AMATERASU!!
IT'S MY ANCESTORS' KEY!!

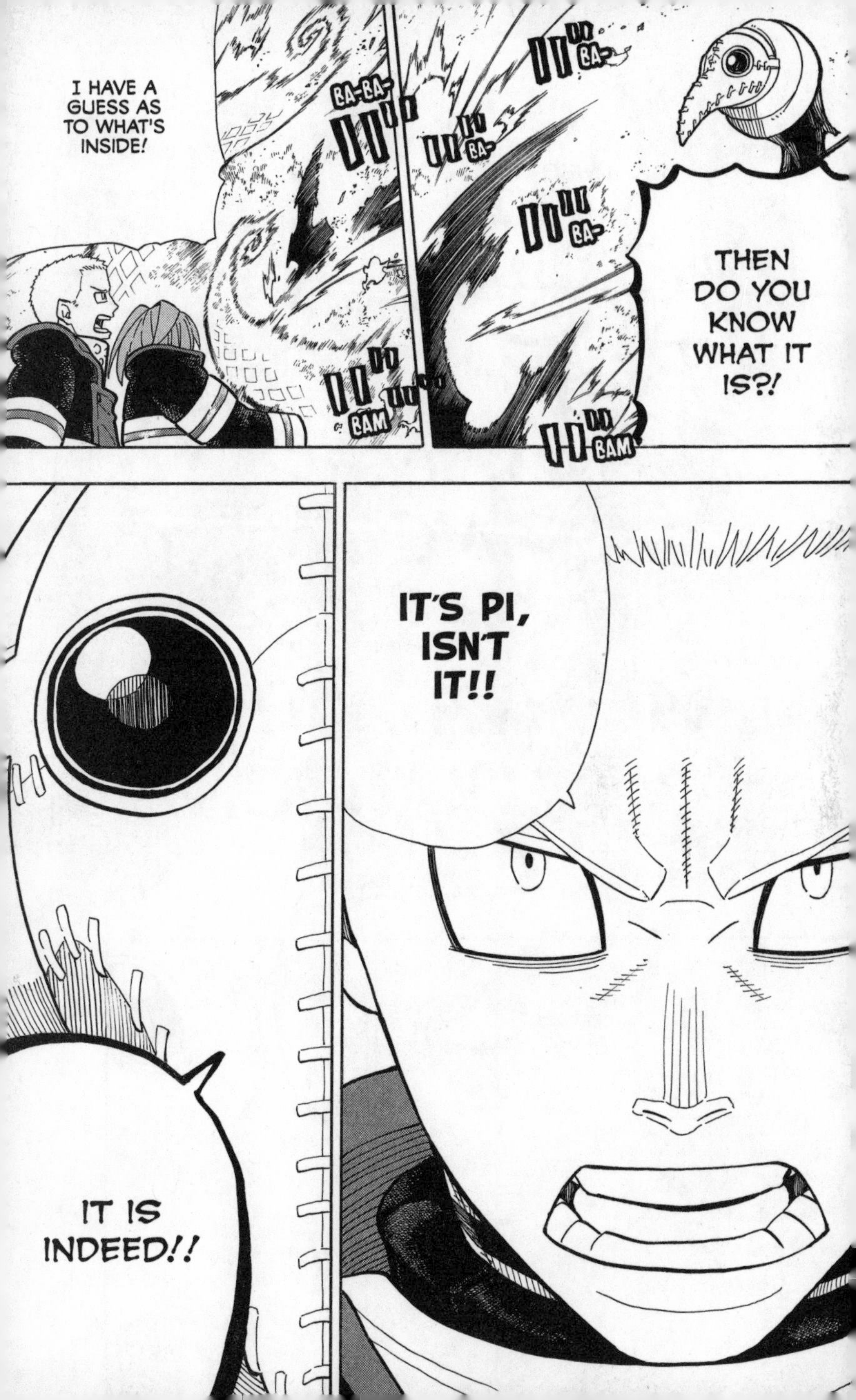
I HAVE A GUESS AS TO WHAT'S INSIDE!
BA-
BA-
BA-BA-
BA-
BAM
BAM
THEN DO YOU KNOW WHAT IT IS?!
IT'S PI, ISN'T IT!!
IT IS INDEED!!

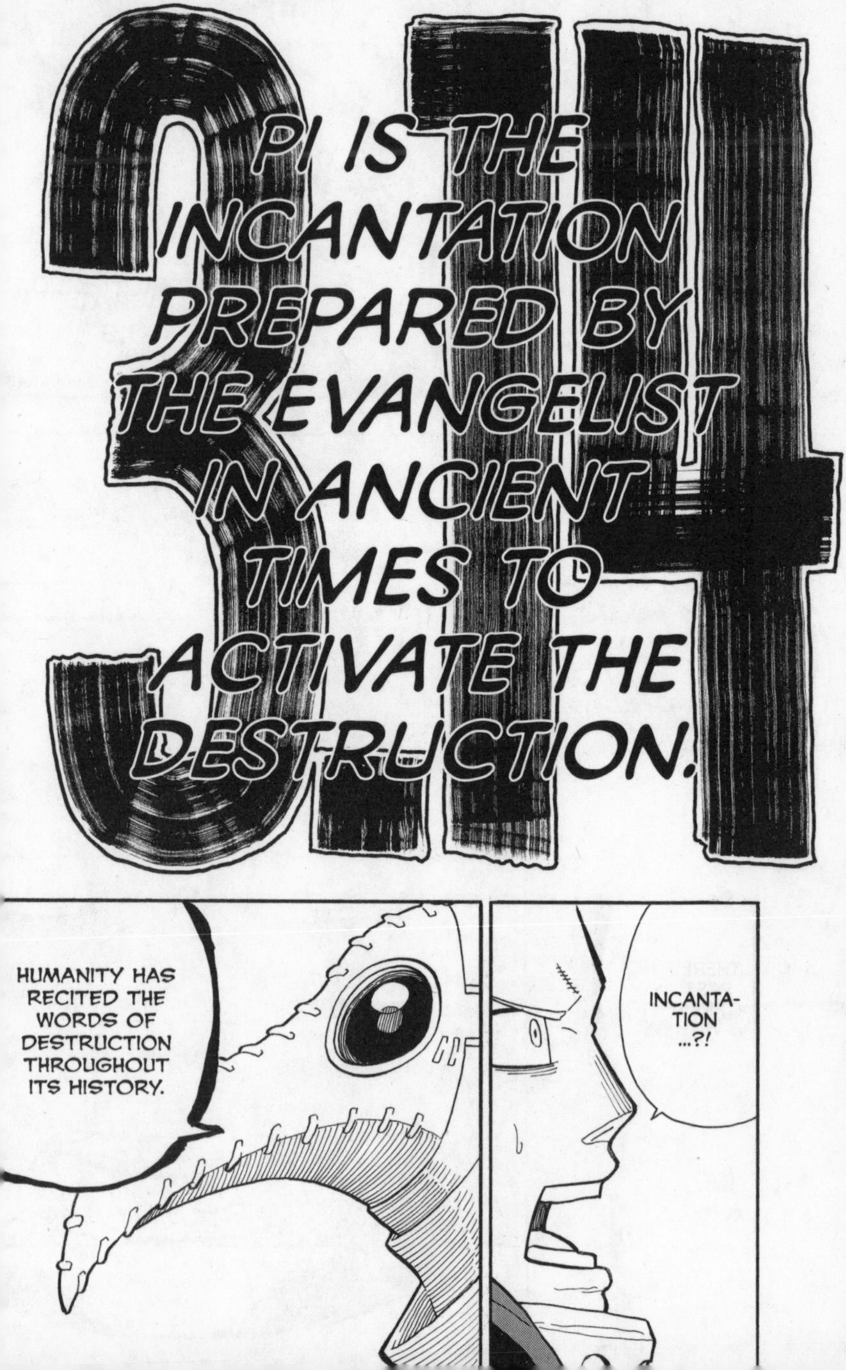
314
PI IS THE INCANTATION PREPARED BY THE EVANGELIST IN ANCIENT TIMES TO ACTIVATE THE DESTRUCTION.
INCANTATION...?!
HUMANITY HAS RECITED THE WORDS OF DESTRUCTION THROUGHOUT ITS HISTORY.

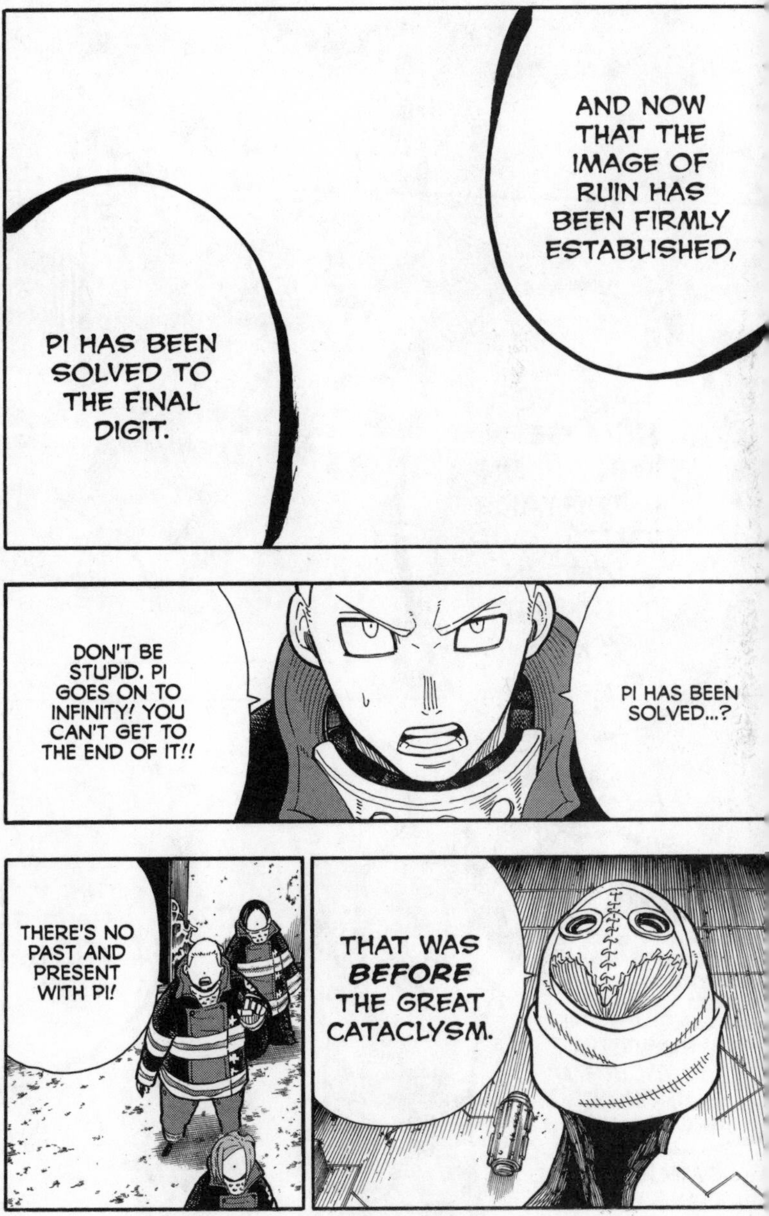
AND NOW THAT THE IMAGE OF RUIN HAS BEEN FIRMLY ESTABLISHED,
PI HAS BEEN SOLVED TO THE FINAL DIGIT.
PI HAS BEEN SOLVED...?
DON'T BE STUPID. PI GOES ON TO INFINITY! YOU CAN'T GET TO THE END OF IT!!
THAT WAS *BEFORE* THE GREAT CATACLYSM.
THERE'S NO PAST AND PRESENT WITH PI!

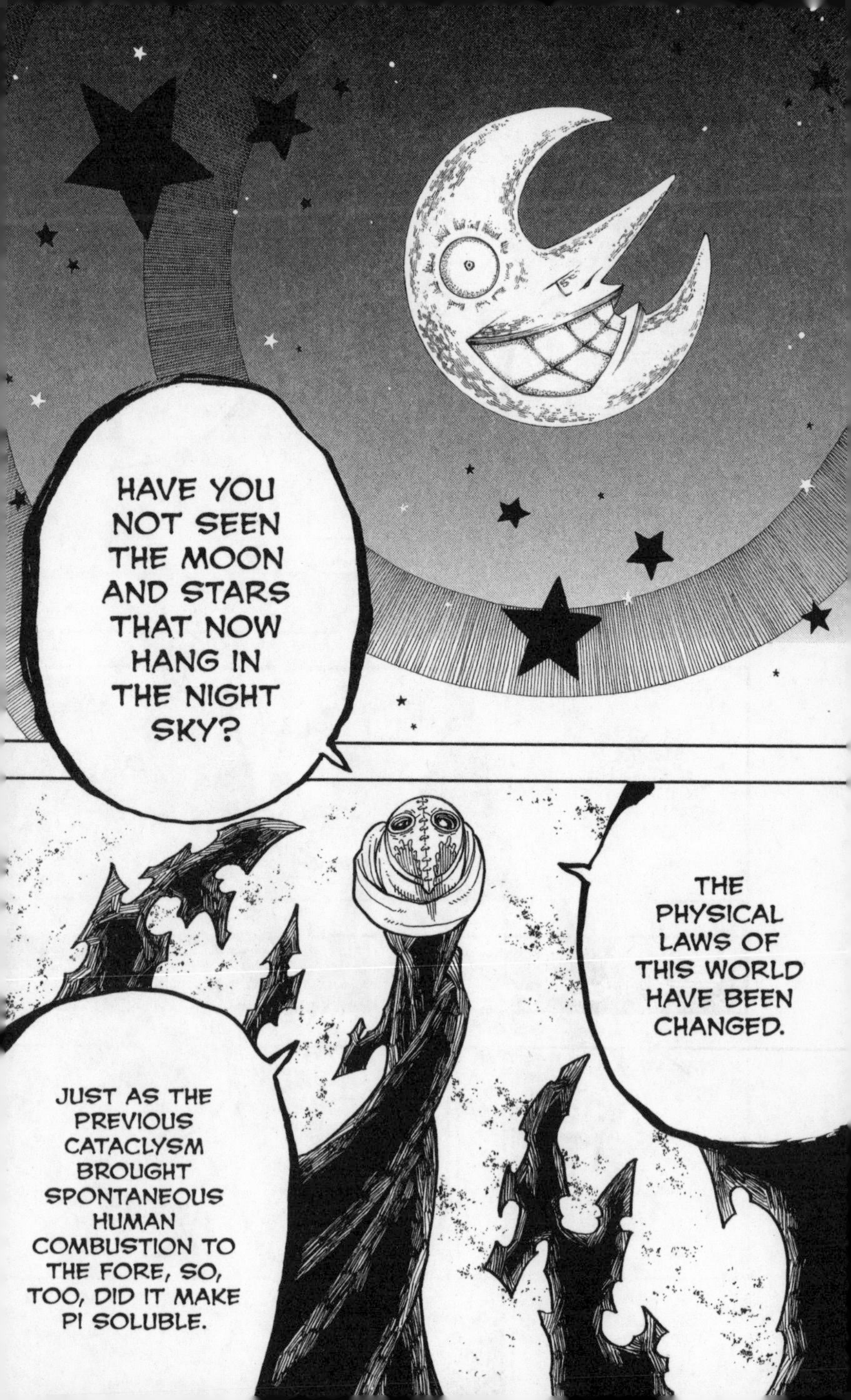
HAVE YOU NOT SEEN THE MOON AND STARS THAT NOW HANG IN THE NIGHT SKY?
THE PHYSICAL LAWS OF THIS WORLD HAVE BEEN CHANGED.
JUST AS THE PREVIOUS CATACLYSM BROUGHT SPONTANEOUS HUMAN COMBUSTION TO THE FORE, SO, TOO, DID IT MAKE PI SOLUBLE.

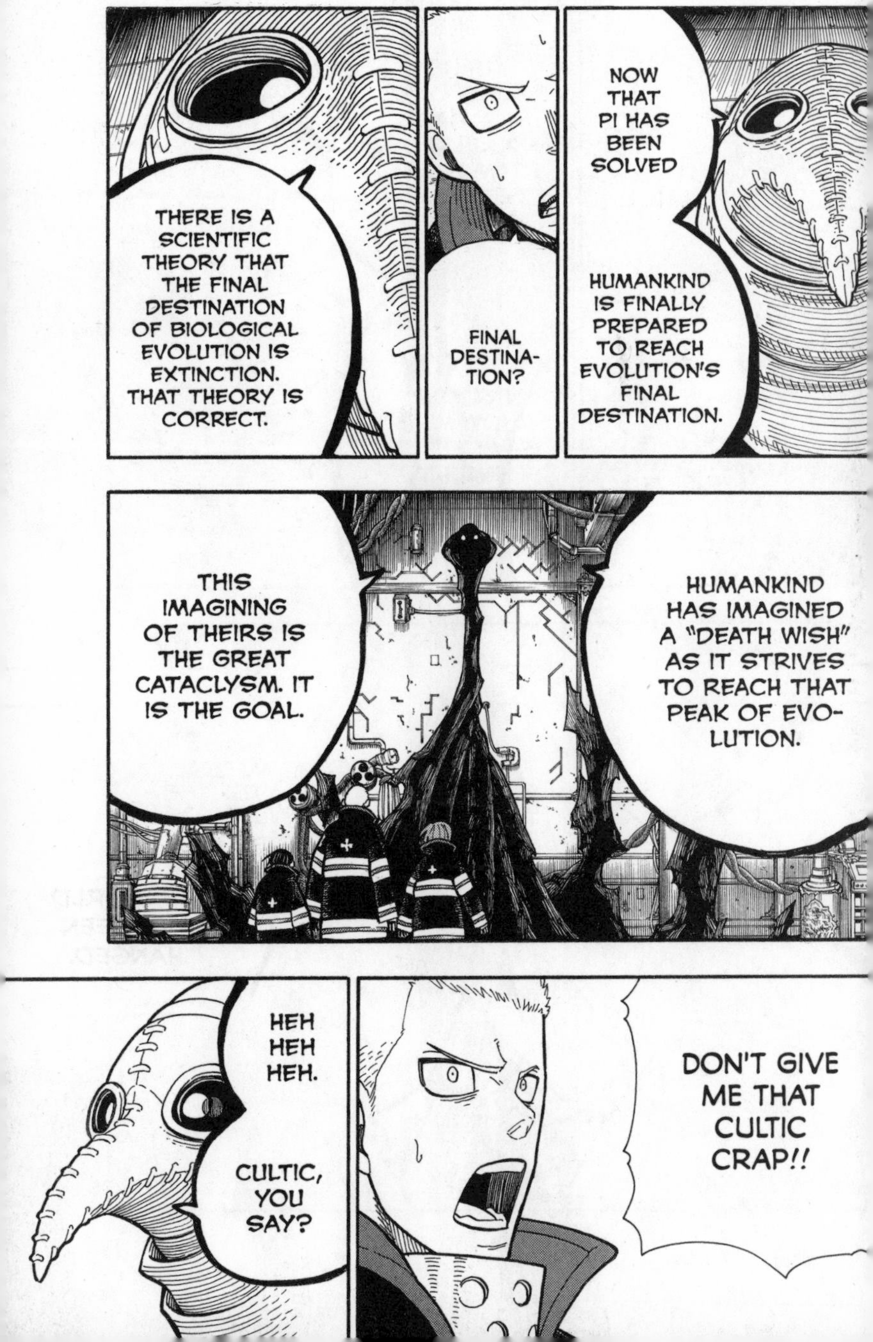
NOW THAT PI HAS BEEN SOLVED
HUMANKIND IS FINALLY PREPARED TO REACH EVOLUTION'S FINAL DESTINATION.
FINAL DESTINA-TION?
THERE IS A SCIENTIFIC THEORY THAT THE FINAL DESTINATION OF BIOLOGICAL EVOLUTION IS EXTINCTION. THAT THEORY IS CORRECT.
HUMANKIND HAS IMAGINED A "DEATH WISH" AS IT STRIVES TO REACH THAT PEAK OF EVO-LUTION.
THIS IMAGINING OF THEIRS IS THE GREAT CATACLYSM. IT IS THE GOAL.
DON'T GIVE ME THAT CULTIC CRAP!!
HEH HEH HEH.
CULTIC, YOU SAY?

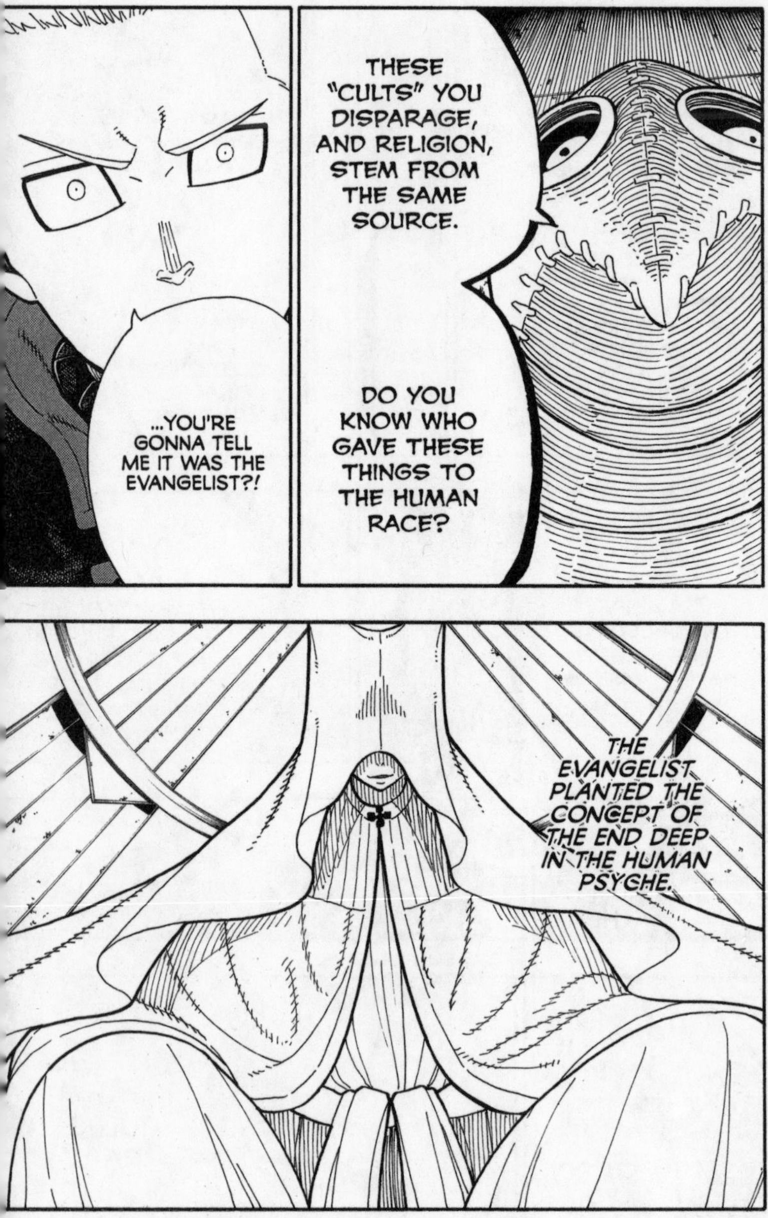
THESE "CULTS" YOU DISPARAGE, AND RELIGION, STEM FROM THE SAME SOURCE.
DO YOU KNOW WHO GAVE THESE THINGS TO THE HUMAN RACE?
...YOU'RE GONNA TELL ME IT WAS THE EVANGELIST?!
THE EVANGELIST PLANTED THE CONCEPT OF THE END DEEP IN THE HUMAN PSYCHE.

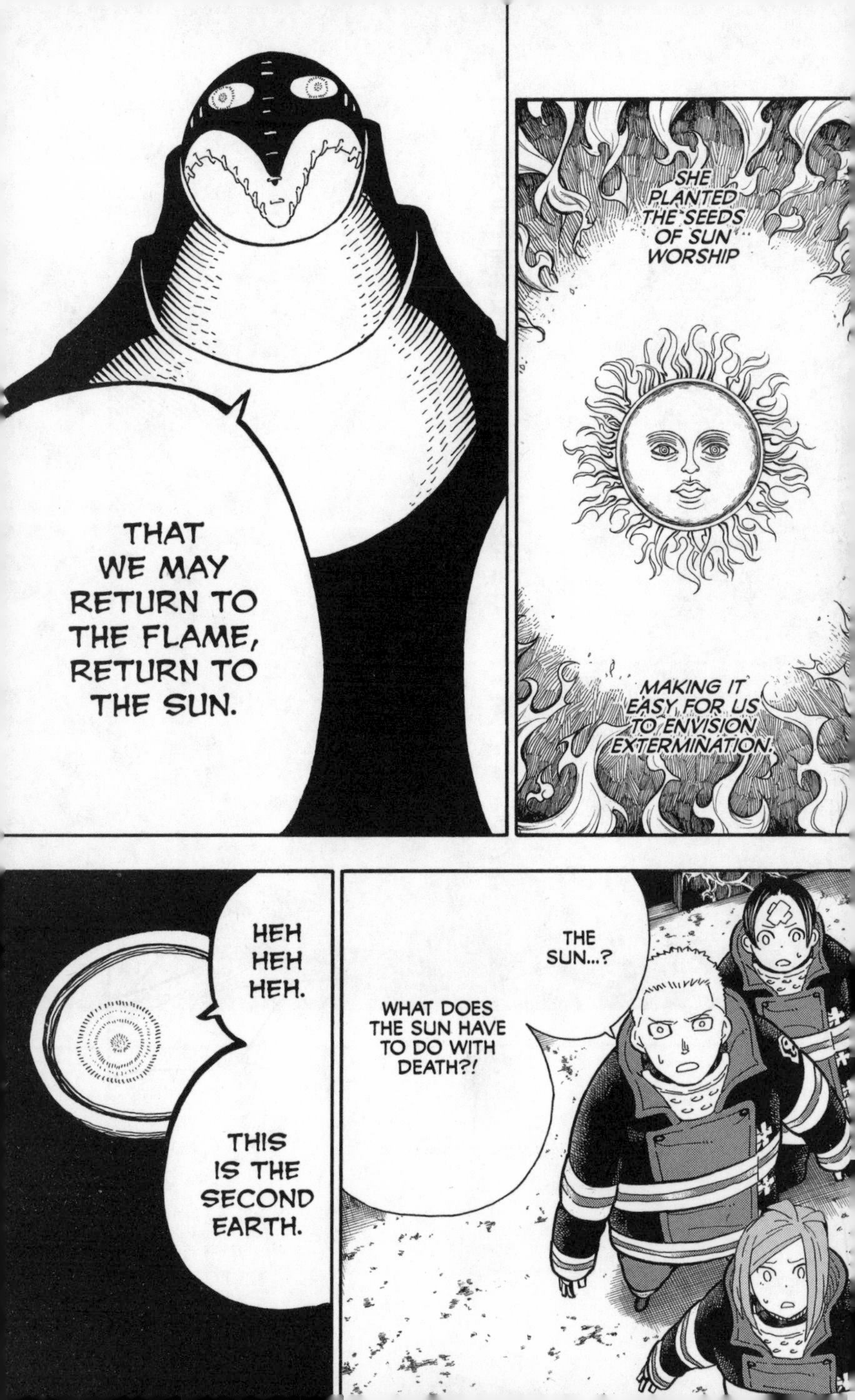
SHE PLANTED THE SEEDS OF SUN WORSHIP
MAKING IT EASY FOR US TO ENVISION EXTERMINATION.
THAT WE MAY RETURN TO THE FLAME, RETURN TO THE SUN.
THE SUN...?
WHAT DOES THE SUN HAVE TO DO WITH DEATH?!
HEH HEH HEH.
THIS IS THE SECOND EARTH.

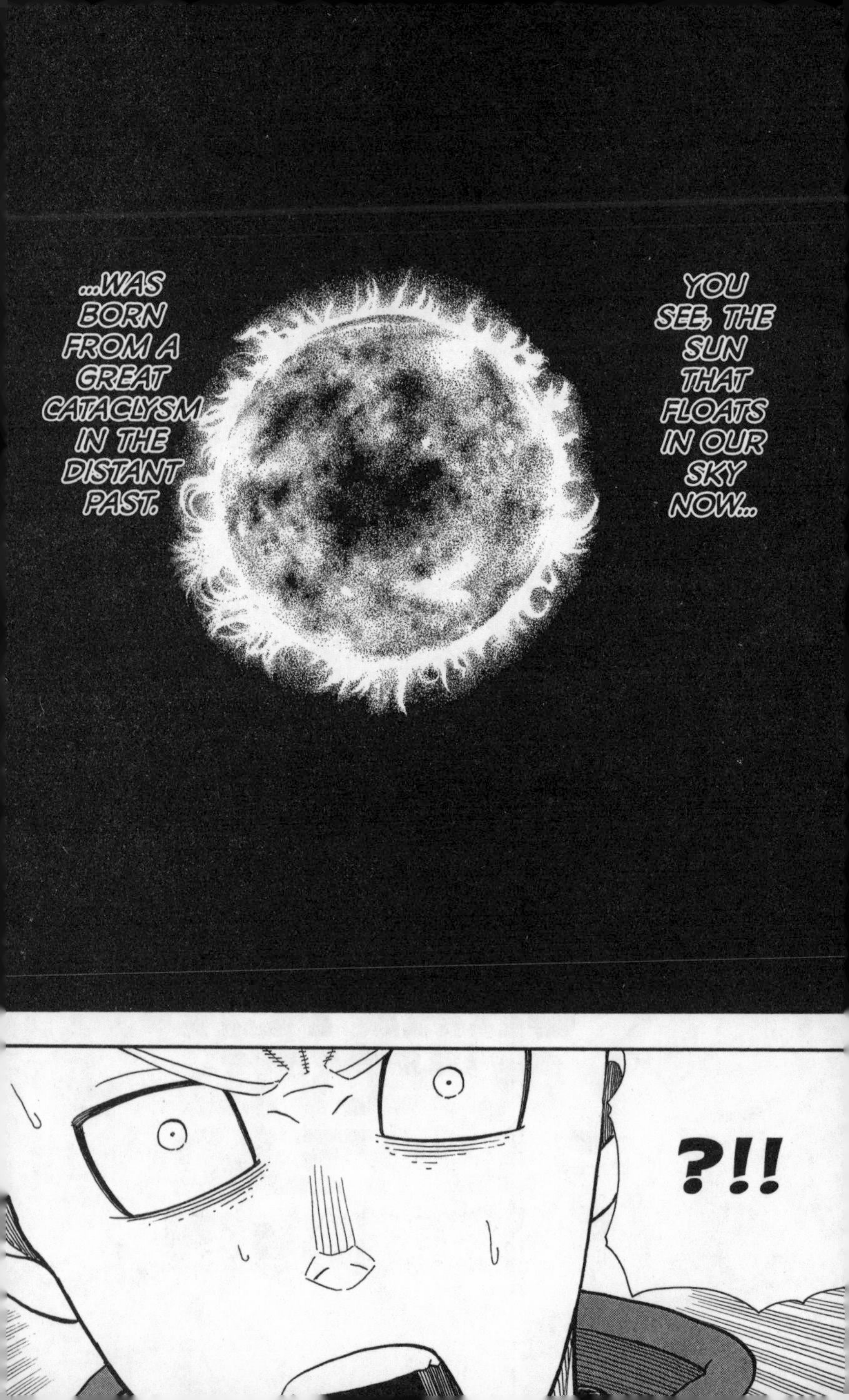
YOU SEE, THE SUN THAT FLOATS IN OUR SKY NOW...
...WAS BORN FROM A GREAT CATACLYSM IN THE DISTANT PAST.
?!!

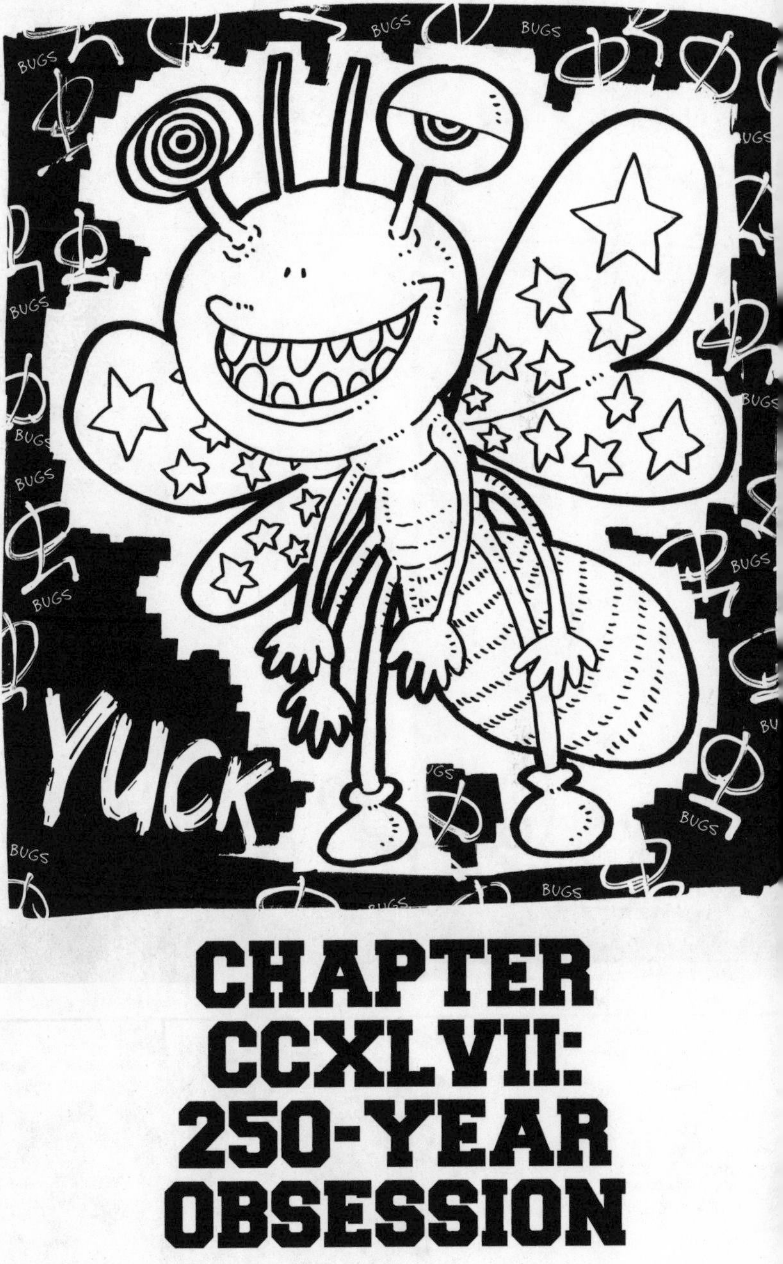
BUGS
YUCK

CHAPTER CCXLVII: 250-YEAR OBSESSION

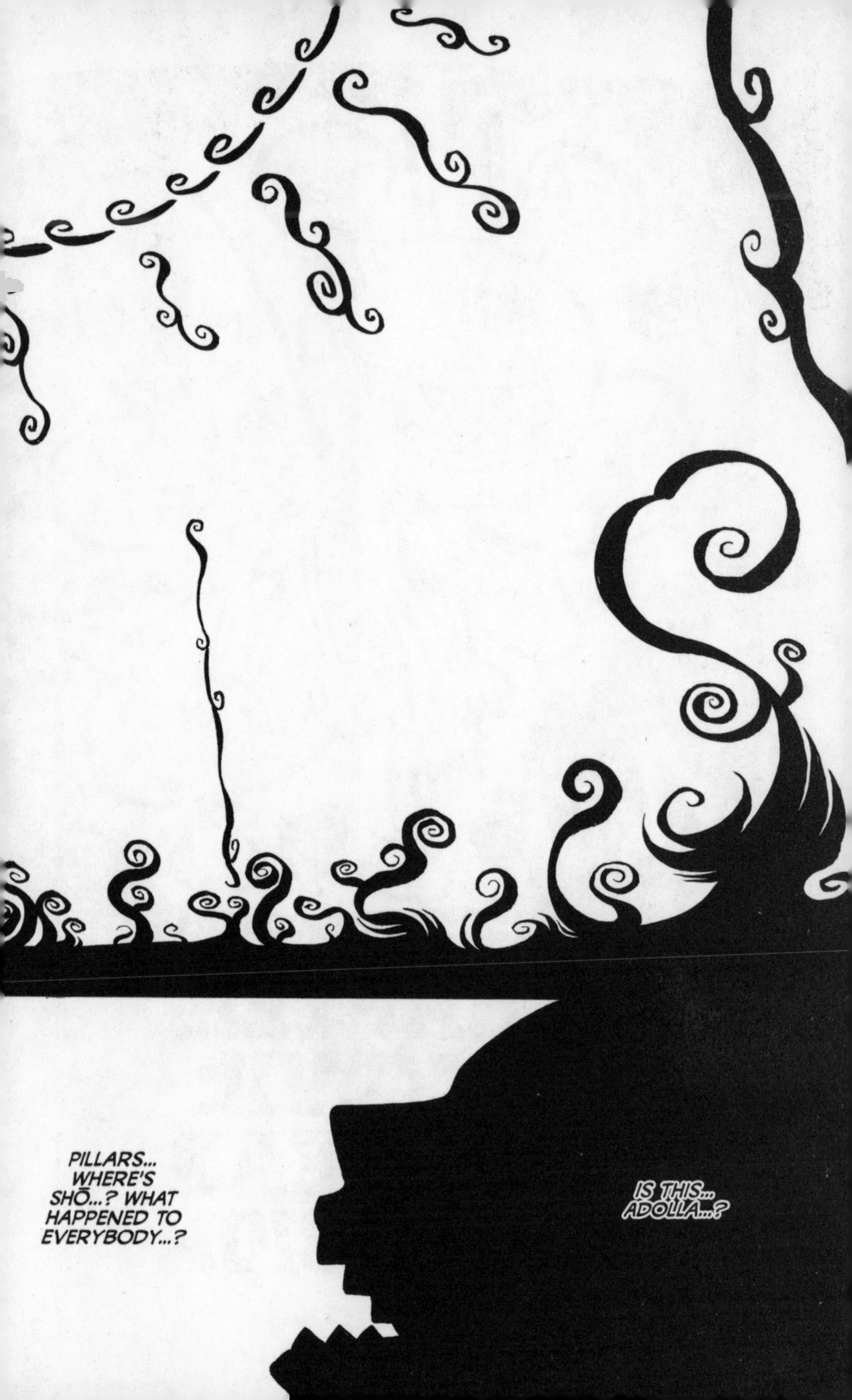
IS THIS... ADOLLA...?
PILLARS... WHERE'S SHŌ...? WHAT HAPPENED TO EVERYBODY...?

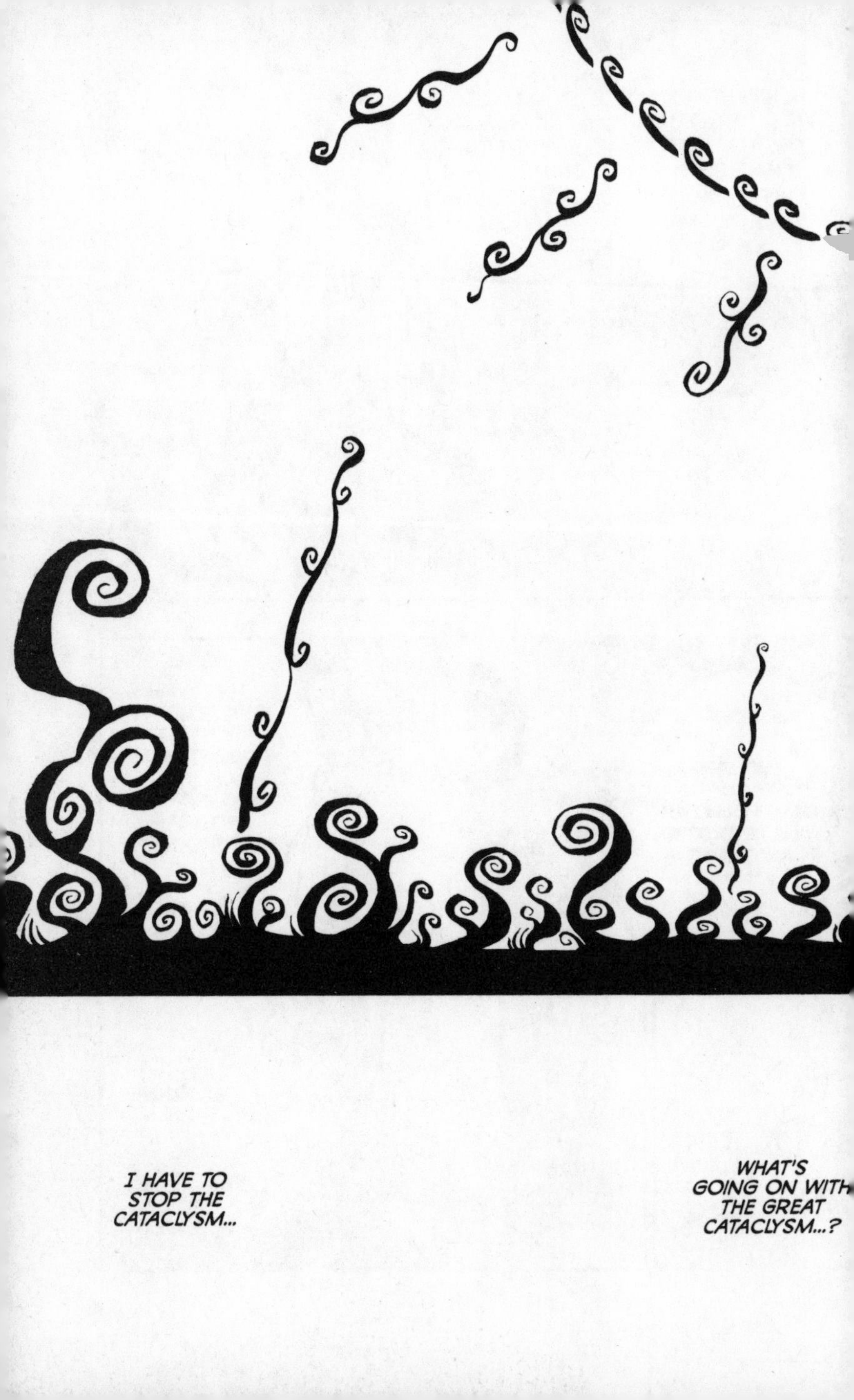
WHAT'S GOING ON WITH THE GREAT CATACLYSM...?
I HAVE TO STOP THE CATACLYSM...

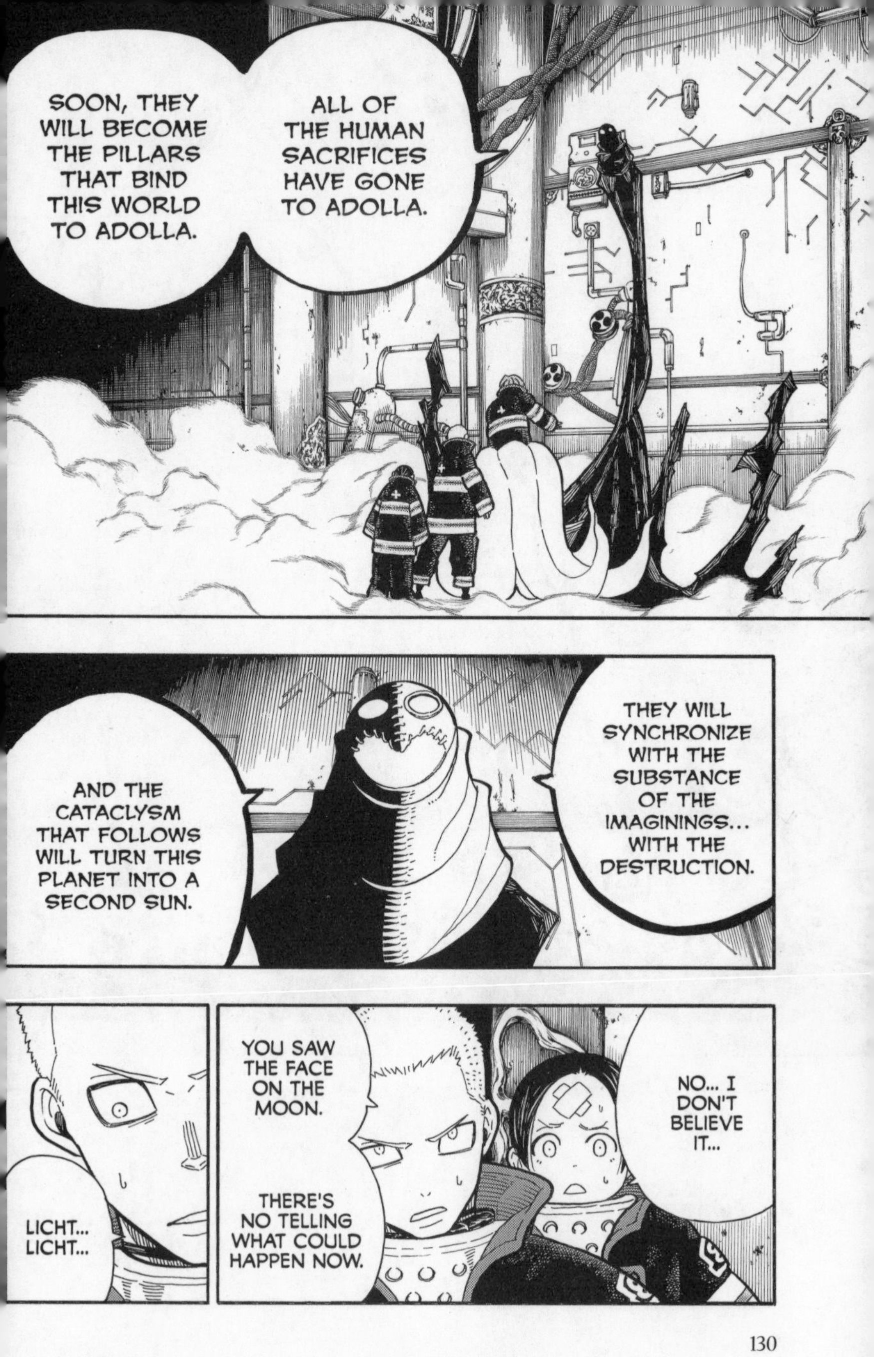
ALL OF THE HUMAN SACRIFICES HAVE GONE TO ADOLLA.
SOON, THEY WILL BECOME THE PILLARS THAT BIND THIS WORLD TO ADOLLA.
THEY WILL SYNCHRONIZE WITH THE SUBSTANCE OF THE IMAGININGS... WITH THE DESTRUCTION.
AND THE CATACLYSM THAT FOLLOWS WILL TURN THIS PLANET INTO A SECOND SUN.
NO... I DON'T BELIEVE IT...
YOU SAW THE FACE ON THE MOON.
THERE'S NO TELLING WHAT COULD HAPPEN NOW.
LICHT... LICHT...

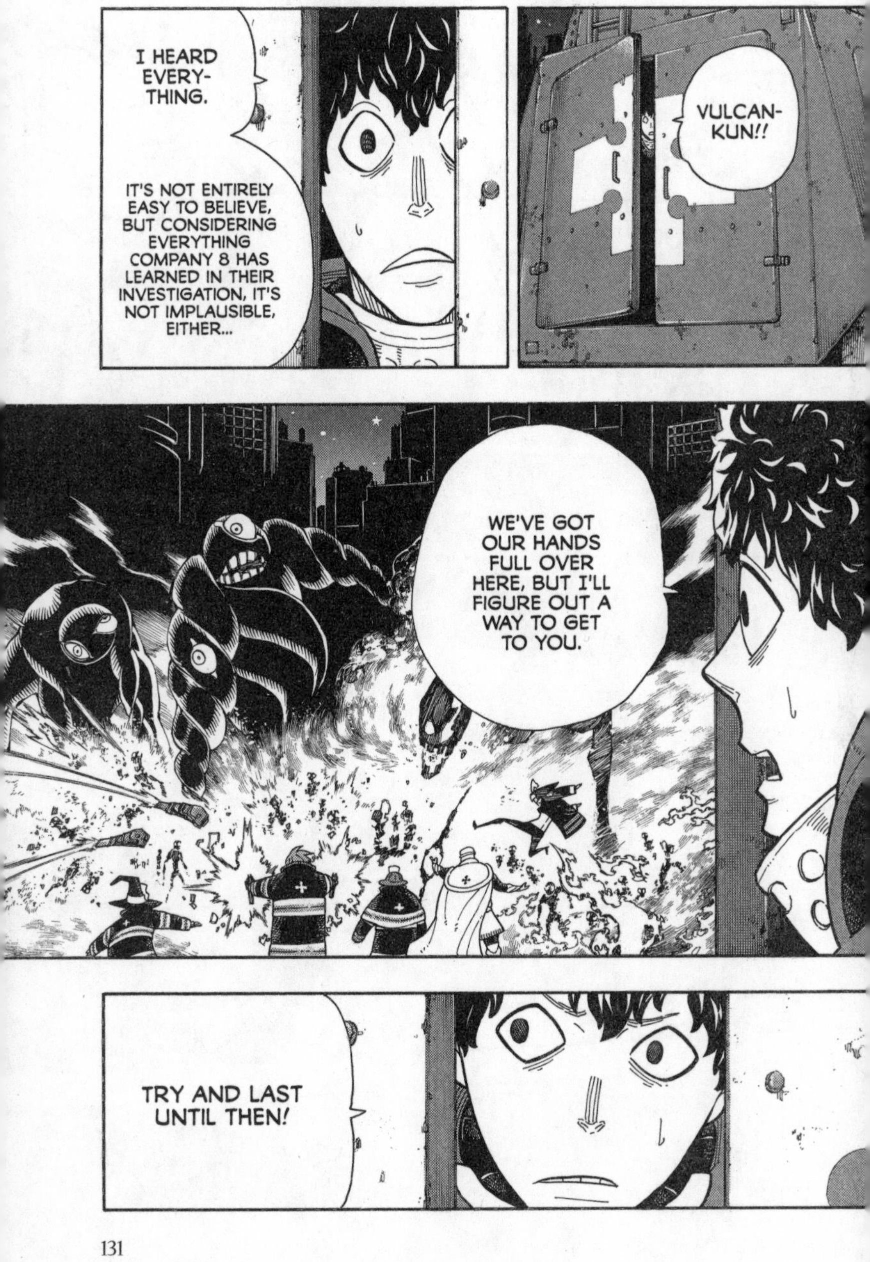
VULCAN-KUN!!
I HEARD EVERYTHING.
IT'S NOT ENTIRELY EASY TO BELIEVE, BUT CONSIDERING EVERYTHING COMPANY 8 HAS LEARNED IN THEIR INVESTIGATION, IT'S NOT IMPLAUSIBLE, EITHER...
WE'VE GOT OUR HANDS FULL OVER HERE, BUT I'LL FIGURE OUT A WAY TO GET TO YOU.
TRY AND LAST UNTIL THEN!

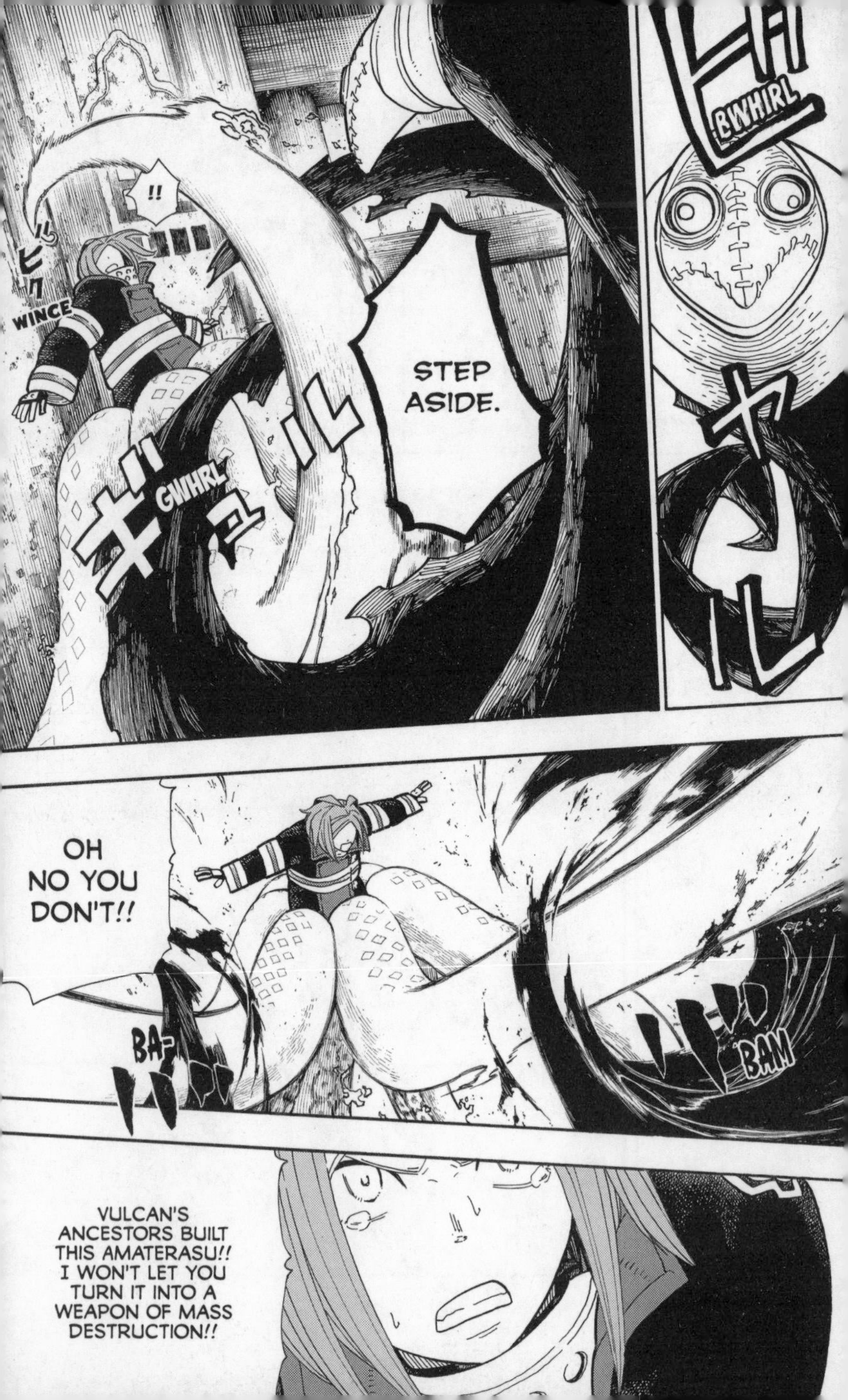
BWHIRL
!!
WINCE
STEP ASIDE.
GWHIRL
OH NO YOU DON'T!!
BAM
BA-
VULCAN'S ANCESTORS BUILT THIS AMATERASU!! I WON'T LET YOU TURN IT INTO A WEAPON OF MASS DESTRUCTION!!

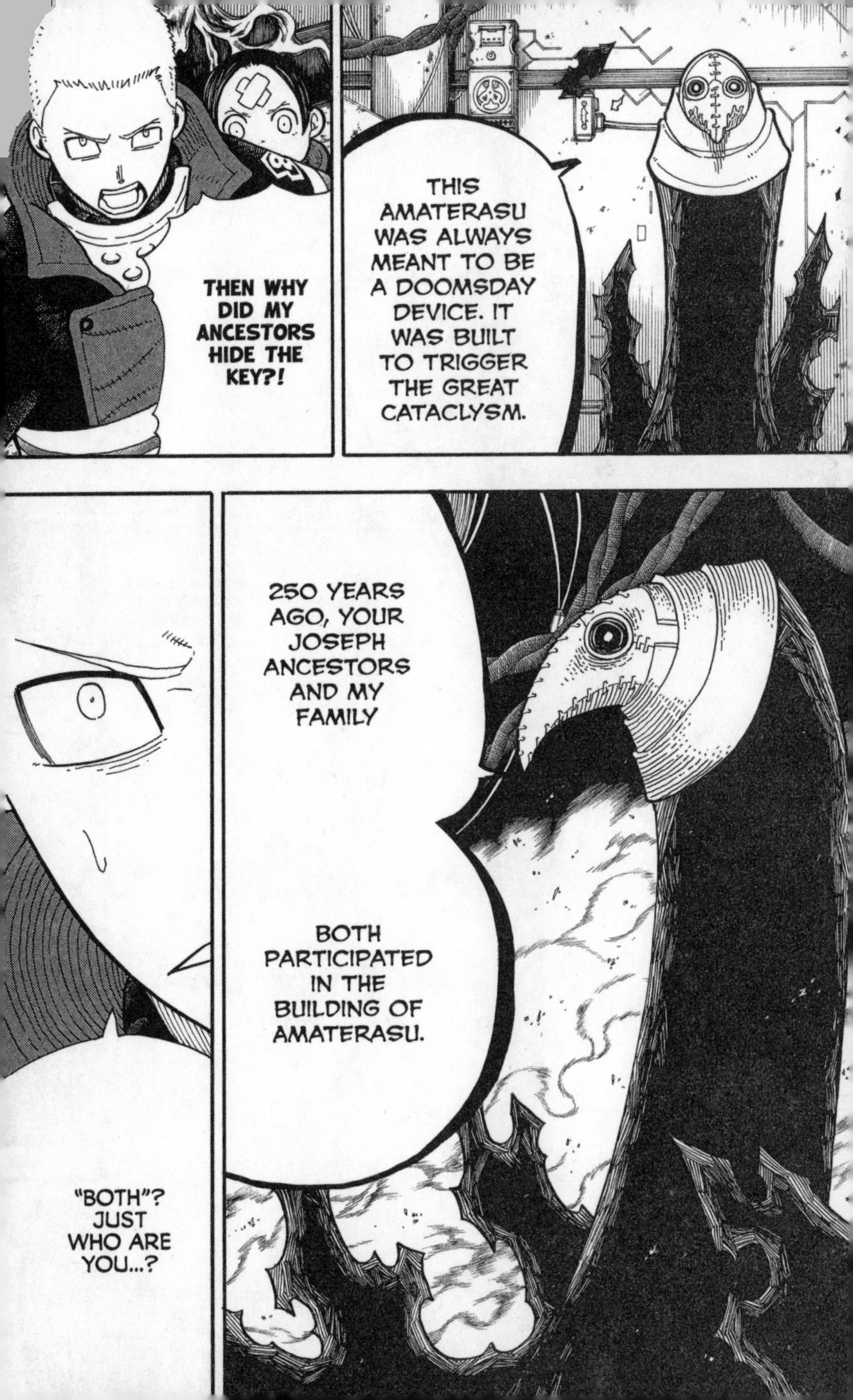
THIS AMATERASU WAS ALWAYS MEANT TO BE A DOOMSDAY DEVICE. IT WAS BUILT TO TRIGGER THE GREAT CATACLYSM.
THEN WHY DID MY ANCESTORS HIDE THE KEY?!
250 YEARS AGO, YOUR JOSEPH ANCESTORS AND MY FAMILY
BOTH PARTICIPATED IN THE BUILDING OF AMATERASU.
"BOTH"? JUST WHO ARE YOU...?

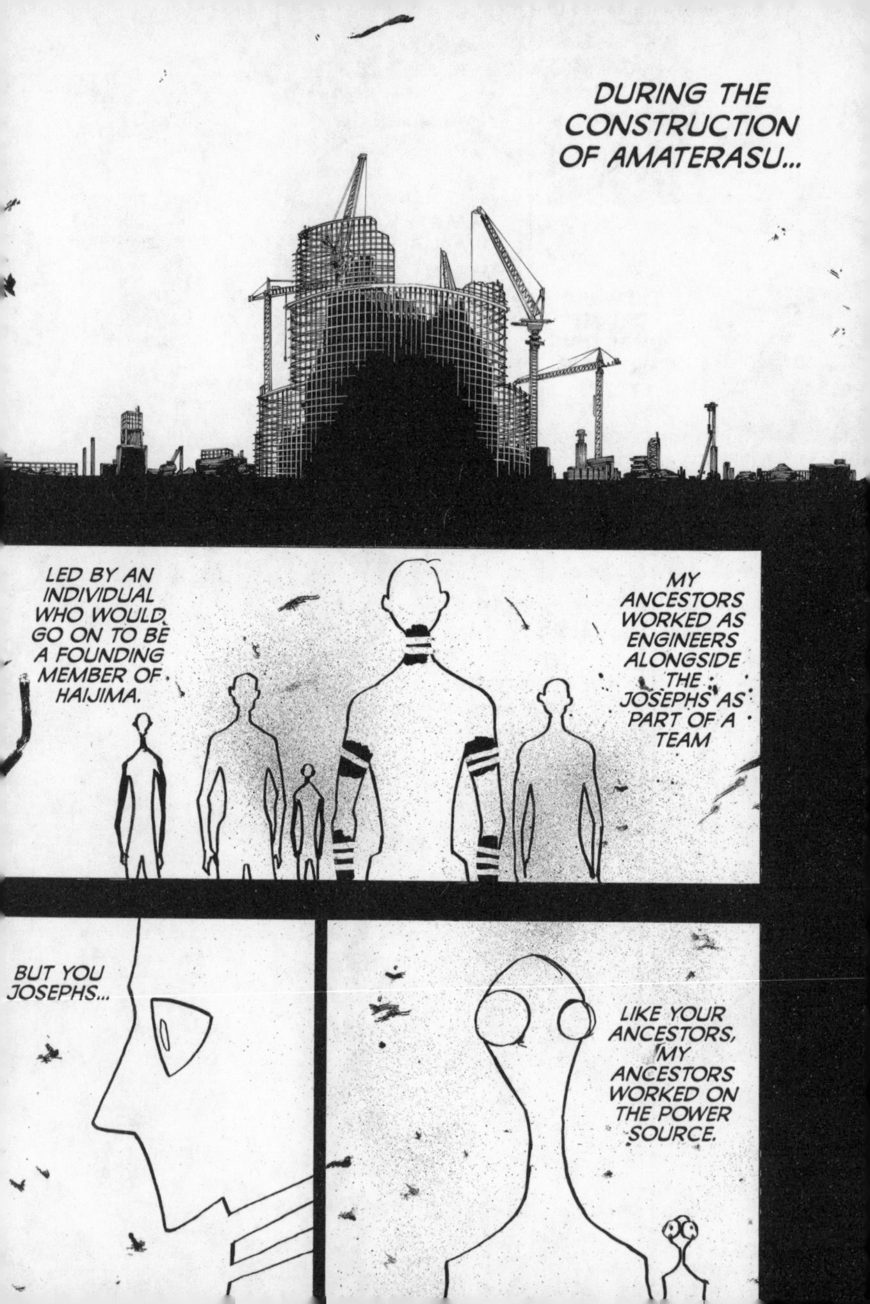
DURING THE CONSTRUCTION OF AMATERASU...
MY ANCESTORS WORKED AS ENGINEERS ALONGSIDE THE JOSEPHS AS PART OF A TEAM
LED BY AN INDIVIDUAL WHO WOULD GO ON TO BE A FOUNDING MEMBER OF HAIJIMA.
LIKE YOUR ANCESTORS, MY ANCESTORS WORKED ON THE POWER SOURCE.
BUT YOU JOSEPHS...

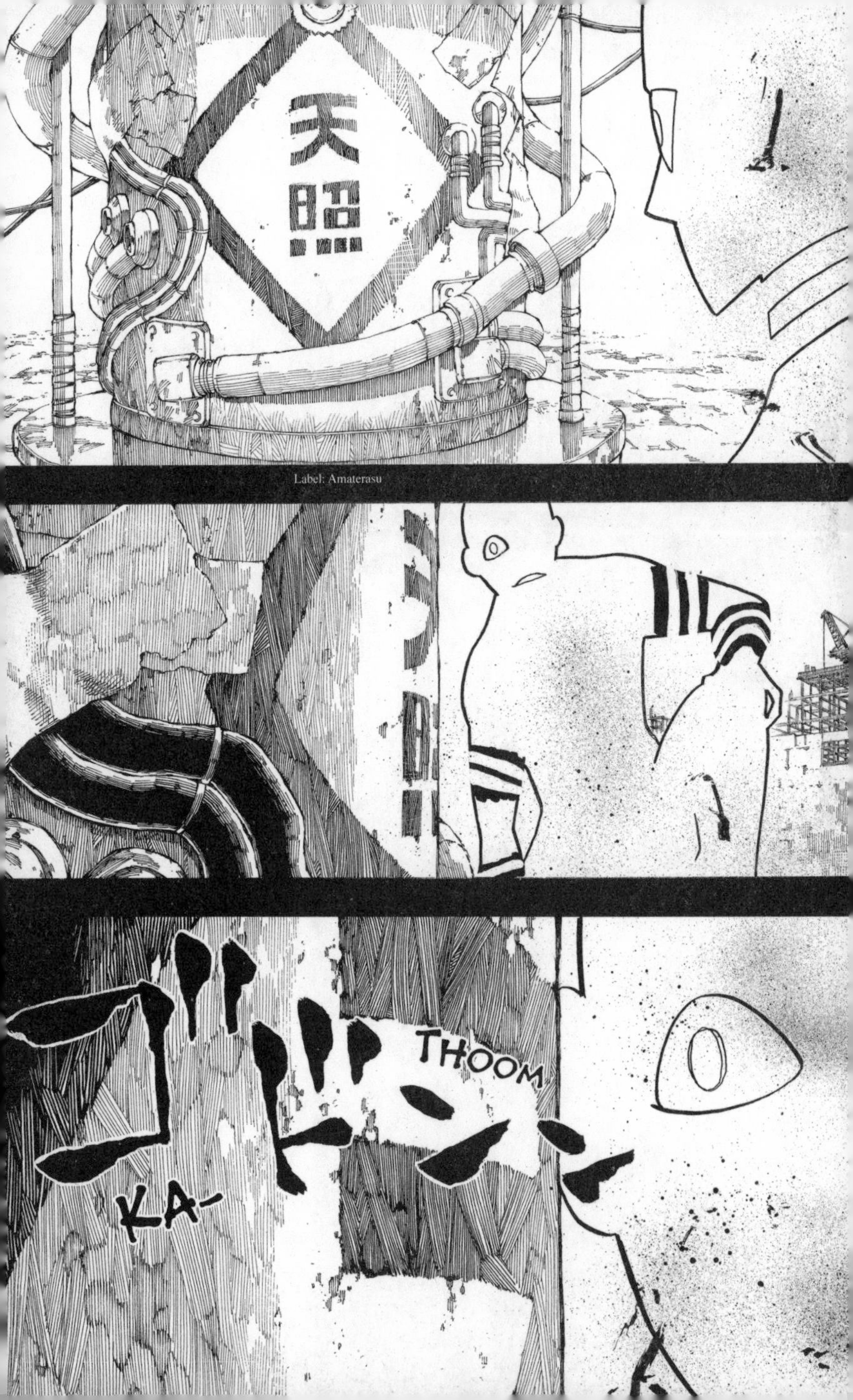
天照
Label: Amaterasu
THOOM
KA-

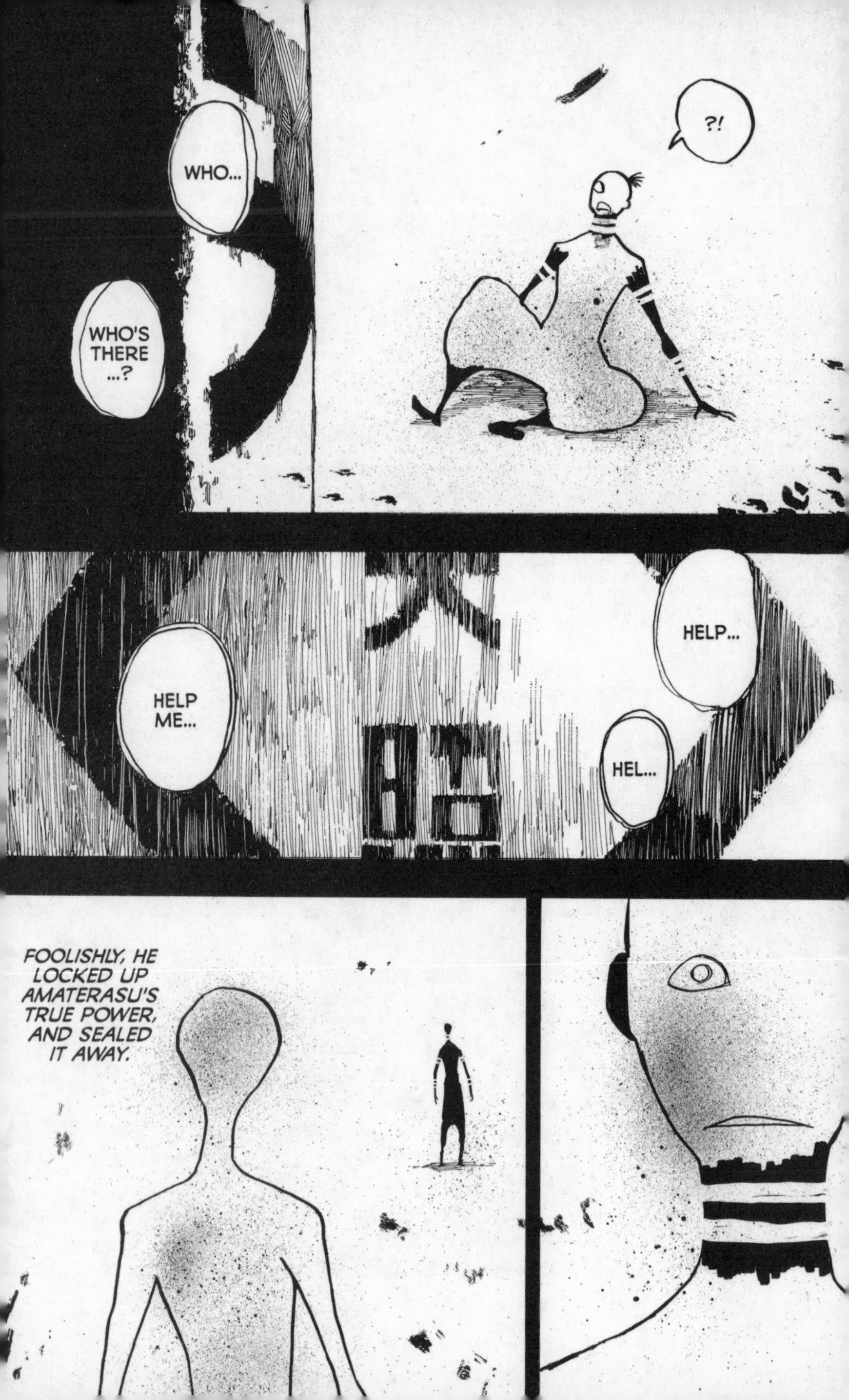
?!
WHO...
WHO'S THERE ...?
HELP...
HEL...
HELP ME...
FOOLISHLY, HE LOCKED UP AMATERASU'S TRUE POWER, AND SEALED IT AWAY.

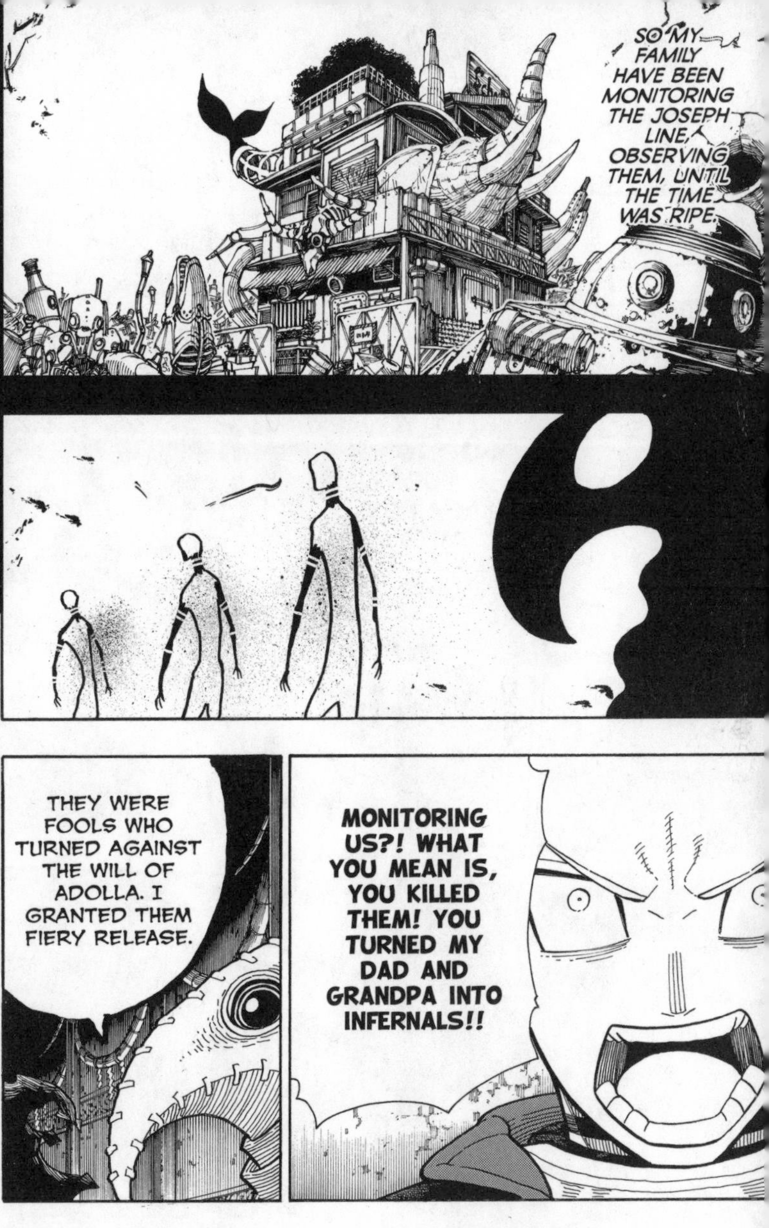
SO MY FAMILY HAVE BEEN MONITORING THE JOSEPH LINE, OBSERVING THEM, UNTIL THE TIME WAS RIPE.
MONITORING US?! WHAT YOU MEAN IS, YOU KILLED THEM! YOU TURNED MY DAD AND GRANDPA INTO INFERNALS!!
THEY WERE FOOLS WHO TURNED AGAINST THE WILL OF ADOLLA. I GRANTED THEM FIERY RELEASE.

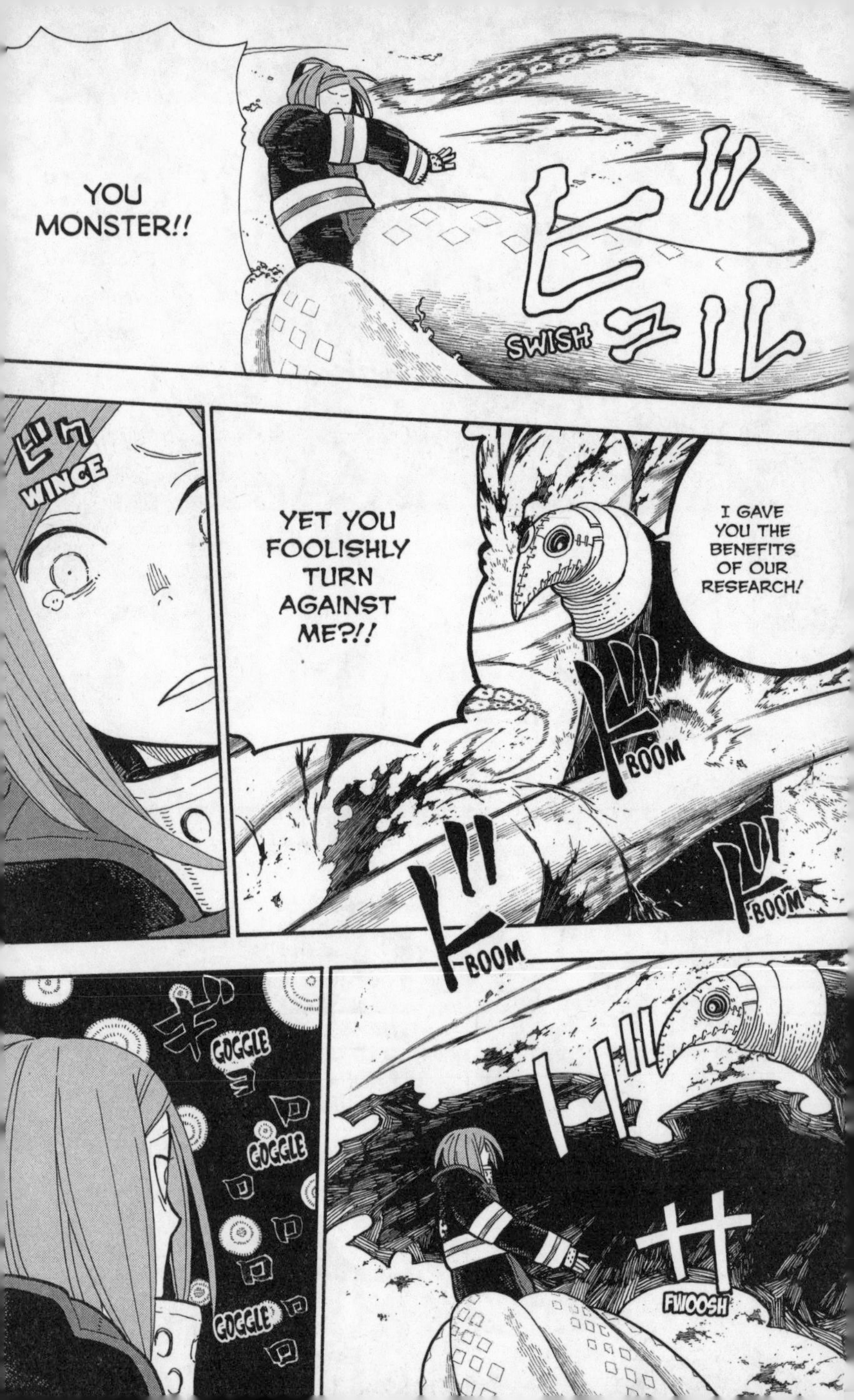
YOU MONSTER!!
SWISH
I GAVE YOU THE BENEFITS OF OUR RESEARCH!
YET YOU FOOLISHLY TURN AGAINST ME?!!
BOOM
BOOM
BOOM
WINCE
FWOOSH
GOGGLE
GOGGLE
GOGGLE

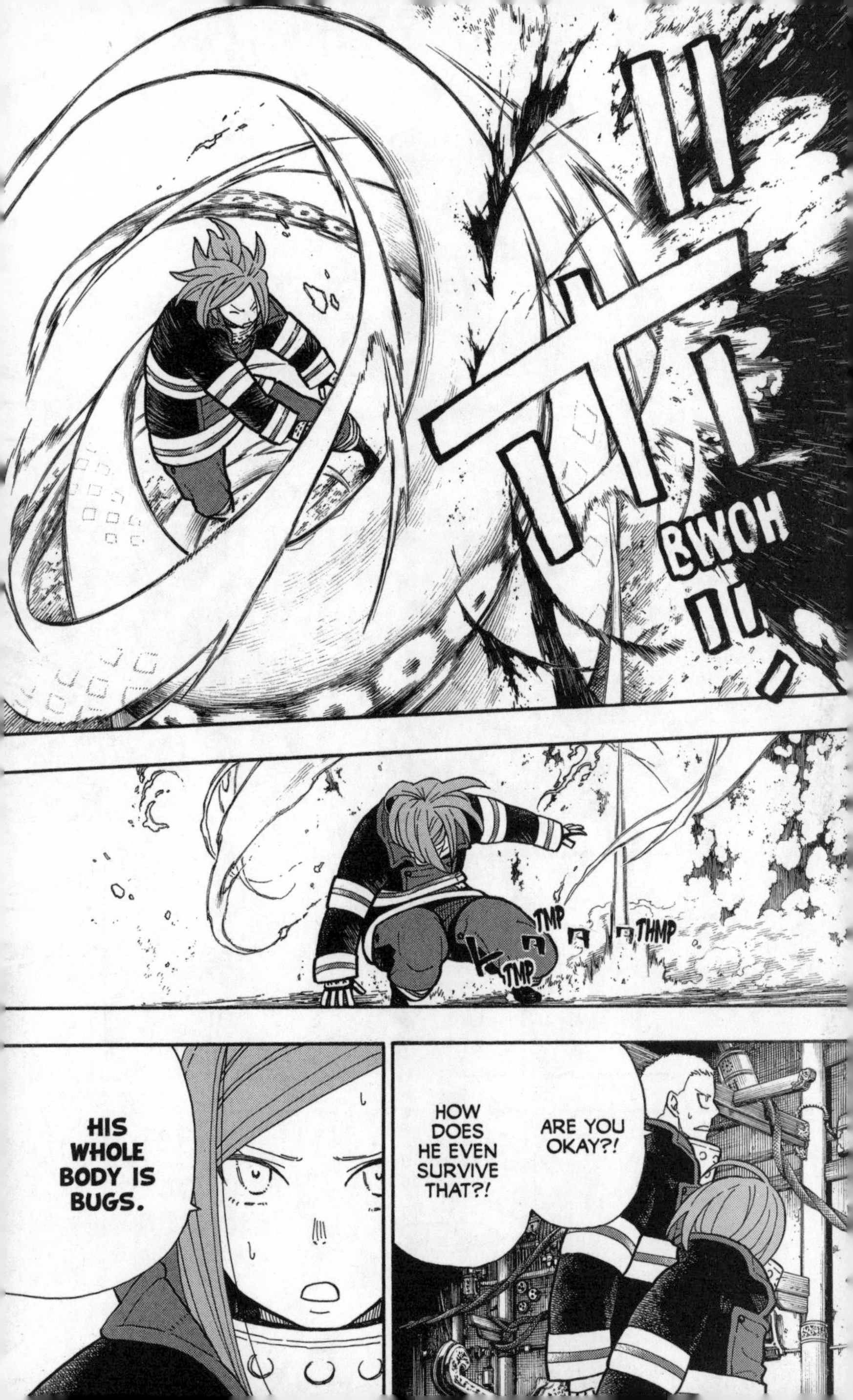
BWOH
THMP
TMP
TMP
ARE YOU OKAY?!
HOW DOES HE EVEN SURVIVE THAT?!
HIS WHOLE BODY IS BUGS.

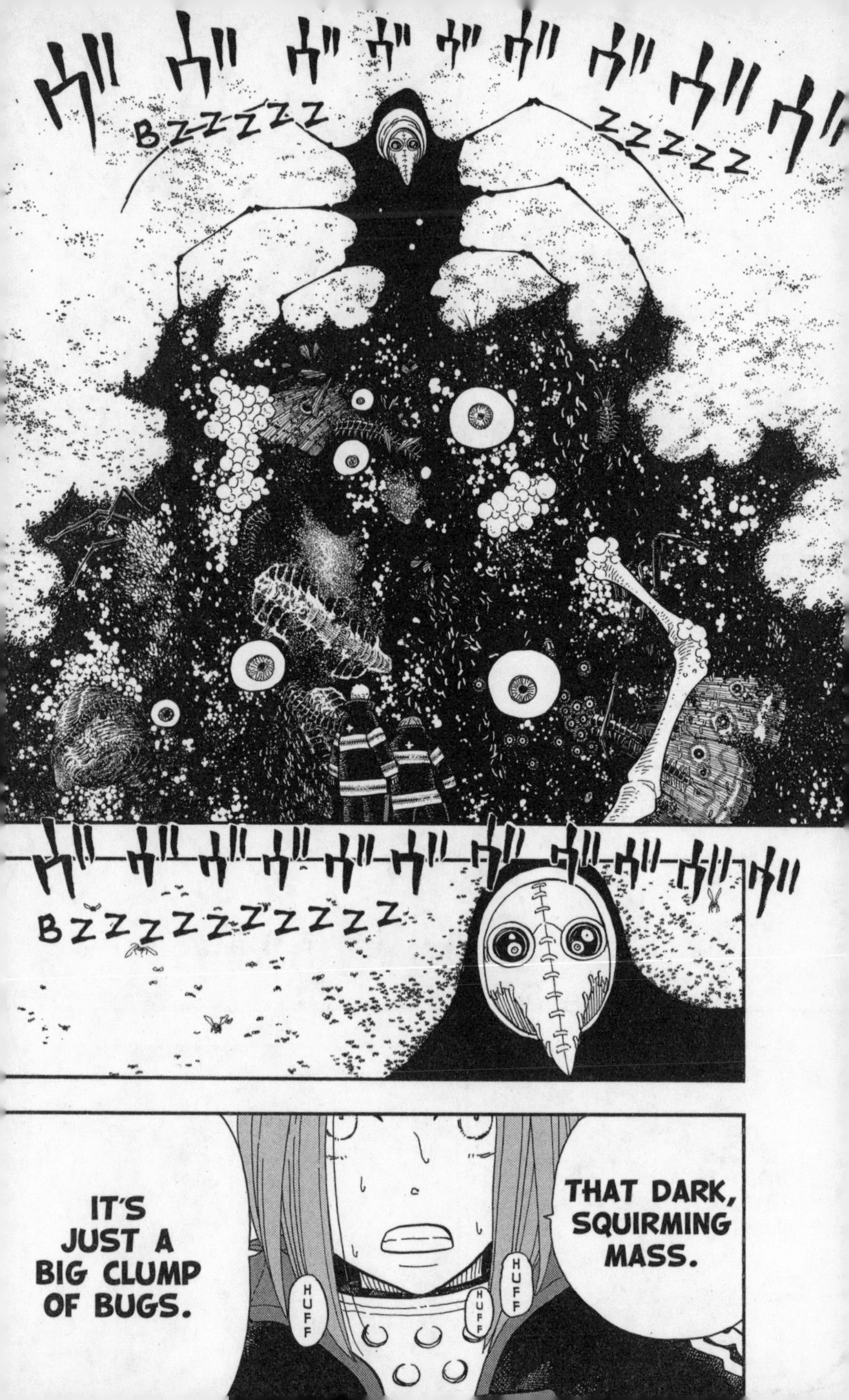
BZZZZZZ
ZZZZZZ
BZZZZZZZZZZZ
THAT DARK, SQUIRMING MASS.
HUFF HUFF
HUFF HUFF
IT'S JUST A BIG CLUMP OF BUGS.

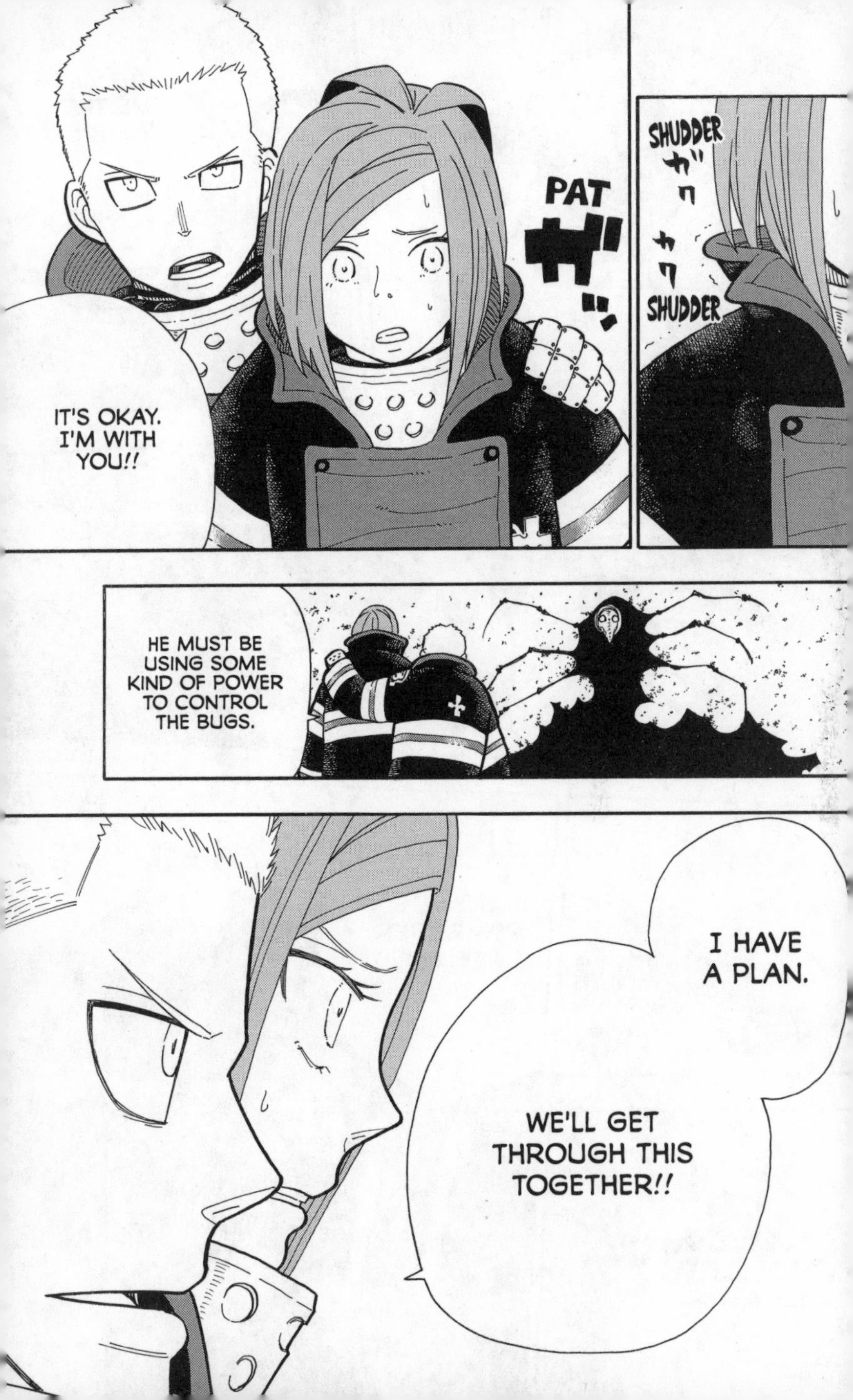
SHUDDER
ガクガク
SHUDDER
PAT
ガッ
IT'S OKAY. I'M WITH YOU!!
HE MUST BE USING SOME KIND OF POWER TO CONTROL THE BUGS.
I HAVE A PLAN.
WE'LL GET THROUGH THIS TOGETHER!!

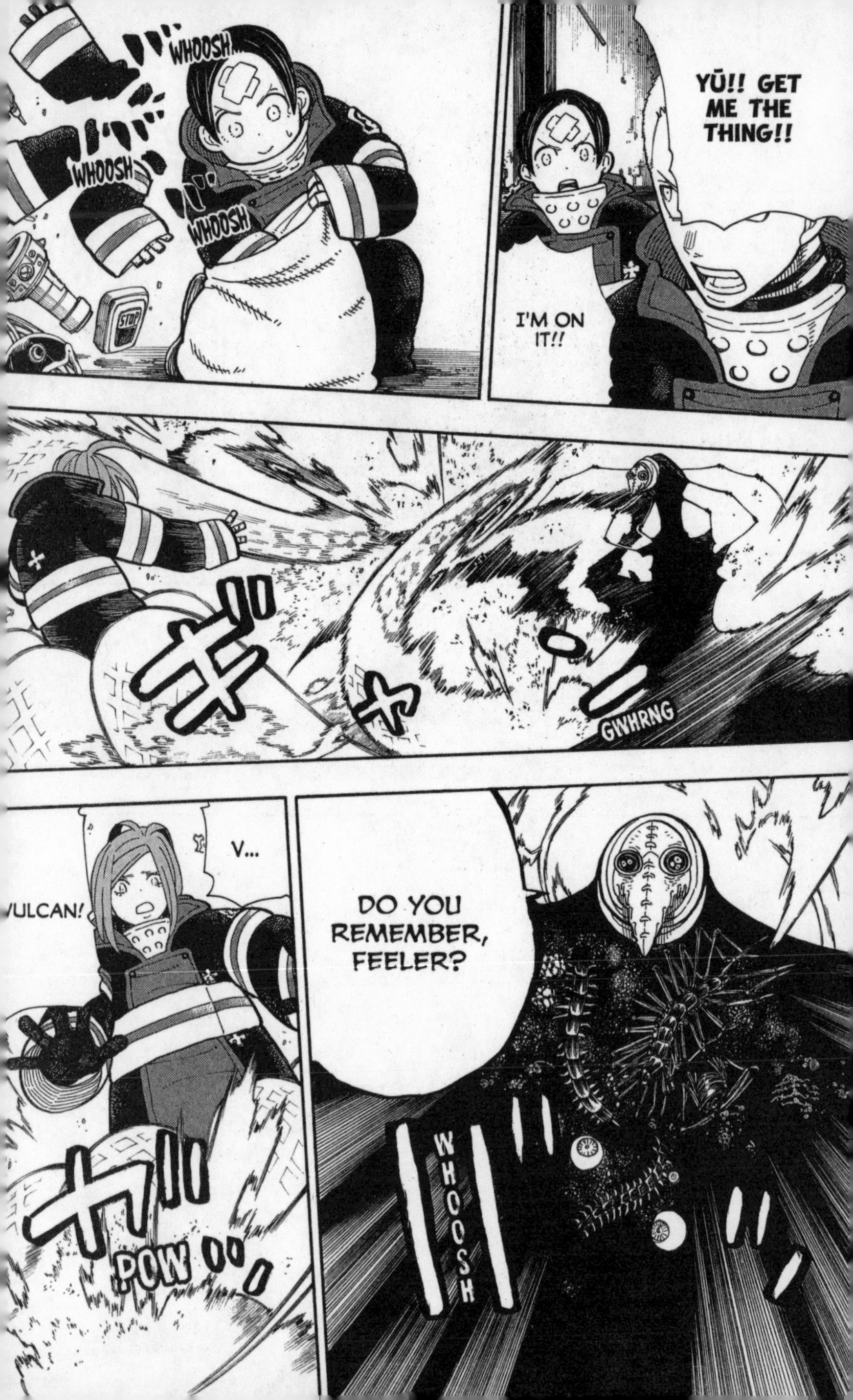
YŪ!! GET ME THE THING!!
I'M ON IT!!
WHOOSH
WHOOSH
WHOOSH
GWHRNG
DO YOU REMEMBER, FEELER?
WHOOSH
V...
VULCAN!
POW

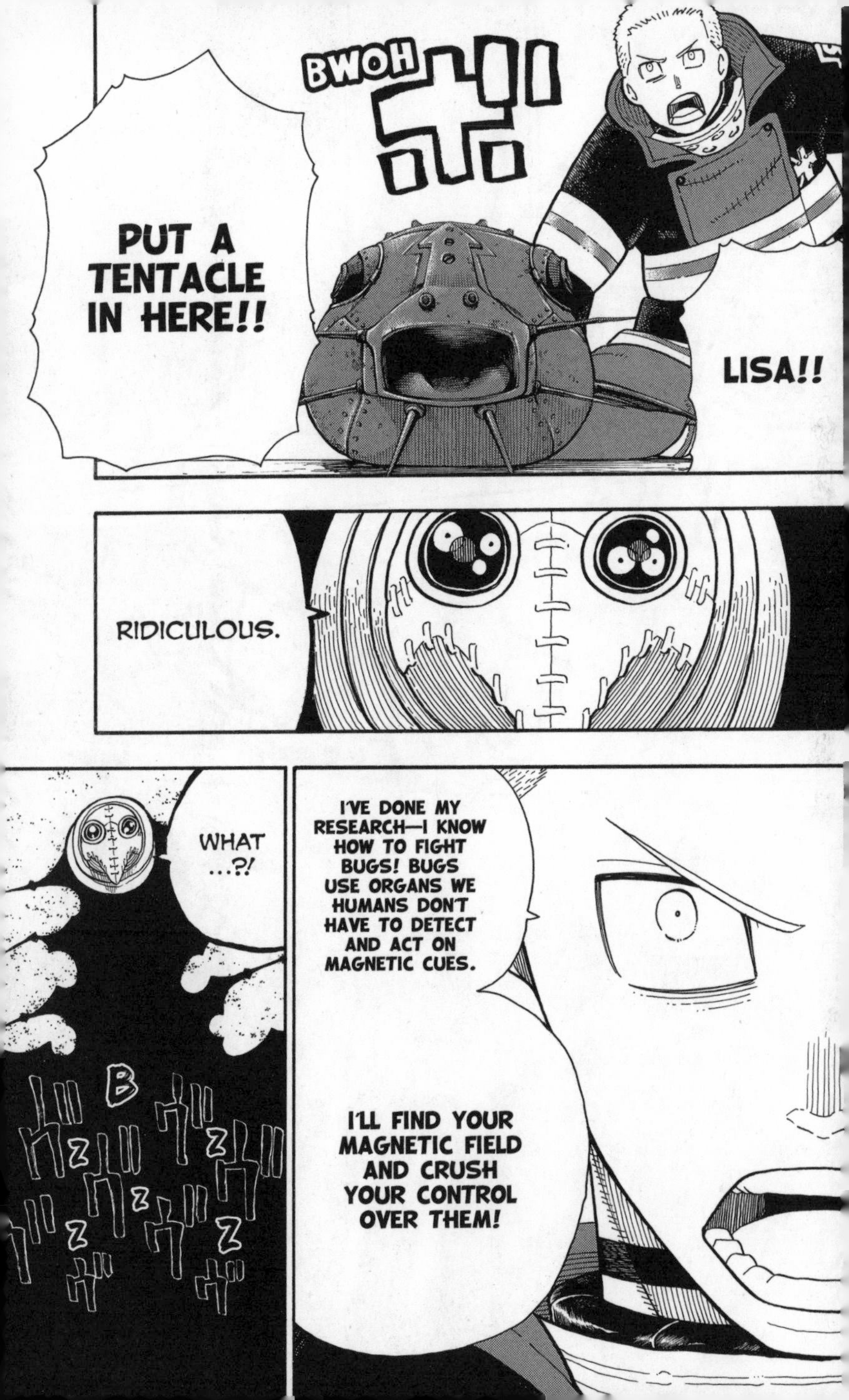
BWOH!!
LISA!!
PUT A TENTACLE IN HERE!!
RIDICULOUS.
I'VE DONE MY RESEARCH—I KNOW HOW TO FIGHT BUGS! BUGS USE ORGANS WE HUMANS DON'T HAVE TO DETECT AND ACT ON MAGNETIC CUES.
I'LL FIND YOUR MAGNETIC FIELD AND CRUSH YOUR CONTROL OVER THEM!
WHAT ...?!
BZZZZZ

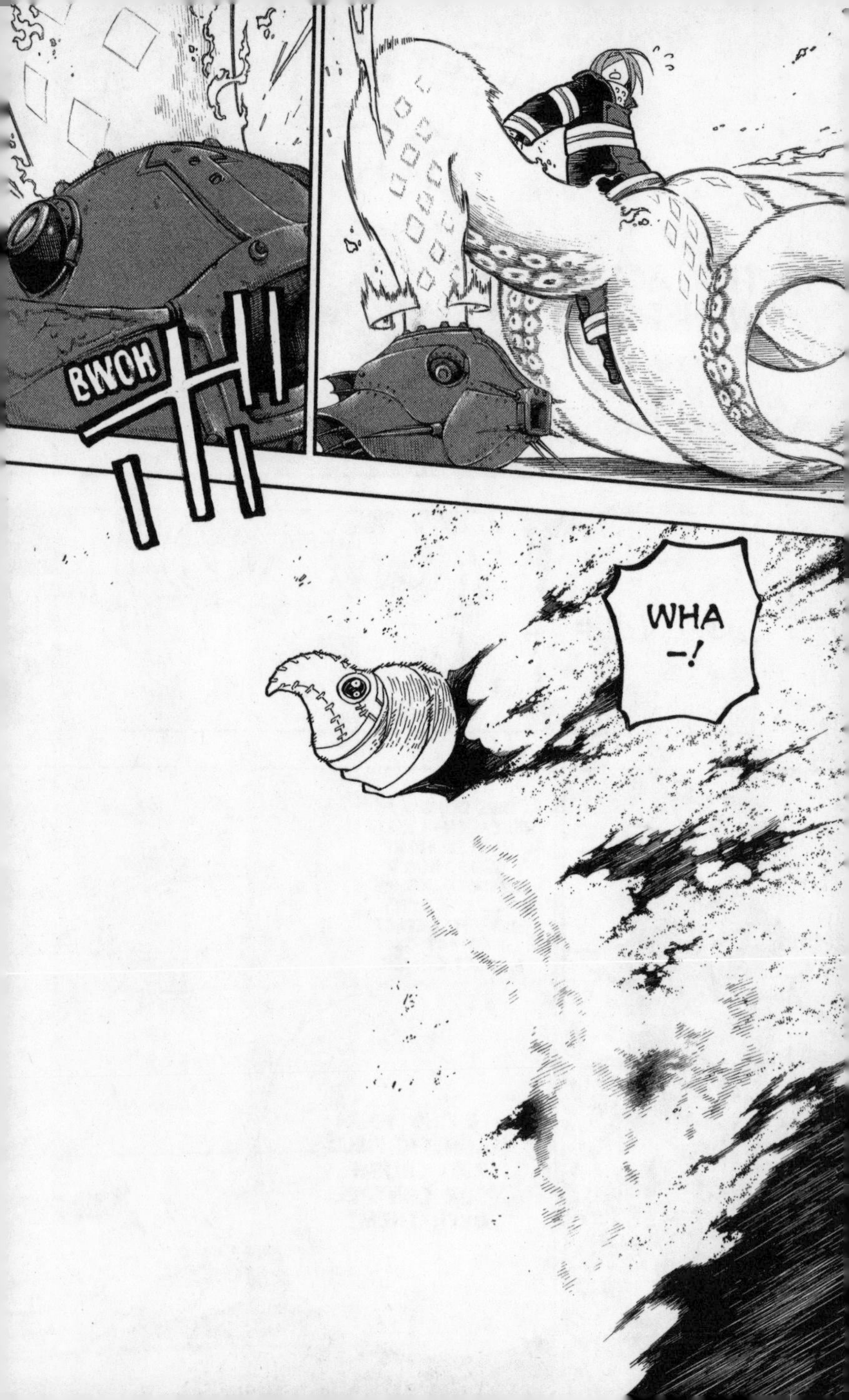
BWOH
WHA—!

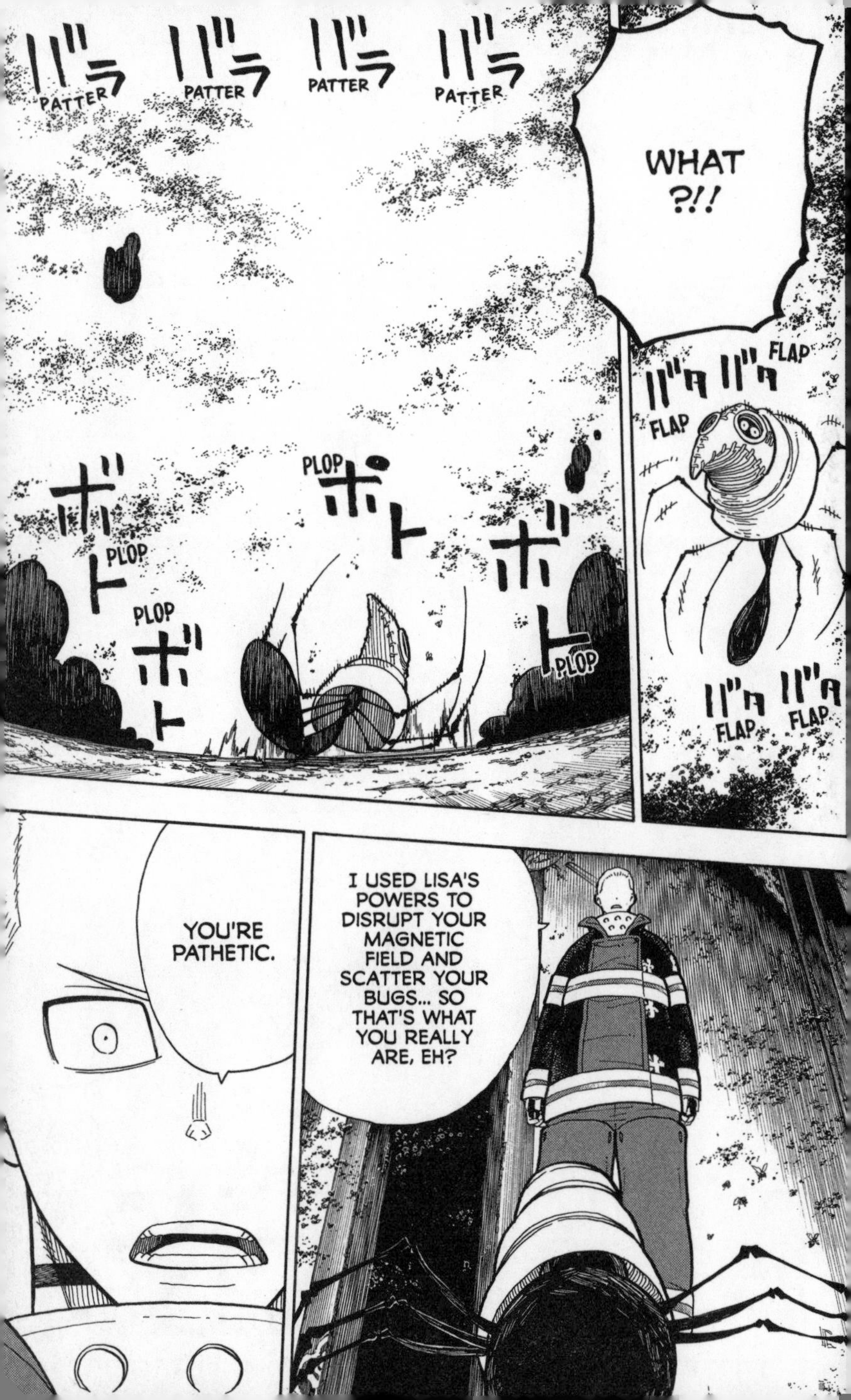
WHAT ?!!
バタバタ FLAP FLAP
バタ FLAP
バタ FLAP
バラ PATTER
バラ PATTER
バラ PATTER
バラ PATTER
ボト PLOP
ボト PLOP
ボト PLOP
ボト PLOP
I USED LISA'S POWERS TO DISRUPT YOUR MAGNETIC FIELD AND SCATTER YOUR BUGS... SO THAT'S WHAT YOU REALLY ARE, EH?
YOU'RE PATHETIC.

FIRE FORCE

ART: GREAT CATACLYSM

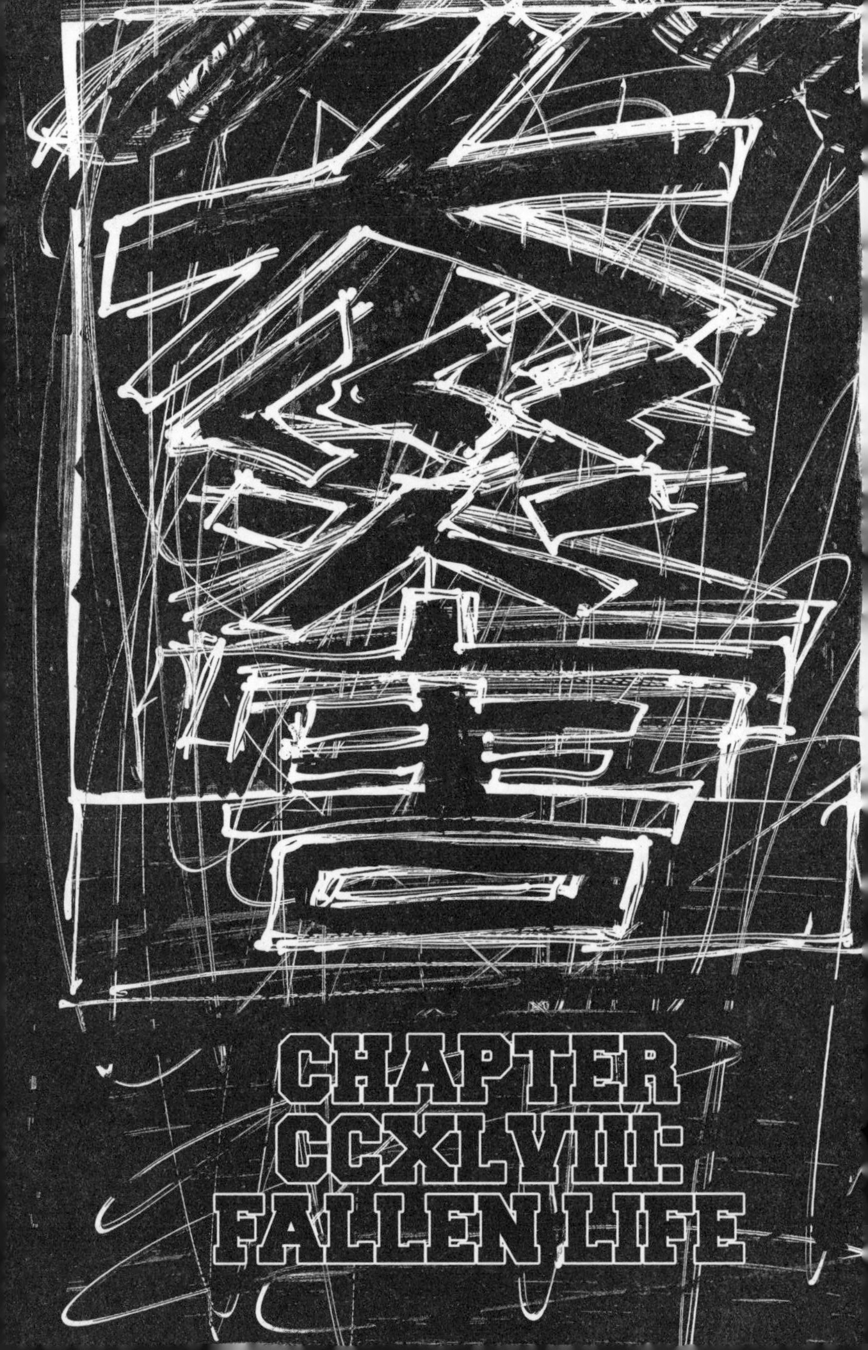

CHAPTER CCXLVIII: FALLEN LIFE

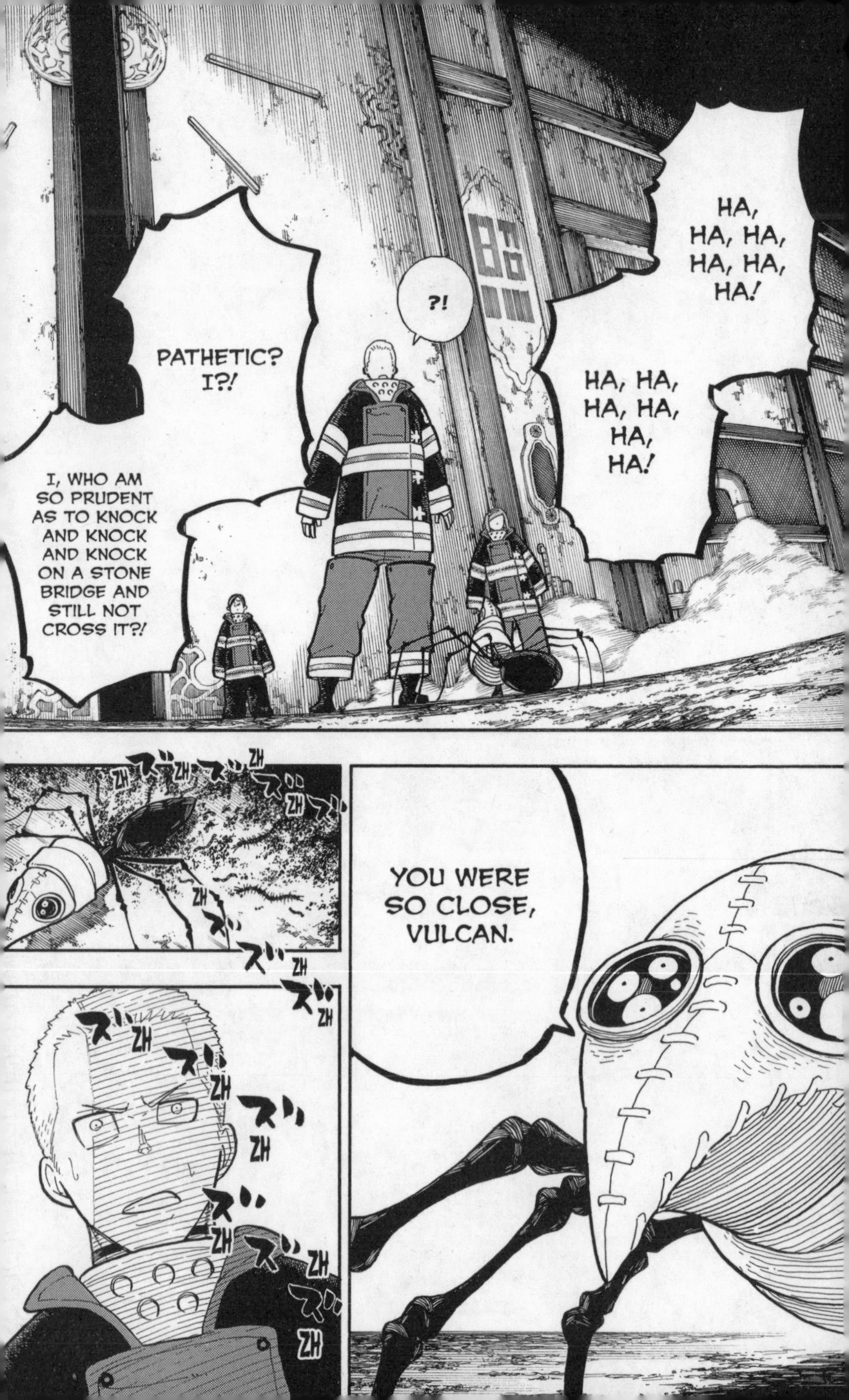
HA, HA, HA, HA, HA, HA!
HA, HA, HA, HA, HA, HA!
?!
PATHETIC? I?!
I, WHO AM SO PRUDENT AS TO KNOCK AND KNOCK AND KNOCK ON A STONE BRIDGE AND STILL NOT CROSS IT?!
YOU WERE SO CLOSE, VULCAN.
ZH ZH ZH ZH
ZH ZH ZH
ZH ZH ZH ZH ZH ZH

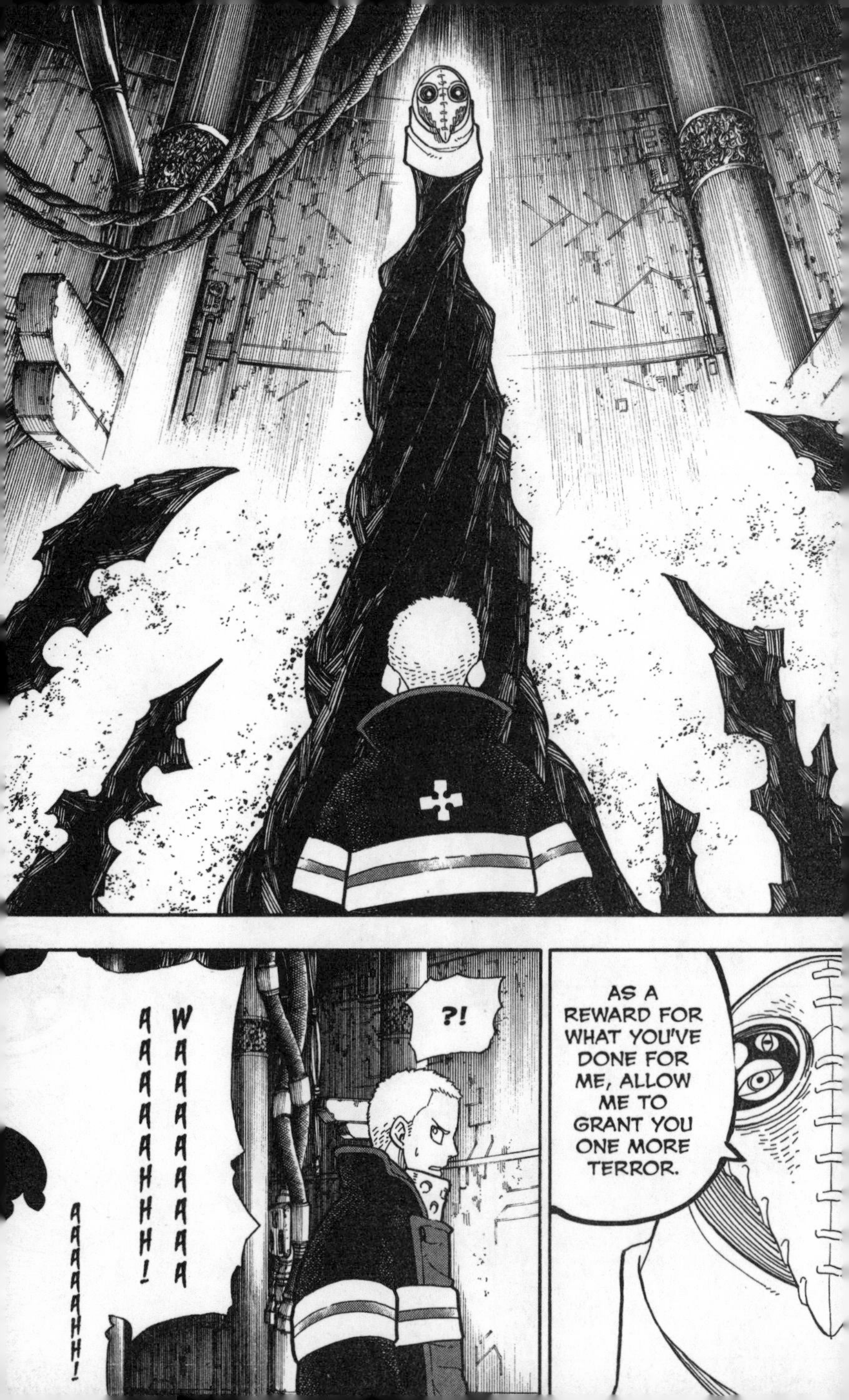
AS A REWARD FOR WHAT YOU'VE DONE FOR ME, ALLOW ME TO GRANT YOU ONE MORE TERROR.
?!
WAAAAAAAAAAAAAHHH!
AAAAAHH!

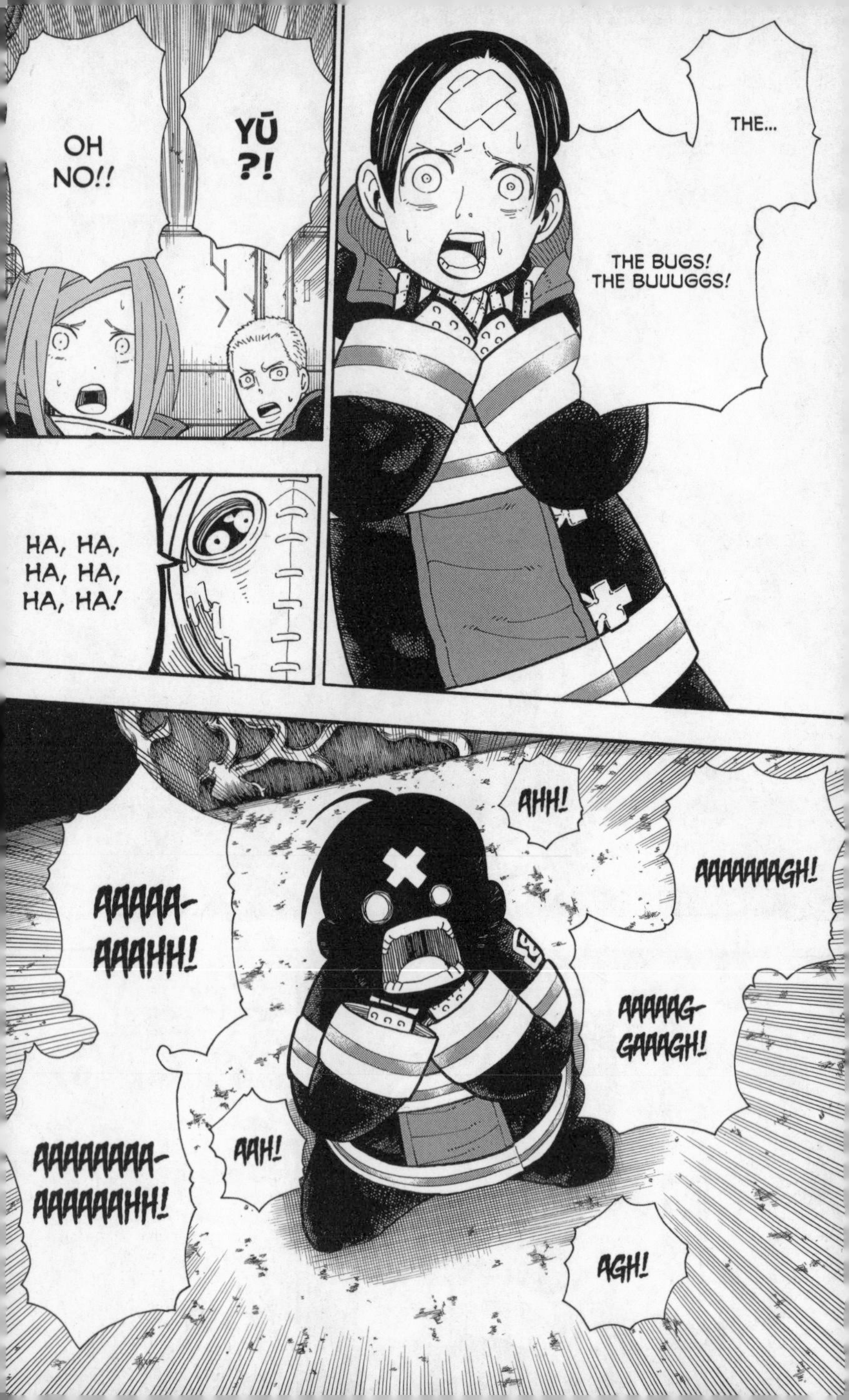
THE...
THE BUGS! THE BUUUGGS!
YŪ ?!
OH NO!!
HA, HA, HA, HA, HA, HA!
AHH!
AAAAAAAGH!
AAAAA-AAAHH!
AAAAAG-GAAAGH!
AAH!
AAAAAAAA-AAAAAAAHH!
AGH!

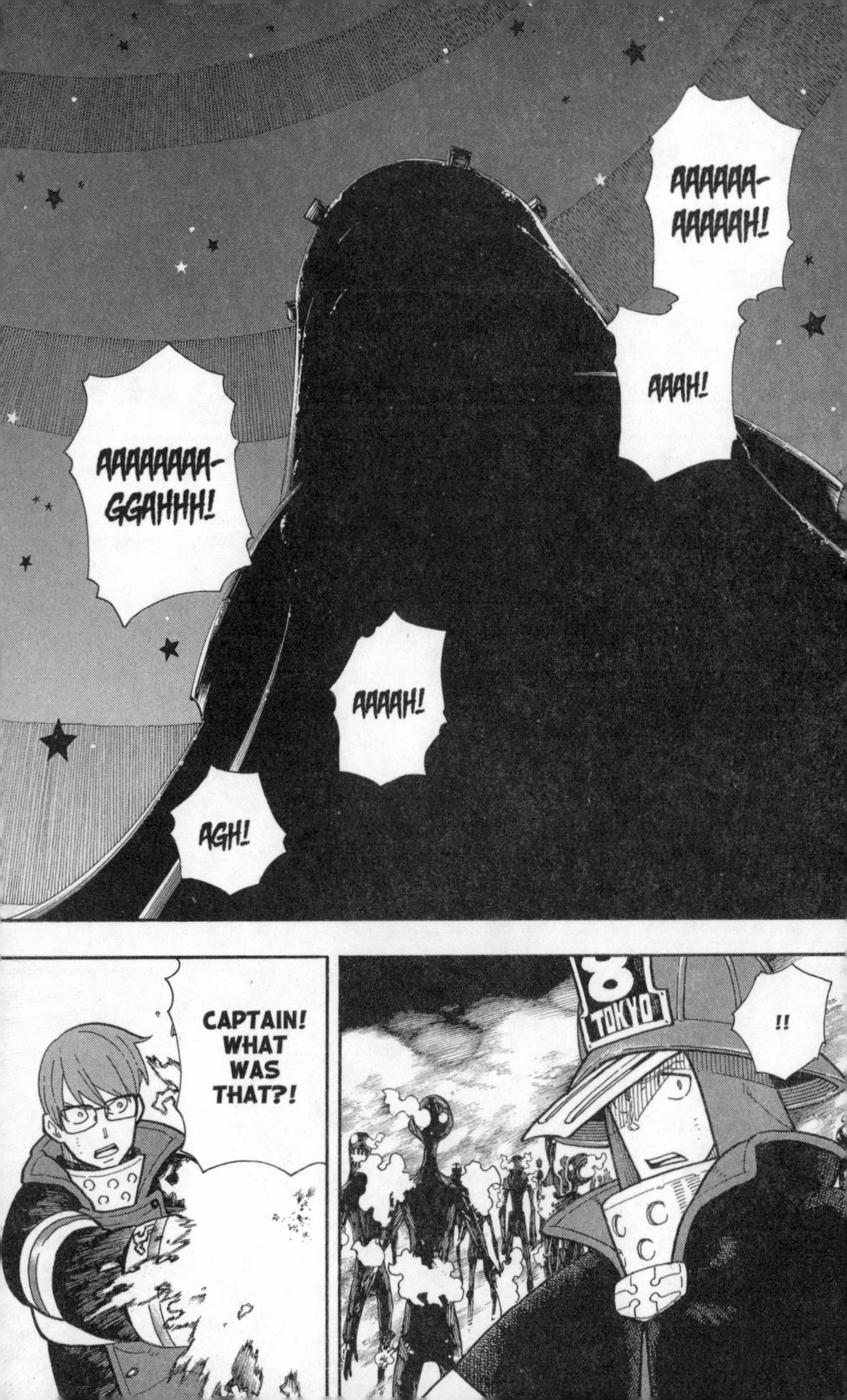
AAAAAA-AAAAAH!
AAAH!
AAAAAAAA-GGAHHH!
AAAAH!
AGH!
!!
CAPTAIN! WHAT WAS THAT?!

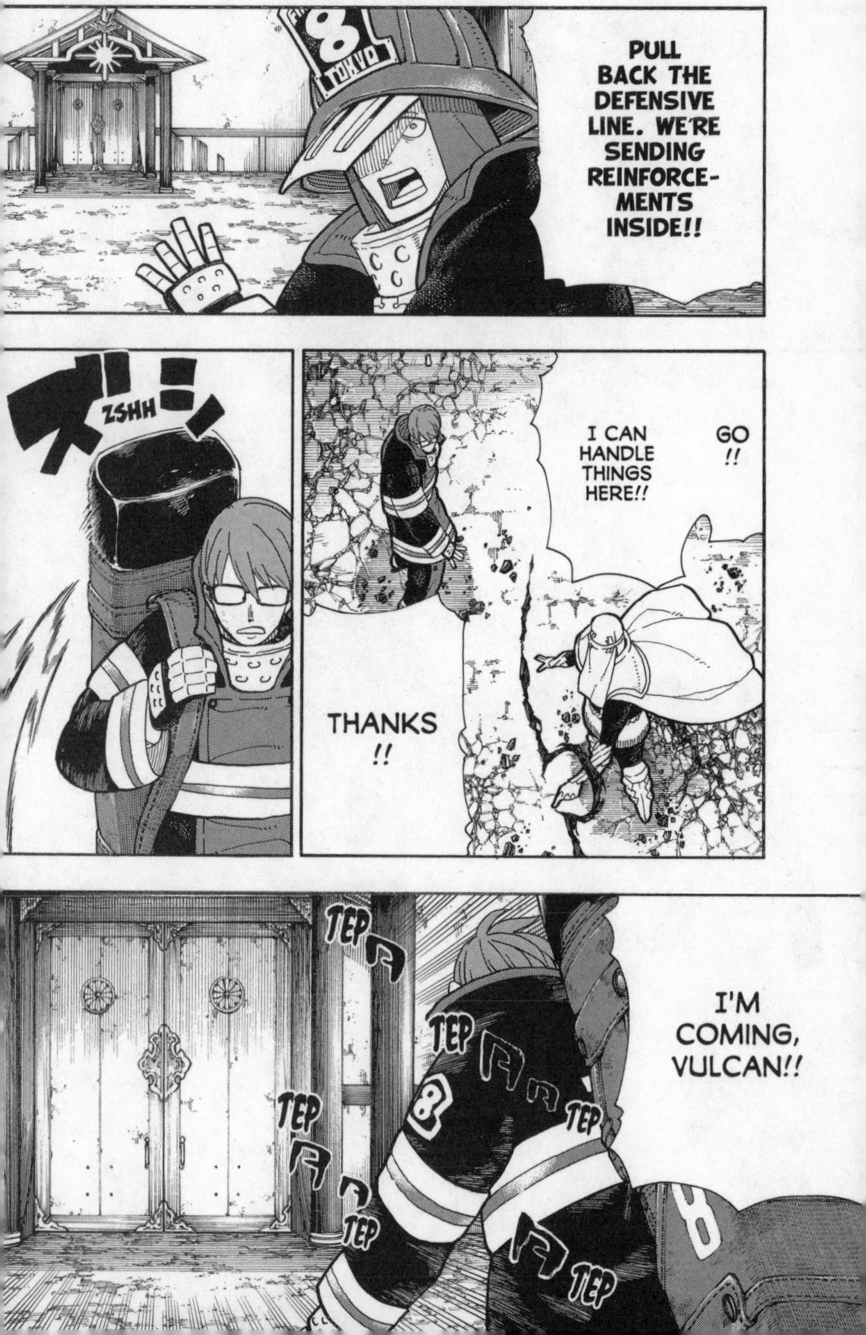
PULL BACK THE DEFENSIVE LINE. WE'RE SENDING REINFORCE-MENTS INSIDE!!
I CAN HANDLE THINGS HERE!!
GO!!
THANKS!!
ZSHH
I'M COMING, VULCAN!!
TEP
TEP
TEP
TEP
TEP
TEP

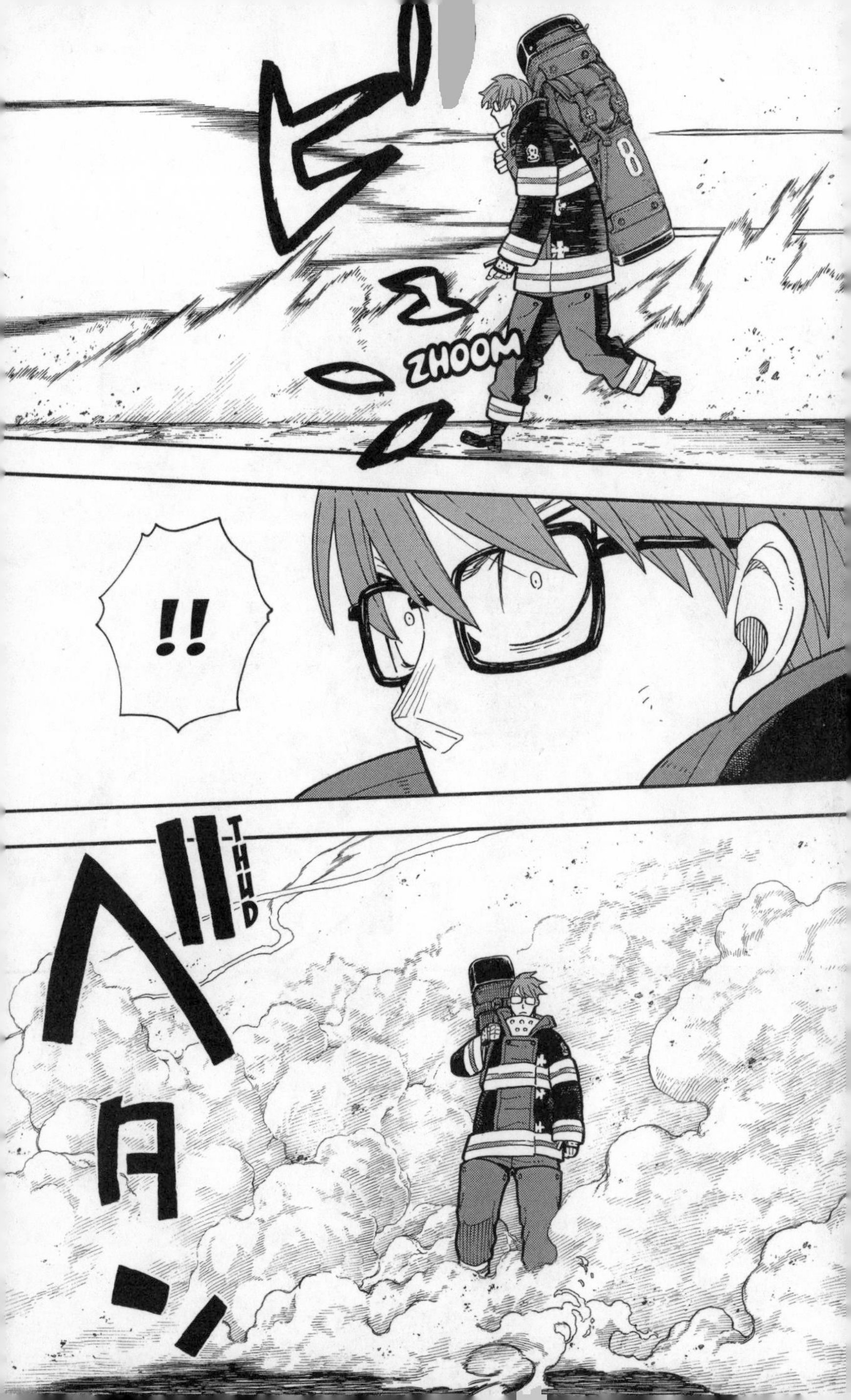
ZHOOM
!!
THUD

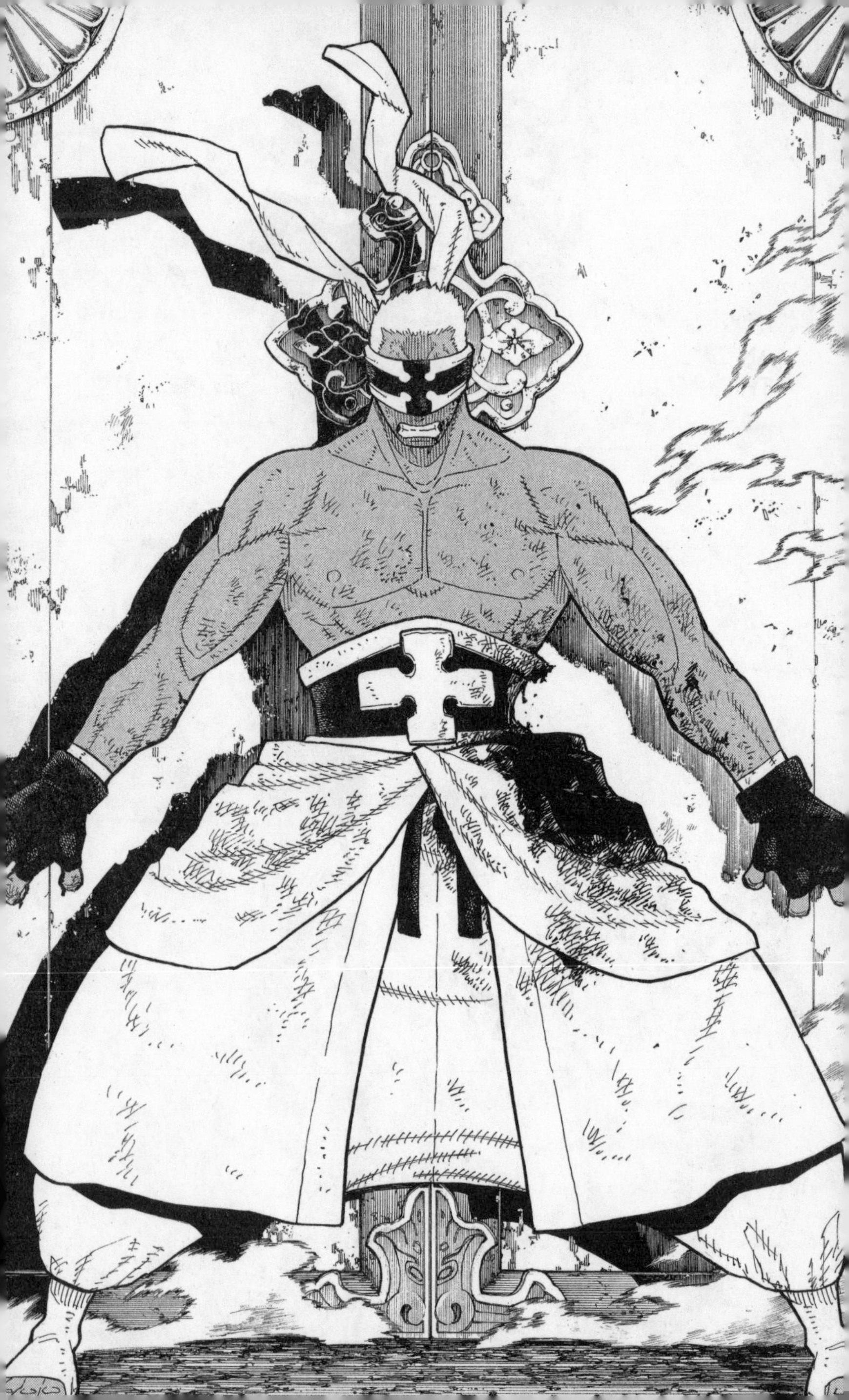

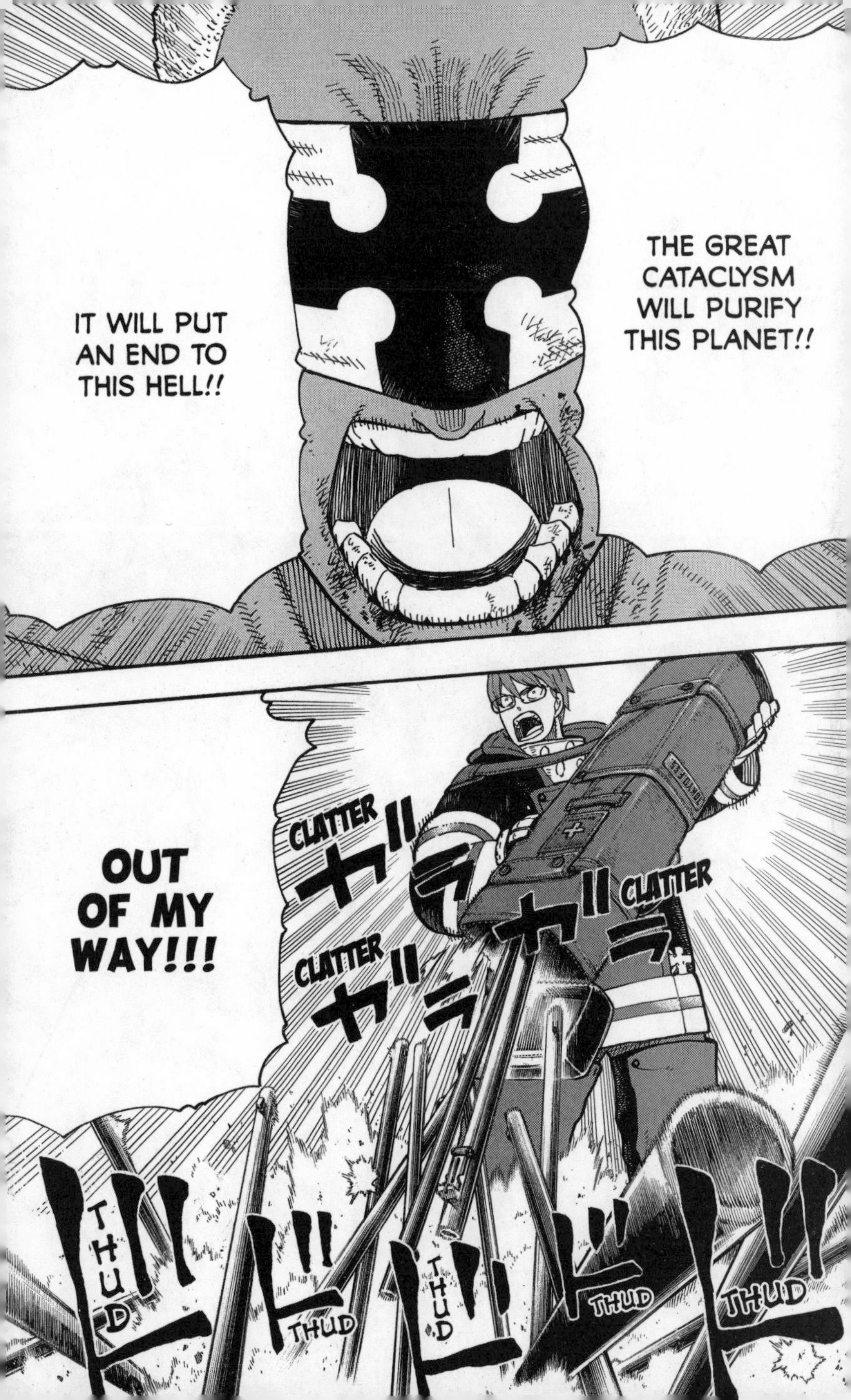

THE GREAT CATACLYSM WILL PURIFY THIS PLANET!!
IT WILL PUT AN END TO THIS HELL!!
CLATTER
CLATTER
CLATTER
OUT OF MY WAY!!!
THUD
THUD
THUD
THUD
THUD

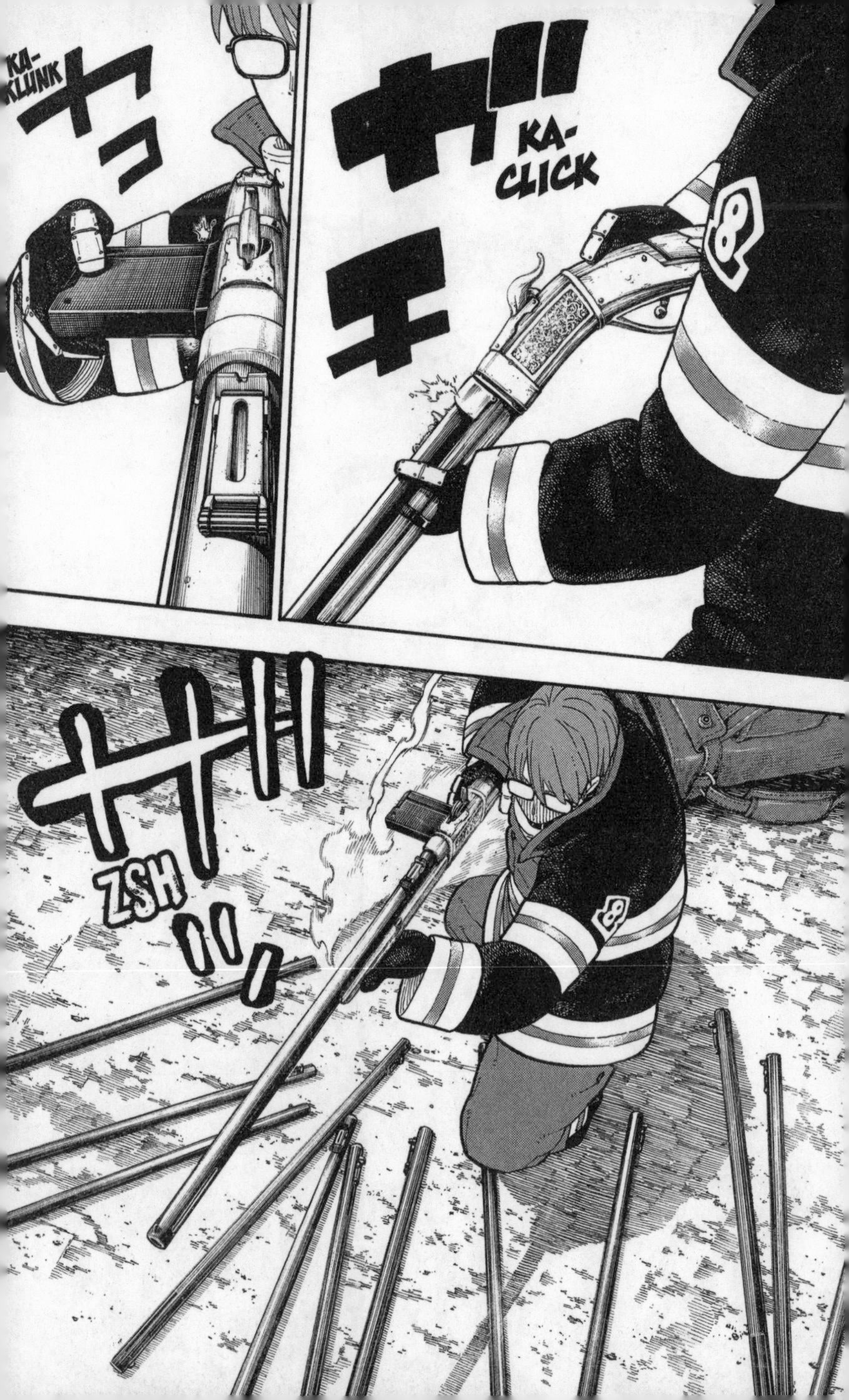
KA-
CLICK
KA-
KLUNK
ZSH

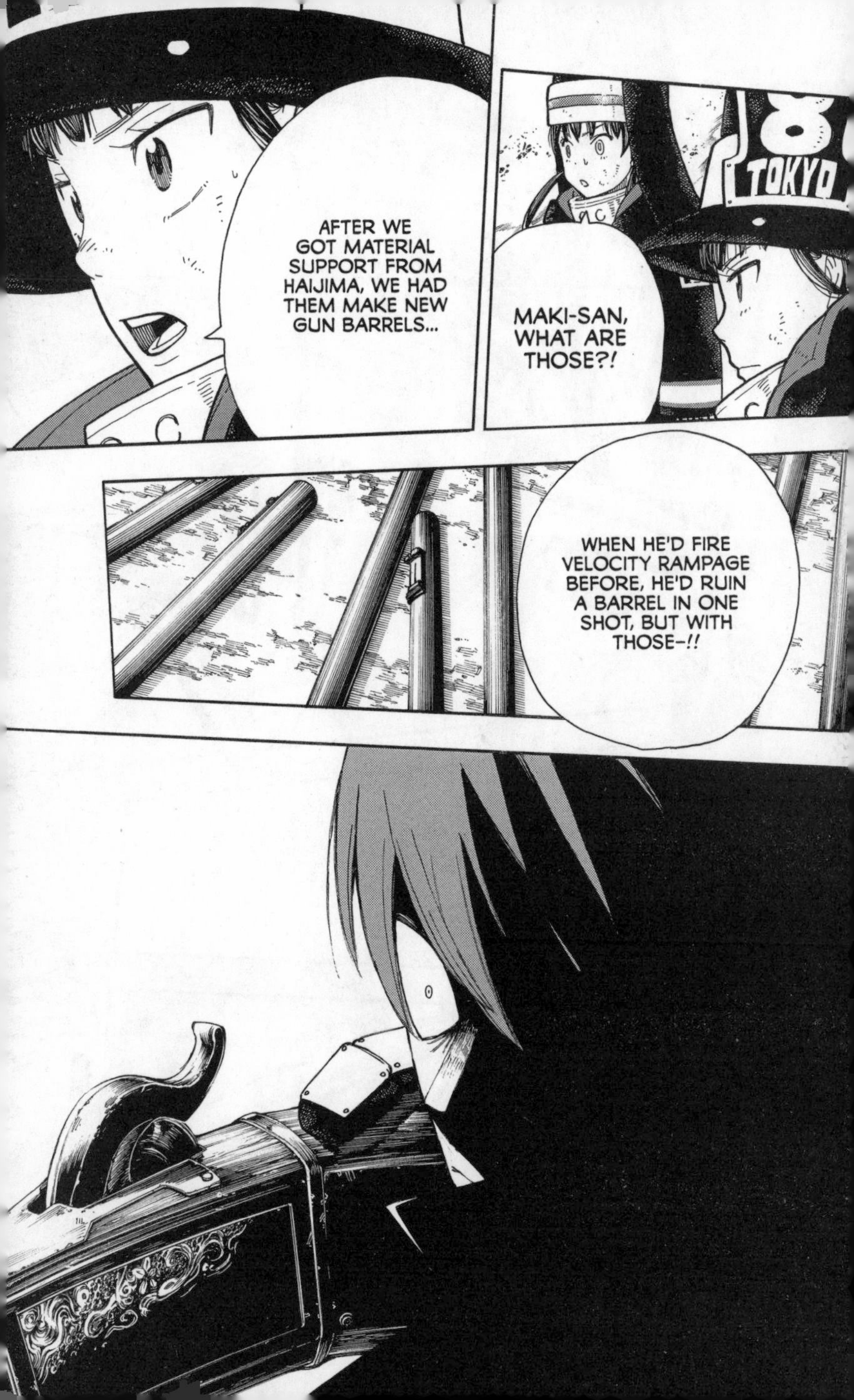
TOKYO
MAKI-SAN, WHAT ARE THOSE?!
AFTER WE GOT MATERIAL SUPPORT FROM HAIJIMA, WE HAD THEM MAKE NEW GUN BARRELS...
WHEN HE'D FIRE VELOCITY RAMPAGE BEFORE, HE'D RUIN A BARREL IN ONE SHOT, BUT WITH THOSE–!!

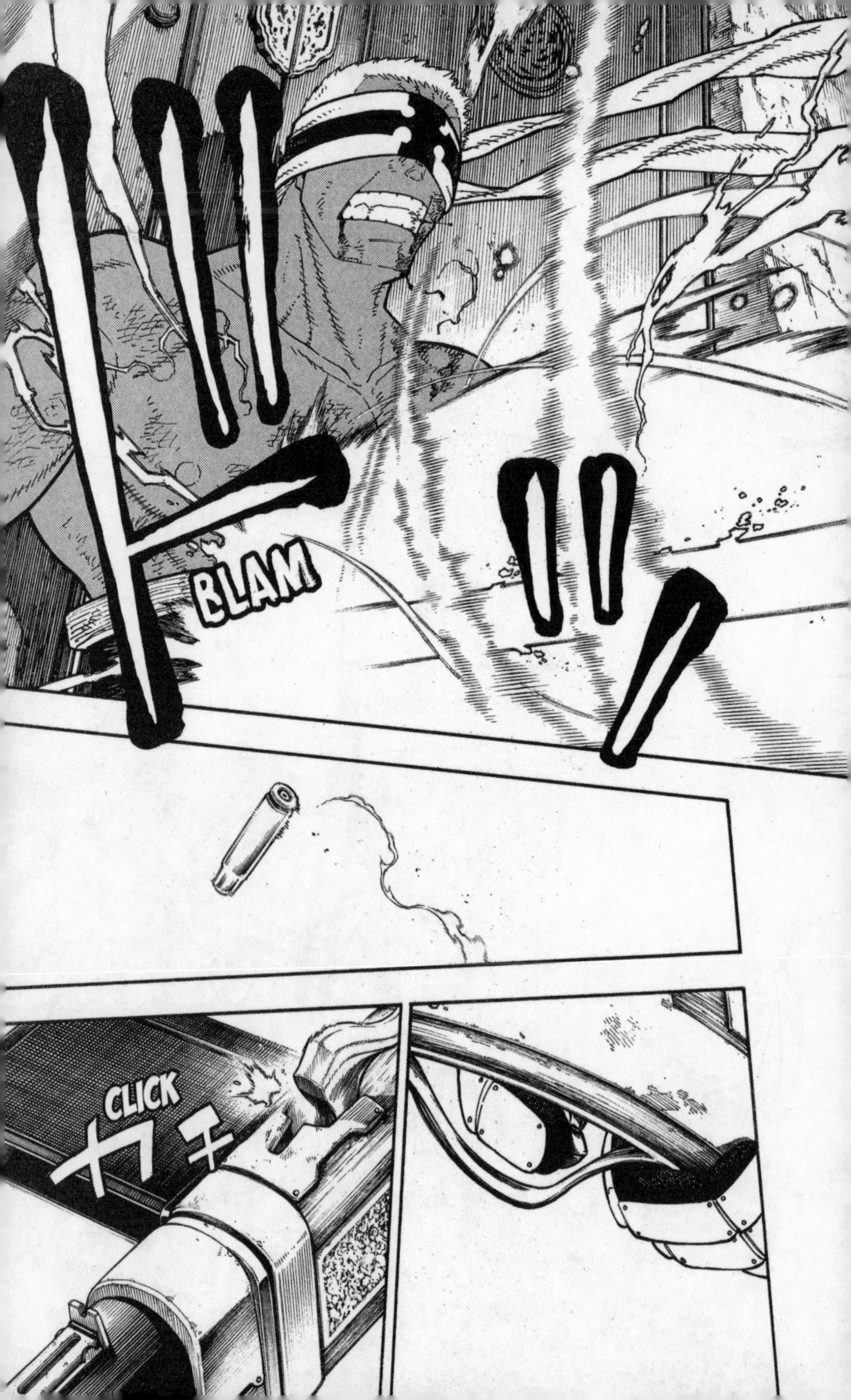
BLAM
CLICK
カチ

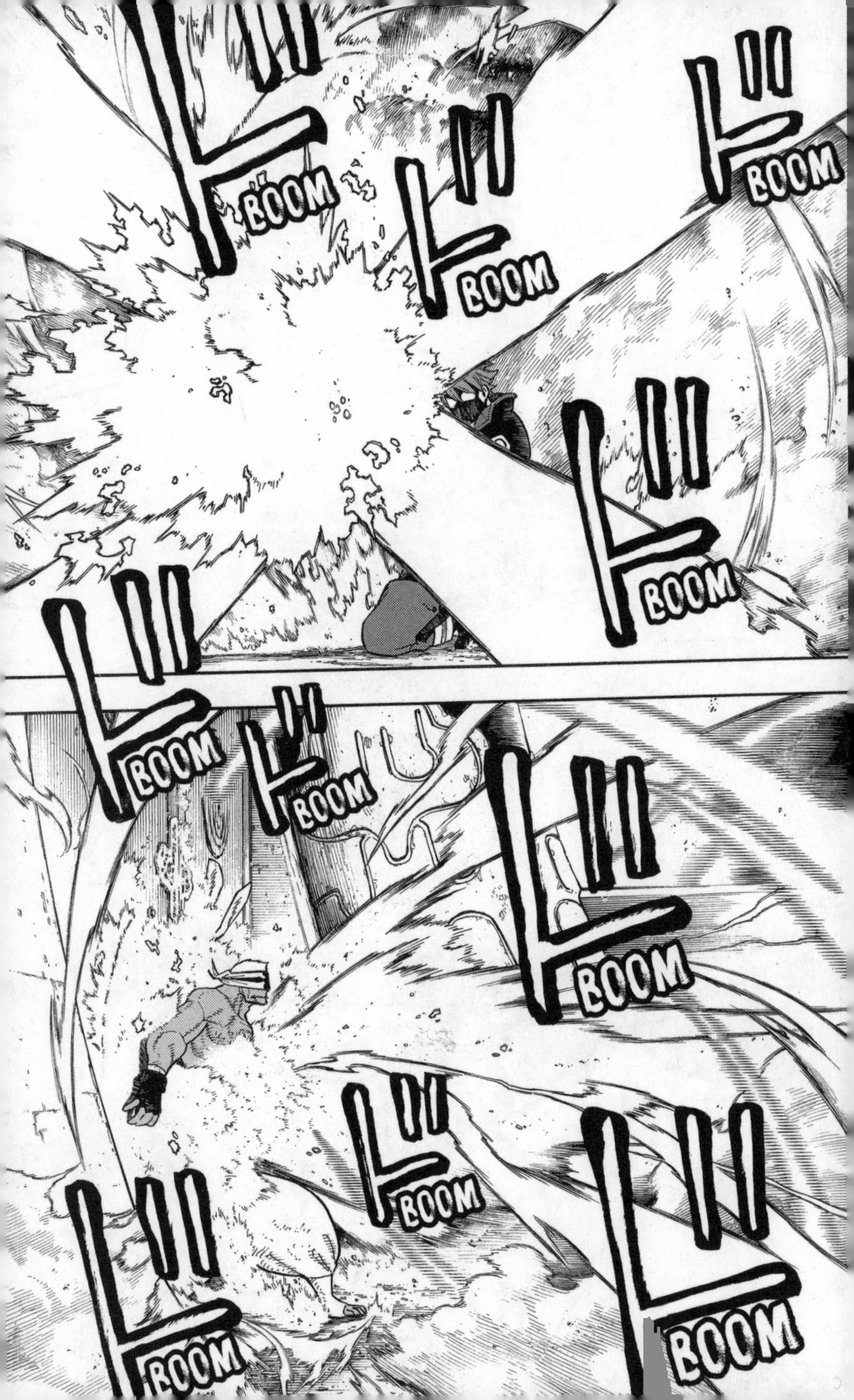
ド BOOM
ド BOOM
ド BOOM
ド BOOM
ド BOOM
ド BOOM
ド BOOM
ド BOOM
ド BOOM
ド BOOM

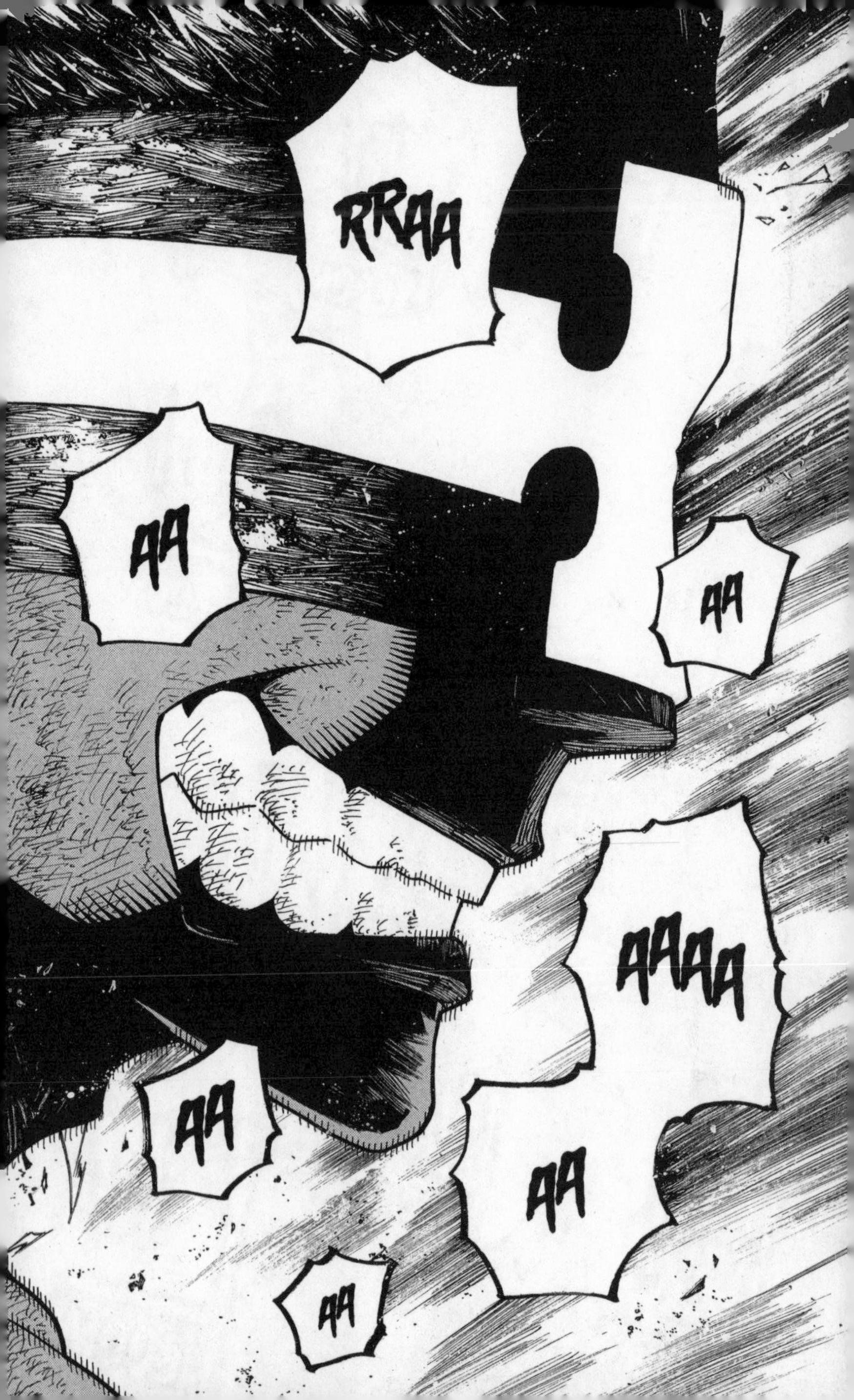
RRAA
AA
AA
AAAA
AA
AA
AA

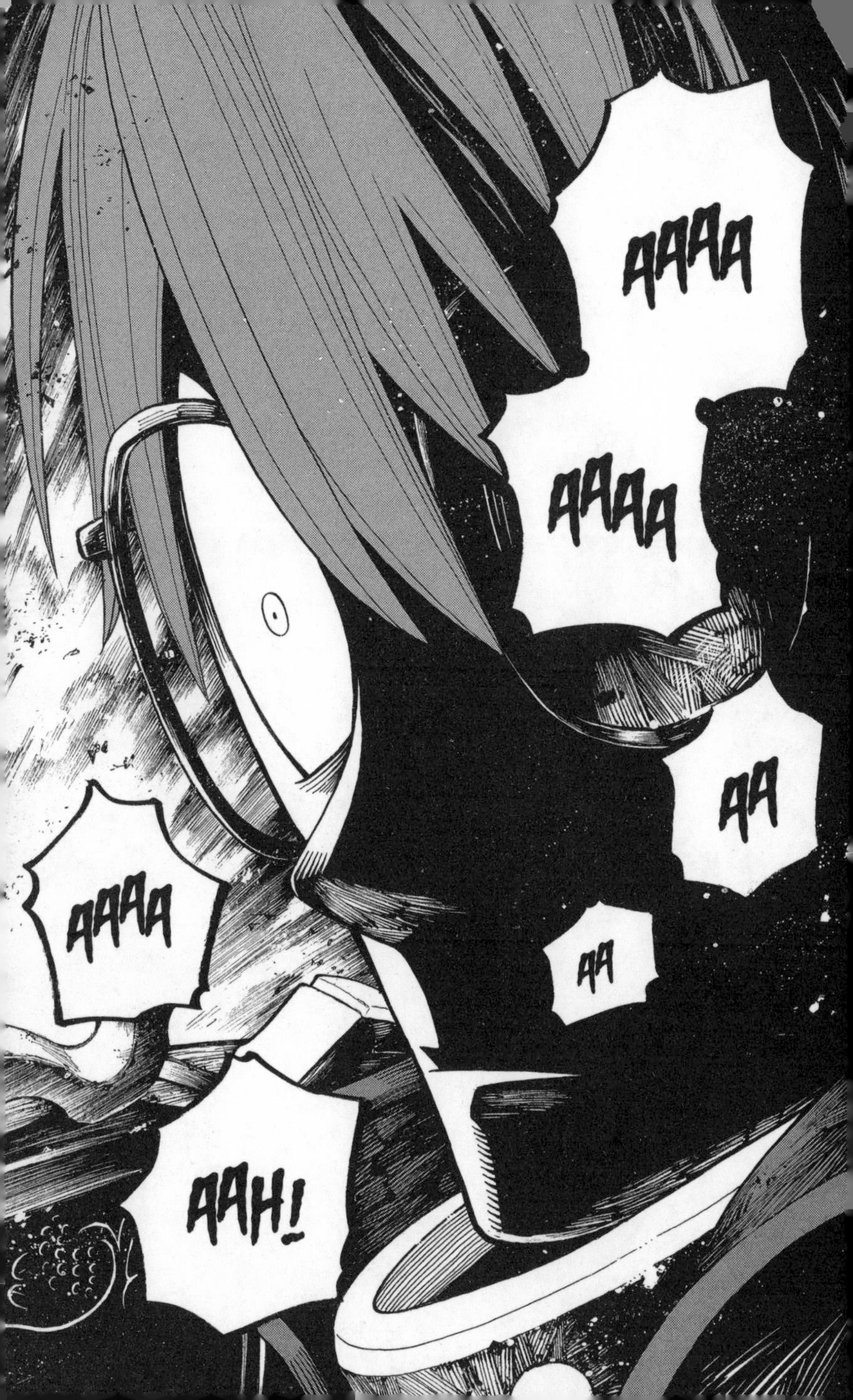
AAAA
AAAA
AA
AA
AAAA
AAH!

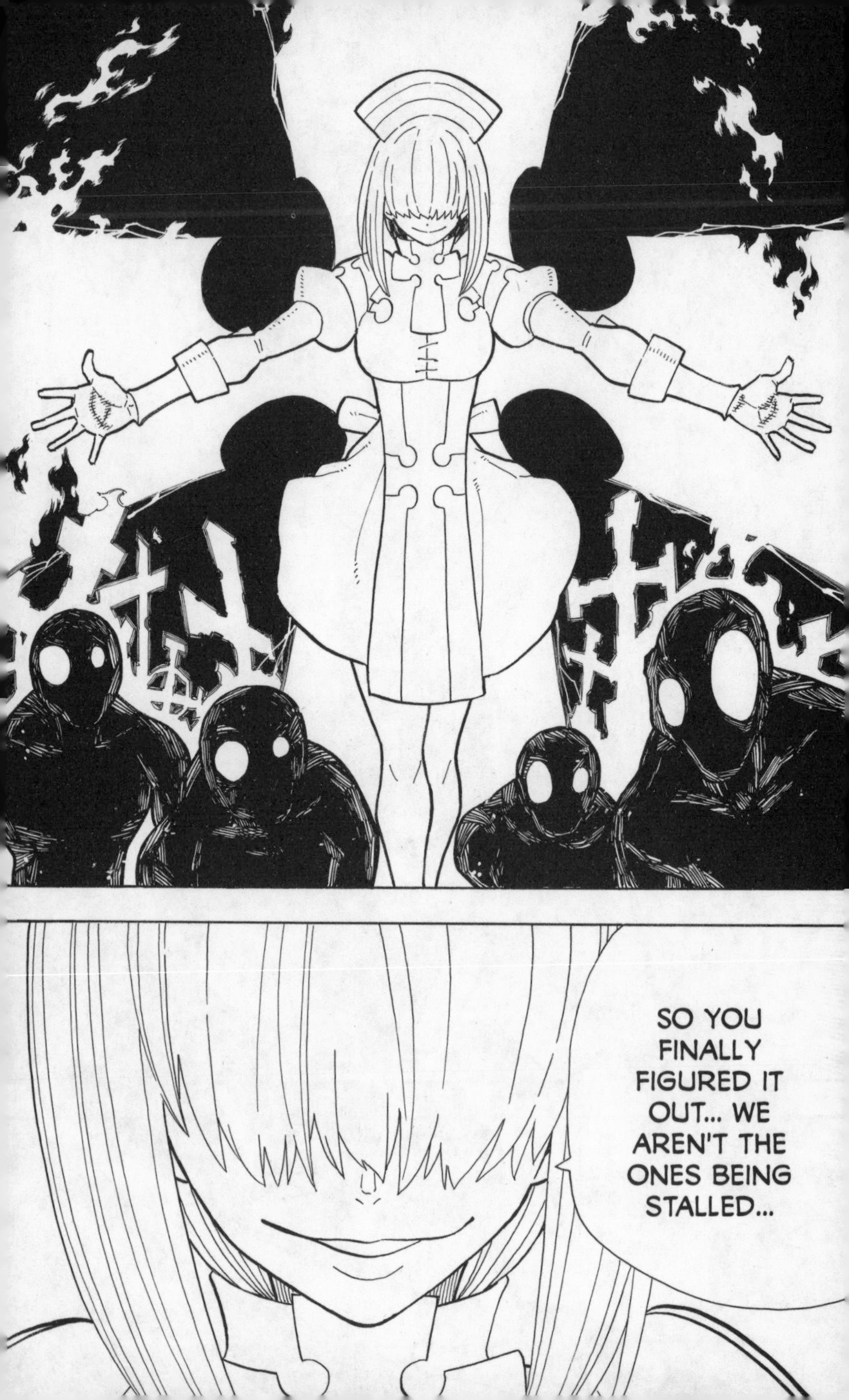
SO YOU FINALLY FIGURED IT OUT... WE AREN'T THE ONES BEING STALLED...

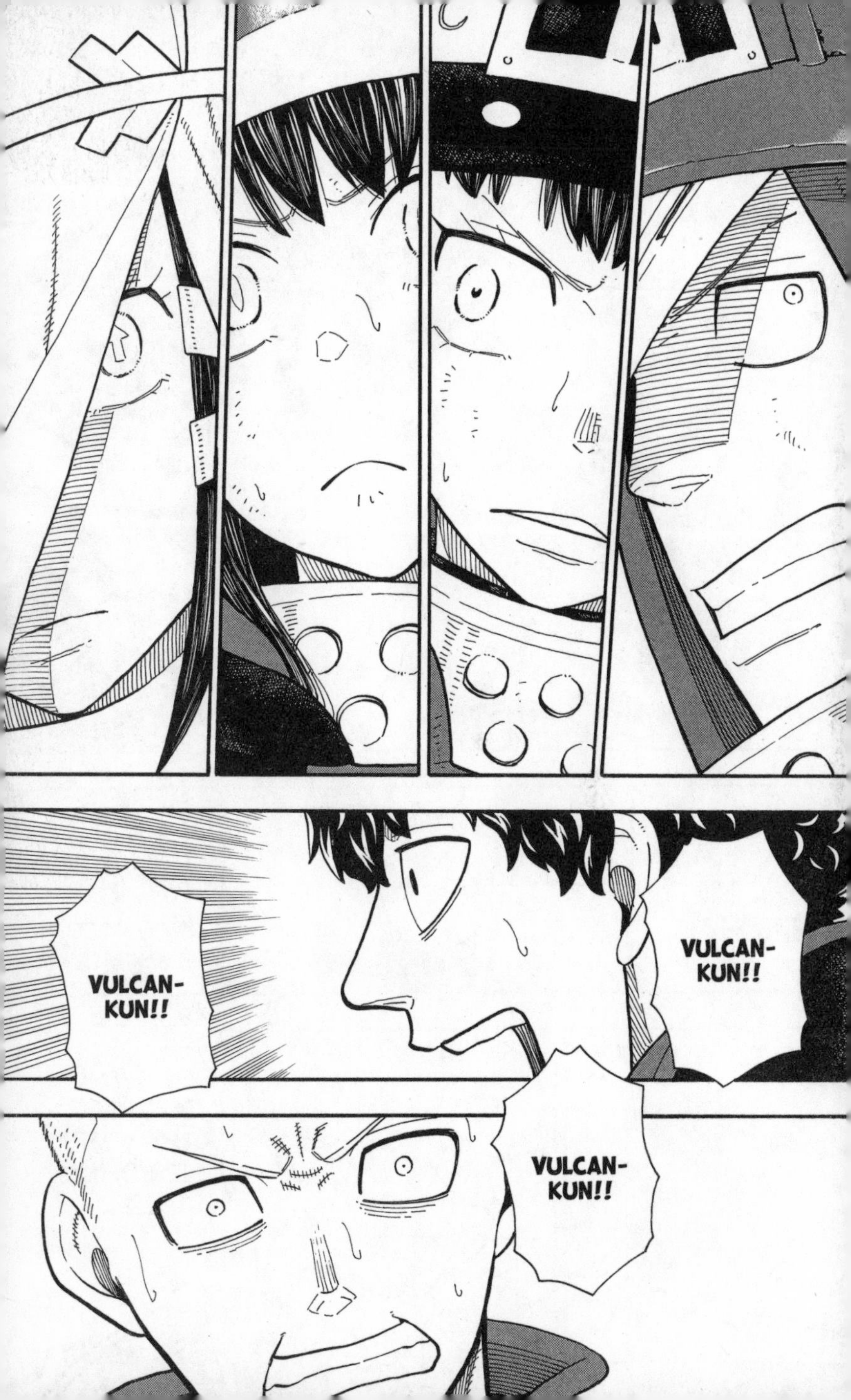
VULCAN-KUN!!
VULCAN-KUN!!
VULCAN-KUN!!

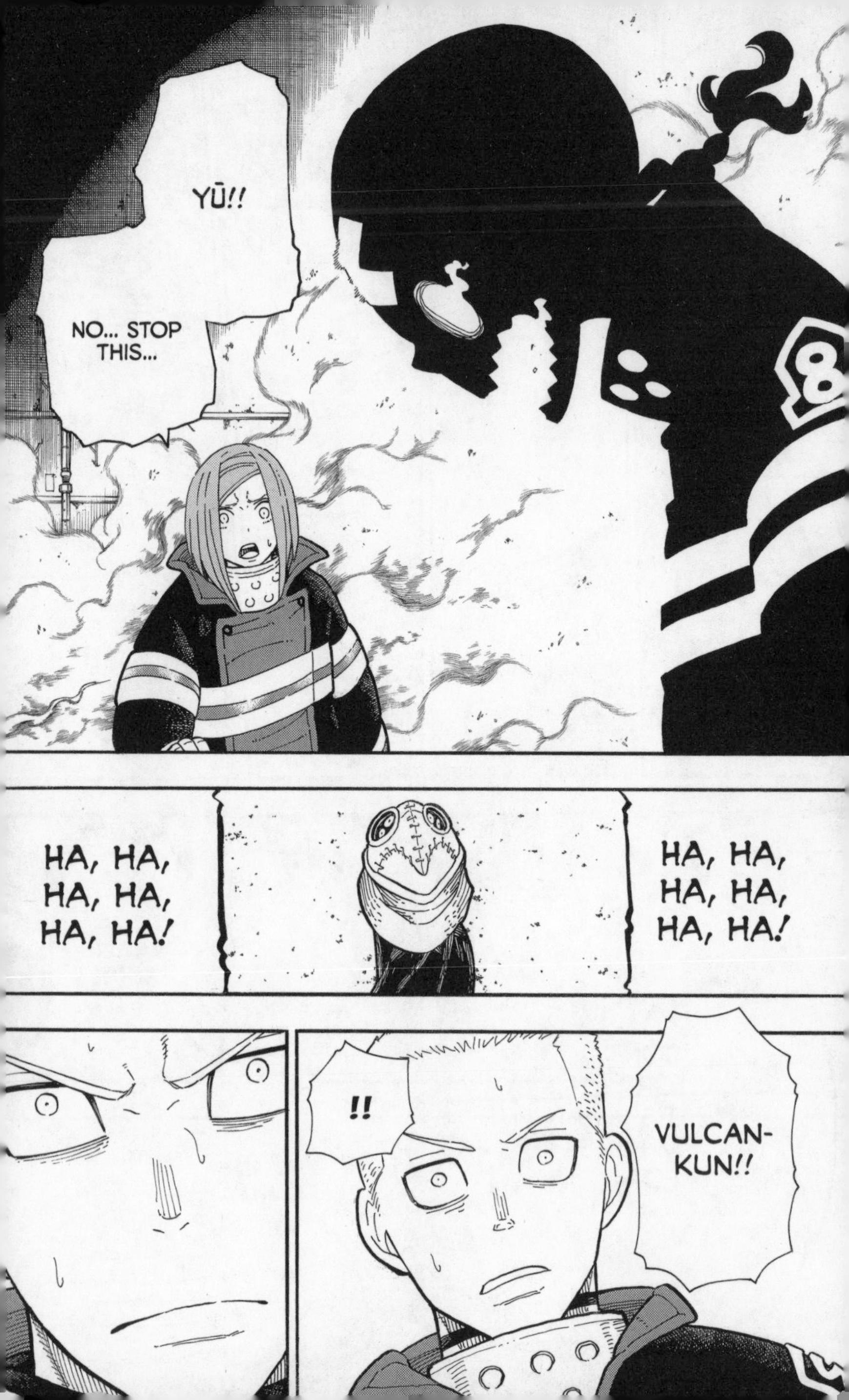
YŪ!!
NO... STOP THIS...
HA, HA, HA, HA, HA, HA!
HA, HA, HA, HA, HA, HA!
VULCAN-KUN!!
!!

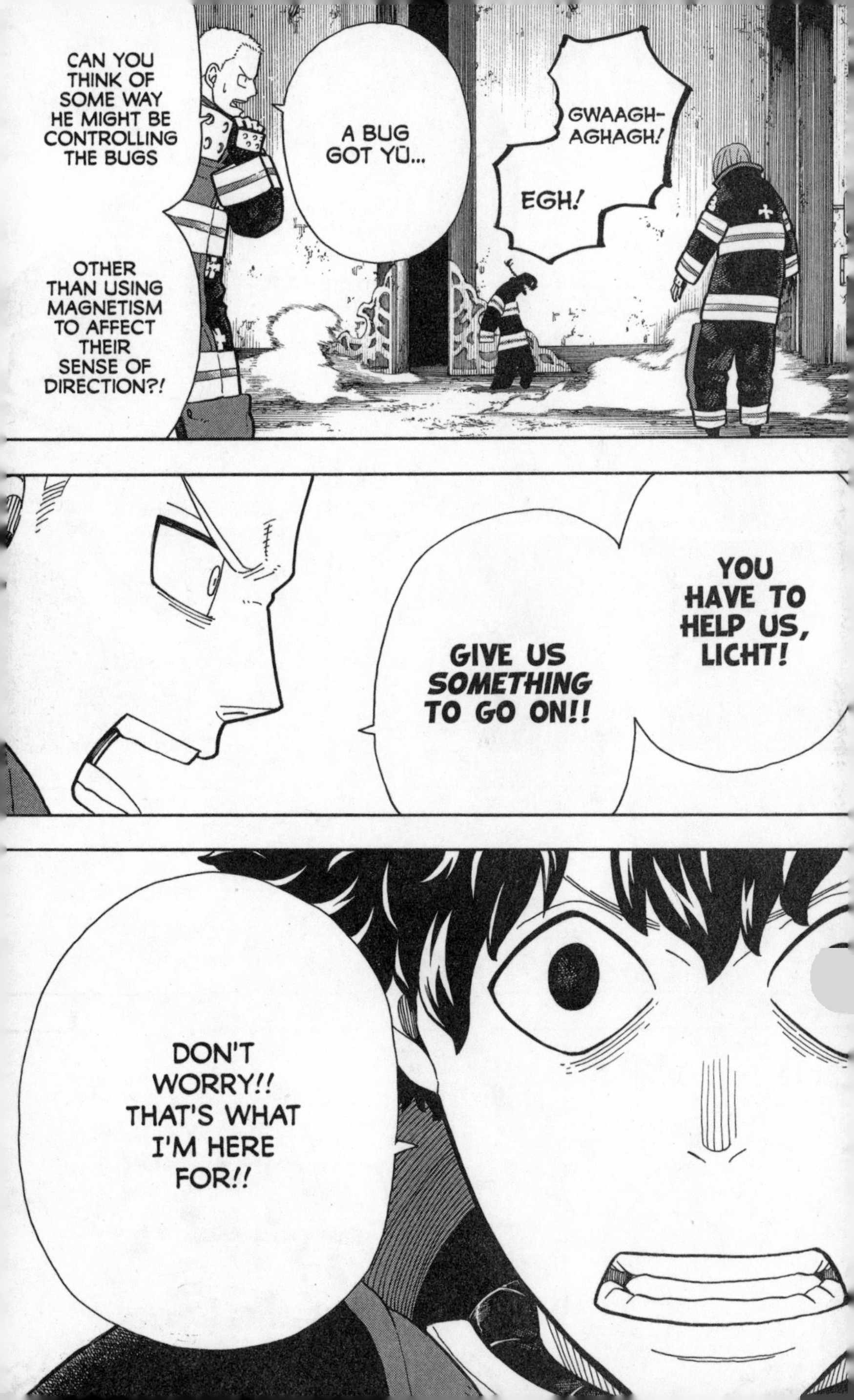
GWAAGH-AGHAGH!
EGH!
A BUG GOT YŪ...
CAN YOU THINK OF SOME WAY HE MIGHT BE CONTROLLING THE BUGS
OTHER THAN USING MAGNETISM TO AFFECT THEIR SENSE OF DIRECTION?!
YOU HAVE TO HELP US, LICHT!
GIVE US SOMETHING TO GO ON!!
DON'T WORRY!! THAT'S WHAT I'M HERE FOR!!

FIRE FORCE

CHAPTER CCXLIX: WAITING ON THE OTHER SIDE OF DESPAIR

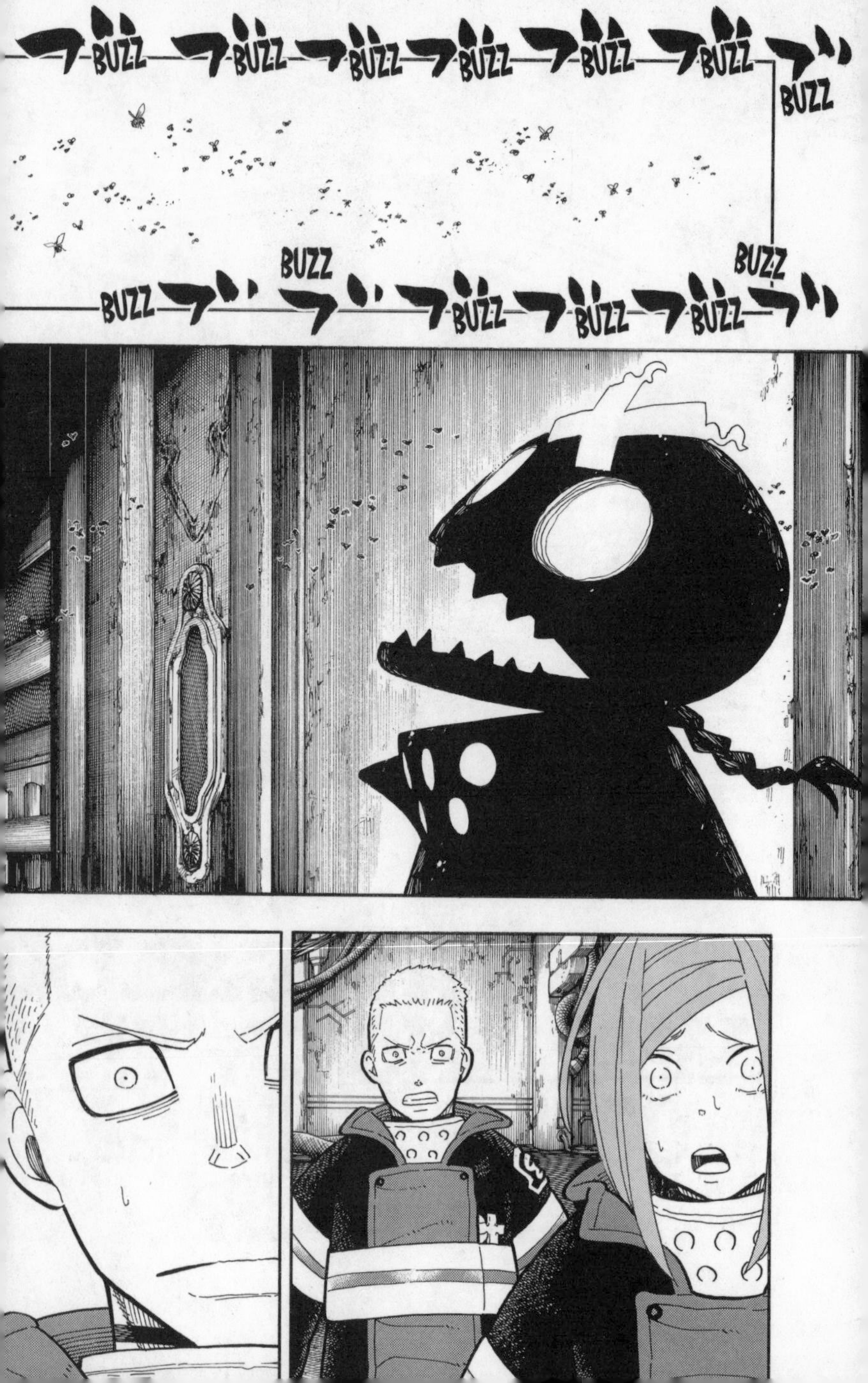
BUZZ BUZZ BUZZ BUZZ BUZZ BUZZ BUZZ
BUZZ BUZZ BUZZ BUZZ BUZZ BUZZ

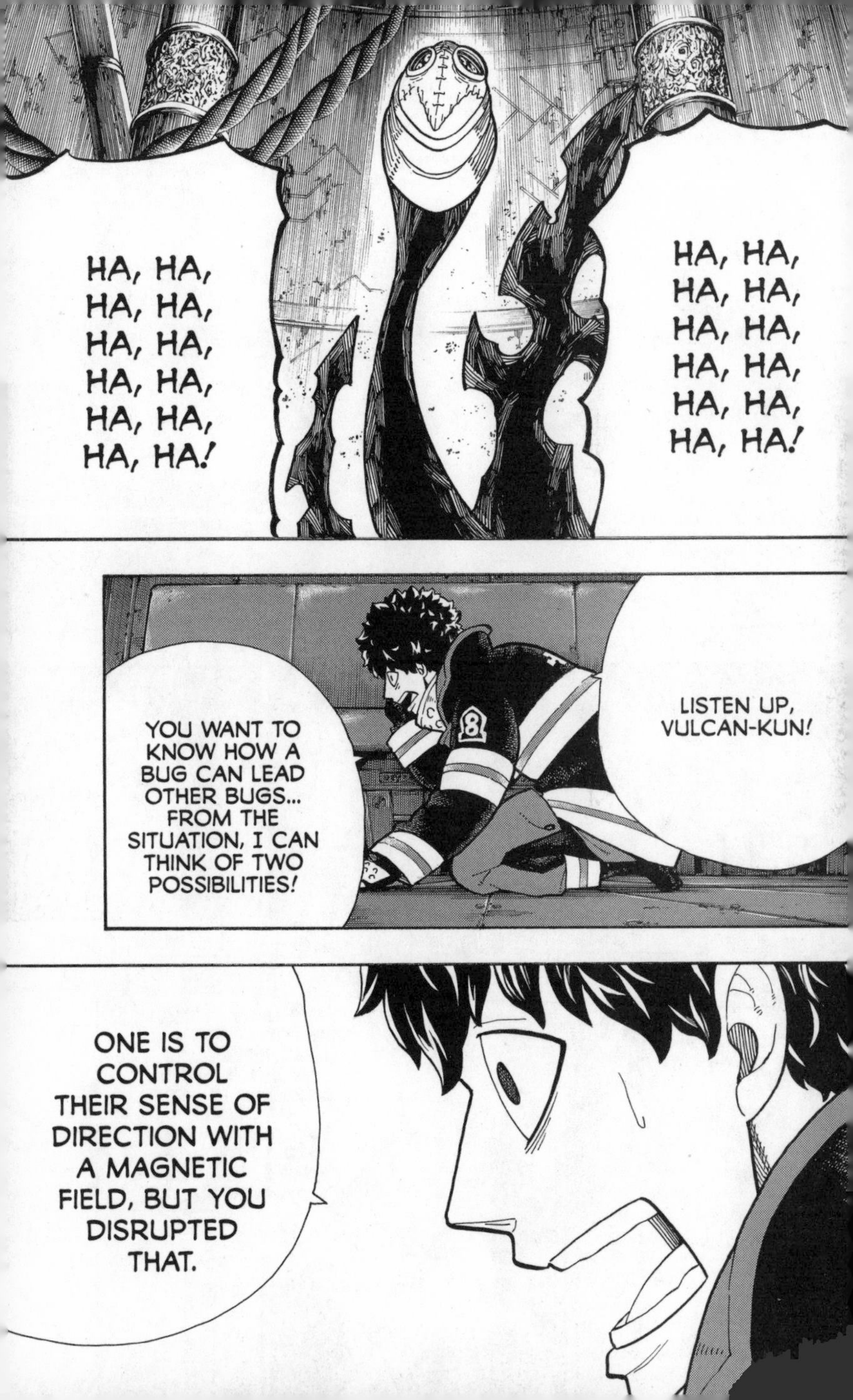
HA, HA, HA, HA, HA, HA, HA, HA, HA, HA, HA, HA!
HA, HA, HA, HA, HA, HA, HA, HA, HA, HA, HA, HA!
LISTEN UP, VULCAN-KUN!
YOU WANT TO KNOW HOW A BUG CAN LEAD OTHER BUGS... FROM THE SITUATION, I CAN THINK OF TWO POSSIBILITIES!
ONE IS TO CONTROL THEIR SENSE OF DIRECTION WITH A MAGNETIC FIELD, BUT YOU DISRUPTED THAT.

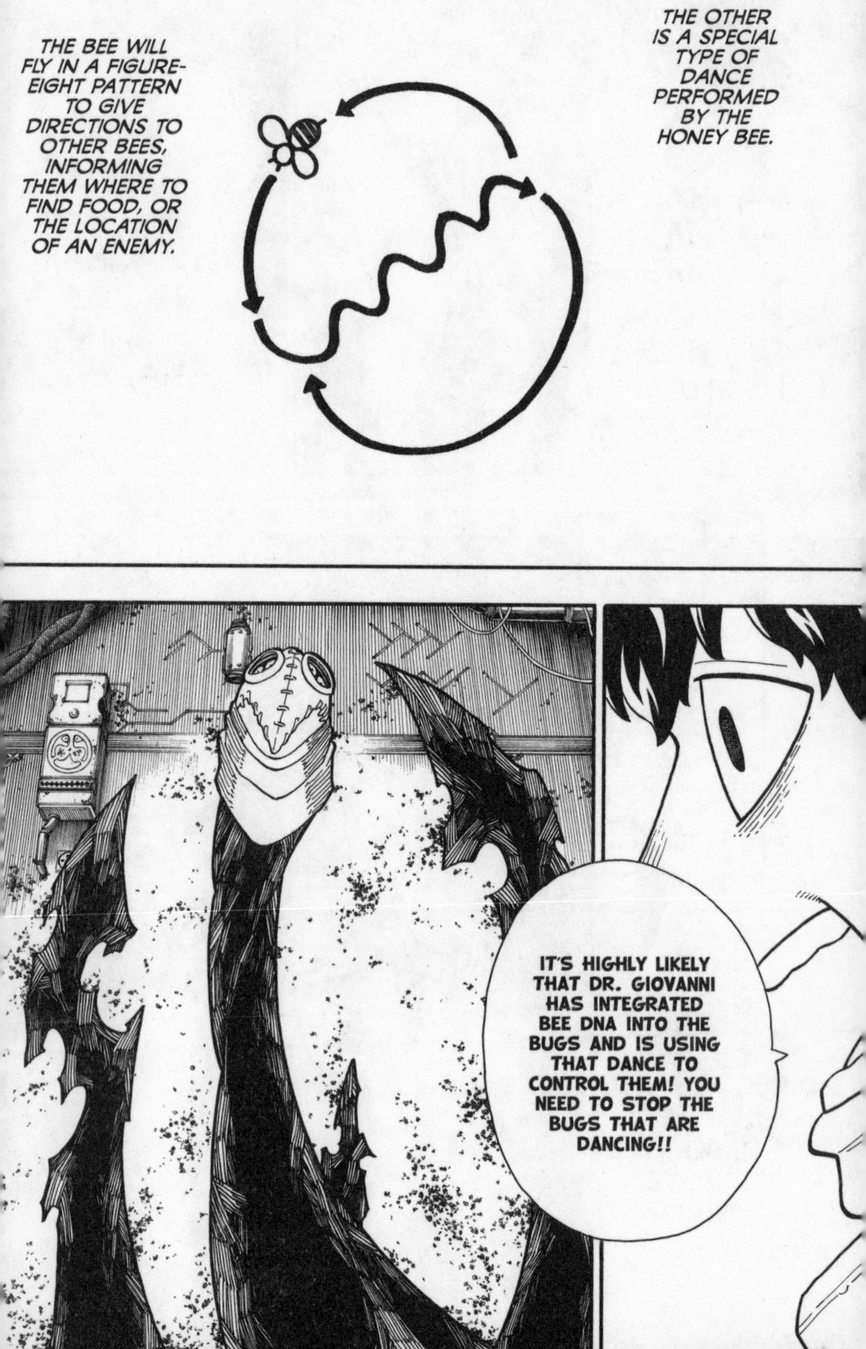
THE OTHER IS A SPECIAL TYPE OF DANCE PERFORMED BY THE HONEY BEE.
THE BEE WILL FLY IN A FIGURE-EIGHT PATTERN TO GIVE DIRECTIONS TO OTHER BEES, INFORMING THEM WHERE TO FIND FOOD, OR THE LOCATION OF AN ENEMY.
IT'S HIGHLY LIKELY THAT DR. GIOVANNI HAS INTEGRATED BEE DNA INTO THE BUGS AND IS USING THAT DANCE TO CONTROL THEM! YOU NEED TO STOP THE BUGS THAT ARE DANCING!!

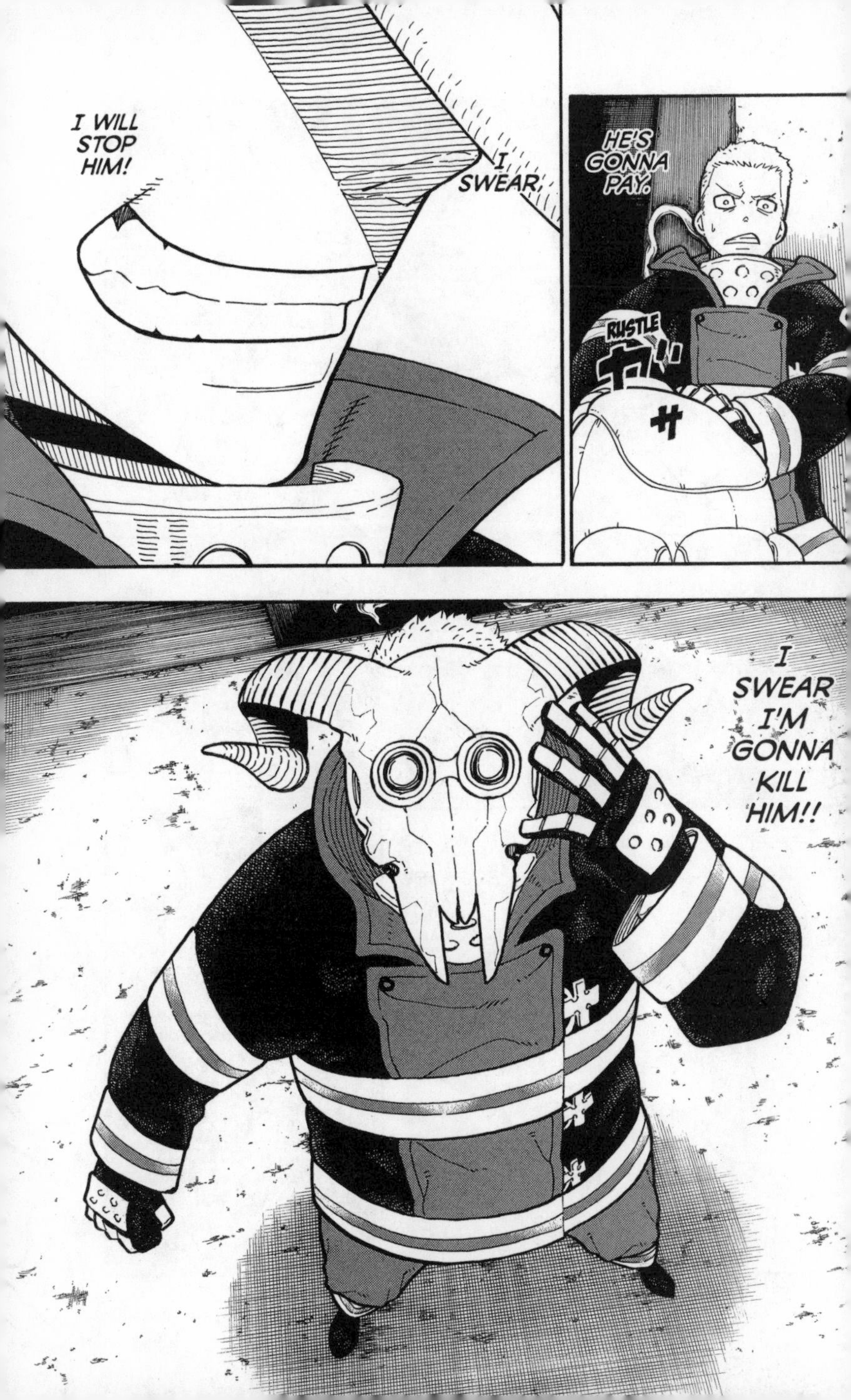
HE'S GONNA PAY.
RUSTLE
I WILL STOP HIM!
I SWEAR.
I SWEAR I'M GONNA KILL HIM!!

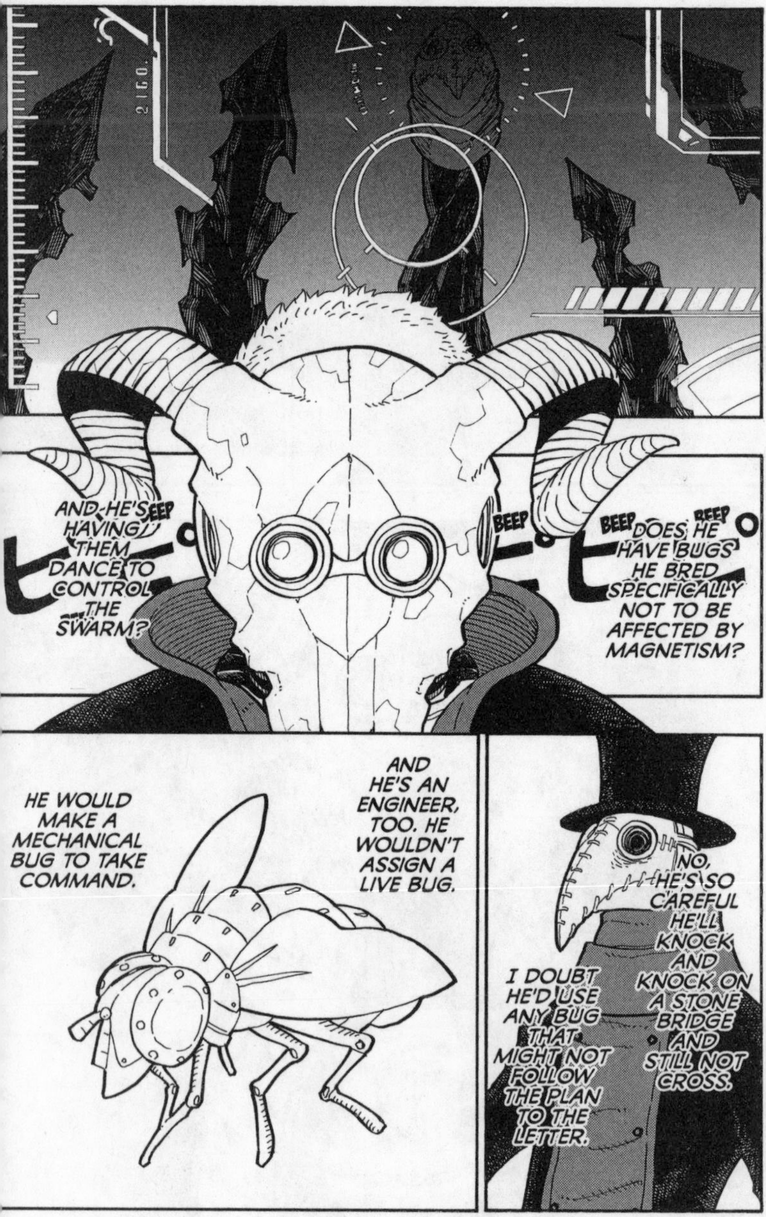
BEEP
BEEP
DOES HE HAVE BUGS HE BRED SPECIFICALLY NOT TO BE AFFECTED BY MAGNETISM?
BEEP
BEEP
AND HE'S HAVING THEM DANCE TO CONTROL THE SWARM?
NO, HE'S SO CAREFUL HE'LL KNOCK AND KNOCK ON A STONE BRIDGE AND STILL NOT CROSS.
I DOUBT HE'D USE ANY BUG THAT MIGHT NOT FOLLOW THE PLAN TO THE LETTER.
AND HE'S AN ENGINEER, TOO. HE WOULDN'T ASSIGN A LIVE BUG.
HE WOULD MAKE A MECHANICAL BUG TO TAKE COMMAND.

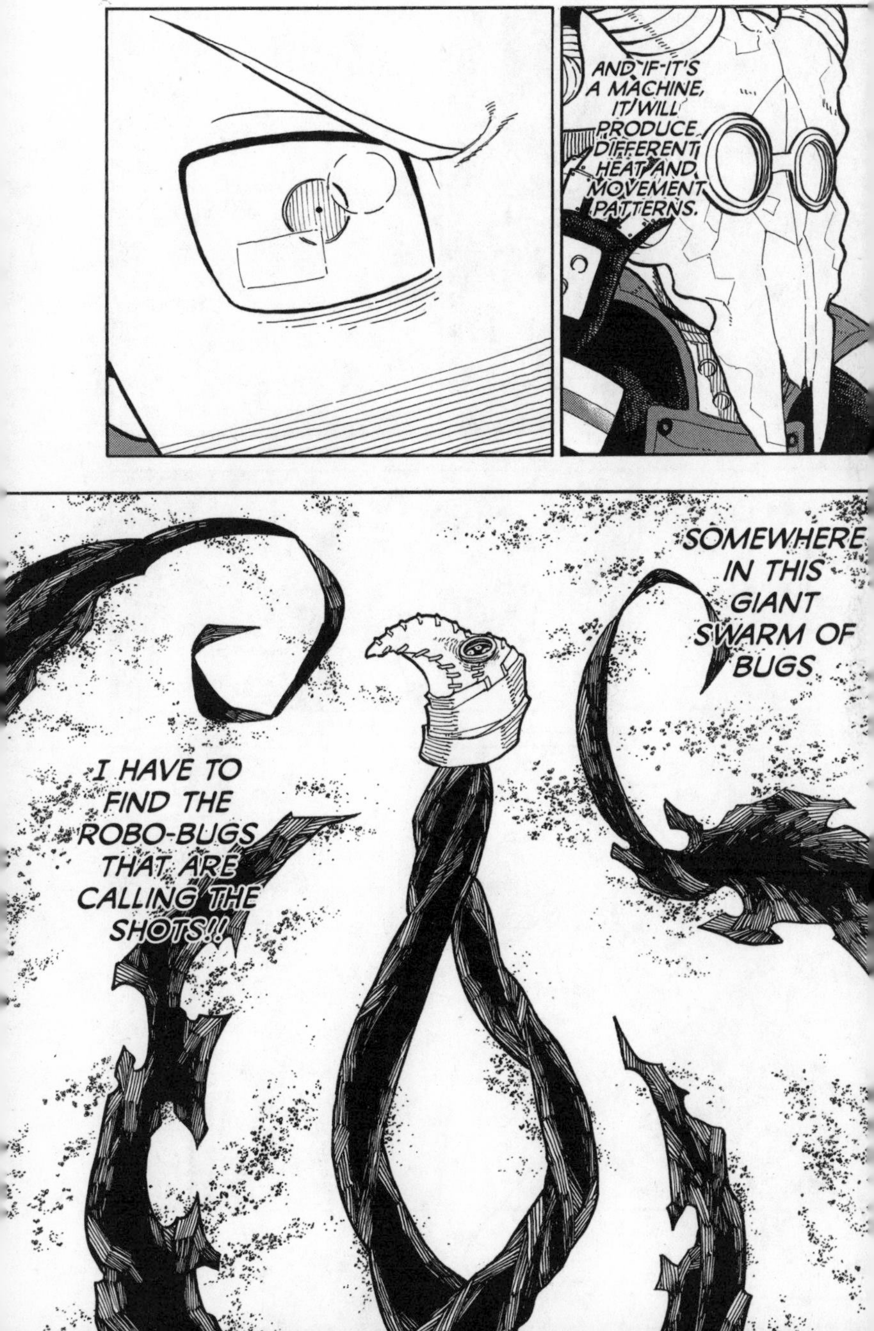
AND IF IT'S A MACHINE, IT WILL PRODUCE DIFFERENT HEAT AND MOVEMENT PATTERNS.
SOMEWHERE IN THIS GIANT SWARM OF BUGS
I HAVE TO FIND THE ROBO-BUGS THAT ARE CALLING THE SHOTS!!

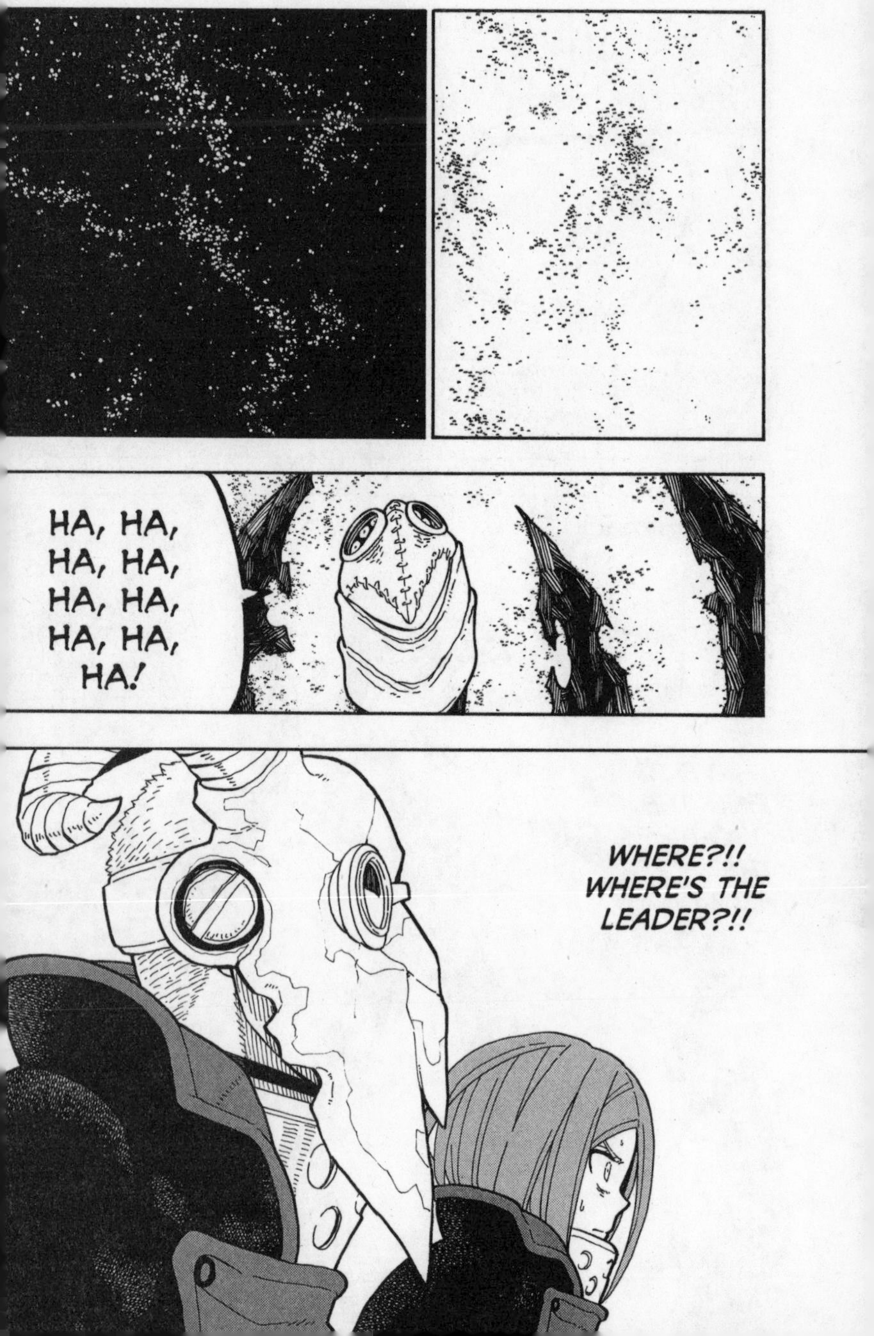
HA, HA, HA, HA, HA, HA, HA, HA, HA!
WHERE?!! WHERE'S THE LEADER?!!

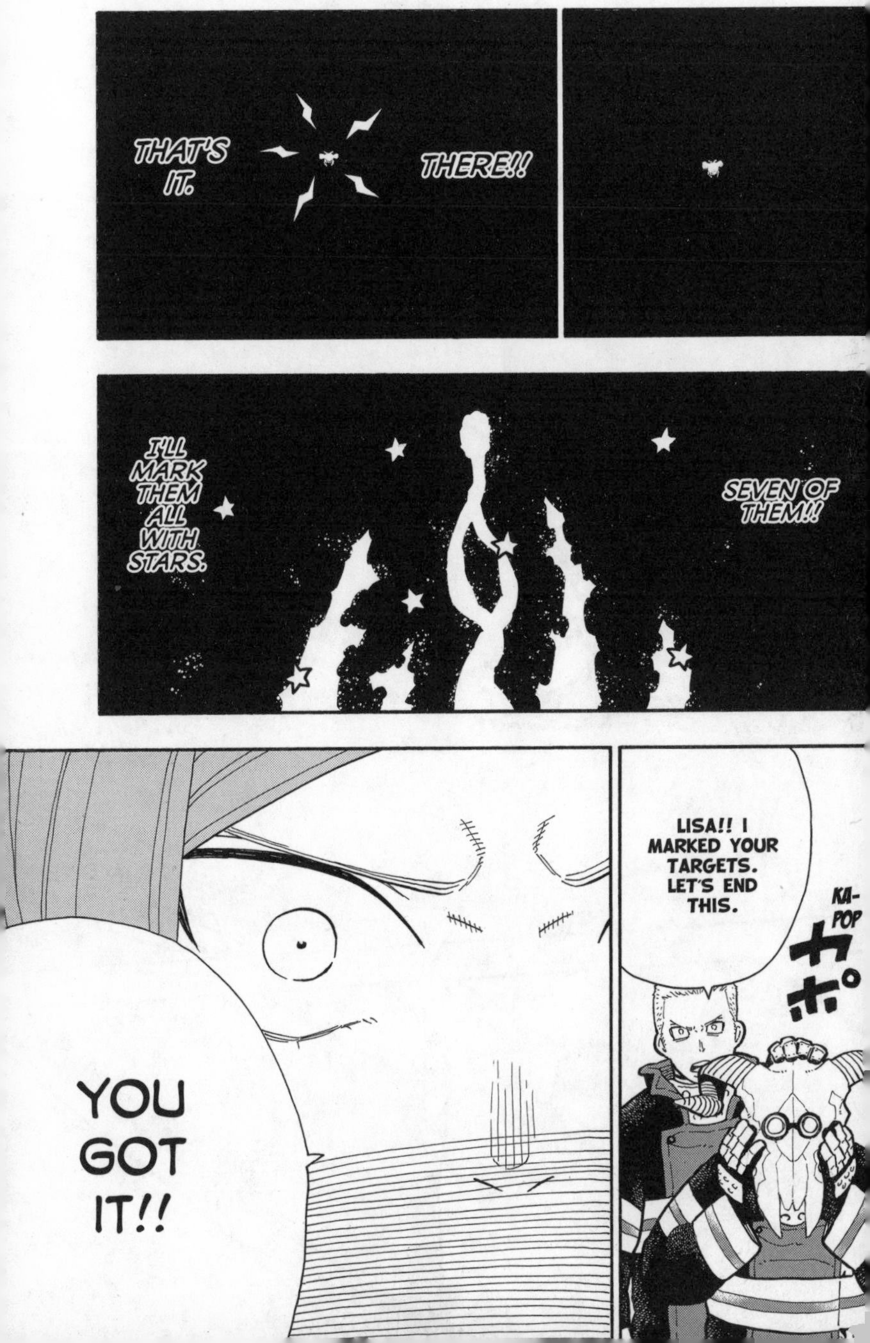
THAT'S IT.
THERE!!
SEVEN OF THEM!!
I'LL MARK THEM ALL WITH STARS.
LISA!! I MARKED YOUR TARGETS. LET'S END THIS.
KA-POP
YOU GOT IT!!

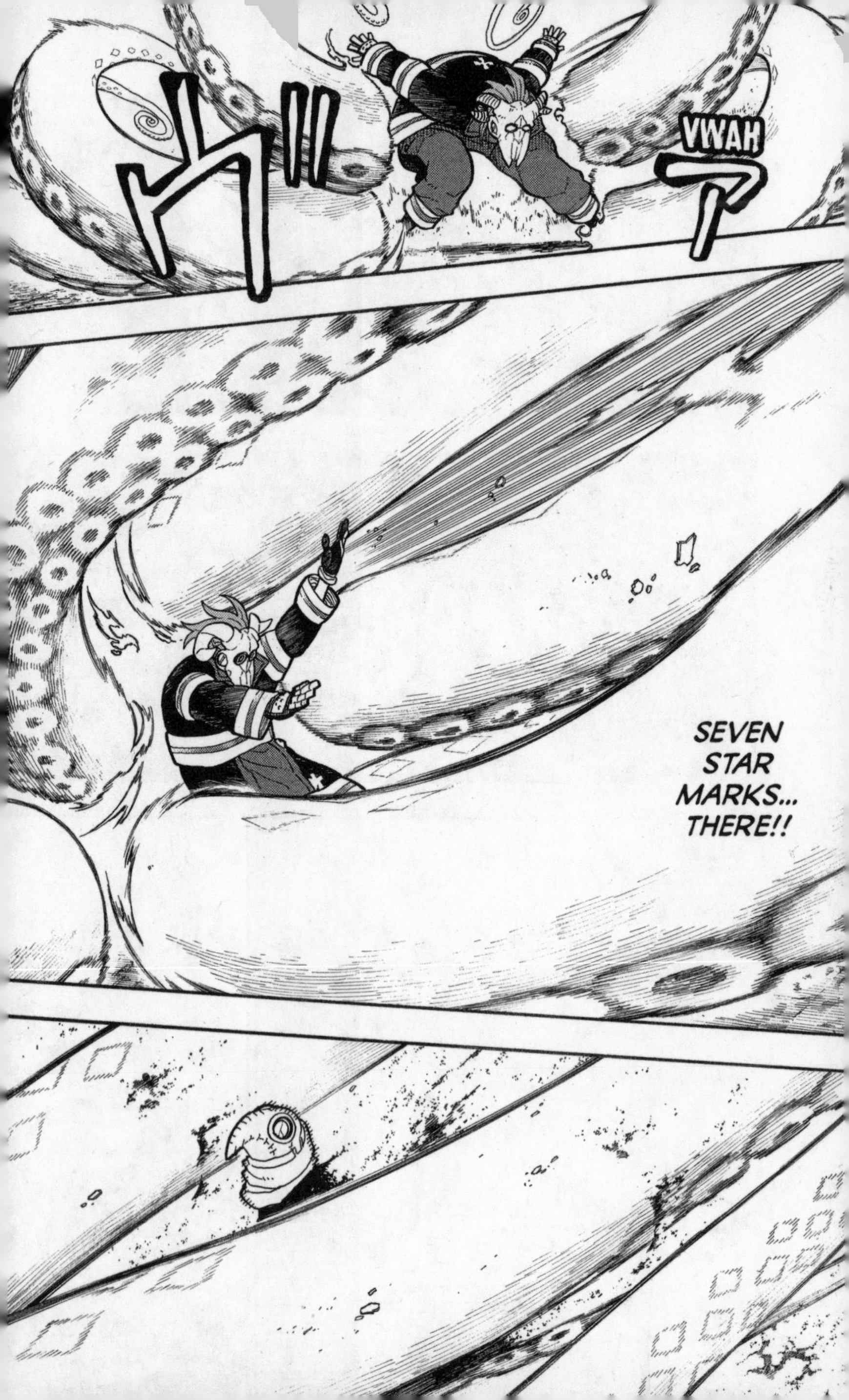
VWAH
SEVEN STAR MARKS... THERE!!

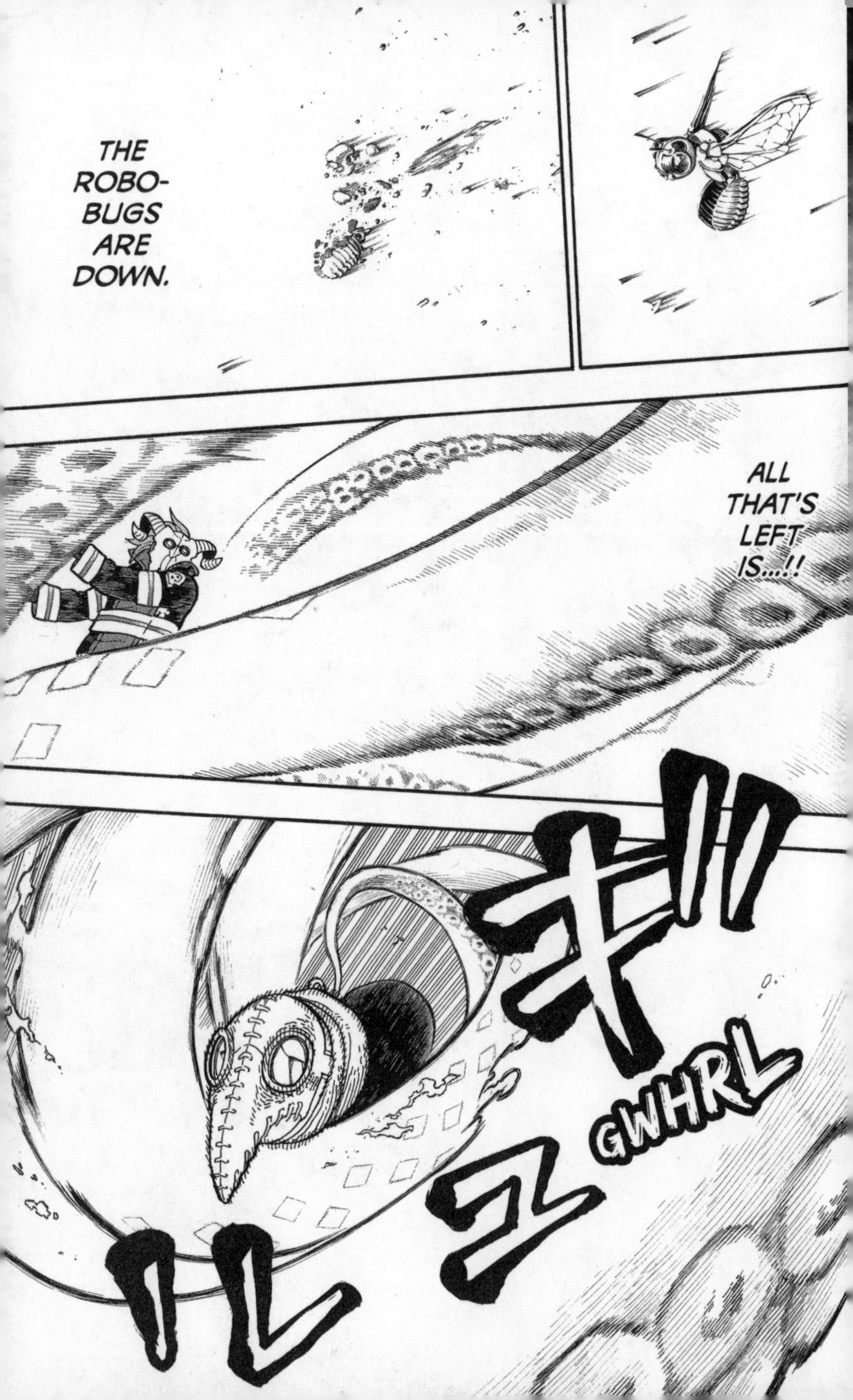
THE ROBO-BUGS ARE DOWN.
ALL THAT'S LEFT IS...!!
ギュルン
GWHRL

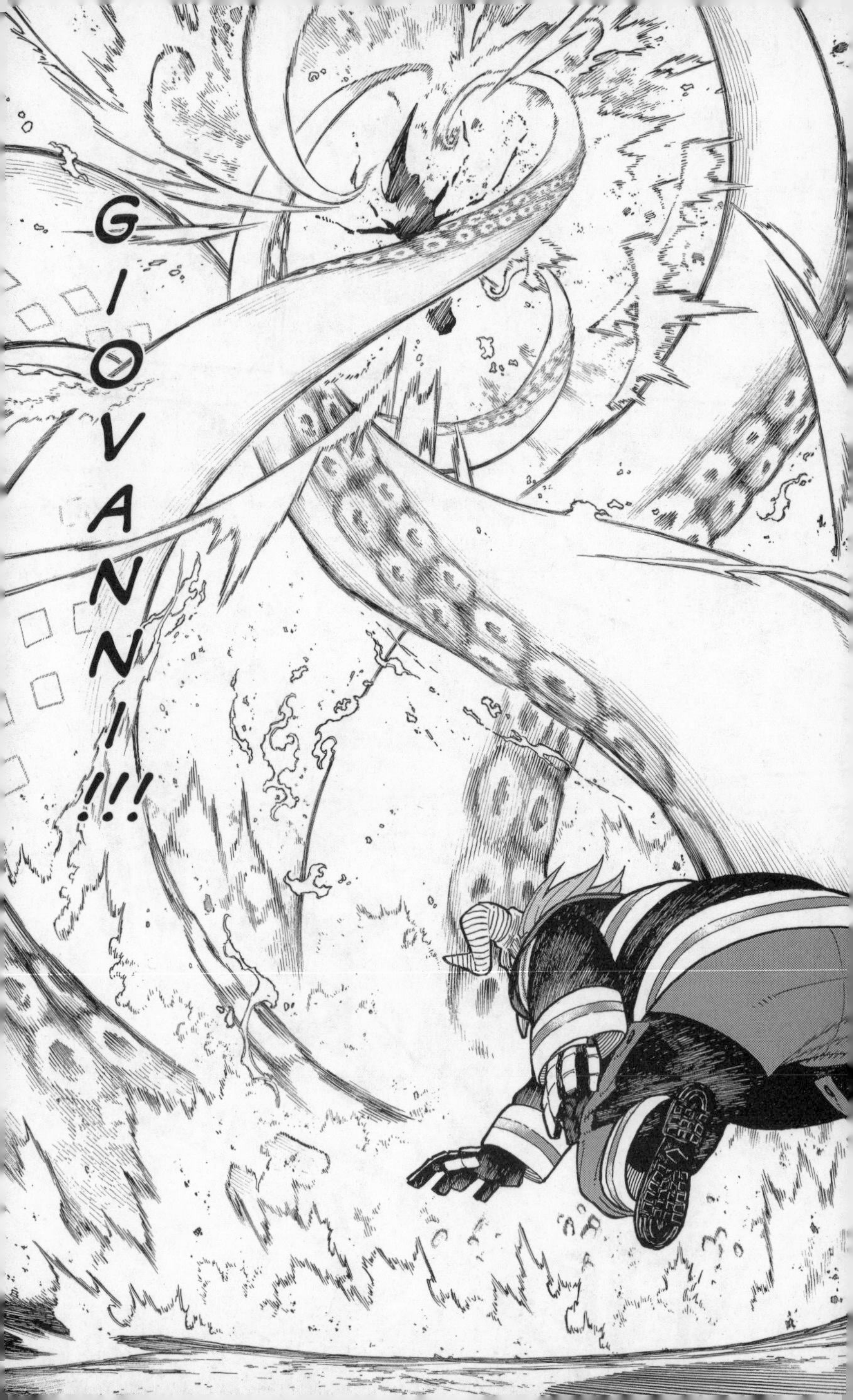
GIOVANNI!!!

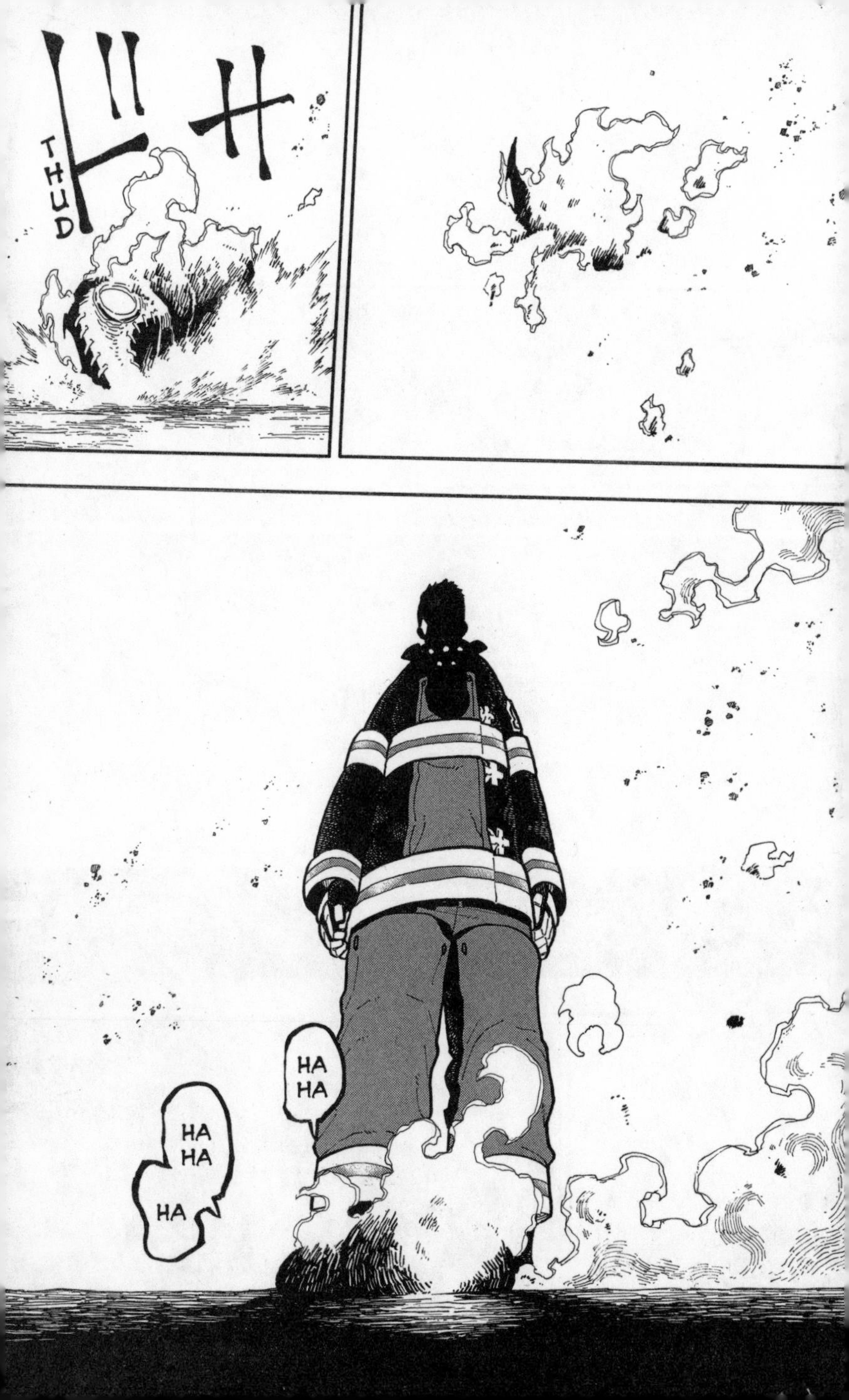
ドサ
THUD
HA HA
HA HA
HA

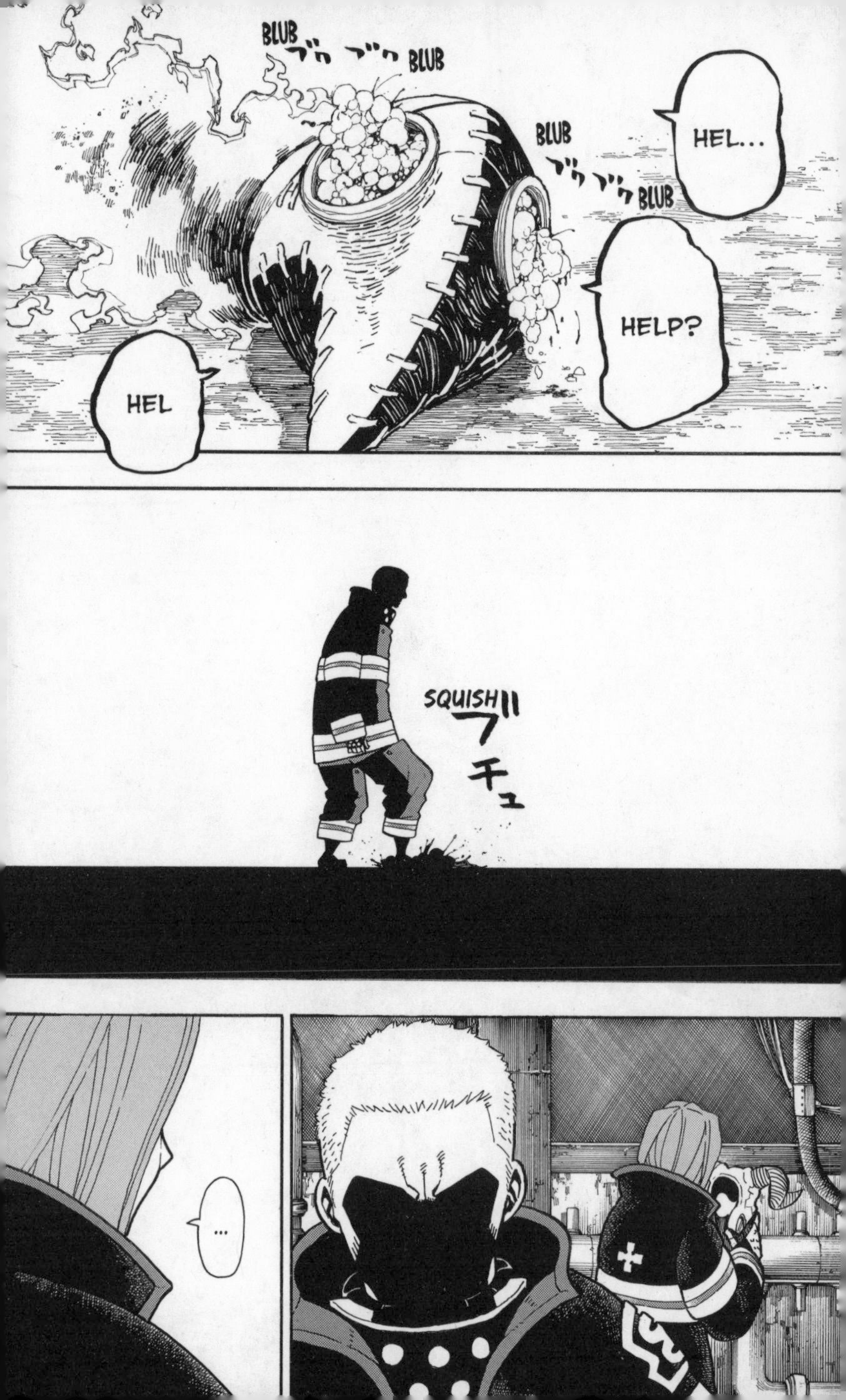
HEL...
BLUB BLUB
BLUB ブク ブク BLUB
HELP?
HEL
SQUISH
ブチュ
...

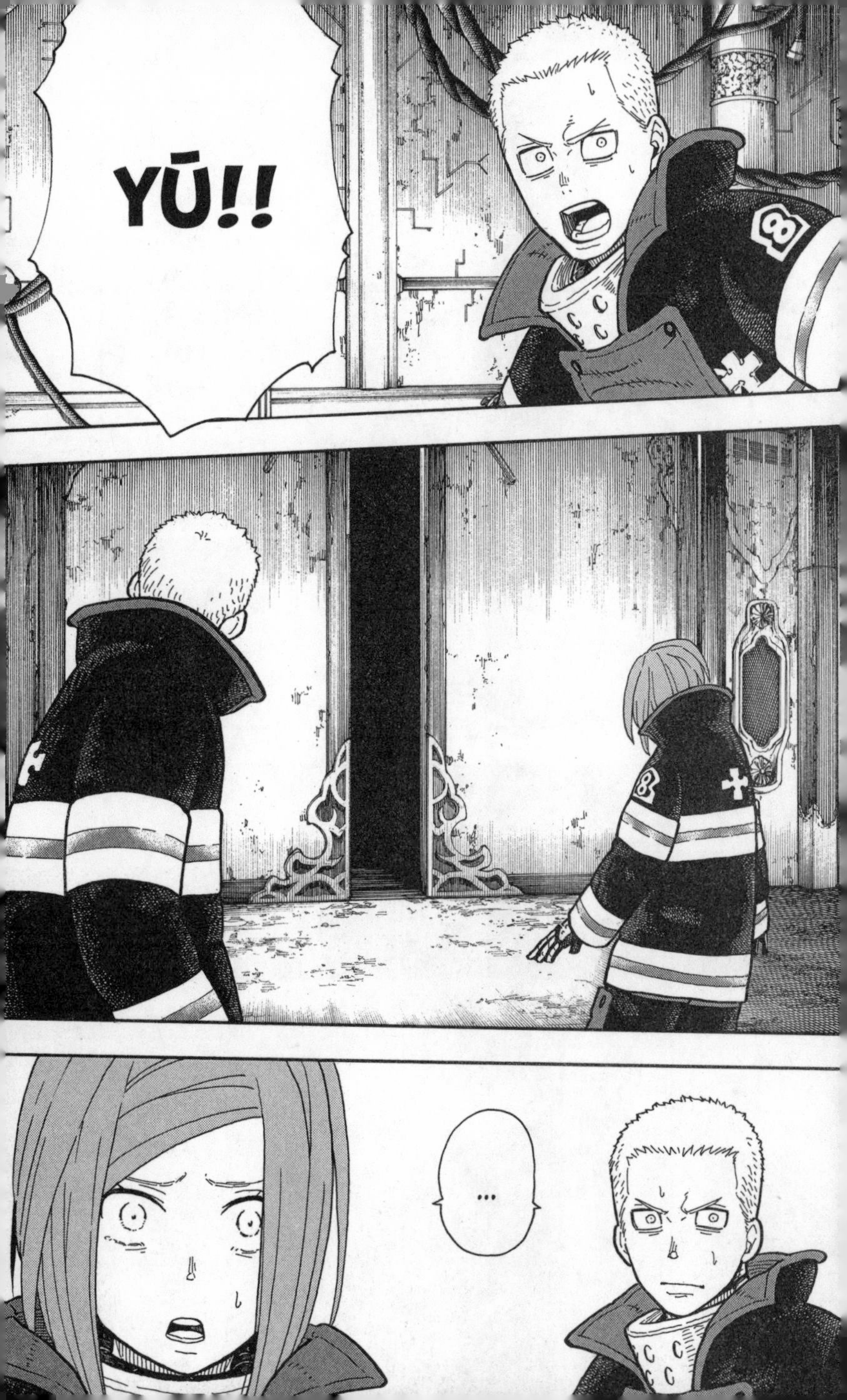
YŪ!!
...

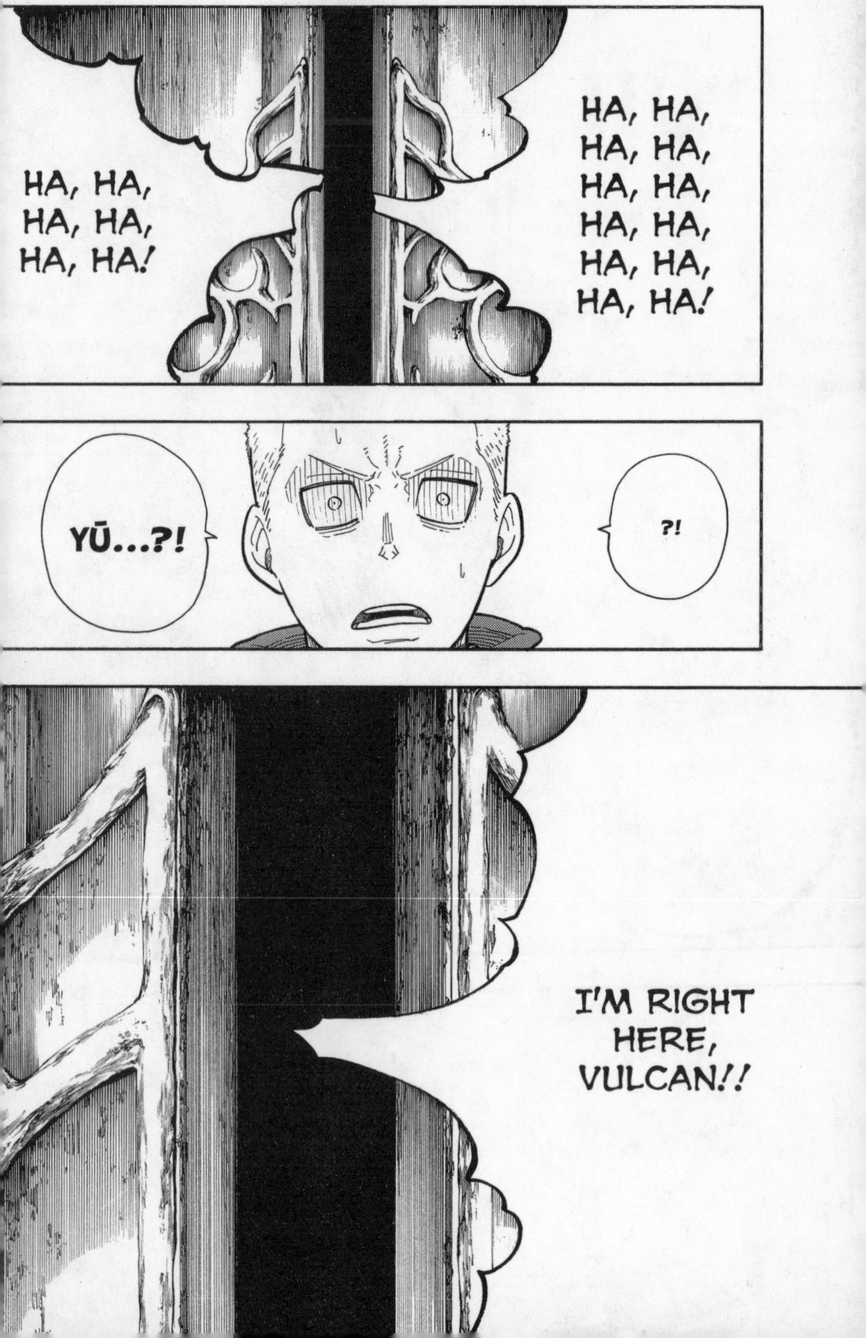
HA, HA, HA, HA, HA, HA, HA, HA, HA, HA, HA, HA!
HA, HA, HA, HA, HA, HA!
?!
YŪ...?!
I'M RIGHT HERE, VULCAN!!

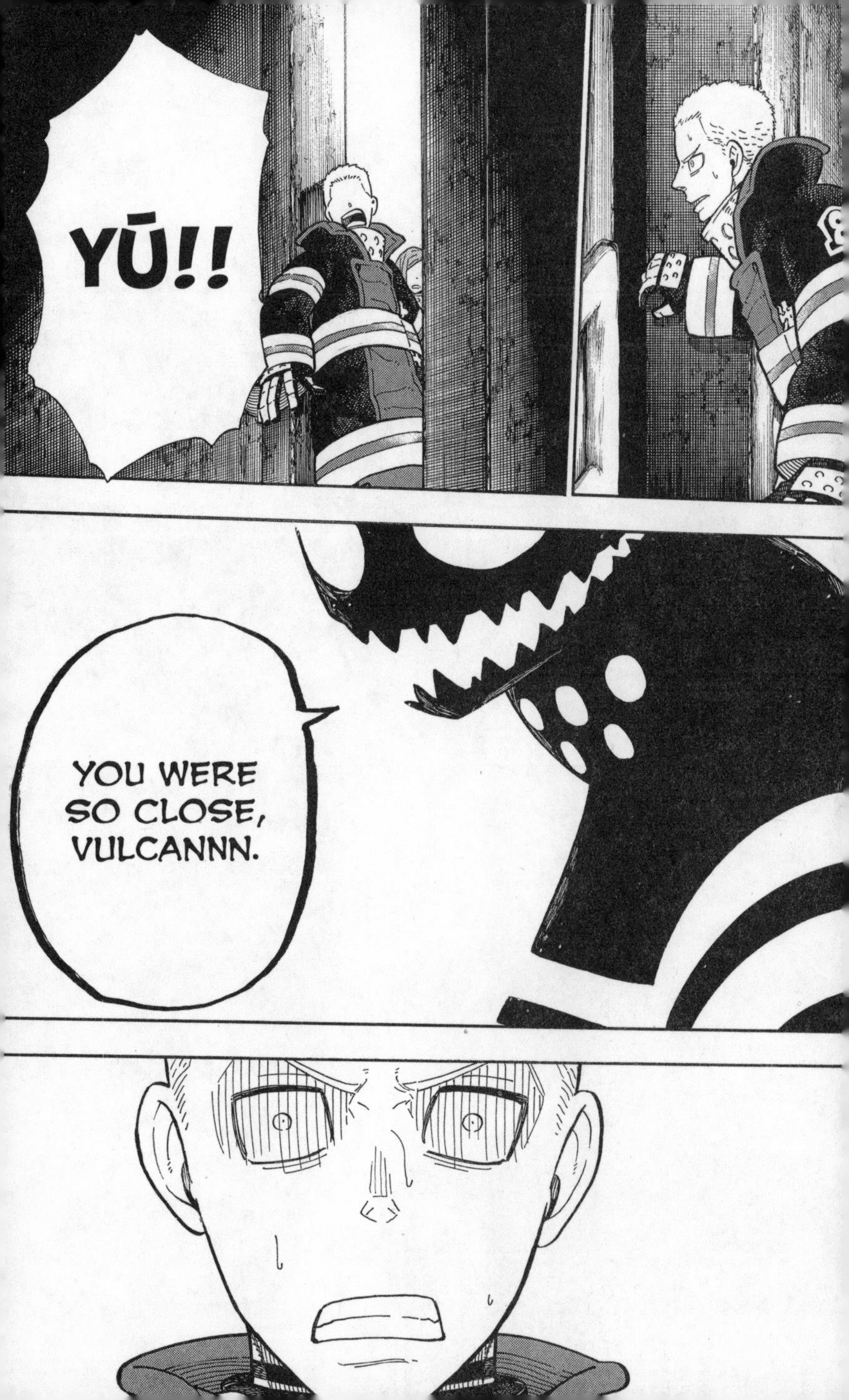
YŪ!!
YOU WERE SO CLOSE, VULCANNN.

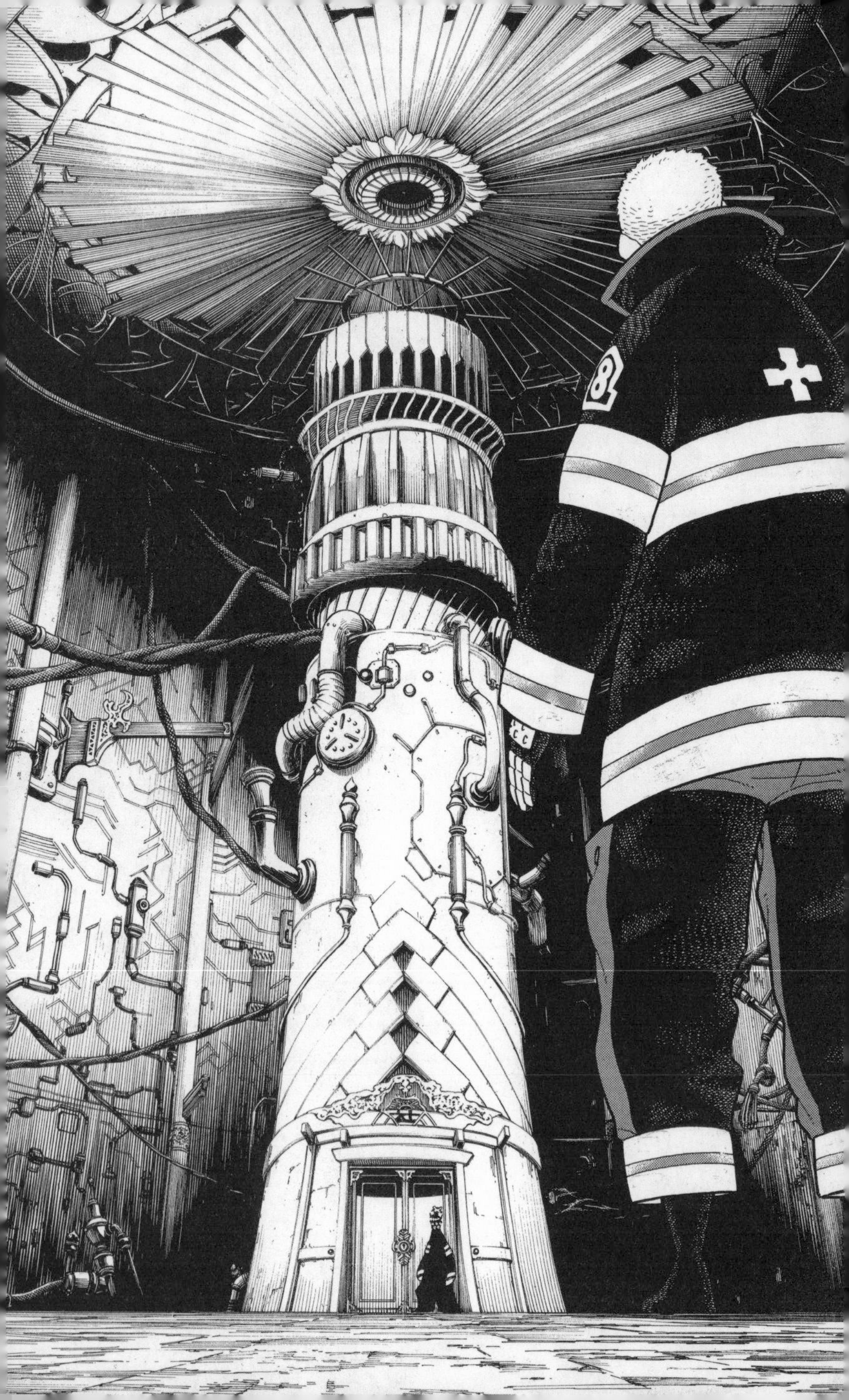

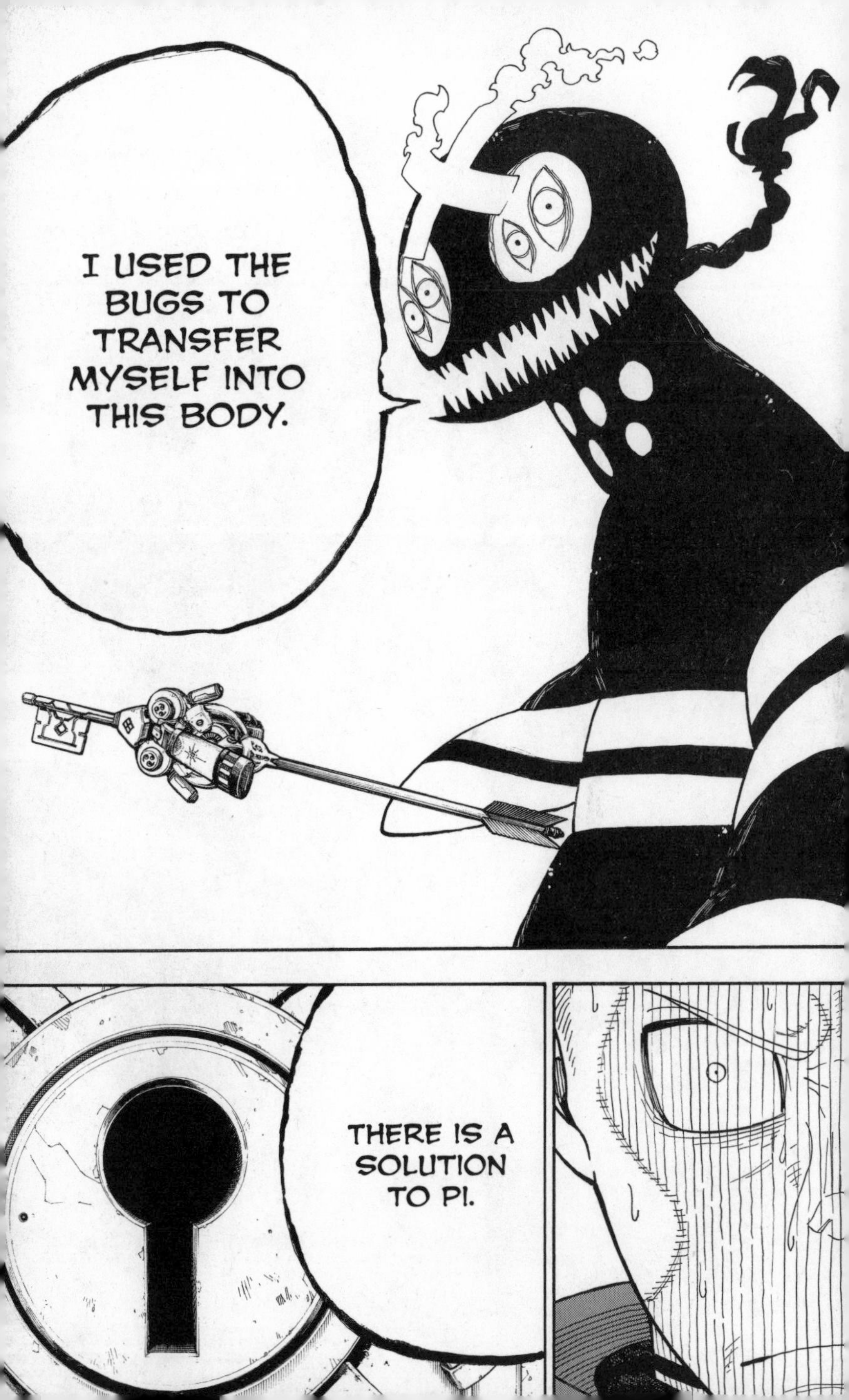
I USED THE BUGS TO TRANSFER MYSELF INTO THIS BODY.
THERE IS A SOLUTION TO PI.

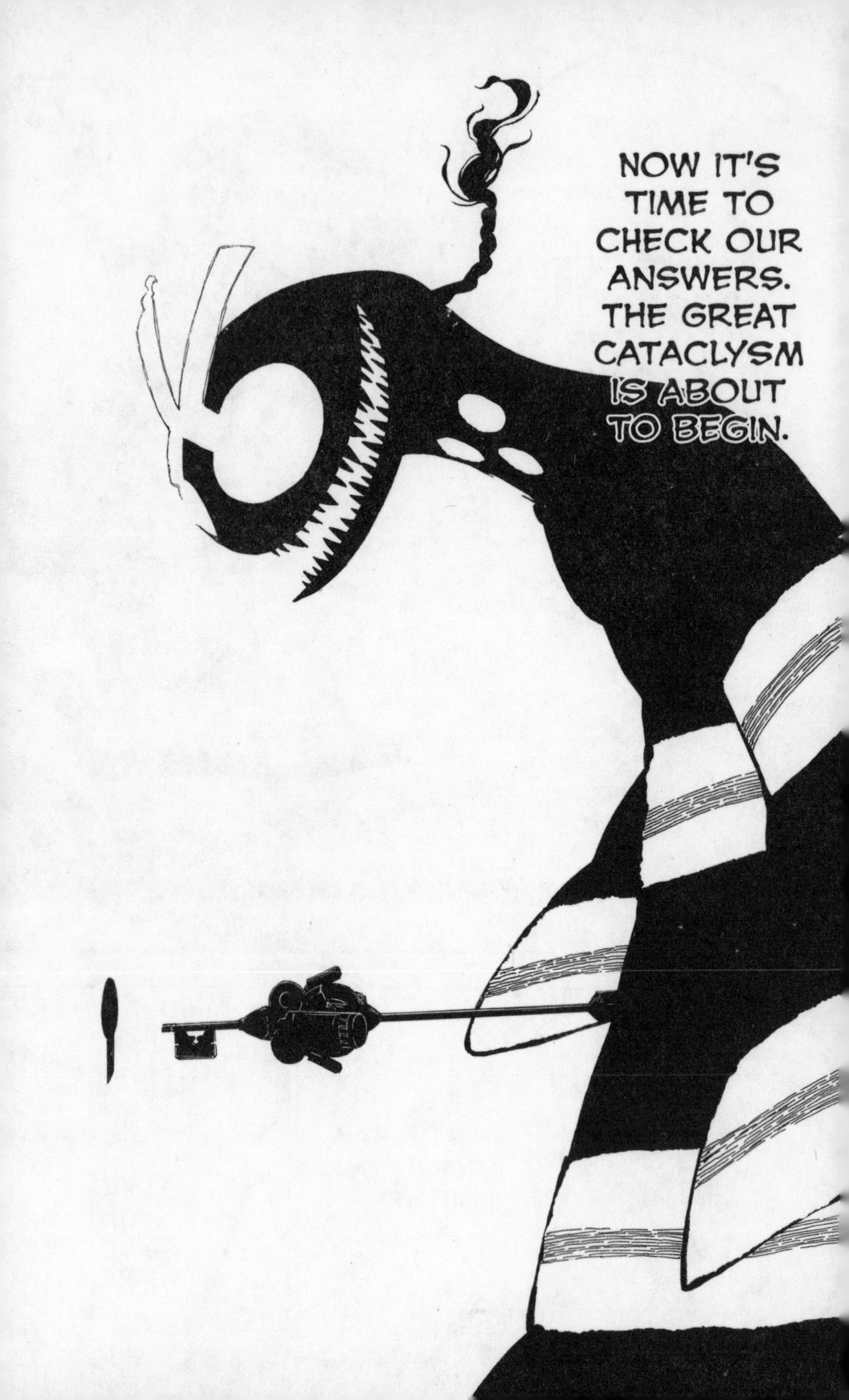
NOW IT'S TIME TO CHECK OUR ANSWERS. THE GREAT CATACLYSM IS ABOUT TO BEGIN.

TO BE CONTINUED IN VOLUME 29!!

AFTERWORD MANGA: ATSUSHIYA

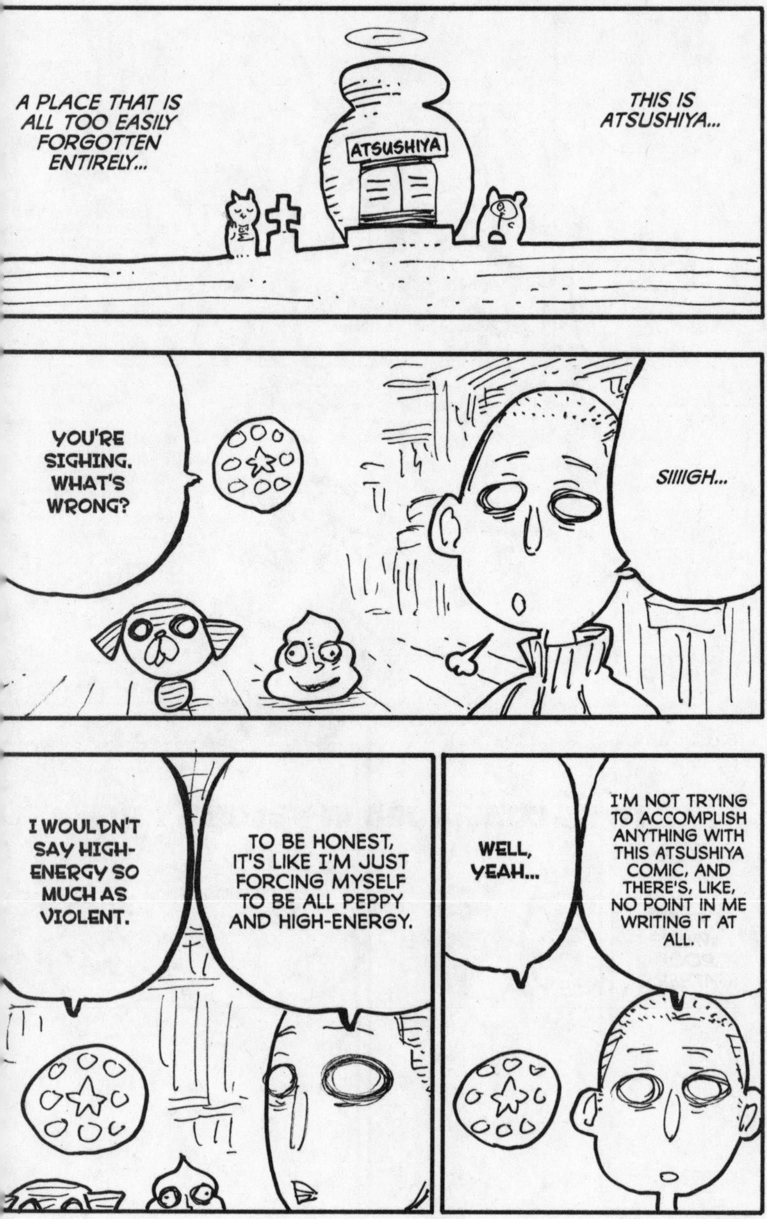
THIS IS ATSUSHIYA...
A PLACE THAT IS ALL TOO EASILY FORGOTTEN ENTIRELY...
ATSUSHIYA
SIIIGH...
YOU'RE SIGHING. WHAT'S WRONG?
I'M NOT TRYING TO ACCOMPLISH ANYTHING WITH THIS ATSUSHIYA COMIC, AND THERE'S, LIKE, NO POINT IN ME WRITING IT AT ALL.
WELL, YEAH...
TO BE HONEST, IT'S LIKE I'M JUST FORCING MYSELF TO BE ALL PEPPY AND HIGH-ENERGY.
I WOULDN'T SAY HIGH-ENERGY SO MUCH AS VIOLENT.

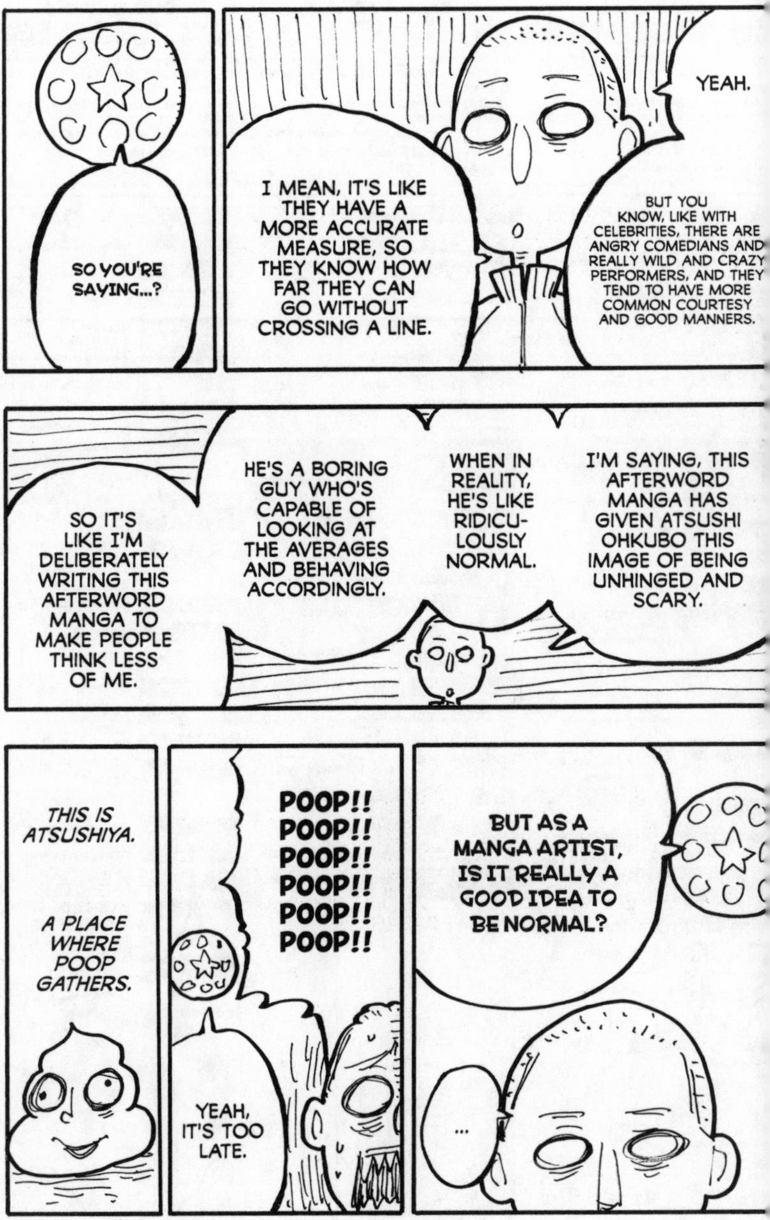
YEAH.
BUT YOU KNOW, LIKE WITH CELEBRITIES, THERE ARE ANGRY COMEDIANS AND REALLY WILD AND CRAZY PERFORMERS, AND THEY TEND TO HAVE MORE COMMON COURTESY AND GOOD MANNERS.
I MEAN, IT'S LIKE THEY HAVE A MORE ACCURATE MEASURE, SO THEY KNOW HOW FAR THEY CAN GO WITHOUT CROSSING A LINE.
SO YOU'RE SAYING...?
I'M SAYING, THIS AFTERWORD MANGA HAS GIVEN ATSUSHI OHKUBO THIS IMAGE OF BEING UNHINGED AND SCARY.
WHEN IN REALITY, HE'S LIKE RIDICU-LOUSLY NORMAL.
HE'S A BORING GUY WHO'S CAPABLE OF LOOKING AT THE AVERAGES AND BEHAVING ACCORDINGLY.
SO IT'S LIKE I'M DELIBERATELY WRITING THIS AFTERWORD MANGA TO MAKE PEOPLE THINK LESS OF ME.
BUT AS A MANGA ARTIST, IS IT REALLY A GOOD IDEA TO BE NORMAL?
...
POOP!! POOP!! POOP!! POOP!! POOP!! POOP!!
YEAH, IT'S TOO LATE.
THIS IS ATSUSHIYA.
A PLACE WHERE POOP GATHERS.

OGUN MONTGOMERY

AFFILIATION: SPECIAL FIRE FORCE TRAINING ACADEMY
RANK: SECOND-YEAR, TOP OF CLASS
ABILITY: THIRD GENERATION PYROKINETIC

Controls tattoos that raise his physical abilities using thermal energy.

Height	Height: 161cm [5'3'']
Weight	54kg [119lbs.]
Age	14
Birthday	March 3
Sign	Pisces
Bloodtype	B
Nickname	Black Star
Self-Proclaimed	Burger King
Favorite Foods	Hamburgers
	Anything that doesn't fill me up
Favorite Music	Reggae, hip hop
Favorite Animal	Hawk
Favorite Color	Orange
Favorite Type of Girl	Like, the girl I like is my type
Who He Respects	Guys who used to earn money playing sports when that was a thing
Who He Hates	I don't hate anybody
Who He's Afraid Of	That guy who complains when all we're doing is playing in the park
Hobbies	Basketball and sports involving boards, like skateboarding
Daily Routine	Playing sports in the park
Dream	I want to be in one of those big sporting events, like the "Olympics" they used to have
Shoe Size	25cm [7]
Eyesight	1.5 [20/12.5]
Favorite Subject	History, math
Least Favorite Subject	Language arts

ARTHUR BOYLE

AFFILIATION: SPECIAL FIRE FORCE TRAINING ACADEMY
RANK: SECOND-YEAR, HIGHEST FIREPOWER IN PRACTICAL EXAMS
ABILITY: THIRD GENERATION PYROKINETIC

Emits a blade of flame from the hilt of his sword

Height	153cm [5'0'']
Weight	44kg [97lbs.]
Age	14
Birthday	July 10
Sign	Cancer
Bloodtype	A
Nickname	Stupid
Self-Proclaimed	Knight King
Favorite Foods	Fry bread!
Least Favorite Food	Wet cardboard! (The tissue was okay)
Favorite Music	K Sugiyama!
Favorite Animal	Dragon Quest!
Favorite Color	Sparkle!
Favorite Type of Girl	Anyone, as long as she's a princess!
Who He Respects	Y Horii!
Who He Hates	People who hold grudges!
Who He's Afraid Of	Dragon King Dracon!
Hobbies	SNES!
Daily Routine	Leveling up!
Dream	To be the Knight King
Shoe Size	25cm [7]
Eyesight	1.5 [20/12.5]
Favorite Subject	Meals and break time
Least Favorite Subject	Everything other than breaks

SHINRA KUSAKABE

AFFILIATION: SPECIAL FIRE FORCE TRAINING ACADEMY
RANK: SECOND-YEAR, FASTEST IN PRACTICAL EXAMS
ABILITY: THIRD GENERATION PYROKINETIC

Emits fire from his feet

Height	159cm [5'2.5'']
Weight	49kg [108lbs.]
Age	17
Birthday	October 29
Sign	Scorpio
Bloodtype	AB
Nickname	The Devil's Footprints
Self-Proclaimed	Hero
Favorite Foods	Ramen Hamburgers Fried Chicken
Least Favorite Food	None
Favorite Music	Maru-kun theme song, hero version
Favorite Animal	Leopard, Anything fast
Favorite Color	Red
Favorite Type of Girl	Pretty girls
Who He Respects	My mother
Who He Hates	Arthur
Who He's Afraid Of	People at the facility
Hobbies	Soccer Futsal
Daily Routine	Breakdancing
Dream	To become a hero
Shoe Size	25.5cm [7.5]
Eyesight	2.0 [20/10]
Favorite Subject	Math
Least Favorite Subject	Language Arts

190

Young characters and steampunk setting,
like *Howl's Moving Castle* and *Battle Angel Alita*

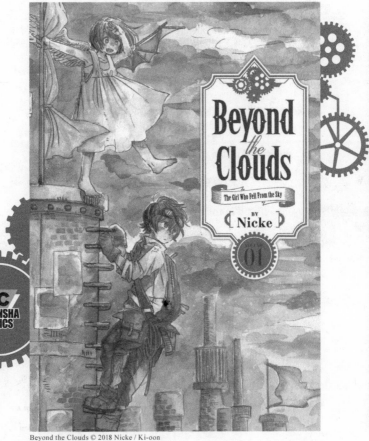

Beyond the Clouds © 2018 Nicke / Ki-oon

A boy with a talent for machines and a mysterious girl whose wings he's fixed will take you beyond the clouds! In the tradition of the high-flying, resonant adventure stories of Studio Ghibli comes a gorgeous tale about the longing of young hearts for adventure and friendship!

HRYA

A Kodansha Comics Trade Paperback Original
Fire Force 28 copyright © 2021 Atsushi Ohkubo
English translation copyright © 2022 Atsushi Ohkubo

All rights reserved.

Published in the United States by Kodansha Comics, an imprint of Kodansha USA Publishing, LLC, New York.

Publication rights for this English edition arranged through Kodansha Ltd., Tokyo.

First published in Japan in 2021 by Kodansha Ltd., Tokyo.

ISBN 978-1-64651-520-2

Printed in the United States of America.

www.kodansha.us

9 8 7 6 5 4 3 2 1
Translation: Alethea Nibley & Athena Nibley
Lettering: AndWorld Design
Editing: Greg Moore
Kodansha Comics edition cover design by Phil Balsman

2022

OCT

Publisher: Kiichiro Sugawara

Director of publishing services: Ben Applegate
Director of publishing operations: Dave Barrett
Associate director, publishing operations: Stephen Pakula
Publishing services managing editors: Madison Salters, Alanna Ruse